Morris Goodman, Ph. D.
1 Cypress Street
Maplewood, N. J. 07040.

D1570272

# The Limits
# of Biological Treatments
# for Psychological Distress

*Comparisons with
Psychotherapy and Placebo*

# The Limits
# of Biological Treatments
# for Psychological Distress

*Comparisons with
Psychotherapy and Placebo*

*Edited by*
Seymour Fisher
Roger P. Greenberg
*State University of New York
Health Science Center, Syracuse*

1989

LAWRENCE ERLBAUM ASSOCIATES, PUBLISHERS
Hillsdale, New Jersey          Hove and London

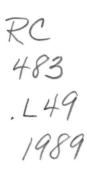

Lawrence Erlbaum Associates, Inc., Publishers
365 Broadway
Hillsdale, New Jersey 07642

**Library of Congress Cataloging-in-Publication Data**
The limits of biological treatments for psychological distress: Comparisons
  with psychotherapy and placebo / [edited by] Seymour Fisher and Roger P.
  Greenberg.
    p. cm.
  Includes index.
  ISBN 0-8058-0138-3
  1. Psychopharmacology—Evaluation.   2. Electroconvulsive therapy—
Evaluation.   I. Fisher, Seymour.   II. Greenberg, Roger P.
  [DNLM:   1. Mental Disorders—drug therapy.   WM402 H847]
RC483.H68     1989
616.89'18—dc19
DNLM/DLC
for Library of Congress                                                89-1300
                                                                           CIP

Printed in the United States of America
10  9  8  7  6  5  4  3  2  1

To my family: *Drs. Rhoda, Jerid,* and *Eve Fisher*—
and *Dr. Mark Whitmore*
With further regards to *Dr. Hippocrates* who recognized
the temptation to be too aggressively therapeutic.

S.F.


To my wife *Vicki* and my son *Michael* who—
without benefit of statistics—keep me
aware of what is meaningful in life.

R.P.G.

# CONTENTS

# CONTRIBUTORS

**Sidney E. Cleveland** ● Baylor College of Medicine, Houston, TX 77024

**Montosh J. Dewan** ● Department of Psychiatry, State University of New York Health Science Center, and Veterans Administration Medical Center, Syracuse, NY 13210

**Seymour Fisher** ● Department of Psychiatry, State University of New York Health Science Center, Syracuse, NY 13210

**Roger P. Greenberg** ● Department of Psychiatry, State University of New York Health Science Center, Syracuse, NY 13210

**Silas Halperin** ● Department of Psychology, Syracuse University, Syracuse, NY 13210

**Bertram P. Karon** ● Department of Psychology, Michigan State University, East Lansing, MI 48824

**Marvin Koss** ● Department of Psychiatry, State University of New York Health Science Center, and Veterans Administration Medical Center, Syracuse, NY 13210

**Ronald S. Lipman** ● Department of Research and Evaluation, Friends Hospital, Philadelphia, PA 19124

**Diane McGuinness** ● University of South Florida, Fort Myers, FL 33913

**Edward J. Murray** ● Department of Psychology, University of Miami, Miami, FL 33158

**Harold A. Sackeim** ● Department of Psychiatry, Columbia University, New York, NY 10032

# PREFACE

This book is devoted to finding out how effective the somatic therapies widely used in treating "mental disorders"[1] truly are. Vast quantities of effort and money are being channeled into drug therapies of various kinds. It has been estimated that 10% to 12% of the adult population in the United States uses a psychoactive drug at least once during a calendar year (Klerman, 1986). We feel there are quasi-mythic images circulating concerning the power of "biological psychiatry" that need to be examined. Issues pertaining to therapeutic efficacy are always politicized. The resident therapeutic experts on the scene are often biased because they have already invested their reputations in claims advertised to large numbers of patients. Our intention is to examine as objectively and fairly as possible the existing scientific data bearing on the value of the somatic treatment modes dominant in 20th century psychiatry. The need for such evaluation is pointed up by Valenstein's (1986) book *Great and Desperate Cures*, which depicts the eventual calamitous results for psychiatry of launching inadequate scientific appraisals of such treatments as lobotomy and insulin shock therapy. He suggests that the same forces that fostered these treatments, that in retrospect were grossly irrational, "are still active today."

In an earlier enterprise we (Fisher & Greenberg, 1985) undertook to evaluate the scientific credibility of many of Freud's primary psychodynamic notions and also the efficacy of the psychoanalytic therapy he devised. This proved to be a complicated enterprise, but we eventually came up with

---

[1] However, one major category, viz., bipolar disturbance, was not examined.

definitive conclusions concerning which areas of Freud's work were or were not scientifically sound. The present volume represents an analogous probe into the somatic armamentarium for "mental disorders." The time is propitious for a broad survey of the somatic therapies being offered to people who are psychologically in a state of disequilibrium. Which of these therapies are actually most dependable? How much better are they than nonsomatic approaches? What are the physiological costs and threats associated with them? Are there any exaggerations or distortions in the therapeutic claims being made? Where do we really stand at this point in time with reference to the proven advantages of the somatic therapies?

Biological treatment approaches for psychological problems have several built-in seductive appeals for both practitioners and patients that could color objective evaluation. Obviously, there is a need to do something when people feel disabled by their emotions and behaviors. Faced with a cry for help from an individual displaying puzzling or seemingly irrational behavior, clinicians may feel more secure knowing they can point to a relatively easily applied procedure, such as pill taking, to comply with the demand that something be done. The biological perspective has an evident attraction for patients too, in that it suggests that they are not accountable for the creation of their symptoms (because symptoms are due to chemical imbalances) and that they are not responsible for playing an active role in the solution to their discomforts. Dressed in the cloak of hard science, biological treatment approaches also radiate an aura of precision and specificity that is not as readily associated with the seemingly softer behavioral sciences. It is easy to lose sight of the fact that although the treatments can be delivered with exact measurement of chemical composition and dosage level, the results are being gauged in terms of feelings and judgments about behavior. The medicalized treatments with their images of hard tech, hard science control, quiet the unpleasant idea of people's actions being governed by irrational, disordered feelings, thoughts, and impulses. We raise these ideas not to discount the possible benefits of somatic approaches, but to point out how the pressing demand for simple, comfortable, blame-free treatments could skew evaluations of their effectiveness.

Our strategy in evaluating the therapies had been deliberately provocative. We wanted to take nothing for granted and to feel free to raise questions no matter how naive they might appear to be. Our assumption is that there is good reason to approach any established structure of therapeutic practices with skepticism and the expectation that the "Emperor's clothes" may not be what they appear to be. The long-term practitioners of therapeutic modes are inclined to become complacent and to encrust themselves with exaggerated claims. We assume that probing for weakness and looking for cracks in treatment rationales will eventually benefit consumers as well as practitioners of such treatments. Our selection of contributors to this volume was guided by our intent to be fresh and questioning. We chose persons whom we considered to be challenging and at least a bit anti-authoritarian. But as a first priority, we chose persons who had a proven track record of scholarly capability and who were expertly acquainted with the fundamental issues involved in evaluating treatment outcomes. Incidentally, we wanted contributors who were not too identified with or invested in treatment roles. Although several were engaged in clinical practice, they also had major work investments outside the clinical realm.

We called upon our contributors to burrow into the research pertinent to most of the heralded somatic approaches current in the treatment of psychologically disturbed individuals. A number of the major drug treatments are critiqued, as is electric shock therapy. In the drug area, we (Greenberg and Fisher) embark upon a broad appraisal of the scientific literature concerned with the power of antidepressant agents. We also take an excursion into the realm of placebos and highlight the puzzling dilemma of whether to use active or inactive placebos in drug research trials. Edward Murray focuses microscopically upon the outcome measures customarily employed to evaluate the effects of antidepressants and points up the advantages and disadvantages of a number of them. Ronald Lipman examines the evidence bearing on the efficacy of the antianxiety agents, and Bertram Karon compares the outcomes deriving from treatment of schizophrenics with drugs as contrasted with psychotherapy. Diane McGuinness probes the vast literature dealing with the use of stimulant drugs to cope with the so-called hyperactive or Attention Deficit child. Mantosh Dewan and Marvin Koss present us with a wide-ranging survey of the physiological side effects of many of the major therapeutic drugs. At still another level, Sidney Cleveland pulls together the literature concerned with the psychological mediators of drug effects. Further, Silas Halperin takes a critical look at the statistical procedures widely used in studies of antianxiety and antidepressant agents. Harold Sackeim completes the overall project by reviewing what is known about the therapeutic power of electric convulsive therapy. In a final overview we survey the major conclusions of the various chapters and ponder a number of urgent questions and issues that emerge.

As is seen, the evaluation of treatment modes is a tricky matter. The scientific literature bearing on treatment outcomes is not only of great volume, but also often surprisingly vague, contradictory, and susceptible to multiple interpretations. It does not take much bias either for or against a drug to slant one's interpretations of the available pertinent data. It is all too easy to dismiss one study because it has some "defect" (no matter how minor) or to accept another because it "so clearly" demonstrates a positive or negative effect. If one is to be honest, one must from the outset admit that bias is rampant. It is probably impossible to interpret the current mass of treatment outcome findings without being pulled by hidden agendas. Let the reader and also the consumer of somatic treatments beware. At this stage of the game, claims and conclusions should be treated as tentative. Even when one is able to discern that a particular treatment is "significantly" more effective than a placebo control, the nagging question remains as to how large the treatment advantage must be to represent a viable choice for a real life person in distress. Considering the financial costs and not inconsiderable and uncomfortable side effects of most somatic treatments, is a 20% advantage over placebo sufficient? Or does the advantage have to be 30% or 40%? How consistently must the scientific literature demonstrate a given magnitude of advantage before it has real life implications? What if 50% of the studies indicate a 40% advantage, but 50% show only a 20% advantage or less? What if more recent studies indicate less of an advantage than did earlier ones?

This leads into the question of what consumers should be told about the therapeutic potential of any somatic treatment offered to them. Obviously, they cannot be apprised of the full complexity of the accumulated research literature. Should they be expected to take on faith that "This will help you"? Should there be at least a rough quantitative statement of the probable advantage of the treatment as compared to doing nothing? Or as compared to alternative forms of treatment? There is little consensus about such questions. Many think the consumer should be willing to put his faith in the "expert clinician." Many worry that giving too much information to the consumer will destroy potentially important placebo effects. Obviously, such views fall outside of the purview of science and represent political and ethical schemas.

Beyond the confusion already mentioned, we also ask the reader to wonder a bit about the scientific security of present methods for testing therapeutic effectiveness. We think there is evidence of a false sense of assurance about the safeguards provided by the double blind or other variant paradigms. We are not the first to discern cracks in apparently blind designs. However, past criticisms have simple been superficially acknowledged and then substantially ignored. The problem may be more serious than we have been willing to admit. We had better shake off our inertia and attend to a matter that has potentially serious unsettling implications for what we think we know about the therapeutic power of various substances and procedures.

## REFERENCES

Fisher, S., & Greenberg, R. P. (1985). *The scientific credibility of Freud's theories and therapy.* New York: Columbia University Press.

Klerman, G. L. (1986). Drugs and psychotherapy. In S. L. Garfield & A. E. Bergin (Eds.), *Handbook of psychotherapy and behavior change* (pp. 777–818). New York: Wiley.

Valenstein, E. S. (1986). *Great and desperate cures.* New York: Basic Books.

# 1 EXAMINING ANTIDEPRESSANT EFFECTIVENESS: FINDINGS, AMBIGUITIES, AND SOME VEXING PUZZLES

Roger P. Greenberg
Seymour Fisher
*State University of New York*
*Health Science Center*

Since Kuhn (1958) detected an apparent antidepressant effect for imipramine, many studies have explored this phenomenon. Despite some past skeptical opinions (Jenner, 1977; Porter, 1970; Wechsler, Grosser, & Greenblatt, 1965), it is now widely accepted that the therapeutic effectiveness of the antidepressants, especially the tricyclics, has been indubitably demonstrated. However, although this chapter does not question that antidepressants are therapeutic, it does question the magnitude of the effect and some of its underlying causes. As we surveyed the literature dealing with antidepressants, we detected some inconsistences and methodological gaps in current claims and clinical practices. The history of treatment modes for psychological disturbance bristles with examples (e.g., insulin therapy, lobotomy) that were widely accepted and ultimately proved to fall short of early claims. This is, of course, also true in other areas of treatment (Benson & McCallie, 1979). A cautious attitude about treatment claims is dictated by what has gone before. Among other things, this chapter focuses on the way in which the double-blind design has typically been used to evaluate the therapeutic value of the antidepressants and suggests that it has not been applied satisfactorily. More specifically, our intent is the following:

1. To appraise the effectiveness of the antidepressants across multiple reviews and studies. It should be noted, however, that the appraisal restricts itself to the effectiveness for relieving depression and does not deal with other symptom categories to which antidepressants have been applied.

2. To examine the stability of findings involving the antidepressants, with

a special focus on whether reported levels of effectiveness have changed in more recent appraisals.

3. To compare the effectiveness of antidepressants to the outcomes for psychotherapies specifically designed to treat depression.

4. To probe the objectivity of the typical double-blind design employed to evaluate antidepressants, especially in relation to the issue of using placebos that are inactive.

5. To offer suggestions of possible ways of balancing deficiencies in current approaches to measuring the effectiveness of antidepressants and other therapeutic agents.


## PAST REVIEWS OF ANTIDEPRESSANT DRUG EFFICACY

Since the introduction of antidepressant drugs, many studies have attempted to assess their effectiveness, and a variety of reviewers have tried their hand at summarizing the reports that have appeared in the literature. The reviewers have focused on the antidepressant effects of tricyclic compounds and monoamine oxidase inhibitors (MAOIs). Obviously there is overlap in the studies summarized by different authors. However, there is occasional disagreement among reviewers in categorizing the same investigation as showing evidence for or against drug use. Results have generally been compressed into either box scores comparing the number of studies showing drugs to be superior to placebos versus those showing no difference in outcome or compilations of the percentage of patients significantly improving on drugs as opposed to placebos. A search of the literature revealed 15 such reviews. Six assessed the drug effects as relatively positive and superior to placebos and 7 suggested more modest, cautious, or equivocal conclusions about drug effects. Two reviews took a somewhat different tack and attempted to measure the degree to which groups treated with antidepressant drugs have exceeded non-drug control groups. Note that these 15 reviews were largely written in the 1960s.

Perhaps a presentation of the positive reviews should begin with the work of Cole (1964) who, in providing an early impressionistic discussion of drug treatments, noted that two thirds of 15 placebo-controlled studies of depressed inpatients showed imipramine to be superior. Three placebo-controlled studies of outpatients also declared imipramine to be the more effective treatment. Similarly, Davis (1965) detailed a box score account of 47 antidepressant drug studies. Most of these reports were placebo controlled and double-blind. The drug was declared superior to placebos in 68% of the studies. At a later date, Davis, Klerman, and Schildkraut (1968) tabulated box scores for 52 double-blind placebo-controlled studies of tricyclics and 28 similarly controlled investigations of MAOIs. Drugs were declared superior to placebos in 79% of the tricyclic studies and in 54% of the MAOI studies.

Klerman and Cole (1965) found 23 studies comparing imipramine to placebo. Eighteen of these studies (78%) indicated that the drug outcome was better. However, the authors of 3 of these 18 positive papers felt that their investigations as a whole did not present really convincing evidence of imipramine's general superiority to the controls. Overall, the authors of the studies felt that the drug was convincingly superior 15 times in the 23 trials (65%). Incidentally, even this figure may be an overestimation of the number of trials in which imipramine exceeded placebo. Thus, a commentary (Beck, 1967) on this review indicated that many studies were counted by Klerman and Cole as showing positive results even though the superiority of the drug was slight and short of statistical significance on a number of indices.

Klerman and Cole also combined the data across all the studies, permitting an overall judgment as to whether the patients had or had not improved. They concluded that 65% of the 550 imipramine-treated patients improved, whereas 31% of the 459 controls evidenced similar improvement. They went on to suggest that this improvement difference between drugs and placebo might not be as large as the percentages indicated because some of the improved patients were not improved enough to satisfy either themselves or their physicians. Therefore, imipramine was deemed "not entirely satisfactory treatment in many of the depressed patients to whom it was given" (p. 282).

Klein and Davis (1969) reviewed 65 studies comparing tricyclics with placebo and indicated that 50 showed the drug to be superior (77%). They found no striking overall outcome differences among the tricyclics. Although there were differences in diagnostic groupings and types of measurement among studies, it was felt that combining samples might give an approximate summary statement of the efficacy of antidepressants. Therefore, the percentages of improvement reported by the various studies were pooled. The number of patients rated at least moderately improved was combined within the drug and placebo groups respectively and compared with the number found to be slightly improved, unchanged, or worse. In this way the reviewers derived a figure of 70% as the rate of improvement on imipramine and 39% as the placebo improvement rate. Overall it was concluded that imipramine was superior to a placebo, although "not overwhelmingly so," with a treatment superiority of about 30% more improvement for the active drug than for the placebo. Similarly, in fewer studies, amitriptyline was found to be more beneficial than placebo (62% vs. 24%).

In a more recent, widely cited review, Morris and Beck (1974) looked at 146 double-blind studies on antidepressant drugs utilized in the United States in 1972. Two thirds of the 93 studies of tricyclics indicated that the drug was superior to a placebo, whereas one third of the reports found no difference. The box score outcome for the MAOIs revealed somewhat less success, with an overall superiority over placebo in only 33% of the papers. When MAOI results were limited to only FDA approved drugs, the success rate rose to 61% in favor of the drugs, but Morris and Beck cautioned that this average value could be misleading in view of the considerable variability in efficacy among the MAOIs.

Although the tone of the six reviews cited to this point indicates a superiority of the antidepressant drugs over placebos, seven other reviews indicate more cautious or equivocal conclusions. Brady, in a 1963 review of placebo-controlled studies of imipramine, found that 52% (13 of 25 studies) of these comparisons yielded no significant difference in outcome (cited in Beck, 1967). Atkinson and Ditman (1965) examined 16 reports where the patients were given similar depressive diagnoses and in which an MAOI (tranylcypromine) was used as the sole treatment. Ten of the 16 studies employed a pre-post design without control groups. Study outcomes were divided into three groups: favorable, equivocal, or unfavorable. Of the comparisons, 68% were deemed equivocal or unfavorable.

Friedman, Granick, Cohen, and Cowitz (1966) located 21 reports appearing between 1957 and 1964 of double-blind controlled studies comparing imipramine with placebo on hospitalized endogenous or psychotic depressed patients. Eleven of the 21 studies claimed that imipramine was superior to a placebo. However, Friedman et al. stated that on close inspection even the 11 studies reporting positive effects for the drug with psychotic depressives were inconclusive. Only 2 of the 11 studies claimed the results were statistically significant and patients in the "positive" studies turned out to be a mixed sample of endogenous and nonendogenous depressives. In short, Friedman et al. could not find a single double-blind controlled study that demonstrated clearly favorable results with a sample of hospitalized psychotic depressives. Overall, Friedman and his colleagues concluded that the matter of treating endogenous or psychotic depression with imipramine is "unsettled." Their investigation of this question in an additional carefully done study presented in the same paper indicated that if all outcome indices were considered, there was equivalent relief from depression when hospitalized psychotic depressives were treated with either imipramine or an active placebo.

McNair (1974), in studying how frequently different self-rating scales indicate antidepressant effectiveness, analyzed the results of 72 research publications reporting on 75 largely antidepressant drug trials (almost all double-blind) published between 1955 and 1972. The studies produced an average of six comparisons per trial by utilizing a variety of measures with various subscores and sometimes having more than one evaluation period. Significant treatment effects were found in only 21% of the 451 comparisons. Although this represents a greater number of significant effects than would be expected by chance, the results are modest. Another overview suggesting conservative conclusions was presented by Rogers and Clay (1975), who examined 30 trials comparing imipramine to placebo. They used the global ratings of improvement in each of the studies and submitted each to Fisher's Exact Test. Although the authors attempted to report results in a sympathetic manner, they found drugs superior to placebo in only 10 of 30 comparisons (33%).

Wechsler et al. (1965), in a review of 103 publications that appeared over a 5-year period, raised questions about the actual magnitude of the antidepressant drug effect. They found the size of the effect to be related to the type of research design. Treatments were found to be more effective when placebo controls were not employed. The association between improvement rates and research design is highlighted by viewing the work on imipramine, the treatment studied most frequently. Imipramine was found to be at least 65% effective in only 1 of the 9 studies comparing it to a placebo, as opposed to 7 out of 9 studies without a control group and 11 out of 17 reports comparing it to another active treatment.

A. Smith, Traganza, and Harrison (1969) presented a "comprehensive overview of antidepressant literature published in the English language." More than 2,000 articles were screened resulting in a distillation of 490 trials of the efficacy of one or more drugs used in the treatment of depression. The authors discovered, as had Wechsler et al. (1965), that the sophistication of the research design was a dominant factor in determining the level of reported improvement. The more stringently controlled the study, the lower the reported drug improvement rate. Improvement rates for drugs were significantly lowered by either the presence of a control group or the use of blind techniques. Interestingly, increasing study sophistication had the opposite effect on placebo response. The more stringent the controls, the more improvement noted for placebo. Overall, the authors suggested that the methodology of antidepressant research is more significant than the drug being studied in determining the outcome of a clinical trial. They concluded that "the differences between the effectiveness of antidepressant drugs and placebo are not impressive" (p. 19). When studies were restricted to those having placebo controls and blind techniques, active medications had only about a 15% improvement advantage over placebo (with respective median improvement rates of 61.1% vs. 46.3%). Skepticism about the conclusions reached by most authors was raised by the finding that only 18% of the studies in the literature up to that time used statistical tests to decide whether the active drugs were effective. Most frequently (in 67% of the studies) authors simply used global improvement judgments (without statistical comparisons) to reach conclusions about efficacy. The literature review did not indicate what percentage of the time a statistically significant difference was found between drugs and placebos in studies that tested for a difference.

M. L. Smith, Glass, and Miller (1980), utilizing an effect size statistic, determined the degree to which drug treatment groups exceeded control groups on outcome measures drawn from a representative sample of published studies. Their analysis of 75 antidepressant drug effect sizes indicated that the average antidepressant drug effect size is .40. This means that the average person treated with antidepressants is at the 66th percentile of the placebo control group or, conversely, that the average person treated with placebos will do better than 34% of those treated with antidepressants. The typical patient's standing on outcome variables was bettered by 16 percentile points because of taking drugs rather than a placebo. The fact that this is a relatively modest drug effect is underlined by the finding that of the three major types of psychotropic medications (antipsychotic, antidepressant, and antianxiety), antidepressants produced the smallest effects.

Another meta-analysis, reported by a group from Australia and New Zealand (Quality Assurance Project 1983), also analyzed the results for controlled trials of drug treatments for depression. Results were separately assessed for neurotic (69 studies) and endogenous depressions (54 studies) treated with tricyclics (or other approaches). The effect size (ES) for the treatment of neurotic depression with tricyclics (ES = .52) was slightly higher than the effect size obtained by Smith et al. (1980). A larger effect size was obtained for tricyclic treatment of endogenous depressions (ES = .79). However, the data indicated that the largest effect size for treating neurotic depression occurred with psychotherapy (ES = 1.00) and the largest effect size for dealing with endogenous depressions (where no comparisons with psychotherapy were made) occurred in studies of Electroconvulsive Therapy (ECT) (ES = .93). There were differences in criteria for including studies, handling data, and measuring outcome between the Australian and American meta-analyses, which may account for differential results. Oddly, the Australian/New Zealand analysis found no relationship between research design characteristics and effect size, whereas the M. L. Smith et al. (1980) project discovered— consistent with other researchers—that effect size was related to such design characteristics as degree of blindness in assessing outcome and randomness of assignment to treatment and control groups.

## COMMENTARY ON THE REVIEWS

After looking at modern textbooks in psychiatry, a reading of the antidepressant drug literature may come as something of a surprise. Although textbooks frequently proclaim that drugs are a significant solution to the problem of depression, research findings help to place this conclusion in perspective. Even the most positive reviews indicate that 30% to 40% of the studies show no difference in response to drugs and placebos (M. L. Smith et al., 1980). In terms of the percentage of improvement, supporters of medication use suggest that about one third of patients do not improve with antidepressant treatment, one third improve with placebos, and an additional one third show a response to medication that they would not have achieved with placebos. Thus, with the most positive outlook, about two thirds of the cases—placebo responders and those who do not respond to anything—would do as well or better with placebo treatment as they would do if treated by an active medication. Furthermore, as we have already noted, review evidence suggests that the average depressed person taking placebos will attain a better outcome than 34% of those individuals taking an active medication (M. L. Smith et al., 1980).

The strength of conclusions about antidepressant efficacy is of course limited by the strength of the data from which those conclusions are drawn, and there are a number of problems common to the bulk of studies reviewed by the investigators we have cited. Klein, Gittleman, Quitkin, and Rifkin (1980) have suggested that some of these problems may have decreased the size of the difference between drug-treated and placebo-treated groups. For example, the lack of clear consistent inclusion criteria for diagnosing depression may have created a heterogenous population in many studies and thereby obscured the unique benefits of drugs for certain types of depression. Yet over the years, reviewers of empirical work have been in disagreement as to whether drugs work best with any particular type of depressive group, such as neurotic or psychotic depressives (Beck, 1967; Bielski & Friedel, 1976; Friedman et al., 1966; Raskin & Crook, 1975), and some recent studies utilizing objective, reliable diagnostic criteria have not found any relationship between an endogenous–nonendogenous factor and the outcome of treatment (Blackburn, Bishop, Glen, Whalley, & Christie, 1981; Hersen, Bellack, Himmelhoch, & Thase, 1984; Rush, Beck, Kovacs, & Hollon, 1977).

Clearly, there have been major difficulties in trying to define homogenous diagnostic subgroups of depressed patients. This problem is highlighted by the work of Katschnig and his colleagues (see overview by Katschnig, Nutzinger, & Schanda, 1986) who found vagueness, looseness in terminology, and little overlap among nine different diagnostic systems purporting to distinguish between endogenous and neurotic depression. Furthermore, in their research on 176 depressed inpatients, none of the endogenous/nonendogenous distinctions made by any of the definitions showed an association with preceding life stress, illness course, or a number of outcome measures over a 2- to 3-year period following discharge.

On the other hand, Bielski and Friedel (1976), in reviewing studies predicting response to tricyclic antidepressants, did find a few reports citing evidence for a relationship between positive response to tricyclic medications and individual symptoms that have been associated with an endogenous diagnosis (e.g., anorexia, weight loss, and middle or late insomnia). Yet they note, with some surprise, that the conclusion regarding a relationship between drug response and endogenous symptoms is based on relatively few controlled studies.

Prusoff, Weissman, Klerman, and Rounsaville (1980), in speaking of the clinical folklore surrounding the subtype of depression labeled "endogenous," underlined the difficulties in dealing with the concept because of a lack of consensus and imprecision about definition. In their work they used the Research Diagnostic Criteria to define depression subtypes. For most subtypes of depression they found no difference in outcome for four different types of treatment (e.g., interpersonal psychotherapy, drugs, a combination of interpersonal psychotherapy and drugs, or supportive psychotherapy on patient demand). Situational depressions (where there was an indication of a precipitating event) seemed to respond best to either drugs or psychotherapy (depending on the outcome measure) with the combination of both adding nothing to either treatment alone. In contrast, endogenous depressions responded better to a combination of psychotherapy and drugs than to drugs alone. In this study psychotherapy alone proved to be ineffective as a treatment for endogenous depression. Interestingly, the diagnoses used for this work were based on several independent symptoms. It was not known whether some symptoms were more predictive of response than others. The criteria used for diagnosis also allowed patients to be placed in more than one diagnostic category at a time. Unlike the widely accepted clinical lore, it was possible in this scheme for a patient's depression to be labeled both situational *and* endogenous. Of the 26 patients (out of 81) in this investigation who were diagnosed endogenous, 7 were also labeled as having situational depression.

It has been speculated, too, that some of the early studies did not use a high enough medication dose to attain maximum drug–placebo differences (Klein et al., 1980). Although a few researchers have supported this idea (Quitkin, Rabkin, Ross, & McGrath, 1984), there is room for debate on this issue because others, such as Wechsler and his colleagues (1965), found no relationship between the percentage of improvement reported in a large number of studies and either dosage level or the length of treatment. Similarly, the large-scale Australian and New Zealand meta-analysis of antidepressant outcome studies found no relationship between effect size (a measure of outcome magnitude) and dosage level (Quality Assurance Project, 1983). Despite much emphasis by some observers concerning the importance of using sufficiently high dosages to attain therapeutic effects (see overview by Quitkin, 1985), the truth is that little relevant empirical work comparing dosage levels has been done. We have found only two studies explicitly concerned with this issue. One (Watt, Crammer, & Elkes, 1972) did demonstrate a clear therapeutic superiority for a higher dose (150 vs. 300 mg of desmethylimipramine), although only a modest 50% of the patients improved on the higher dose and the raters of improvement were not blind to dosage level. Another (Simpson, Lee, Cuculic, & Kellner, 1976) actually indicated only a borderline advantage for a 300 mg dose of imipramine as compared to a 150 mg dose.

Research on dosage levels may be an inefficient means for gathering evidence on antidepressant efficacy because dosage and blood plasma levels of antidepressants do not appear to be highly related. However, the picture does not become totally clear if one attempts to associate plasma levels (rather than dosage levels) with clinical outcome. Although several studies have shown an association between plasma levels and outcome for some drugs, the magnitude of the relationship and its consistency have raised some concerns. Complicating the attempts to find evidence for a direct relationship between plasma level and outcome are wide interindividual biochemical and pharmacokinetic variations (e.g., Moller et al., 1985). As Simpson, Edmond, and White (1983) note after reviewing this area, "efforts to relate plasma levels to therapeutic outcome have, in general, been disappointing" (p. 27), and the relationships, although "extensively studied since 1962, remain controversial" (p. 29).

Research on the association of blood level concentrations of drugs and outcome has shown a moderate relationship in some clinical groups and no consistent relationship in others (APA Task Force, 1985; Glassman, Perel, Shostak, Kantor, & Fleiss, 1977; Reisby et al., 1977). One report indicated that plasma level was correlated with treatment response in only one third of the patients (Blackwell, 1982). Work with different drugs has also yielded different conclusions. Although there have not been many independent studies, the relationship between blood level measurement and clinical response has shown a degree of consistency with some drugs (e.g., imipramine) and none with others (e.g., amitriptyline) (APA Task Force, 1985). The size of the correlation found in studies that do report a significant relationship suggests that an individual's blood level of medication accounts, at best, for only a minor part of the "drug effect" (Glassman et al., 1977; Reisby et al., 1977).

Friedel (1982), in concluding that only the antidepressants nortriptyline and imipramine have shown some relationship between plasma level and therapeutic response, suggests that the relationship holds only for those patients with an endogenous type of diagnosis. He wrote:

It is important to recognize that the reported relationships between antidepressant plasma levels and therapeutic response have been determined for the most part in patients with endogenous depression or, as defined in DSM-III, major depressive disorder with melancholea. Patients who have other depressive subtypes that are not typically responsive to the tricyclics, e.g., those with psychotic symptoms, atypical depressions, or neurotic and reactive depressions, cannot be expected to demonstrate a correlation between antidepressant plasma levels and therapeutic outcome. (p. 40)

However, even the conclusion that there is a relationship between clinical response and plasma concentration for endogenous depression has not received consistent support. For example, a carefully done study on 90 inpatients (with 85% endogenous and 15% psychotic depression diagnoses) showed virtually no significant linear or curvilinear relationships between any measure of plasma concentration and any of several measures of clinical response to either imipramine or amitriptyline (Kocsis, Hanin, Bowden, & Brunswick, 1986).

There are some characteristics of drug studies that exaggerate the differential effects of drugs and placebo. Prominent among these is the type of study design. In general, the less blind the study participants and drug administrators are to whether drugs or placebos are being administered, the greater the drug–placebo differences become (M. L. Smith et al., 1980). This is a particularly important finding because, as we show, there is good reason to believe that most antidepressant drug studies are not conducted under truly double-blind conditions (Ainslie, Stiefel, & Jones, 1966). Relatedly, studies that rely on global impressionistic ratings of change are more likely to obtain significant drug–placebo outcome differences than are investigations making use of more objective, structured measures of psychological symptoms or adjustment (McNair, 1974; M. L. Smith et al., 1980). McNair found that global ratings were unique in yielding significant differences between antidepressant drugs and placebos and that no other type of measure showed differences even 20% of the time. He noted that global ratings do not necessarily reflect only changes in depressive symptomatology and that an individual may express any type of perceived change—such as in anxiety or sleep patterns—with such ratings. Similarly, Klerman and Cole (1965) discovered that significant differences between antidepressants and placebos dropped 42% when morbidity scores based on signs or symptoms rather than global ratings were used.

A word is in order at this point about a common practice in antidepressant drug research designs that artificially reduces apparent placebo response rates. It is by now a fairly standard procedure to initiate drug trials with a "washout" phase (single-blind, from 7 to 10 days) during which all prospective candidates for the study are placed on placebo, and those who show significant improvement are eliminated. Those who do not respond are then randomly assigned to the usual double-blind (drug versus placebo) design. One of the major purposes of the "washout" period is to "eliminate from the clinical trial patients whose symptoms remit, improve, or rapidly fluctuate within a short time span" (Rabkin et al., 1986, p. 274). Obviously, though, it also eliminates individuals who may be sensitive to the therapeutic impact of the placebo experience. One study (Rabkin et al., 1987) that systematically probed the positive response rate during washout preliminary to an antidepressant study found that the rate was in the 19%–20% range. Thus, a significant segment of the potential placebo responders was eliminated even before the formal comparison of placebo versus drug response was initiated. This means that the placebo response rates of all studies using washout phases may be substantially understating what the placebo response rate is in the real world population of depressed persons seeking treatment. One could perhaps reason that if some of the variance of improvement in the actual drug group is due to placebo, the washout phase would ultimately reduce the improvement rate in that group too. That may well be, and there are complex questions that can be debated in this regard. But, in any case, the fact remains that in the context of washout procedures the formal statistics concerning explicit improvement rates in placebo control groups are probably seriously understated (compared to the real world).

Rabkin et al. (1987) investigated the characteristics of depressed patients who improve during the washout phase and found they are typified by "milder illness symptoms" than those who do not so improve. They also reported that the washout responders differ from those patients who were not eliminated from the study and who subsequently responded to placebo during a 6-week period. The washout responders were "more mildly ill," "more chronic," and characterized by "fewer illness precipitants." It is an interesting curiosity that Rabkin et al. (1987) also discovered that the "proportion of placebo washout responders declined in the winter months (p. 9).

The variability in outcome reported among studies and differences in improvement assessments by different raters indicate powerful bias and attitudinal mediators in how drug outcome will be experienced, interpreted, or assessed. A similar conclusion is suggested by some multicenter studies that use the same drug and the same criteria for patient selection, but then find that patients improve significantly more at certain of the centers than they do at others. For example, in a single study, Greenblatt, Grosser, and Wechsler (1964) compared improvement rates obtained by three antidepressant drugs and a placebo used at three different hospitals. The rank order of treatment effectiveness among the hospitals was found to be approximately the same no matter what the treatment was. One hospital consistently produced the best results, whereas another produced the worst. Results with imipramine showed that marked improvement occurred 67% of the time at the most effective hospital and 31% of the time at the least effective center. A more recent example comes from a study comparing imipramine, alprazolam, and placebo in the treatment of depression at five different settings (Feighner, Aden, Fabre, Rickels, & Smith, 1983). Although the pooled data showed the drugs to be more effective than the placebo, an examination of the results from each of the centers demonstrated considerable variability. For instance, after 6 weeks of treatment, every one of the six outcome measures showed imipramine to be equivalent to placebo in two or more of the five centers. Two of the centers found a difference favoring imipramine on only 1 of 12 comparisons. An equivalent 1 out of 12 comparisons favored placebos. Variability in outcome extends to placebos as well, with some investigators finding relatively low rates of response and others finding improvement in as many as 80% of those treated with placebo (Jenner, 1977).

## MORE CURRENT FINDINGS: COMPARISONS
## WITH PSYCHOTHERAPEUTIC TREATMENTS

Recent research on drug effects is less plagued by some of the major questions that have surrounded earlier work. For the most part the criteria for inclusion into a depressive sample and the measures of outcome are more objective and clearly spelled out. Duration of treatment tends to be longer and drugs are usually prescribed at accepted dosage levels. It is interesting, therefore, to raise the question of whether the drug effects achieved in recent studies are superior, inferior, or equivalent to past findings. Since the efficacy of the major tricyclics has been generally accepted (despite the inconsistencies in the literature), most current research focuses on testing the adequacy of newly introduced drugs. However, one area where findings on the older accepted tricyclics have continued to be collected is in the comparison of drugs to the psychotherapeutic procedures developed specifically to deal with major depressions. Studies of cognitive therapy, interpersonal psychotherapy, behavior therapy, and social skills training have used the widely prescribed antidepressant medications as standards against which psychotherapy efficacy can be tested. We decided to look at such studies to see what improvement rates for drugs look like under more careful methodology of modern studies. Newer studies may differ from many of the older reports in the bias of the investigators. One would expect these authors to be somewhat less invested in finding powerful medication effects. They are more likely to utilize measures, such as the Beck Depression Inventory, that are more precise and objective than the global ratings earlier work relied on. The standards for significant improvement are probably also more stringent in that the newer measures often permit a precise comparison of patients' depression scores at the end of treatment with normative depression scores.

Eight trials comparing a specified type of psychotherapy (for depression) to antidepressant drugs have been reported in seven studies. Three of these trials indicated that psychotherapy was equivalent to medication in fostering improvement (Blackburn et al., 1981, Hospital Outpatient Sample;[1] Murphy, Simons, Wetzel, & Lustman, 1984; Weissman, Prusoff, DiMascio, Neu, Goklaney, & Klerman, 1979) and five indicated that psychotherapy was superior to the drug in promoting substantial change (Bellack, Hersen, & Himmelhoch, 1981;[2] Beutler et al., 1987; Blackburn et al., 1981, General

---

[1]Results for this trial were also reported by Blackburn and Bishop (1981).

[2]Two reports of a follow-up study that included additional patients and results after 6 months of maintenance treatment showed that social skills training continued to be superior to the drug on measures of social skills. There were no differences between social skills training and dynamic psychotherapy on the social skills measures. In the expanded sample both types of psychosocial treatments produced outcomes equivalent (rather than superior) to medication on measures of depression (Bellack, Hersen, & Himmelhoch, 1983; Hersen et al., 1984).

Practice Sample; McLean & Hakstian, 1979; Rush et al., 1977). None of the trials showed the drug to be superior. One of the studies used a relaxation group as a control (McLean & Hakstian, 1979). This group was presumed to be equivalent to a placebo because there was no reason to believe that relaxation by itself would be an effective treatment for depression. Results showed no difference between treatment with relaxation and treatment with drugs.

Eleven trials presented evidence on whether adding drugs to psychotherapy produced better results. In nine, the addition of drugs made no difference in treatment outcome (Beck, Hollon, Young, Bedrosian, & Budenz, 1985; Bellack et al., 1981; Beutler et al., 1987; Blackburn et al., 1981, General Practice Sample; DeRubeis, 1983; Murphy et al., 1984; Roth, Bielski, Jones, Parker, & Osborn, 1982; Rush & Watkins, 1981; Wilson, 1982). The other two trials showed that the combination of drugs and psychotherapy was better than either alone (Blackburn et al., 1981, Hospital Outpatient Sample; DiMascio et al., 1979; Weissman et al., 1979). Weissman and her collaborators, in finding the combination treatment preferable, indicated that drugs and psychotherapy affected different aspects of the clinical picture. Psychotherapy had its main effect on mood, apathy, suicidal ideation, work, and interest, whereas medication mainly influenced sleep and appetite. Differential treatment response was also noted between those classified as endogenous depression and those diagnosed as situational depression (Prusoff et al., 1980). Endogenous depressed patients responded best to a combination of interpersonal psychotherapy and medication, whereas those with situational depression responded well to interpersonal psychotherapy with no added benefits if drugs were included in the treatment.

Conte and her colleagues (Conte, Plutchik, Wild, & Karasu, 1986) provide an additional perspective in a review of studies published between 1974 and 1984 comparing the outcome of combined treatment (psychotherapy and drug therapy) with either psychotherapy or medication administered alone. They used an elaborate statistical procedure that weighted studies according to their design adequacy. Seventeen reports on 11 patient samples were surveyed. Included in the analysis were some early reports on psychotherapies that were not specifically designed for treating depression in a focused way (e.g., marital psychotherapy, dynamic group psychotherapy, and psychotherapy to prevent relapse in patients who had been responsive to previous drug treatment). The authors of the review concluded that the combined treatment was "slightly" more efficacious than either drugs or psychotherapy when applied alone. However, they also note that the results might be interpreted as showing that most often there is no difference between combined treatments and psychotherapy or drugs administered alone. Indeed, the data showed that there was a four times greater likelihood that the combined condition would equal psychotherapy than be superior to it and that it was twice as likely that the combined treatment would equal drug treatment alone rather than exceed it.

Some may speculate that the constraints of adhering to an experimental design might render drug therapy less effective in study trials than it would be in "real life" where physicians feel free to flexibly change drugs or dosages. There is at present no empirical evidence for such a speculation. In fact, there are indications in the literature that treatment with medications, as typically used in practice, would not produce significantly better results. Teasdale, Fennell, Hibbert, and Amies (1984) compared treatment outcomes for 34 general practice patients with a major depressive disorder (91% meeting the Research Diagnostic Criteria for definite or probable endogenous major depressive disorder). Patients were randomly assigned to continue the treatment they would normally receive (which typically relied on antidepressant medication) or to receive sessions of cognitive psychotherapy in addition to treatment as usual. Following treatment, patients receiving cognitive therapy, in addition to usual medical treatment, showed a significantly superior outcome on blind and independently assessed measures of symptom severity (i.e., the Hamilton Rating Scale for Depression and the Montgomery Asberg Depression Scale). At termination, patients receiving cognitive therapy also rated themselves as less depressed (on the Beck Depression Scale) than those getting just the usual treatment. Post-treatment, 82% of the psychotherapy patients rated themselves as not depressed (on the Beck Scale) compared to 23% in the treatment as usual condition. Improvement for the usual treatment condition rose to 58% post-treatment if patients rated mildly depressed were included. At 3-month follow-up, results for the usual treatment group improved to a level comparable to the psychotherapy patients.

Another interesting point regarding trials comparing drugs and psychotherapy is made by Hollon and DeRubeis (1981). They note that studies most often use placebo-plus-psychotherapy combinations to represent psychotherapy in comparative trials. According to data they derived from several studies, the placebo-plus-psychotherapy combination is not equivalent to psychotherapy alone and therefore potentially misleading in assessing relative outcomes. In particular, they discovered that psychotherapy alone was more likely to exceed comparative treatments than was psychotherapy-plus-placebo. If proven correct, their arguments indicate that reviews of the literature may underestimate the efficacy of psychotherapy when compared to medication.

Perhaps the findings most relevant to the present chapter concern the percentage of patients who improved substantially as a result of drug treatment. These figures provide an approximation of a "cure rate." Of the 7 samples that provided this type of data, 5 showed that the rate of substantial or marked improvement was between 14% and 27% (Beck et al., 1985; Blackburn & Bishop, 1981, General Practice Sample; Hersen et al., 1984; McLean & Hakstian, 1979; Rush et al., 1977). The remaining 2 samples showed substan-

tial improvement rates of 56% (Murphy et al., 1984) and 77% (Blackburn &
Bishop, 1981, Hospital Outpatient Sample). The median percentage of patients who substantially improved on antidepressants in these 7 samples was
25%. This finding suggests that antidepressant medications may be significantly less potent in fully alleviating depressions than some reviews have
implied.

A statistical meta-analysis of 56 outcome studies comparing the relative
effectiveness of treating unipolar depression in adults with drugs or psychotherapy augments the findings cited earlier on specific types of psychotherapy for
depression. The meta-analysis (Steinbrueck, Maxwell, & Howard, 1983)
synthesized the results of studies on psychotherapy outcome for depression
and studies of drug therapy outcome for depression. The psychotherapy and
the drug therapy did not have to occur within the same study to be included,
although each treatment had to be compared to a control group. Treatment
effectiveness was measured by the computation of effect sizes for each study.
It was concluded that, on average, psychotherapy outcome was superior to
drug therapy outcome (with an average effect size that was approximately
twice as large). This conclusion needs to be viewed with some caution being
that the drug studies and the psychotherapy studies were not conducted under
exactly comparable conditions. Therefore, differences in outcome might be
due to differences in study characteristics rather than differences in the type of
treatment. Some of the differences may have favored psychotherapy outcome,
whereas other differences favored drug treatment. For example, a bias in favor
of psychotherapy outcome may have resulted from drug studies more often
employing double-blind procedures. In contrast, drug outcome was favored by
the treatment duration differences. The average duration of the drug therapy
in the studies reviewed was almost twice as long as the psychotherapy duration
(7 vs. 4 weeks). It was not possible in the integration of these diverse studies
to statistically ensure that the results were due only to differences in the
treatments.

Initial findings of the National Institute of Mental Health Treatment of
Depression Collaborative Research Program (Elkin et al., 1986) help to round
out the current picture. The study, conducted at three different sites, tested
the relative efficacy of two forms of psychotherapy (interpersonal psychotherapy and cognitive behavior therapy) and a standard drug treatment (imipramine) combined with clinical management. A pill-placebo control group with
clinical management was also included. Treatments were carefully defined
and standardized, and patients were objectively diagnosed using research
criteria. First reports on the results indicate no significant differences in
outcome between either of the psychotherapies and imipramine in reducing
depressive symptoms or affecting overall functioning. By 16 weeks, all treatments (including the placebo condition) resulted in a significant reduction in
symptoms of depression. The difference in outcome between active treatments

and placebo was more marked for the severely depressed patients. Improvement for all treatment groups was across a broad range of measures without differential effects in specific areas for different treatments. A more detailed presentation of the results, as well as work on significant predictors of treatment response, is promised for the future.

In summary, a growing number of carefully done trials comparing active, focused psychotherapies (such as cognitive or interpersonal therapy) to antidepressant drug treatment suggests that depressed outpatients receiving psychotherapy do at least as well, and sometimes better, than those receiving drugs. Although drugs may help patients with their sleep disturbances, research shows they are often less efficient than psychotherapy in helping patients with depression and apathy (DiMascio et al., 1979) and frequently ineffective in aiding patients in their social adjustment, interpersonal relationships, or work performance (Lyons, Rosen, & Dysken, 1985; Weissman, Klerman, Paykel, Prusoff, & Hanson, 1974). In contrast, psychotherapy with similar depressed outpatients has led to improvements in overall adjustment, interpersonal communication, and work performance while reducing interpersonal friction and anxious rumination (Weissman et al., 1974).

As our review notes, there are a few indications in the literature that drugs seem to work best with a subgroup of depressed patients who exhibit symptoms that have been associated with an endogenous classification (e.g., anorexia, weight loss, and insomnia). Presently, the studies demonstrating this are relatively few and the definitions utilized by different investigators are not always consistent with each other. Furthermore, as we have previously indicated, some investigators have not found endogenicity to predict either a unique response to drugs or a response that cannot be attained with non-drug treatment. There are also scattered suggestions in the literature that depressed patients with delusions, suicidal ideation, hypochondriacal concerns, or hysterical personality features may have a poor response to tricyclic medications (see review by Bielski & Friedel, 1976). In an update of the Bielski and Friedel review (1976) of predictors of antidepressant response, Friedel (1983) concluded that specific symptoms serve as better predictors of drug response than do diagnostic classifications. Diagnostic categories, even when determined by objective operational criteria such as the Feighner Criteria, the Research Diagnostic Criteria, or the DSM III Criteria for major depressive disorders, seem to produce groupings that are still too heterogeneous to allow for high-level prediction of tricyclic response. The update notes that psychomotor retardation now appears to be the strongest predictor of medication response. It remains for future research, which controls for depression severity and provides clear operational definitions for symptoms, diagnostic conditions, and treatments, to clarify whether the hints in the literature will result in specific, reliable personality predictors for good and poor response to antidepressant drugs.

RELAPSE

The literature suggests that after a period of recovery, depressed individuals frequently experience a return of their previously troubling symptoms. The reality of this observation is carefully documented in a review by Belsher and Costello (1988) who, after highlighting the ambiguities and inconsistencies in how relapse and recovery have been defined, show that approximately 50% of depressed patients relapse within 2 years of recovery. Overall, although the cumulative probability of relapse was proven to increase with time (i.e., 30% at 6 months, 40% at 12 months, and 50% at 2 years), individual patients were less likely to relapse the longer they stayed well. The review noted several factors that increased the likelihood of relapse. Included were the following: recent environmental stress, the lack of social support from family, a history of depressive episodes, and persistent neuroendocrine dysfunction following recovery.

Some researchers have proposed that antidepressant medication may be of particular value in staving off relapse in patients afflicted with *recurrent* unipolar depression who initially respond positively to the medication. For example, Prien and Kupfer (1986) reviewed six studies where such patients were either continued on antidepressants or switched to a placebo after responding positively to the initial trial on medication. On average, 50% of the patients relapsed when switched to a placebo, whereas only 22% of those continuing on the antidepressant relapsed. Prien and Kupfer went on to suggest that relapse was less likely if *responsive* patients were continued on the active drug until they had ben free of symptoms for 16 to 20 weeks. This research is consistent with some other indications that the nonpsychotic, nonbipolar depressions treated with drugs may not have a particularly positive long-term course once treatment stops. Kovacs, Rush, Beck, and Hollon (1981), in analyzing data from both their study and the work done in Boston and New Haven by Weissman and her co-workers (Weissman, Kasl, & Klerman, 1976), found that approximately two thirds of the patients became symptomatic again at some point during the first year after ceasing to take medication (irrespective of whether they had been on the medication for longer than 1 year or for only 3 months). Although rate of relapse for the 1 year following cognitive therapy seemed lower than the rate for those treated with drugs (44% vs. 65%), the relatively small number of patients involved rendered the differences in clinical course not statistically significant.

Hints are beginning to emerge that the protection against relapse afforded by medication may be at least equaled, and perhaps surpassed, by psychotherapy. Blackburn, Eunson, and Bishop (1986) presented follow-up results for patients with unipolar depression who had initially been assigned randomly for treatment with either cognitive psychotherapy or pharmacotherapy, or a combination of both therapies. Following symptom remission, recovered patients were continued for 6 months on maintenance trials of their respective treatments. Relapse rates (as defined by symptom scores) were shown to vary with the type of maintenance treatment. Within 6 months, 30% of those on medication maintenance had relapsed, compared to 6% for those receiving booster sessions of psychotherapy, and a zero rate for those maintained on the combination of both treatments. Recurrence rates at 2 years (as defined through the use of hospital records and case notes) were 78% medication maintenance, 23% psychotherapy, and 21% for the combination treatment. These data suggest that periodic psychotherapy sessions were more effective in preventing relapse than were maintenance dosages of the medication. However, these findings are based on a relatively small number of subjects and we do not know from these results if the patients initially treated with medication would have been better maintained with psychotherapy than they were with maintenance medication.

Kupfer and Frank (1987) present some initial data suggesting that relapse rates can be held to less than 10%, 4 months after recovery, if a combined treatment consisting of psychotherapy, an educational workshop, and medication is administered during both the acute and the continuation phases of treatment to patients with recurrent (mainly endogenous) depressions. They specifically attribute the low relapse rate they obtained to the addition of psychotherapy to maintenance medication, because other trials with similar patients receiving drug maintenance alone had been much less effective in preventing relapse. As these authors point out, to more definitively confirm the advantages of combined treatments over drug-only approaches in preventing relapse, the results need to be replicated and compared in a randomized trial to results for patients being continued on drug therapy alone and, we would add, to results for patients being continued on psychotherapy alone.

## NEW ANTIDEPRESSANT–PLACEBO STUDIES

A review of the literature on newer antidepressants by Kane and Lieberman (1984) created a unique opportunity for viewing drug effects from another vantage point. The review analyzed 49 efficacy studies of the drugs amoxapine, maprotiline, and trazodone. Of particular interest to us, however, was a subset of 20 studies that looked at one of the newer drugs in comparison to one of the standard tricyclic drugs (i.e., imipramine or amitriptyline) and placebos. All of these studies met the additional criteria (as stipulated by Kane and Lieberman) of appearing in English language publications, including only patients with depression, and having a minimum duration of 3 weeks for drug trial. We decided to focus on the results comparing the effectiveness of placebo to one of the standard drugs in each of the studies where such a comparison was possible. Our aim was to see if the work performed under the more sophisticated conditions of modern studies would show any change from the older literature in the effectiveness of the standard tricyclic drugs (imipramine or amitriptyline) when compared to placebo. These studies, of course, also offered the advantage of comparing the effectiveness of the standard tricyclics to a placebo in a situation where proving the efficacy of the standard drug was not a prime concern. In general, compared to the older literature the new studies used more careful, clear depression criteria for including patients and utilized currently accepted standards for drug dosage levels and treatment duration.

In order to develop an overall impression of outcome from the available studies, we followed Kane and Lieberman's decision to look at response rates in each of the studies. We examined each study to see if there was a significant difference in response rates between drug and placebo. Like Kane and Lieberman we were interested in "clinically meaningful" differences and we used the measures that they selected for their review. Therefore, the data from each study were included if any of the following three measures was available, listed in order of decreasing priority: the percentage of patients achieving (a) a specified final score on the Hamilton Depression Scale (HAM-D) that could be considered indicative of complete or near complete recovery; (b) a clinical global improvement rating of moderate or marked; or (c) a 50% reduction in scores from baseline to end point on the HAM-D or a comparable scale.

Of the 20 studies, 16 provided data on at least one of the three specified measures. Table 1.1 presents a list of the 16 studies along with information for each study on patient status, type of drug used, drug dosage, duration of drug trial, and significance of the drug–placebo difference. For purposes of categorization, studies that allowed maximum imipramine doses of 200 to 300 mg per day were considered high dosage (11 of 13 studies) and those that permitted amitriptyline doses up to 200 mg per day were classified as high dosage (3 of 3 studies). As can be seen, all but 2 of the studies permitted doses up to the commonly accepted maximum levels. In 2 of the studies, statistical tests for significance were not reported and had to be computed from the data presented. Two other studies did not report the percentage of improvement, but did indicate if there was or was not a statistically significant drug–placebo difference in the percentage of patients improving on one of the specified measures.

An overview of all 16 studies indicates that the majority (62%) show no difference in the percentage of patients benefiting from an active drug as opposed to a placebo. Additional analyses were conducted to see if drug–placebo outcome differences were affected by a number of patient or study variables: in- or outpatient status, duration of drug trial, dosage level, sample size. It might be assumed that hospitalized patients have a more severe form of depression and that this might affect results. Therefore, we separated the studies into those dealing with inpatients and those performed on outpatients. Both the majority of studies with inpatients (57%) and the majority of studies with outpatients (67%) showed no difference in the percentage of patients

TABLE 1.1
Summary of Newer Drug Trials Comparing Standard Tricyclics to Placebo

| Study | Patient Status Inpatient (I); Outpatient (O) | Drug Imipramine (Im); Amitriptyline (A) | Drug Dosage High (H); Low (L) | Duration of Trial (in weeks) | Significance of Drug-Placebo Difference (Sig. or N.S.) |
|---|---|---|---|---|---|
| Dominquez et al., 1981 | O | Im | H | 6 | N.S.[a] |
| Escobar et al., 1980 | I | Im | H | 4 | Sig. |
| Fabre et al., 1979 | I | Im | H | 4 | Sig. |
| Feighner, 1980 | I | Im | H | 4 | N.S. |
| Gershon et al., 1981 | O | Im | H | 4 | Sig. |
| Goldberg & Finnerty, 1980 | O | A | H | 6 | N.S. |
| Goldberg et al., 1981 | O | A | H | 6 | Sig. |
| Keiv & Okerson, 1979 | O | Im | L | 6 | N.S. |
| Kellams et al., 1979 | I | Im | H | 4 | N.S. |
| Mann et al., 1981 | O | Im | H | 4 | N.S. |
| Rickels & Case, 1982 | O | A | H | 6 | Sig. |
| Rickels et al., 1981 | O | Im | H | 6 | N.S. |
| R.C. Smith, 1975 | O | Im | L | 6 | N.S. |
| Steinbook et al., 1979 | I | Im | H | 4 | N.S. |
| Trapp et al., 1979 | I | Im | H | 4 | N.S. |
| Van Der Velde, 1981 | O | Im | H | 4 | Sig.[a] |

[a]Significance calculated from data presented

significantly improving on drugs as opposed to placebos. To see if longer lasting clinical trials produced better results than shorter trials, the studies were divided according to treatment duration. Nine of the studies had a treatment duration of 4 weeks and 7 of the studies had a 6-week treatment duration. Treatment duration made no difference in outcome. The majority of both shorter duration studies (56%) and longer duration studies (71%) showed no significant difference in the percentage of patients who responded to drugs or placebos. As previously noted, only 2 of the studies used a "low dose" of the drug and those studies were segregated from the higher dose studies to see if dosage made a difference. Neither of the low-dose studies revealed a drug–placebo difference. The majority of high-dose studies (57%) also showed no difference. Because a small sample size might diminish the probability of finding a statistically significant difference between drug and placebo treatments, the studies were divided into those that included sample sizes of 15 or more patients in each treatment group and those that did not. Seventy-five percent of the studies with the smaller sample sizes showed no significant drug–placebo difference and 50% of the large sample size studies showed no difference. The difference in outcome due to sample size was not significant. In sum, a series of chi-square analyses examining the number of studies showing significant drug–placebo differences and the number not showing differences indicated that inpatient status, treatment duration, dosage level, and sample size all played no role in determining significance. Only 4 of the 16 studies (all using outpatients) were conducted with a combination of the longer trial duration, higher dose levels and larger sample sizes. Half of these 4 studies showed significant results and half did not. In order to get a sense of overall improvement in these studies, reports of the percentage of patients who improved in each study were combined. On average, 59% of the patients on tricyclics were rated as improved, whereas 36% of the placebo-treated patients improved. The percentage of improvement on either drugs or placebos tended to be lower for inpatient (drugs 49%; placebos 21%) than it was for outpatients (drugs 67%; placebos 47%).

The review, therefore, does not support the idea that the effectiveness of the standard antidepressant drugs is more clearly demonstrated by newer drug trial investigations. Drug–placebo differences in outcome tended to be modest (with a median difference of 21%) and the majority of studies showed no difference in the percentage of patients *significantly* improved by drugs in contrast to placebos. There is no indication that current studies using more objective inclusion criteria, longer treatment durations, and acceptable medication dosages are achieving better outcomes than older studies did, and the overall drug–placebo outcome difference is frequently smaller than the 30% to 35% figure commonly reported in the older literature. The instability of response to drugs or placebos was readily apparent across the new drug trial studies. For drug treatment the percentage of patients improving ranged from 20% to 80%; whereas for placebo treatment the percentage of patients improving ranged from 0% to 91%. It could, of course, be argued that trials of longer than 6 weeks would show more significant drug effects; however, there are indications that many improved patients show a worsening during weeks 7 to 12 that necessitates an increase in dosage or a change of drug (Prien & Levine, 1984). It might also be argued that studies *allowing* adequate maximum drug dosages do not actually utilize the maximum dosage and therefore obscure drug effects. For the present, however, we must conclude that current research shows only modest drug effects. It should be added that the earlier review of the recent literature dealing with psychotherapeutic treatment of depression also underlines the relative modesty of antidepressant drug effects from still another perspective.


## DOUBLE-BLIND DESIGN

It goes without saying that unless a drug treatment produces a therapy result substantially exceeding that obtained from placebo and/or spontaneous recovery it has little value. This is especially true if one considers the not inconsiderable and sometimes life-threatening negative side effects that some drugs initiate. This point is widely accepted (Lasagna, 1979) and underlies the fact that the double-blind placebo design is considered essential for establishing therapeutic efficacy. There are acknowledged difficulties in applying the double-blind design. Foremost among these is the fact that the participants pick up cues that sometimes make it possible to differentiate between the patients receiving the active drug and those receiving the placebo (Jenner, 1977; Marini, Sheard, Bridges, & Wagner, 1976; Nash, 1962, Rabkin et al., 1986; Stallone, Mendlewicz, & Fieve, 1975). This is a serious problem because previous studies have shown that the less controlled the evaluation of a therapeutic procedure the more an experimenter can bias the outcome. The previously cited review by Wechsler et al. (1965) of the antidepressant literature nicely illustrates this point. They looked at more than 100 studies and reported that whereas 17 of 30 no-control studies reported at least 65% improvement, only 5 of 22 placebo-controlled studies showed that much improvement. Interestingly, too, Wechsler et al. discovered a significant positive correlation between degree of therapeutic efficacy of the active drug in each study and the efficacy of the placebo. If the drug effect was large, the placebo effect was also large. This suggests that despite the use of the double blind there was a spread of intensity of therapeutic expectation for the active drug to the placebo. A similar pattern, indicating that a placebo often has one half the efficacy of the active drug with which it is being compared, has also been described (Jospe, 1978).

By and large, the early, largely uncontrolled (non-double-blind) studies initiated by enthusiasts for a drug treatment are those that come up with the most dramatic therapeutic results. Karlowski et al. (1975) have actually shown that the breaking of the double blind by patients influences the patients' ratings of their symptoms. It should be acknowledged that some studies have not shown such an effect. There are many sources of uncontrolled information that can undermine a double-blind design. These have been reviewed elsewhere. They may variously involve differences between the active drug and the placebo with reference to the quantity and specific sites of their side effects, and also with reference to the time frames in which they generate responses (Guy, Gross, & Dennis, 1967; Jospe, 1978).

A serious source of interference with the double-blind are the cues supplied by the body sensations aroused by an agent. Hill, Haertzen, Wolbach, and Miner (1963) discovered that patients learn to discriminate between drug and placebo largely from cues provided by body sensations and symptoms. Examination of studies of the effectiveness of the antidepressants indicates that such agents produce different patterns of body sensations than do inert placebos. A substance like imipramine usually initiates clearly defined body experiences (e.g., dry mouth, tremor, sweating, constipation). Inactive placebos used in studies of antidepressants also apparently initiate some body sensations, but they are fewer, more inconsistent, and less intense as indicated by the fact that they are less often cited by patients as a source of discomfort causing them to drop out of treatment (Klein et al., 1980). Probably in the great majority of studies of the effectiveness of antidepressants involving a comparison with an inactive placebo there have been significant differences in the body experiences of the drug and placebo groups. Such differences could signal to the patients involved whether they were receiving an active or inactive agent and they could, further, supply discriminating cues to all personnel (e.g., nurses) responsible for the patients' day-to-day treatment. In the case of the personnel, one would expect that they would adopt different attitudes toward those they identified as being "on" versus "off" active treatment and consequently communicate contrasting expectations. Porter (1970) and also Rabkin et al. (1986) actually reported that in a double-blind study of imipramine it was possible by means of side effects to identify a significant number of the patients taking the active drug. Those patients receiving an inactive placebo have fewer signals (from self and from others) indicating they are being actively treated and should be improving. By the same token, patients taking an active drug like imipramine receive multiple signals that may well amplify potential placebo effects linked to the therapeutic context. Is it possible that a large proportion of the difference in effectiveness often reported in comparisons of antidepressants with inactive placebos can be explained as a function of body sensation discrepancies? It is conceivable, and fortunately there are research data that shed light on the matter.

## ACTIVE PLACEBO STUDIES

Let us begin with an analysis by Thomson (1982). He reviewed all the double-blind placebo-controlled studies of tricyclic antidepressants completed between 1958 and 1972 that he could find. He discovered that 68 of the studies had employed an inert placebo and 7 an active one (atropine) that produced a variety of body sensations. When the outcomes of the studies were computed, he found that whereas 59% of the designs in which an inert placebo was employed indicated that the tricyclic had a superior therapeutic effect, this was true in only one study (about 14% of the designs) in which the active placebo was utilized. The difference was statistically significant. Using an active placebo in the experimental designs eliminated any therapeutic advantage for the tricyclics. To check on the reliability of his own judgments, Thomson had a second rater evaluate the therapeutic outcomes that were described in the active placebo studies and this rater's judgments were in perfect agreement. Thomson raised the question whether the atropine employed as the active placebo might, because of its anticholinergic effects, have had an antidepressant effect. He wondered, too, whether researchers careful enough to incorporate an atropine placebo might simply have been more rigorous in their experimental designs. In any case, his findings did forcefully document the possibility that the active placebos produced greater therapeutic "amplification" than did the inert ones. It is important to emphasize that the failure to find drug–placebo differences in the studies cited by Thomson was not due to low rates of improvement in patients receiving antidepressants, but rather results largely from the elevated improvement rates in patients receiving the active placebos. Other findings in the literature suggest that an active substance increases placebo potency (Brune et al., 1962; Kast & Loesch, 1961). There are also data suggesting that the side effects associated with active drugs may enhance the drugs' therapeutic efficacy (Dinnerstein & Halm, 1970; Penick & Fisher, 1965).

Searching the literature concerned with the antidepressants, we found four other instances in which active placebos (or reasonable equivalents) were utilized, but which were not available to the Thomson analysis. In these studies differences between the antidepressant and the active placebo were of a low order. We briefly consider each here. Fahy, Imlah, and Harrington (1963) compared the efficacy of imipramine, electroconvulsive therapy, and thiopentone sleep treatments in treating patients with "moderately severe" depressive symptoms. Thiopentone sleep was considered to be a placebo. No significant differences among the three treatment conditions occurred. McLean and Hakstian (1979) tested the relative therapeutic power of amitriptyline, short-term psychotherapy, behavior therapy, and a control condition somewhat analogous to an active placebo. The control condition involved teaching patients how to relax their muscles and getting them to "appreciate the relation between muscle tension and depression" (p. 821). It was in the main focused on changing body experience. The patients who participated were "moderately clinically depressed." No differences were detected between the drug and control groups for any of several outcome measures. Weintraub and Aronson (1963/1964) examined the effects of imipramine and an active placebo (atropine). The majority of patients were classified as "moderately" to "severely" depressed. Although a group of resident physicians rated their patients as significantly more improved on imipramine than on placebo, the chief residents who performed the same set of ratings could not discern a significant difference. An MMPI measure of improvement that was included showed a modest significant advantage for imipramine. Friedman (1975) looked at the relative effectiveness of amitriptyline and an active placebo (atropine) in treating depression. This was done in the context of a "marital therapy" condition and a "minimal personal contact" condition. The actual design involved drug-marital therapy, drug-minimal contact, placebo-marital therapy, and placebo-minimal contact. All patients had a primary diagnosis of depression. At the end of 10 weeks of treatment there were only minor differences between the drug and placebo categories, as defined by rating scales. The effects of the drugs and placebos were more alike than different. Almost all of the ratings indicated an absence of significant differences. During a 2-week period subsequent to treatment when no drug or placebo was administered, differences in relapse rates could not be detected. Also, self-ratings by patients gave largely negative results with respect to drug versus placebo differences. The findings just reviewed are of the same tenor as Thomson reported in his analysis of the comparative efficacies of tricyclics and active placebos.

The fact that increasing the activity of a placebo intensifies its efficacy has been documented in other contexts too. For example, Kast and Loesch (1961) treated patients with "functional digestive disorders" with meprobamate and tridihexyliodide. They showed that adding atropine to the treatment and focusing the patients' attention on the "dry mouth" sensations associated with it changed the "improvement rate" significantly up or down, as a function of psychological sets they suggested. The addition of the "dry mouth" experience could be manipulated to alter improvement rates. Interestingly, Lipman, Park, Rickels, and Chase (1966) likewise found a variable impact on improvement rates of anxious patients treated with either chlordiazepoxide hydrochloride or chlordiazepoxide plus atropine, or placebo (inactive), or atropine. More specifically, focusing the patient's attention on "dry mouth" (produced by atropine) in the context of a physician describing "dry mouth" as a positive therapeutic indicator had a relatively more negative effect on improvement than did such focusing when the physician adopted a neutral attitude toward "dry mouth." Overall, the active placebo (atropine) was found under a "neutral set" condition to produce a poorer response than inactive placebo at one of the clinics participating in the study and a "marginally better" response at the two other participating clinics. Baker and Thorpe (1957) reported that a placebo had greater therapeutic efficacy than mepazine because the particularly sweet taste of the placebo was so sensorially impressive to the subjects. Fangman (1963) contrasted morphine with an inactive placebo and with an active placebo (phenobarbital) in the treatment of pain. Phenobarbital is not usually regarded as an analgesic but it does from the perspective of naive subjects

produce side effects similar to those for morphine. Although morphine proved
to be significantly more analgesic than the inactive placebo, it was only
marginally, or not at all, more analgesic than the active placebo. Rickels,
Lipman, and Raab (1966) indirectly highlighted the fact that the efficacy of
a placebo is influenced by how obviously it can be identified as non-active.
They carried out crossover studies in which patients received a placebo after
first being on either "therapeutically active" or "inactive" drugs. There was a
66% improvement rate for the placebo in those who had first received the
"inactive" drug; whereas the improvement rate was only 37% in those who
had initially received the "active" medication. The difference was statistically
significant. It was concluded: "In other words, when offering a patient the
possibility for a direct comparison between drugs, he frequently differentiates
between active agent and placebo, and the more effective clinically the first
agent, the worse is the subsequent placebo response" (p. 549). Apropos of
this observation, one must take a conservative and even somewhat skeptical
attitude toward reports in the literature (Prien & Kupfer, 1986) describing
substantial differences in the relapse rates of depressed patients who have
significantly improved as the result of antidepressant treatment and who are
either allowed to continue on their antidepressant medication or placed on
placebo. Patients who remain on their medication are roughly 35% less likely
to relapse than are those shifted to placebo. Obviously, those given the
placebo would receive numerous bodily cues that they were now ingesting an
inert substance and also the possibility would be afforded of an unusually vivid
direct comparison with the active agent.                                  .

Overall, one may conclude that the active placebo is more powerful than
the inactive placebo and this probably reflects the fact that the active placebo
more convincingly arouses body sensations that affirm that a potent agent has
been taken into one's body. Interestingly, the efficacy of a placebo may in
some contexts be significantly correlated with the number of side effects it
produces (Moertel, Taylor, Roth, & Tyce, 1976; Shapiro, Struening, Barten,
& Shapiro, 1975). In the Shapiro et al. study it was demonstrated that both
positive and negative effects of a placebo may be enhanced by a large number
of "side effects." Joyce (1959) found evidence that placebo responders may be
particularly sensitive to the autonomic changes occurring in their body, and
one may surmise that such responders unrealistically magnify the side effects
aroused by a placebo. Evidence exists that many of the effects of active drugs
may at times be linked simply to the changes in body experience they induce.
Karniol, Dalton, and Lader (1978) reported that the ratings by normal subjects
of their "well-being" after ingesting lithium chloride did not correlate with
plasma or erythrocyte lithium concentrations, but rather with amount of
nausea experienced. The peripheral effects of lithium (viz., nausea) and not
blood concentration levels were best predictive of subjective drug effects
reported. After reviewing the literature on response variability to psychotropic

drugs Janke (1983) concluded: "The usual assumption is that there is a substantial correlation between dosage level, concentration of the drug in the blood in nervous tissue, on the one hand, and behavioral changes on the other hand. Substantial correlations have been found sometimes, but not very frequently" (p. 40).

## BODY PERCEPTION

Research dealing with body perception indicates the need, in a trial context, for using active placebos capable of generating clear-cut body sensations. The prominence of one's own body in one's perceptual field has significant behavioral effects. When an active drug like imipramine is taken into the body it initiates body experiences that, in the light of past research (Fast & Fisher, 1971; Fisher, 1970, Fisher, 1986), can be said to increase body awareness. However, an inactive placebo would be less likely to enhance such awareness. This discrepancy could well bear on possible therapeutic effects. Consider the following: It has been shown (Duval & Wicklund, 1972) that procedures intensifying body awareness (e.g., being confronted with one's mirror image) increase the likelihood that people will behave in a conventional, self-controlled fashion. Several experiments have demonstrated that higher levels of body awareness inhibit deviant or antisocial behavior. Note that Greenberg and Fisher (1973) demonstrated that intensifying body awareness increases projective responses indicative of ability to plan ahead thoughtfully and restrain impulsive expression of affect. Obviously, one of the pathways to becoming a depressed patient in need of treatment or hospitalization is to display poorly controlled responses (e.g., crying, suicidal threats). Thus, an active drug like imipramine might result in an improvement in symptoms by virtue of the increased body awareness it induces. An inactive placebo would be less likely to do so. Note, too, that studies (Gibbons, 1977; Scheier & Carver, 1977) have indicated that with heightened body awareness there is an increased ability to discriminate whether one has been given an inactive placebo. This suggests that in a double-blind study of a drug like imipramine those taking the imipramine would, by virtue of their heightened body focus, be more accurately tuned into the attributes of the drug. Those taking the imipramine could be more certain they were not receiving an inactive treatment. Those on the inactive placebo would presumably be less accurately cognizant of what was happening to them. Such a difference in degree of assurance about what treatment one was receiving could have therapeutic consequences. Gibbons and Gaeddert (1984) summarized studies indicating that amount of body awareness affects responses to a placebo.

Incidentally, there are other known facts about the effects of intensified body awareness that may prove to be relevant to drug therapy research.

Evidence exists that men are made more anxious by increased body awareness than are women (Fisher, 1986). This raises the possibility that drugs that cause a rapid, vivid build-up of body sensations might be reacted to more sensitively by men and therefore result in their having a greater or smaller therapeutic response. It may prove profitable to examine sex differences in the effectiveness of drugs falling into such a category. Indeed, Glassman et al., (1977) reported that several studies have found a sex difference in response to imipramine. Brunswick, Amsterdam, Potter, Caroff, and Rickels (1983) summarize a number of findings demonstrating that the correlations between clinical responses to antidepressants and the plasma levels of such antidepressants tend to be significantly positive in women but not in men. Hamilton, Alagna, and Pinkel (1984) also describe a sex difference in the effects of an antidepressant upon self-perception. It is perhaps pertinent, too, that women who are depressed are more likely than depressed men to respond to the experience of being depressed by channeling their attention into self-examination (Nolen-Hoeksema, 1987) that could potentially magnify body sensations. Note, finally, that we (Greenberg, Fisher, & Shapiro, 1973) showed that degree of masculinity–femininity mediates the attitudes and even the side effect responses of certain classes of patients to antipsychotic medications.

Another interesting point derives from research based on body landmark functions that indicates that stimulation of specific body sectors selectively affects feelings about self and responses to classes of stimuli (Fisher, 1962; Gottschalk & Uliana, 1976). Past research (Fisher, 1970; Fisher, 1986; Fisher & Cleveland, 1958) has shown that augmenting sensations in the skin or muscle increases body boundary definiteness, whereas intensifying body interior sensations has the opposite effect. Drugs that have selectively arousing effects on such exterior versus interior body sites could, then, influence the sense of boundary definiteness and this, in turn, could affect levels of personal insecurity. In another context (Fisher, 1970), it was found that a vibratory stimulus to the back of the body affects selective learning for words that have dirt or contaminatory connotations. Or stimulation to the mouth affects selective memory for words with hostile-aggressive implications (Fisher, 1970). Consider the possible implications of the last example just cited with respect to a drug like imipramine. A salient side effect of imipramine is the sensation of "dry mouth." This probably magnifies the prominence of the mouth in the body scheme, which, in turn, could conceivably modify reactions to hostile themes. A widely discussed psychodynamic formulation about depression focuses on the manner in which hostile impulses are channeled. Therefore, the selective highlighting of the mouth by imipramine might, by virtue of its effects on the processing of hostile themes, have an impact on level of depression. Incidentally, it may be pertinent to this point that Leyburn (1967) cites reports of a "relation between the doctor's ratings of improvement and the frequency of dry mouth" (p. 1137) in patients participating in a study utilizing imipramine.

Conceivably, various drugs could, quite analogously, mobilize awareness of certain major body areas that are associated with specific emotional themes and thereby indirectly influence psychodynamic processes involved in particular clinical syndromes. Because inactive placebos less often mobilize focused and sustained awareness of a specific body sector, they would be less likely to exert such an influence. The body image literature indicates that any agent affecting body experience can potentially influence behavior. It is an oversimplification to assume that the effects of drugs used in psychiatry need only be considered in the context of their direct CNS action. The ways in which they alter body perception may also be of consequence.

## EXPANDING THE DOUBLE-BLIND DESIGN

The material reviewed earlier indicates that the double-blind design has not been realistically applied to the evaluation of antidepressant drugs. It is amazing that so much care has been devoted to controlled research designs, but with a gross neglect of the need for utilizing an active placebo. This has been true despite sporadic questioning about this matter (Blumenthal, Burke, & Shapiro, 1974; Rohsenow & Marlatt, 1981). One cannot but wonder about this oversight. It is apparent that the oversight applies not only to the evaluation of the antidepressants but also all other drugs (e.g., antipsychotic, antianxiety) used in psychiatric treatment. Until a respectable number of studies are completed for each of the drugs currently used that would compare active placebo with drug results, we must consider that an adequate scientific appraisal has not yet occurred for such drugs. This is a matter that urgently needs to be confronted. We have not systematically included other safeguards in the typical double-blind design to ensure that the participants have not breached the double-blind. In view of what we know, it would seem important to plan the following as part of all drug evaluation designs:

1. Frequent reports by patients of what they perceive their treatment to be.

2. Systematic measurement not only of patients' "side effects" but also of the patterning of their body experiences (Fisher, 1970) when they receive "treatment" agents. Such measures would permit an analysis of whether drug and placebo were being experienced differently, even if patients could not explicitly discriminate whether they were receiving drug or placebo. This

would be especially important to do if patients were receiving an active placebo.

3. Frequent reports by personnel involved in the patient's care as to their perceptions of what treatment the patient is receiving.

Only a few scattered studies have attempted even approximations of such evaluations.

Others who have criticized the double-blind design have offered suggestions that might help to balance its deficiencies. For example, Guy et al., (1967) proposed using neutral raters and data evaluators who would be recruited outside the ranks of those carrying out the study and who would therefore be more resistant to biasing factors. There have also been novel suggestions about ways of elaborating the design so that more information is available as to the role of placebo effects in therapeutic results. Thus, Rohsenow and Marlatt (1981) sketch the following paradigm that was originally proposed by Ross, Krugman, Lyerly, and Clyde (1962); expect drug/receive drug, expect drug/receive placebo, expect no drug/receive drug, expect no drug/receive placebo. They manipulate expectancies systematically, with the active drug either present or replaced by a placebo. They cite findings indicating that such a design has been helpful in disentangling placebo and drug effects in studies of alcohol. Plutchik, Platman, and Fieve (1969) suggest analogously that designs for drug studies need not simply seek to eliminate placebo effects, but rather can include conditions that manipulate these effects. They propose pushing the effects to their limits in order to ascertain their maximum impact. Illustratively, they visualize using patients and psychiatrists who are extremely positive toward a particular drug and then measuring how much this enhances its efficacy. They reason that one could accumulate information about the psychological context that most reinforces an active drug and try to duplicate that context whenever the drug is administered.

Apropos of the power of the placebo, Dinnerstein, Lowenthal, and Blitz (1966–1967), after reviewing the placebo literature, arrived at the following provocative formulation:

> As drugs are normally employed in laboratory studies, clinical research, or clinical practice involving pain or anxiety, they have no predictable effects on a given person except as modifiers of the placebo effects. Rather than producing direct and unambiguous pharmacological effects on a subject's pain or anxiety, drugs act primarily as amplifiers or inhibitors of the placebo effects. (p. 104)

Although this perspective is almost shocking in its extremeness, it calls attention to the fact that we have been inclined to exclude or get rid of placebo effects rather than to recognize their centrality in most of the published research dealing with drug treatment of psychological difficulties.

Overall, we would underscore that the purpose of our critique is to raise questions about the magnitude of the therapeutic efficacy of the antidepressants and also the scientific methodology employed to test that efficacy. It is important to emphasize that we are not suggesting that antidepressants are simply dramatic placebos. It may well be that the action of, for example, the tricyclics at specific brain sites significantly decreases depressive symptomatology. However, until adequate studies involving active placebos are carried out, it is difficult to disentangle the direct physiological variance from that due to placebo amplification. Depressed patients who detect improvement in their state, upon receiving an antidepressant may perceive this as a dramatic signal that there is hope of recovery. Such an expectation plus the vivid body experiences that are usually initiated by antidepressants plus the perceived positive therapeutic expectation of those administering the treatment may well synergistically result in considerable clinical improvement. Overall, it is difficult to see how a fair therapeutic evaluation can be attained unless an active placebo is included in experimental designs. If one generalizes, this would apply also to the evaluation of any drug directed at symptoms with a large psychological component.

## REFERENCES

APA Task Force (1985). Tricyclic antidepressants—Blood level measurements and clinical outcome. *American Journal of Psychiatry, 142,* 155–162.

Ainslie, J. D., Stiefel, J. R., & Jones, M. B. (1966). Practical drug evaluation method. *Archives of General Psychiatry, 15,* 368–372.

Atkinson, R. M., & Ditman, K. S. (1965). Tranylcypromine: A review. *Clinical Pharmacology and Therapeutics, 6,* 631–655.

Baker, A. A., & Thorpe, J. G. (1957). Placebo response. AMA *Archives of Neurology & Psychiatry, 78,* 57–60.

Beck, A. T. (1967). *Depression: Causes and treatment.* Philadelphia: University of Pennsylvania Press.

Beck, A. T., Hollon, S. D., Young, Y. E., Bedrosian, R. C. & Budenz, D. (1985). Treatment of depression with cognitive therapy and amitriptyline. *Archives of General Psychiatry, 42,* 142–148.

Bellack, A. S., Hersen, M., & Himmelhoch, J. (1981). Social skills training compared with pharmacotherapy and psychotherapy in the treatment of unipolar depression. *American Journal of Psychiatry, 138,* 1562–1567.

Bellack, A. S., Hersen, M., & Himmelhoch, J. (1983). A comparison of social-skills training, pharmacotherapy and psychotherapy for depression. *Behavior Research and Therapy, 21,* 101–107.

Belsher, G., & Costello, C. G. (1988). Relapse after recovery from unipolar depression: A critical review. *Psychological Bulletin, 104,* 84–96.

Benson, H., & McCallie, D. P. Jr. (1979). Angina pectoris and the placebo effect. *New England Journal of Medicine, 300,* 1424–1429.

Beutler, L. E., Scogin, F., Kirkish, P., Schretlen, D., Corbishley, A., Hamblin, D., Meredith, K., Potter, R., Bamford, C. R., & Levenson, A. I. (1987). Group cognitive therapy and alprazolam in the treatment of depression in older adults. *Journal of Consulting and Clinical Psychology, 55,* 550–556.

Bielski, R. J., & Friedel, R. O. (1976). Prediction of tricyclic antidepressant response. *Archives of General Psychiatry, 33,* 1479–1489.

Blackburn, I. M., & Bishop, S. (1981). Is there an alternative to drugs in the treatment of depressed ambulatory patients? *Behavioral Psychiatry, 9,* 96–104.

Blackburn, I. M., Bishop, S., Glen, A. I. M., Whalley, L. J., & Christie, J. E. (1981). The efficacy of cognitive therapy in depression: A treatment trial using cognitive therapy and pharmacotherapy, each alone and in combination. *British Journal of Psychiatry, 139,* 181–189.

Blackburn, I. M., Eunson, K. M., & Bishop, S. (1986). A two-year naturalistic follow-up of depressed patients treated with cognitive therapy, pharmacotherapy and a combination of both. *Journal of Affective Disorders, 10,* 67–75.

Blackwell, B. (1982). Antidepressant drugs: Side effects and compliance. *Journal of Clinical Psychiatry, 43,* 14–18.

Blumenthal, D. S., Burke, R., & Shapiro, A. K. (1974). The validity of "identical matching placebos." *Archives of General Psychiatry, 31,* 214–215.

Brune, G., Morpurgo, C., Bielkus, A., Kobayashi, T. Tourlentes, T., & Himwich, H. (1962). Relevance of drug induced extrapyramidal reactions to behavioral changes during neuroleptic treatment. Treatment with trifluoperazine singly and in combination with trihexyphenidyl. *Comprehensive Psychiatry, 3,* 227–234.

Brunswick, D. J., Amsterdam, J. D., Potter, L., Caroff, S., & Rickels, K. (1983). Relationship between tricyclic antidepressant plasma levels and clinical response in patients treated with desipramine or doxepin. *Acta Psychiatrica Scandinavica, 67,* 371–377.

Cole, J. O. (1964). Therapeutic efficacy of antidepressant drugs. A review. *Journal of the American Medical Association, 190,* 124—131.

Conte, H. R., Plutchik, R., Wild, K. V., & Karasu, T. B. (1986). Combined psychotherapy and pharmacotherapy with treatment of depression: A systematic analysis of the evidence. *Archives of General Psychiatry, 43,* 471–479.

Davis, J. (1965). Efficacy of tranquilizing and anti-depressant drugs. *Archives of General Psychiatry, 13,* 552–572.

Davis, J., Klerman, G., & Schildkraut, J. (1968). Drugs used in the treatment of depression. In D. H. Efron (Ed.), *Psychopharmacology: A review of progress (1957–1967)* (pp. 719–747). Public Health Service Publication, No. 1,836.

DeRubeis, R. J. (1983, December). *The cognitive–pharmacotherapy project: Study design, outcome, and clinical followup.* Paper presented at the American Association of Behavior Therapy, Washington, D.C.

DiMascio, A., Weissman, M. M., Prusoff, B. A., Neu, C. Zwilling, M., & Klerman, G. L. (1979). Differential symptom reduction by drugs and psychotherapy in acute depression. *Archives of General Psychiatry, 36,* 1450–1456.

Dinnerstein, A. J., & Halm, J. (1970). Modification of placebo effects by means of drugs: Effects of aspirin and placebos on self-rated moods. *Journal of Abnormal Psychology, 75,* 308–314.

Dinnerstein, A. J., Lowenthal, M., & Blitz, B. (1966–67). The interaction of drugs with placebos in the control of pain and anxiety. *Perspectives in Biology & Medicine, 10,* 103–117.

Dominguez, R. A., Jacobson, A. F., Weiss, B. L., Goldstein, B. J., & Steinbook, R. M. (1981). A placebo-controlled comparison of amoxapine and imipramine in the treatment of depressed outpatients. *Current Therapeutic Research, 29,* 714–727.

Duval, S., & Wicklund, R. A. (1972). *A theory of objective self-awareness.* New York: Academic Press.

Elkin, I., Shea, T., Imber, S., Pilkonis, P., Sotsky, S., Glass, D., Watkin, J., Leber, W., & Collins, J. (1986, October). *NIMH treatment of depression collaborative research program:*

*Initial outcome findings.* Paper presented at the meeting of the American Association for the Advancement of Science, Philadelphia, PA.

Escobar, J. I., Gomez, J., Constain, C., Rey, J., & Santacruz, H. (1980). Controlled clinical trial with trazodone, a novel antidepressant. A South American experience. *The Journal of Clinical Pharmacology, 20,* 124–130.

Fabre, L. F., McLendon, D. M., & Gainey, A. (1979). Trazodone efficacy in depression: A double-blind comparison with imipramine and placebo in day-hospital type patients. *Current Therapeutic Research, 25,* 827–834.

Fahy, P., Imlah, N., & Harrington, J. (1963). A controlled comparison of electroconvulsive therapy, imipramine and thiopentone sleep in depression. *Neuropsychiatry, 4,* 310–314.

Fangman, J. J. (1963). *The effects of morphine on two forms of experimental pain.* Unpublished master's thesis, Fordham University, Bronx, NY.

Fast, G., & Fisher, S. (1971). The role of body attitudes and acquiescence in epinephrine and placebo effects. *Psychosomatic Medicine, 33,* 63–84.

Feighner, J. P. (1980). Trazodone, a triazolopyridine derivative, in primary depressive disorder. *Journal of Clinical Psychiatry, 41,* 250–255.

Feighner, J. P., Aden, G. C., Fabre, L. F., Rickels, K., & Smith, W. T. (1983). Comparison of alprazolam, imipramine, and placebo in the treatment of depression. *Journal of the American Medical Association, 249,* 3057–3064.

Fisher, S. (1962). Theme induction of localized somatic tension. *Journal of Nervous & Mental Disease, 134,* 34–47.

Fisher, S. (1970). *Body experience in fantasy and behavior.* New York: Appleton-Century-Crofts.

Fisher, S. (1986). *Development and structure of the body image.* (Vols. 1 & 2). Hillsdale, NJ: Lawrence Erlbaum Associates.

Fisher, S., & Cleveland, S. (1958). *Body image and personality.* Princeton, NJ: Van Nostrand.

Friedel, R. O. (1982). The relationship of therapeutic response to antidepressant plasma levels: An update. *Journal of Clinical Psychiatry, 43,* 37–42.

Friedel, R. O. (1983). Clinical predictors of treatment response: An update. In J. M. Davis & J. W. Maas (Eds.), *The affective disorders* (pp. 379–384). Washington, DC: American Psychiatric Press.

Friedman, A. S. (1975). Interaction of drug therapy with marital therapy in depressive patients. *Archives of General Psychiatry, 32,* 619–637.

Friedman, A. S., Granick, S., Cohen, H. W., & Cowitz, B. (1966). Imipramine (tofranil) vs. placebo in hospitalized psychotic depressives. (A comparison of patients' self-ratings, psychiatrists' ratings and psychological test scores). *Journal of Psychiatric Research, 4,* 13–36.

Gershon, S., Mann, J., Newton, R., & Gunther, B. J. (1981). Evaluation of trazodone in the treatment of endogenous depression: Results of a multicenter double-blind study. *Journal of Clinical Psychopharmacology, 1,* 39S–44S.

Gibbons, F. X. (1977, April). *Self-focused attention and the attribution of arousal: Inhibition of the placebo effect.* Paper presented at 48th annual meeting of Eastern Psychological Association, Boston.

Gibbons, F. X., Gaeddert, W. P. (1984). Focus of attention and placebo utility. *Journal of Experimental Social Psychology, 20,* 159–176.

Glassman, A. H., Perel, J. M., Shostak, M., Kantor, S. J., & Fleiss, J. L. (1977). Clinical implications of imipramine plasma levels for depressive illness. *Archives of General Psychiatry, 34,* 197–204.

Goldberg, H. L., & Finnerty, R. J. (1980). Trazodone in the treatment of neurotic depression. *Journal of Clinical Psychiatry, 41,* 430–434.

Goldberg, H. L., Rickels, K., & Finnerty, R. (1981). Treatment of neurotic depression with a new antidepressant. *Journal of Clinical Psychopharmacology, 1,* 35S–38S.

Gottschalk, L. A., & Uliana, R. L. (1976). A study of the relationship of nonverbal to verbal behavior: Effect of lip caressing on hope and oral references as expressed in the content of speech. *Comprehensive Psychiatry, 17,* 135–152.

Greenberg, R. P., & Fisher, S. (1973). A muscle awareness model for changes in Rorschach human movement responses. *Journal of Personality Assessment, 37,* 512–518.

Greenberg, R. P., Fisher, S., & Shapiro, J. (1973). Sex-role development and response to medication by psychiatric in-patients. *Psychological Reports, 33,* 675–677.

Greenblatt, M., Grosser, G. H., & Wechsler, H. (1964). Differential response of hospitalized depressed patients to somatic therapy. *American Journal of Psychiatry, 120,* 935–943.

Guy, W., Gross, M., & Dennis, H. (1967). An alternative to the double blind procedure. *American Journal of Psychiatry, 123,* 1505–1512.

Hamilton, J. A., Alagna, S. W., & Pinkel, S. (1984). Gender differences in antidepressant and activating drug effects on self-perceptions. *Journal of Affective Disorders, 7,* 235–243.

Hersen, M., Bellack, A. S., Himmelhoch, J. M., & Thase, M. E. (1984). Effects of social skill training, amitriptyline and psychotherapy in unipolar depressed women. *Behavior Therapy, 15,* 21–40.

Hill, H. E., Haertzen, C. A., Wolbach, A. B., Jr., & Miner, E. J. (1963). The Addiction Research Center Inventory: Appendix. I. Items comprising empirical scales for seven drugs. II. Items which do not differentiate placebo from any drug condition. *Psychopharmacologia, 4,* 184–205.

Hollon, S. D., & DeRubeis, R. J. (1981). Placebo-psychotherapy combinations: Inappropriate representations of psychotherapy in drug-psychotherapy comparative trials. *Psychological Bulletin, 90,* 467–477.

Janke, W. (1983). Response variability of psychotropic drugs: Overview of the main approaches to differential pharmacopsychology. In W. Janke (Ed.), *Response variability to psychotropic drugs* (pp. 33–65). Elmsford, NY: Pergamon Press.

Jenner, F. A. (1977). Some of the problems and difficulties associated with clinical studies of antidepressant agents. *British Journal of Clinical Pharmacology, 4,* 199S–207S.

Jospe, M. (1978). *The placebo effect in healing.* Lexington, MA: Lexington Books.

Joyce, C. R. B. (1959). Consistent differences in individual reactions to drugs and dummies. *British Journal of Pharmacology, 14,* 512–521.

Kane, J. M., & Lieberman, J. (1984). The efficacy of amoxapine, maprotiline and trazodone in comparison to imipramine and amitriptyline: A review of the literature. *Psychopharmacology Bulletin, 20,* 240–249.

Karlowski, T. R., Chalmers, T. C., Frenkel, L. D., Kapikian, A. Z., Lewis, T. L., & Lynch, J. M. (1975). Ascorbic acid for the common cold. A prophylactic and therapeutic trial. *Journal of the American Medical Association, 231,* 1038–1042.

Karniol, I. G., Dalton, J., & Lader, M. H. (1978). Acute and chronic effects of lithium chloride on physiological and psychological measures in normals. *Psychopharmacology, 57,* 289–294.

Kast, E. C., & Loesch, J. (1961). Influence of the doctor-patient relationship on drug action. *Illinois Medical Journal, 119,* 390–393.

Katschnig, H., Nutzinger, D., & Schanda, H. (1986). Validating depressive subtypes. In H. Hippius, G. L. Klerman, & N. Matussek (Eds.), *New results in depression research* (pp. 36–44). Berlin Heidelberg: Springer Verlag.

Kellams, J. J., Klapper, M. H., & Small, J. G. (1979). Trazodone, a new antidepressant: Efficacy and safety in endogenous depression. *Journal of Clinical Psychiatry, 40,* 390–395.

Kiev, A., & Okerson, L. (1979). Comparison of the therapeutic efficacy of amoxapine with that of imipramine. *Clinical Trials Journal, 16,* 68–72.

Klein, D. F., & Davis, J. M. (1969). *Diagnosis and drug treatment of psychiatric disorders.* Baltimore: Williams & Wilkins.

Klein, D. F., Gittleman, R., Quitkin, F., & Rifkin, A. (1980). *Diagnosis and drug treatment of psychiatric disorders: Adults and children* (2nd ed.). Baltimore: Williams & Wilkins.

Klerman, G. L., & Cole, J. O. (1965). Clinical pharmacology of imipramine and related antidepressant compounds. *Pharmacological Reviews, 17*, 101–141.

Kocsis, J. H., Hanin, I., Bowden, C., & Brunswick, D. (1986). Imipramine and amitriptyline plasma concentrations and clinical response in major depression. *British Journal of Psychiatry, 148*, 52–57.

Kovacs, M., Rush, A. J., Beck, A. T., & Hollon, D. (1981). Depressed outpatients treated with cognitive therapy or pharmacotherapy. A one-year follow-up. *Archives of General Psychiatry, 38*, 33–39.

Kuhn, R. (1958). The treatment of depressive states with G-22355 (imipramine hydrochloride). *American Journal of Psychiatry, 115*, 459–464.

Kupfer, D. J., & Frank, E. (1987). Relapse in recurrent unipolar depression. *American Journal of Psychiatry, 144*, 86–88.

Lasagna, L. (1979). Placebos and controlled trials under attack. *European Journal of Clinical Pharmacology, 15*, 373–374.

Leyburn, P. (1967). A critical look at antidepressant drug trials *The Lancet, 2*, 1135–1138.

Lipman, R. S., Park, L. C., & Rickels, K. (1966). Paradoxical influence of a therapeutic side-effect interpretation. *Archives of General Psychiatry, 15*, 462–474.

Lyons, J. S., Rosen, A. J., & Dysken, M. W. (1985). Behavioral effects of tricyclic drugs in depressed inpatients. *Journal of Consulting & Clinical Psychology, 53*, 17–24.

Mann, J. J., Georgotas, A., Newton, R., & Gershon, S. (1981). A controlled study of trazodone, imipramine, and placebo in outpatients with endogenous depression. *Journal of Clinical Psychopharmacology, 1*, 75–80.

Marini, J. L., Sheard, M. H., Bridges, C. I., & Wagner, E., Jr. (1976). An evaluation of the double-blind design in a study comparing lithium carbonate with placebo. *Acta Psychiatrica Scandinavica, 53*, 343–354.

McLean, P. D., & Hakstian, A. R. (1979). Clinical depression: Comparative efficacy of outpatient treatments. *Journal of Consulting and Clinical Psychology, 47*, 818–836.

McNair, D. M. (1974). Self-evaluations of antidepressants. *Psychopharmacologia, 37*, 281–301.

Moertel, C. G., Taylor, W. F., Roth, A., & Tyce, F. A. J. (1976). Who responds to sugar pills? *Mayo Clinic Proceedings, 51*, 96–100.

Moller, S. E., Reisby, N., Elley, J., Krautwald, O., Ortmann, J., & Larsen, O. B. (1985). Biochemical and diagnostic classification and serum drug levels: Relation to antidepressive effect of imipramine. *Neuropsychobiology, 13*, 160–166.

Morris, J., & Beck, A. (1974). The efficacy of antidepressant drugs. A review of research (1958–1972). *Archives of General Psychiatry, 30*, 667–674.

Murphy, G. E., Simons, A. D., Wetzel, R. D., & Lustman, P. J. (1984). Cognitive therapy and pharmacotherapy, singly and together in the treatment of depression. *Archives of General Psychiatry, 41*, 33–41.

Nash, H. (1962). The double-blind procedure: Rationale and empirical evaluation. *Journal of Nervous & Mental Disease, 134*, 34–47.

Nolen-Hoeksema, S. (1987). Sex differences in unipolar depression: Evidence and theory. *Psychological Bulletin, 101*, 259–282.

Penick, S., & Fisher, S. (1965). Drug-set interaction: Psychological and physiological effects of epinephrine under differential expectations. *Psychosomatic Medicine, 27*, 177–182.

Plutchik, R., Platman, S. R., & Fieve, R. R. (1969). Three alternatives to the double-blind. *Archives of General Psychiatry, 20*, 428–432.

Porter, A. M. W. (1970). Depressive illness in a general practice. A demographic study and a controlled trial of imipramine. *British Medical Journal, 1*, 773–778.

Prien, R. F., & Kupfer, D. J. (1986). Continuation drug therapy for major depressive episodes: How long should it be maintained? *American Journal of Psychiatry, 143*, 18–23.

Prien, R. F., & Levine, J. (1984). Research and methodological issues for evaluating the therapeutic effectiveness of antidepressant drugs. *Psychopharmacology Bulletin, 20*, 250–257.

Prusoff, B. A., Weissman, M. M., Klerman, G. L., & Rounsaville, B. J. (1980). Research Diagnostic Criteria subtypes of depression: Their role as predictors of differential response to psychotherapy and drug treatment. *Archives of General Psychiatry, 37*, 796–801.

Quality Assurance Project (1983). A treatment outline for depressive disorders. *Australian and New Zealand Journal of Psychiatry, 17*, 129–146.

Quitkin, F. M. (1985). The importance of dosage in prescribing antidepressants. *British Journal of Psychiatry, 147*, 593–597.

Quitkin, F. M., Rabkin, J. G., Ross, D., & McGrath, P. J. (1984). Duration of antidepressant drug treatment: What is an adequate trial? *Archives of General Psychiatry, 41*, 238–245.

Rabkin, J. G., McGrath, P., Stewart, J. W., Harrison, W., Markowitz, J. S., & Quitkin, F. (1986). Follow-up of patients who improved during placebo washout. *Journal of Clinical Psychopharmacology, 6*, 274–278.

Rabkin, J. G., Stewart, J. W., McGrath, P. J., Markowitz, J. S., Harrison, W., & Quitkin, F. M. (1987). Baseline characteristics of 10-day placebo washout responders in antidepressant trials. *Psychiatry Research, 21*, 9–22.

Raskin, A., & Crook, T. H. (1975). The endogenous-neurotic distinction as a predictor of response to antidepressant drugs. *Psychological Medicine, 5*, 78–82.

Reisby, N., Gram, L. F., Beck, P., Nagy, A., Petersen, G. O., Ortmann, J., Ibsen, I., Dencker, S. J., Jacobsen, O., Krautwald, O., Sondergaard, I., & Christiansen, J. (1977). Imipramine: Clinical effects and pharmacokinetic variability. *Psychopharmacology, 54*, 263–272.

Rickels, K., & Case, W. G. (1982). Trazodone in depressed outpatients. *American Journal of Psychiatry, 139*, 803–806.

Rickels, K., Case, W. G., Werblowsky, J., Csanalosi, I., Schless, A., & Weise, C. C. (1981). Amoxapine and imipramine in the treatment of depressed outpatients: A controlled study. *American Journal of Psychiatry, 138*, 20–24.

Rickels, K., Lipman, R., & Raab E. (1966). Previous medication, duration of illness and placebo response. *Journal of Nervous & Mental Disease, 142*, 548–554.

Rogers, S. C., & Clay, P. M. (1975). A statistical review of controlled trials of imipramine and placebo in the treatment of depressive illnesses. *British Journal of Psychiatry, 127*, 599–603.

Rohsenow, D. J., & Marlatt, G. A. (1981). The balanced placebo design: Methodological considerations. *Addictive Behaviors, 123*, 1505–1512.

Ross, S., Krugman, A. D., Lyerly, S. B., & Clyde, D. J. (1962). Drugs and placebos: A model design. *Psychological Reports, 10*, 383–392.

Roth, D., Bielski, R., Jones, M., Parker, W., & Osborn, G. (1982). A comparison of self-control therapy and combined self-control therapy and antidepressant medication in the treatment of depression. *Behavior Therapy, 13*, 133–144.

Rush, A. J., Beck, A. T., Kovacs, M., & Hollon, S. (1977). Comparative efficacy of cognitive therapy and pharmacotherapy in the treatment of depressed outpatients. *Cognitive Therapeutic Research, 1*, 17–37.

Rush, A. J., & Watkins, J. T. (1981). Group versus individual cognitive therapy: A pilot study. *Cognitive Therapy and Research, 5*, 95–103.

Scheier, M. F., & Carver, C. S. (1977). Self-focused attention and the experience of emotion: Attraction, repulsion, elation, and depression. *Journal of Personality and Social Psychology, 35*, 625–636.

Shapiro, A. K., Struening, E. L., Barten, H., & Shapiro, E. (1975). Correlates of placebo reaction in an outpatient population. *Psychological Medicine, 5*, 389–396.

Simpson, G. H., Edmond, H. P., & White, K. (1983). Plasma drug levels and clinical response to antidepressants. *Journal of Clinical Psychiatry, 44*, 27–34.

Simpson, G. M., Lee, J. H., Cuculic, A., & Kellner, R. (1976). Two doses of imipramine in hospitalized endogenous and neurotic depressives. *Archives of General Psychiatry*, *33*, 1093–1102.

Smith, A., Traganza, E., & Harrison, G. (1969). Studies on the effectiveness of antidepressant drugs. *Psychopharmacology Bulletin*, *5*, 1–53.

Smith, M. L., Glass, G. V., & Miller, T. I. (1980). *The benefits of psychotherapy*. Baltimore: Johns Hopkins University Press.

Smith, R. C. (1975). Amoxapine, imipramine and placebo in depressive illness. *Current Therapeutic Research*, *18*, 346–353.

Stallone, F., Mendlewicz, J., & Fieve, R. (1975). Double-blind procedure: An assessment in a study of lithium prophylaxis. *Psychological Medicine*, *5*, 78–82.

Steinbook, R. M., Jacobson, A. F., Weiss, B. L., & Goldstein, B. J. (1979). Amoxapine, imipramine and placebo: A double-blind study with pretherapy urinary 3-methoxy-4-hydroxphenylglycol levels. *Current Therapeutic Research*, *26*, 490–496.

Steinbrueck, S. M., Maxwell, S. E., & Howard, G. S. (1983). A meta-analysis of psychotherapy and drug therapy in the treatment of unipolar depression with adults. *Journal of Consulting & Clinical Psychology*, *51*, 856–863.

Teasdale, J. D., Fennell, M. J. V., Hibbert, G. A., & Amies, P. L. (1984). Cognitive therapy for major depressive disorder in primary care. *British Journal of Psychiatry*, *144*, 400–406.

Thomson, R. (1982). Side effects and placebo amplification. *British Journal of Psychiatry*, *140*, 64–68.

Trapp, G. A. Handorf, C. R., & Larach, V. (1979). Trazodone in the treatment of depressed inpatients. *Psychopharmacology Bulletin*, *25*, 25–27.

Van Der Veide, C. D. (1981). Maprotiline versus imipramine and placebo in neurotic depression. *Journal of Clinical Psychiatry*, *42*, 138–141.

Watt, D. C., Crammer, J. L., & Elkes, A. (1972). Metabolism, anticholinergic effects, and the therapeutic outcome of desmethylimipramine in depressive illness. *Psychological Medicine*, *2*, 397–405.

Wechsler, H., Grosser, G. H., & Greenblatt, M. (1965). Research evaluating antidepressant medications on hospitalized mental patients: A survey of published reports during a 5-year period. *Journal of Nervous and Mental Disease*, *141*, 231–239.

Weintraub, W., & Aronson, H. (1963/64). Clinical judgment in psychopharmacological research. *Journal of Neuropsychiatry*, *5*, 65–70.

Weissman, M. M., Kasl, S. V., & Klerman, G. L. (1976). Follow-up of depressed women after maintenance treatment. *American Journal of Psychiatry*, *133*, 757–760.

Weissman, M. M., Klerman, G. L., Paykel, E. S., Prusoff, B., & Hanson, B. (1974). Treatment effects on the social adjustments of depressed patients. *Archives of General Psychiatry*, *30*, 771–778.

Weissman, M. M., Prusoff, B. A., DiMascio, A., Neu, C., Goklaney, M., & Klerman, G. L. (1979). The efficacy of drugs and psychotherapy in the treatment of acute depressive episodes. *American Journal of Psychiatry*, *136*, 555–558.

Wilson, P. H. (1982). Combined pharmacological and behavioral treatment of depression. *Behavior Research and Therapy*, *20*, 173–184.

## 2 MEASUREMENT ISSUES IN THE EVALUATION OF PSYCHOPHARMACOLOGICAL THERAPY

Edward J. Murray
*University of Miami*

The purpose of this chapter is to examine the measures used in drug therapy outcome studies and the impact of issues about these measures on the validity of conclusions about the effectiveness of drug treatment for psychological disorders. We briefly review issues raised in psychotherapy outcome research and then extend these to drug therapy research. We concentrate on measures used in therapy for depression research because there has been a good deal of research and discussion about measurement issues in this area in recent years. The issues in this area are representative of those of drug therapy in general.

## MEASUREMENT IN PSYCHOTHERAPY OUTCOME RESEARCH

In a seminal paper, Strupp and Hadley (1977) suggested that values may be important in psychotherapy outcome evaluation. They recommend that people looking at outcome from different vantage points might have different ways of judging it. For example, a depressed patient may be seen as greatly improved by a psychiatrist, but the patient may not feel that the depression has been alleviated enough to suffer from the side effects of medication. So, too, a change welcomed by the patient may not be welcomed by society. Strupp and Hadley recommend that the effects of psychotherapy, and by extension drug therapy, be evaluated from three perspectives: society, the individual patient, and the mental health professional.

In a similar vein, an NIMH project (Waskow & Parloff, 1975) recom-

mended that a battery of measures be used in evaluating psychotherapy outcome representing several vantage points. From the vantage point of the self
were the Hopkins Symptom Checklist, the MMPI, and Target Complaints.
From the therapist vantage point was Target Complaints. From the vantage
point of an independent evaluator was the Psychiatric Status Schedule. From
the vantage point of relevant others was the Katz Adjustment Scales or the
Personal Adjustment and Role Skills Scales. Although this particular selection
seems somewhat dated and is not a standard battery now, the main point is
that evaluating treatment outcome requires measures from a number of vantage
points. There is no single ultimate criterion.

The most useful and comprehensive recent analysis of treatment outcome
measures that we have found is *The assessment of psychotherapy outcome* by
Lambert, Christensen, and DeJulio (1983). Although this book is oriented
to the evaluation of psychotherapy outcome, the issues are just as applicable
to drug treatment, and in fact, the measures are the same, to a large extent.
In general, the contributors in this book are in favor of multiple measures from
several vantage points; however, they analyze the strengths and weaknesses of
measures of various vantage points.

Self-report measures are reviewed by Beutler and Crago (1983). First,
Beutler and Crago are critical of measures of self-reported improvement,
which are widely used, on the grounds that such ratings are greatly influenced
by the patient's status at the termination of treatment. It is better to directly
assess the patient's status before and after therapy independently. Standardized
personality tests have been used for this purpose, the best of which is the
MMPI. However, the authors conclude that the MMPI is too cumbersome
and insensitive to change to be useful in outcome evaluation, although it may
be useful as a predictor of individual differences in response to treatment.
They recommend, instead, the revised Hopkins Symptom Checklist, the
SCL-90-R, which accesses various symptoms and affective states. When a
specific group of patients, such as anxious or depressed, is studied they recommend specific single-trait measures such as the State–Trait Anxiety Inventory
or the Beck Depression Inventory. They detail a number of problems with
measures of individual target symptoms or scales developed for specific theoretical orientations such as humanistic, analytic, cognitive, or behavioral. Such
measures offer no great advantage over the more general scales and make
comparisons between treatments more difficult. The recommended self-report
scales deal with symptoms and affective states that make them particularly
useful for evaluating the effects of drugs.

An analysis of the use of therapists' evaluation of psychotherapy was
presented by Newman (1983). In general, therapists' evaluations have been
viewed as suspect because of a self-serving bias. Newman cited evidence that
suggests that problems of reliability and accuracy in therapists' evaluations may

be no greater than similar problems in evaluations by patients or independent observers. Furthermore, he believes that sources of bias in therapists' evaluations can be identified and controlled for in various ways. He argued that a major source of bias is impressions formed early in therapy, based on diagnosis, social class, and the nature of referral. He also cited evidence that training improves therapists' ratings; however, he stated that little is known and the demand characteristics of evaluations at termination and follow-up. Of course, it is at termination and follow-up that we are most concerned about possible biases in favor of certain drugs or drug therapy in general. Newman discussed a dozen of the most widely used scales of the more than 100 in the literature. In general, global scales such as Global Assessment Scale, the Menninger Health-Sickness Scale, and the Level of Functioning Scale have the advantage of allowing the therapist to integrate all the information into a single judgment, but have been found to have low reliability. Newman believes training would help in this regard. Other instruments reviewed include the Psychiatric Status Schedule, the Brief Psychiatric Rating Scale, the Clinical Global Impression Scale, and Goal Attainment Scales. However, all of these scales can also be used by independent clinical evaluators. Newman presented an admirable defense of therapists' evaluations and suggestions for improvement, but the problem of bias remains.

The use of ratings by independent clinical evaluations, usually based on interviews after treatment or preferably before and after treatment, is discussed by Auerbach (1983). There are several sources of invalidity in such interview ratings, including the halo effect, or the tendency to rate all traits in the direction of a general impression, the leniency error, or the tendency to rate a patient as more improved than he or she is, and the central tendency error, or the tendency to avoid extreme judgments. In addition, the patient may not give accurate information for a variety of reasons, and the information gained from an interview may not generalize to other situations. Nevertheless, interview ratings are extremely popular in evaluating drug therapy, based largely on the assumption that biases are controlled for by a double-blind design. We return to this issue later.

Auerbach is not satisfied with any of the instruments in common use. For example, the Psychiatric Status Schedule, although reliable, does not correlate well with measures from other sources. Furthermore, it is long and contains a lot of irrelevant questions. Auerbach believes that more information can be gained by an unstructured interview. The Schedule for Affective Diseases and Schizophrenia (SADS) was viewed more favorably but was criticized by Auerbach as too heavily diagnostic. Thus, the depressed patient has to answer a lot of questions designed to rule out schizophrenia. The Structured and Scaled Interview to Assess Maladjustment (SSIAM) has the advantage of covering important areas of social adjustment but has not proved particularly sensitive to therapeutic change. A derivative of the SSIAM, the Social Adjustment Scale (SAS), seems somewhat more sensitive to change but does not relate well to other measures. Auerbach also raised questions about the appropriateness of many of the items. Auerbach recommended using a global rating such as the Global Assessment Scale, but he concedes that the reliability and validity of such scales remain in doubt.

Auerbach did not evaluate the Hamilton Rating Scales for anxiety (HAM-A) or depression (HAM-D), which are widely used in drug treatment. However, the HAM-A is reviewed by Roberts, Aronoff, Jensen, and Lambert (1983), who were impressed by its reliability and psychometric properties. On the other hand, in a recent review Maier, Buller, Philipp, and Heuser (1988) found that although the reliability and concurrent validity of the HAM-A were adequate, there were problems of internal validity, particularly in that anti-anxiety and anti-depressant effects cannot be distinguished. Furthermore, they found that the subscale of somatic anxiety was correlated with the appearance of side effects from medication. In another chapter, Moran and Lambert (1983) conclude that the Hamilton Depression Scale (variously called the HRS, the HRSD, or the HAM-D) is the choice for interviewer-based ratings of depression. They believe that the reliability of the HAM-D is good and that it appears valid in assessing outcome of both psychotherapy and drug therapy. We return to this most widely used interviewer-based rating scale for depression in psychopharmacological treatment.

Davidson and Davidson (1983) review instruments developed to gather data from the third major viewpoint, that is, society or, specifically, significant others such as relatives and friends. They point out that these significant others may also be biased and difficult to communicate with. Many of the measures are adaptations of scales used by mental health professions such as the SSIAM, the SAS, and the PSS. The most widely used is the Katz Adjustment Scale-Relatives Form (KAS-R). This scale appears to have reasonably good reliability, be sensitive to treatment effects, and converge with other measures. Although it was developed for use with severely pathological patients, it seems useful with depressed patients and even normals. An alternative is the Personal Adjustment and Role Skills Scale (PARS). Unfortunately, very few studies of drug therapy, other than for psychosis, have used this source of information.

In summarizing this massive analysis of outcome measures, Lambert and Christensen (1983) believe that the trend is toward understanding that change is multidimensional and measures should reflect that. Furthermore, there is a trend toward greater specificity of measurement for specific populations. As our understanding of the nature of the problems in a specific population increases, specific measures can be developed and used in addition to a multidimensional core battery.

## MEASUREMENT IN PSYCHOPHARMACOLOGICAL THERAPY

Historically, the most common method for evaluating the effects of psycho-pharmacological treatment has been a simple, homemade psychiatric global rating scale. These have been typically unstandardized with no reliability reported. These ratings are sometimes made by the therapist and sometimes by an independent evaluator. We still find such measures as the sole or main measures utilized. For example, in a recent report of the NIMH Collaborative Study Group (Prien et al., 1984) conclusions were based on two global psychiatric ratings, whereas data from a battery of much better developed clinical ratings and self-report scales were not even reported. No reliability was reported for the global ratings.

Furthermore, global psychiatric ratings are often used as the criterion for the validity of other measures. For example, Montgomery and Asberg (1979) developed a new depression scale specifically designed to be sensitive to drug effects and used, as the criterion, the global judgment of an experienced clinician as to whether the patients were responders or nonresponders. In a somewhat more sophisticated study, Cicchetti and Prusoff (1983) evaluated the reliability of several global ratings on depressed patients and found that the reliability ranged from fair to good, with the lowest reliability at the start of therapy. Furthermore, the reliability of global ratings was not noticeably better than that of the Hamilton Rating Scale, which is often validated against such global rating scales. In fact, global psychiatric rating scales are really only crude measures of what the more developed psychiatric rating scales also measure, although they may have the advantage of including more facets of a disturbed state such as depression that may be underemphasized by any one formal rating system.

Sometimes DSM-III diagnoses are used as a method of validating an evaluation instrument. For example, Carr and Smith (1985) validated a self-report measure of depression against DSM-III diagnoses. They found that their self-report measure distinguished depressives from nondepressives and severely melancholic from nonmelancholic depression. However, the DSM-III was designed for diagnostic classification and is not set up to measure change quantitatively. The general consensus among researchers is that a quantitative scale is necessary for evaluating treatment outcome.

One implicit assumption in the widespread use of global, and even quanti-fied, psychiatric ratings is that the clinician's judgment is the ultimate criterion of treatment outcome. Although such a view seems intuitively sound to many, it has been challenged and there are alternative views. As we discussed in reviewing psychotherapy measures, there are sources of bias in evaluating patient improvement from any one of the several vantage points including that of the clinician's judgment.

Nevertheless, judgments from the vantage point of the clinician have been the sole basis for evaluating drug treatment in many studies and continue to be so. For example, in a major study of antidepressant medication conducted by the World Health Organization (1986), 324 depressed patients in seven centers in five countries were given either amitriptyline, imipramine, or maprotiline. The measures were a Clinical Global Impression Schedule, the HAM-D, and the WHO-SADD, as well as several instruments for diagnosis, side effects, and general information. These instruments were all given by a clinical assessor, usually the same assessor for all scales given to a patient at all time periods. Although drug therapy was found to be effective, the reliance on one source of information limits the credibility of the study.

There has been a trend for the inclusion of at least a self-report measure in some of the more recent studies. In a review of the more commonly used measures in depression research, Hughes, O'Hara, and Rehm (1982) found that these measures fall into five classes: Self-report inventories, such as the Beck Depression Inventory; Self-monitoring, which is a more specific and continuous self-report; Ratings by significant others, such as the Katz scales; Clinician's ratings, such as the Hamilton Rating Scale for Depression; and Ward Observations, using an instrument such as the Brief Psychiatric Rating Scale. These measures have been discussed earlier. The most common combination is a clinician rating and a self-report.

In discussing general issues in the design of research evaluating psychopharmacological as well as behavioral treatments, Ackles (1986) commented on the measures that have been used. He categorized clinical ratings and self-report measures as weak and not objective. The most frequently used measures, global clinical impressions, were deemed the least satisfactory because of subjectivity and susceptibility to systematic bias. Ackles argued for the use of more objective direct behavioral measures such as laboratory measures of performance and physiological responding as well as direct behavioral observations. However, outside of special populations such as attention-deficit children and sexual impotence, objective measures have rarely been used. Furthermore, laboratory measures may have problems of their own, particularly in their generalizability to everyday behavior.

There are some promising attempts to develop objective measures. For example, Ulrich and Harms (1985) report on a method to evaluate retardation and agitation in depressed patients before and after drug treatment. Videotapes during interviews were scored by objective ratings of nonverbal behavior. Specific changes in facial expression, hand activity, and restlessness were found. Another type of measure is the EEG during the sleep of depressed patients (e.g., Kerkhofs, Hoffman, DeMartelaere, Linkowski, & Mendlewicz, 1985). Using this method, the effects of drugs on REM sleep can be evaluated, and a much more objective record of insomnia can be obtained than nurses' ratings, which often conflict with patient reports (e.g., Mazure, Nelson, & Price, 1986).

A major recent work on the evaluation of psychopharmacological treatment of depression is *The measurement of depression* by Marsella, Hirschfeld, and Katz (1987). This volume includes chapters on diagnostic, genetic, neurotransmitter, neuroendocrine, and epidemiological measures. More relevant here are papers on clinical, behavioral, and psychological measures.

Rabkin and Klein (1987) reviewed the global and structured clinical interviews and rating scales that we have already covered. They noted that the measures most widely used were introduced over a decade ago and have not been noticeably improved. They believe that there is a pressing need to develop these measures further to increase their sensitivity and applicability to special populations rather than to allow the proliferation of new measures at each research site.

A major theme of *The measurement of depression* is the need to evaluate the effects of psychopharmacological therapy from multiple vantage points. This point is made very clearly by Katz (1987) who describes one of the major studies in the field, the NIMH Collaborative Depression Program on biological treatment. In this study, measures were obtained from experienced clinicians (e.g., HAM-D), nurses on the ward (e.g., Global Ward Behavior Scale), the patients (e.g., SCL-90), and laboratory performance tasks (e.g., reaction time). Neurochemical measures were also obtained. This study can be used as a benchmark for the measurement of drug therapy. Unfortunately, the study has other methodological problems. For example, the design called for a 2-week placebo period and a 4-week treatment period with no control group. This design does not adequately control for placebo effects. Nevertheless, it was possible to identify those who would respond to the drugs much earlier on clinician ratings than on self-reports. This was also true to a lesser degree with nurses' ratings.

Rehm (1987) also emphasized the importance of multiple measures from a behavioral viewpoint. Thus, he included self-report measures as a form of verbal behavior, clinician observations of both verbal and nonverbal behavior, and observations by nurses and others as overt behavior. The ultimate in objectivity is mechanical assessment that would include ratings of videotapes of interviews, therapy, and group therapy. In general, such measures are reliable but do differ from more conventional measures suggesting that a different realm is being investigated.

Lewinsohn and Rohde (1987) also believe that the shortcomings of both clinical ratings and self-report measures can be remedied by the use of behavioral and physiological measures. They mention measures of behavior in the home and on the ward. They also recommend measures of cognitive activity such as expectancies, distortions, causality attributions, and self-reinforce-

ment. This point is amplified by Rush (1987) who reviewed various measures
of cognition related to Beck's theory of depression.

Thus, we see that the standard in the field of measuring outcome of
psychopharmacological treatment has moved from global clinical impressions
to more structured clinical interview scales. Furthermore, complete reliance
on the vantage point of the clinician just recently has given way to a recognition that the vantage points of the patient and other members of society are
valid and should be included. Finally, the need for objective behavioral and
physiological measures has been pointed out, although such measures are not
in widespread use.

Although the use of multiple measures has become the goal of sophisticated
researchers in the evaluation of both psychotherapy and psychopharmacological therapy, such measures present important problems. Thus, Garfield (1980)
raised the issue of what happens if the three or four vantage points do not
agree. He suggests that it is important to investigate the basis for discrepancies,
although he is generally in favor of including measures from several vantage
points.

In fact, an examination of research articles on the evaluation of psychopharmacological treatment over the past decade, particularly for studies with
adults with affective disorders, shows that very few use more than two vantage
points—clinical ratings, usually by a psychiatrist, and patient self-reports. In
the case of depression treatment two specific measures stand out in frequency
of usage and methodological concern—the Hamilton Rating Scale for Depression and the Beck Depression Inventory. In the following sections, we make
a detailed analysis and comparison of these two instruments. We use these
two examples to highlight several important issues in measuring the effects of
drug therapy. We want to emphasize that these two instruments are not the
only nor necessarily the best measures available but that a great deal of research
has been done with them and about them so that important measurement
issues can be discussed.

## THE HAMILTON RATING SCALE FOR DEPRESSION

The most widely used psychiatric rating scale for depression is the Hamilton
Rating Scale for Depression (HAM-D) developed by Hamilton (1960, 1967).
This scale is based on an interview with the patient, although information
from relatives, nurses, and others is sometimes taken into account. In an
open-ended manner, the clinician asks about 17 variables rated on 3- or 5-
point scales. These variables include psychologically oriented items such as
depressed mood, guilt, suicidal ideation, work and interests, loss of insight,
and psychological anxiety symptoms. More somatically oriented items include
insomnia, retardation and agitation, somatic anxiety symptoms, gastrointesti-

nal symptoms, general somatic symptoms, and loss of weight. There is a total score.

The inter-rater reliability of the HAM-D was assessed initially by Hamilton (1960) by having two clinicians score a joint interview. These quasi-independent ratings provided high inter-rater reliability ($r = .90$). Other studies using the joint-interview approach have found similar levels of inter-rater reliability (see Hedlund & Vieweg, 1979). However, the use of joint interviews, as well as the statistical analysis in these early studies, has been criticized by Cicchetti and Prusoff (1983). Using independent raters, they found that, at the beginning of treatment, reliability, assessed by the more appropriate intra-class correlation coefficient, was only .46 for the total score. However, the reliability improved at the end of treatment to .82. They also found that the reliability of the individual items on the HAM-D ranged from poor to excellent, with many more poors than good or excellent. In another study with independent raters (Faravelli, Albanesi, & Poli, 1986) the inter-rater reliability of the HAM-D was found to be .95 using the Pearson method but only .50 using the kappa method. Thus, the reliability of the HAM-D seems to depend on the method of rating, the statistical procedure used, the time of rating, and other factors such as the type of patient population.

The HAM-D has also been factor analyzed in a number of studies (Faravelli et al., 1986; Hamilton, 1960, 1967; Hedlund & Vieweg, 1979; Rhoades & Overall, 1983). Although different factors have been extracted in different studies, four that emerge frequently are Sleep Disturbance, Apathy, Somatization, and Depressive-Anxious Mood. According to the results reported by Cicchetti and Prusoff (1983), the reliabilities of these four factors range from poor to good at the beginning of treatment to good to excellent at the end of treatment. Thus, factor scores also show the effect of time assessed, which is particularly important in assessing treatment outcome.

In general, the concurrent validity of the HAM-D has been evaluated by relating it to other psychiatric ratings (see Hedlund & Vieweg, 1979). An example of this research is that of Knesevich, Biggs, Clayton, and Ziegler, (1977). Hamilton ratings were made by two psychiatrists, based on a joint interview, and then averaged. The Hamilton scores were related to the treating physicians' ratings on an 11-point global scale at the 1st, 3rd, and 6th weeks of drug treatment. The Spearman correlation between the total Hamilton Score and the global rating was .89, $p < .001$. The correlation for change during therapy was also impressive, .68, $p < .001$. Although the Hamilton raters were said to be "blind to treatment," it is difficult to believe that they were unaware that some type of drug was being used or that they were unaware of the time in treatment of individual patients. The validity of the Hamilton has not been satisfactorily answered by studies of this type.

In a more recent study (Faravelli et al., 1986), the HAM-D correlated fairly well (on the order of .70) with two other psychiatric rating scales, the

Wechsler Depression Rating Scale (Wechsler, Grosser, & Busfield, 1963), and the depression section from the Bunney and Hamburg (1963) Rating Scales, as well as a homemade 5-point Global Clinical Impression Scale. However, in this study the ratings for all of these scales were made by two psychiatrists in the course of the same interview. The use of such joint interviews was criticized earlier by Cicchetti and Prusoff (1983) in connection with inter-rater reliability and applies even more to validating one scale against another.

Montgomery and Asberg (1979) report on a similar scale designed to be sensitive to change. They report that their scale is more sensitive to change than the Hamilton, but their results were not statistically significant. Furthermore, both scales were rated in a conjoint interview. One interesting sidelight to this study was that psychomotor retardation was dropped from their final scale for not being sensitive to change. Psychomotor retardation is an important part of the HAM-D.

The internal validity of the HAM-D has been criticized because of the heterogeneity of items that are included. Some of these items are not truly depressive, for example, the anxiety items. Thus, Prien and Levine (1984) point out that the total HAM-D could show a decrease after a supposedly antidepressant drug because of a decrease on items such as anxiety/somatization, sleep disturbance, and weight loss without significant change on other items. Thus, there may have been no real anti-depressant effect but rather an antianxiety effect.

An illustration of the point made by Prien and Levine (1984) is a study by Dunbar, Naarala, and Hijtunen (1985) in which the HAM-D was used to evaluate the effects of two anti-depressant drugs. The HAM-D total score significantly decreased more with mianserin than with clomipramine. However, of the four factor scores only the HAM-D anxiety/somatization measure significantly differentiated the two drugs. Thus the differential effect of the drugs could be due to anxiety rather than depression.

In another study, diazepam, an antianxiety drug, was used as a control for evaluating the effects of antidepressants with an elderly sample (Ather, Ankier, & Middleton, 1985). All medications were highly effective on the HAM-D with no statistically significant differences among treatments, including diazepam. On the other hand, the physician's general assessment suggested that the diazepam was less effective. In another study comparing buspirone and diazepam with anxious patients on both the HAM-A and the HAM-D both drugs were shown to be effective on both measures (Rickels et al., 1982).

Part of the problem here is that people are frequently anxious as well as depressed, and some drugs are anxiolytic as well as antidepressive. Recall that the HAM-A was also criticized as being unable to distinguish between anxiolytic and antidepressant effects by Maier et al., 1988, who felt that its internal validity was faulty. So, too, the internal validity of the HAM-D is faulty. What is needed are two scales that permit the evaluation of depression and anxiety separately.

The construct validity of a psychiatric rating measure is, in many ways, more important than the inter-rater reliability of a given measure or the concurrent or internal validity. This important point was made in a study by Mazure et al. (1986, p. 451). These authors say: "Although it is important to establish how a clinical measure relates to other variables, this approach to validity does not address the basic issue of whether a clinical rating measures what it purports to measure. When a patient reports a symptom, can we assume the symptom is present and that it might be observed in daily behavior outside the interview?"

In this study, these authors used 26 depressive symptom ratings obtained on interviews by clinicians with 62 patients hospitalized with major depression. These clinicians showed very good reliability on the symptoms drawn from the HAM-D and the DSM-III Major Depression Criteria, but as usual they used simultaneous interviews.

Validity was assessed by a behavioral checklist filled out by the nursing staff over a 3-day period in both formal and informal settings. Although the authors point out that there is no agreed-upon "true" measure of depression and no acceptable biological markers, they reasoned that interview measures should be related to generally observable behavior over a longer period of time. The behavioral checklist, whose characteristics were not described nor reliability established, paralleled the interview ratings in content.

In evaluating the concordance between the interview ratings and the behavioral checklist, the symptoms were divided into three groups on the basis of how they were made during the interview: (a) clinical observation only; (b) clinical observation and patient report; and (c) patient report only. The best results were found with the first two categories, which involved at least some use of observational signs. The best of these was "lack of responsiveness" with an $r = .69$, $p < .001$ between interview rating and checklist. This variable is based entirely on observation during the interview and also on observation by the nursing staff. Global severity, hopelessness, and depressed mood also met the authors' criteria for good concordance. In general, the order of magnitude for the relationship between measures involving observation or observation plus patient report was about .50; not an impressive relationship.

On the other hand, the symptoms evaluated on interview on the basis of patient report only showed a poorer concordance with behavioral observations, on the order of .40. The one exception to this was decreased appetite, which was $r = .65$, $p < .001$. The reason for this good prediction was that it was possible to make very clear observations about eating behavior. Obviously, it is more difficult to make objective ratings about loss of energy or difficulty in concentrating.

Interestingly, the validity of items about sleep, such as the classical symptoms of difficulty in falling asleep and early morning wakening, was very low. The authors conclude that patient reports of sleep disturbances may not be valid. However, it may also be that a nurse's observations of sleep behavior may not be valid. For example, a patient may be awake with eyes closed in the early morning. The issue requires the better behavioral and physiological measures of the sleep laboratory.

What can we conclude from this study? First of all, the most clearly observable symptoms of depression and depressed mood seen on interview can also be observed on a hospital ward by the nursing staff. Second, patient reports should be taken seriously. When a really good observational measure such as eating behavior is available, patients prove accurate. When poor behavioral measures, such as judgments of sleep are used, patients may appear to be inaccurate. Third, a lot of depressive content is not readily observable and may be revealed more in one situation than another. That is, some material may be revealed to a psychiatrist but not to a nurse or, equally possible, to a nurse but not to a psychiatrist.

In general, Mazure and associates are to be applauded for addressing the issue of the validity of interview-based symptom ratings. However, in contrast to the care with which the interview-based measures were developed, the behavioral system seems primitive and inadequate in many ways. At this point the only depressive symptom ratings that appear to be validated in this study are those that are extremely obvious to a casual observer.

Dissatisfaction with the Hamilton has led to the development of an improved version called the Clinical Interview for Depression (Paykel, 1985). This psychiatric rating scale was set up more systematically, appears to have good psychometric properties, and is reported to be more sensitive to change than the Hamilton and other ratings. Reliability and validity were established by using separate interviews rather than the usual conjoint interviews. The Clinical Interview for Depression may be the depression rating system of the future. However, as Paykel pointed out, the Hamilton is so widely used and familiar to investigators that it may not be so readily replaced.

To summarize, the HAM-D is very widely used to assess antidepressant medication. Although the HAM-D is generally thought to be highly reliable, most of this work has been based on joint psychiatric interviews. When independent interviews are conducted, the reliability is not very impressive at intake, although it improves at the end of treatment when the rater has more information about the patient. The same is true for the reliability of the factors. The concurrent validity of the HAM-D with other clinician ratings also appears to be good but is marred by the frequent practice of having one rater fill out all the measures. The internal validity of the HAM-D is also questionable because it seems to be sensitive to anxiety and anxiolytic drugs as well as depression and antidepressive drugs. Construct validity has not been adequately evaluated. Thus, the HAM-D has a number of problems that could play a role in its validity as an outcome measure.

## THE BECK DEPRESSION INVENTORY

The most widely used self-report measure of depression is the Beck Depression Inventory (BDI). This measure was originally a 21-item scale developed on the basis of nearly 1,000 psychiatric patients (Beck, Ward, Mendelson, Mock, & Erbaugh, 1961). This inventory was found to have good internal reliability and was validated against clinical ratings. A short, 13-item form of the BDI has also been developed and correlated well with the long form (Beck & Beck, 1972). However, the short form has been criticized on the grounds that, although the cognitive components are adequate, the somatic components of depression, already somewhat weak in the original BDI, are much weaker (Vredenburg, Krames, & Flett, 1985). A revised version of the long form of the BDI was developed (Beck, Rush, Shaw, & Emery, 1979) that improved some of the items and that has about the same internal consistency as the original scale (Beck & Steer, 1984).

The internal consistency of the BDI seems rather good in recent studies (e.g., Beck & Steer, 1984; Gallagher, Nies, & Thompson, 1982; Lightfoot & Oliver, 1985; Reynolds & Gould, 1981). In a comprehensive review of 25 years of research on the BDI, Beck, Steer, and Garbin (1988) concluded that the internal consistency of the instrument has been established in a number of populations. For psychiatric populations the alphas ranged from .76 to .95 with a mean of .86. With nonpsychiatric populations the alphas ranged from .73 to .92 with a mean of .81.

Beck et al. (1988) also reviewed the stability, or test–retest reliability, in 10 studies over time periods ranging from 4 hours to 4 months. For psychiatric patients the Pearson $rs$ ranged from .48 to .86 and for nonpsychiatric populations from .60 to .83. The heterogeneity of populations and time periods makes it difficult to evaluate these results. Perhaps a better example is the study by Gallagher et al. (1981) who retested 77 older patients over a period of 1 to 3 weeks and got a Pearson $r$ of .86.

Factor analytic studies of the BDI have produced a variety of factor structures dependent on method, populations, and other matters (e.g., Reynolds & Gould, 1981; Vredenburg et al., 1985; Weckowitz, Muir, & Cropley, 1967). In their review of some of the better factor analytic studies, Beck et al. (1988) concluded that there is one underlying factor representing the general syndrome of depression, as well as several others depending on the population, but typically: negative attitudes toward the self, performance impairment, and somatic disturbance.

A comprehensive critique of all the major self-report measures of depression has been made by Boyle (1985). He said that earlier positive reviews have overlooked important psychometric deficiencies in these self-report measures. Some of his criticisms are that different scales tap into different facets of depression, have problems with reliability, have been inappropriately factor analyzed, and are usually not assessments of multivariate affective states. In the case of the BDI specifically, Boyle said that it measures symptoms of depression rather than the underlying syndrome of depression that would include psychomotor retardation as well as depressed mood. Boyle also faults the high test–retest reliability and split-half item homogeneity of the BDI on the grounds that such correlations should be moderate. High correlations indicate insensitivity to change or too much item overlap. Poor factor analytic procedures have led to the inconsistent findings on the factor structure of the BDI.

The validity of the BDI has been questioned by Hammen (1980). Typically, in studies of depressed college students, the BDI is used as a screening device. Hammen found that about half of the students scoring at the moderate depressed level were no longer depressed on a re-administration 2 to 3 weeks later. Furthermore, she found that the BDI was not a really fine-tuned predictor of diagnosis of depression using Research Diagnostic Criteria. Lewinsohn and Teri (1982) also found a large number of "false positives" using the Center for Epidemiological Studies Depression Scale, which is similar to the BDI. The authors do not believe that a self-report scale is an adequate measure. Of course these criticisms clash with other evidence of good test–retest reliability and may reflect problems in using college students. Paradoxically, Boyle (1985) criticized the BDI for having too high a test–retest reliability. It is possible that the BDI picks up transient depressed moods as well as more stable ones. Some lability may be important in a therapy assessment device.

The BDI has been validated in a number of ways. First of all, it has been found to be correlated with the MMPI Depression scale, for example, $r = .82$ in one representative study (Holliman & Montross, 1984), as well as with the Zung Self-Rating Depression Scale and the UCLA Loneliness Scale at more modest levels (Reynolds & Gould, 1981). The BDI has been related to content of diaries obtained over a 10-day period (Robbins & Tanck, 1984). The BDI was found to be the best predictor of seeking help at a university psychiatric service (O'Neil, Lancee, & Freeman, 1984). Finally, the BDI has good relationships with psychiatric diagnostic criteria of depression (Gallagher, Breckenridge, Steinmetz, & Thompson, 1983; Oliver & Simmons, 1985). In their comprehensive review, Beck et al. (1988) amass a good deal of evidence supporting the concurrent, discriminant, and construct validity of the BDI.

The internal validity of the BDI was questioned by Boyce (1985). He reviewed evidence that shows that the BDI correlates well with the Taylor Manifest Anxiety Scale and the Eysenck Personality Inventory Neuroticism

Scale. Therefore, he concluded that the BDI may be a measure of emotional instability rather than primarily a measure of depression. Beck et al. (1988) conceded that the BDI is correlated with self-reported anxiety because of some item overlap in the tests and some overlap in the syndromes. They also presented evidence showing that BDI scores are significantly higher in depressed than in anxious patients. Thus, as with the HAM-D there is some concern about this aspect of internal validity.

A major criticism of the BDI has been its relative weakness in assessing certain somatic manifestations of depression, including increased weight and appetite, and excessive sleeping disturbances (Vredenburg et al., 1985a). In addition, it has been suggested that items about psychomotor activity and agitation are needed (Moran & Lambert, 1983). Steer and Beck (1985) replied to those points by suggesting that increased weight and appetite as well as excessive sleeping are atypical symptoms and should not be included in a general depression inventory. Agitation, they said, is clinically observable and not appropriate for a self-report inventory. In reply Vredenburg, Krames, and Flett (1985b) suggested that the addition of such items would make the BDI more generally useful and help in standardizing assessment instruments in the depression area.

In summary, the BDI is the most popular self-report measure of depression. The instrument appears to have good internal consistency and good test-retest reliability. More work needs to be done on its factorial structure. There is some question as to whether the BDI is too stable or too unstable but, although it may pick up transient mood states, it also appears to be appropriate as an outcome measure. In general, there is good evidence for the concurrent, discriminant, and construct validity of the BDI. One remaining problem is that it also seems to pick up anxiety states to some extent, as does the HAM-D. Another problem is that it may not adequately measure some of the somatic aspects of depression.

## THE HAM-D VERSUS THE BDI

A general issue has arisen in the measurement of depression area as to whether a self-report instrument is as valid as a clinician's judgment. In a large part this controversy developed over discrepancies in findings between these two types of measures.

In a large-scale study, Prusoff, Klerman, and Paykel (1972) assessed depressed inpatients, day patients, outpatients, and emergency patients with an expanded version of the Hamilton Scale and a modification of the Symptom Checklist developed at Johns Hopkins, as well as items from the Raskin scale. Patients were assessed at two times: once during the acute phase and at a 10-month period when most of them had recovered. During the acute phase the correlation between the total psychiatric rating score and the total self-report score was only $r = .36$. When individual symptom clusters were examined, the correlations ranged from .11 to .63 with a median correlation of .41. At recovery, the concordance improved, with a correlation of .81 for total psychiatric rating and total self-report scores.

It is interesting that this large discrepancy was explained by assuming that the acutely depressed patient is not an accurate judge of his or her own severity of depression. On the other hand, the psychiatrist can compare the patient with other depressed patients and can also use behavioral data.

Paykel, Prusoff, Klerman, and DeMascio (1973) reported similar divergent findings between their modified Hamilton scale and the Raskin Self-Report Scale. They also found only modest correlations on the order of .45 between change scores on the two measures. They believe that patients, particularly before treatment, may exaggerate their distress, whereas the psychiatrist can put it in better perspective. However, they conceded that there might be other reasons for the discrepancy. They also endorsed the idea of multiple sources of measurement.

Using still another self-report measure of depression, Fava et al. (1986) correlated the Paykel Clinical Interview for Depression, which is the expanded version of the Hamilton, and Kellner's Symptom Questionnaire, which provides a depression scale on hospitalized depressed patients. On admission, the Paykel measure correlated .28 with the depression self-report. On recovery, this correlation rose to .48. Again, the poorest relationship between the psychiatric rating and the self-report measure was when the patients were acutely depressed. Both measures showed improvement after treatment.

The Hamilton Rating Scale for Depression was also compared to the Zung Self-Rating Depression Scale by Carroll, Fielding, and Blashki (1973) using depressed inpatients and day patients as well as psychiatric outpatients. The overall Pearson correlation was .41, not impressive nor clinically meaningful to the authors. The correlation was somewhat better for the outpatients who were presumably less acutely depressed, thus paralleling the results from Prusoff et al. (1972). The authors concluded that the problem with the Zung scale is that it does not stress behavioral and somatic features enough. They reject the Zung scale as a useful instrument.

In a study comparing the Beck Depression Inventory and the Hamilton Rating Scale, Bailey and Coppen (1976) administered both measures on several occasions to hospitalized depressive patients. The psychiatrist administering the Hamilton was not aware of the Beck score administered the same day but was probably aware of the length of time of hospitalization during which time most of the patients recovered. On admission, the Pearson correlation between the two measures was only .21, not significant for patients assessed regularly. By discharge, the correlation had improved to .58, $p <$ .01. The authors attributed these results to the lack of experience of the patients with the Beck Depression Inventory and the "incomplete clinical picture" available to the examining psychiatrist at the time of admission. However, neither of these factors is supposed to influence these measures. The authors, in examining individual patients, pointed out that the two measures showed satisfactory correlations in only two thirds of the cases and produced very divergent results in the rest. The Hamilton scale showed greater improvement than did the Beck Inventory, which suggests that when psychiatrists are aware of how long the patient has been treated and have a more complete clinical picture, the Hamilton Scale may be more biased. In any case, the authors concluded that because of the discrepancies found, both measures should be used in most studies.

Using a somewhat different approach, Bech et al. (1975) related the Hamilton Scale and the Beck Depression Inventory, in a group of depressed inpatients, to an independent, 4-point global clinical assessment scale. Both measures were equally predictive of this global scale, although both tended to underestimate the level of depression in the more severe cases. The authors criticized, statistically, the ability of many of the items to provide a sensitive indication of depression. Of course, all of this assumes some inherent validity in the global clinical assessment scale. In this study, the Hamilton and Beck scales did correlate well (Spearman rank correlation of .72). However, when used as a measure of change or recovery, the correlation was only .56. Of course, the detection of change is our major issue.

The bias in favor of clinician-based rating scales, such as the Hamilton and its derivatives, is very clear. In discussing the HAM-D and the BDI, Rabkin and Klein (1987) noted the discrepancies and stated that "the HRSD remains the preferred measure of the two for assessing depressive severity. . . . In the absence of sufficient clinical resources, or for some specific practical or research questions, the BDI may serve as an acceptable approximation of the HRSD" (p. 65).

In specific response to the criticism leveled at self-report measures, Post et al. (1985) selected a group of depressed patients showing a wide range of severity of depression. They found that scores on the BDI and the MMPI Depression scale were significantly related to stringently defined DSM-III diagnoses but the HAM-D was not. They concluded that clinicians are not necessarily better than patients at defining symptoms.

Beck et al. (1988) presented a more optimistic picture of the relationship between the HAM-D and the BDI than earlier reviews. In 10 studies involving depressed patients, alcoholics, drug addicts, rape victims, medical patients, and college students, they reported relationships between the HAM-D and the BDI ranging from .41 to .86. However, by now the nature of the controversy has changed. Even if the two measures are moderately well correlated, one could show a greater effect of treatment than the other. The belief is that the HAM-D is a more accurate and conservative measure of treatment outcome than the BDI. The reasoning is that the patient overestimates the degree of original depression, as well as the degree of improvement, whereas the clinician has a more balanced and objective view.

The conclusion that the HAM-D is a more conservative measure of treatment effects was buttressed by the review by Moran and Lambert (1983). They examined 18 drug and psychotherapy studies of depression with more than one assessment measure. The most frequent combination of measures found was the HAM-D and BDI in drug treatment studies. They evaluated sensitivity by seeing whether the measure showed a statistically significant effect. Using this approach, they found that the BDI was considerably more sensitive to treatment effects than the HAM-D. This greater sensitivity of the BDI was more apparent in drug treatment than psychotherapy studies.

The methodology used by Moran and Lambert was of the so-called box score type in which the number of studies showing a statistically significant effect are compared with those that do not. This method of comparing groups of studies has been replaced with the method of meta-analysis. In meta-analysis, an effect size (ES) is computed for each measure in each study. The ES is the mean difference between the treatment and control group divided by the standard deviation of the control group. ESs can be aggregated with different measures in which the magnitude of change is taken into account. Meta-analysis has become the accepted way of comparing results in the treatment research area (Smith, Glass, & Miller, 1980; Steinbrueck, Maxwell, & Howard, 1983).

Adopting meta-analysis, Edwards et al. (1984) examined 19 studies in which both the HAM-D and the BDI were used to evaluate the level of depression before and after treatment or control. Treatment included various forms of biological and psychological therapy. Over 1,000 depressed patients were involved in this data analysis. The ES of the improvement in depression was 0.89 for the BDI and 1.29 for the HAM-D. The difference between these ESs was significant using a $t$ test. Thus, the BDI was less liberal than the HAM-D and does not appear to overestimate treatment effects.

In a more comprehensive study, Lambert, Hatch, Kingston, and Edwards (1986) examined the HAM-D and the BDI, and also the Zung Self Rating of Depression in 36 studies of the improvement after psychosocial and pharmacological treatments for depression. Using meta-analysis, they found that the HAM-D had a significantly higher ES than the BDI. Furthermore, the HAM-D was also significantly greater in ES than the Zung, whereas the BDI and the Zung did not differ significantly. The authors point out that the differences between the HAM-D and the self-report measures were larger than the differences ordinarily attributed to treatments.

Lambert et al. (1986) are cautious in drawing conclusions from their work. They said that the results may mean that the HAM-D overestimates improvement or that the HAM-D may be able to pick up somatic signs of improvement not reported by patients. They cited Prusoff et al. (1972) who maintained that the clinician may be more accurate in evaluating acutely or severely depressed patients. However, in this connection, remember in the earlier section of the HAM-D we found that the reliability of the HAM-D was suspect, particularly in the initial assessment. Finally, Lambert et al. pointed out that, from what they could gather, most of the clinical judges were not blind to the fact that patients were in some form of treatment because the studies reviewed included few placebo controls.

In summary, a lack of concordance between Hamilton ratings and self-reports, including the BDI, was interpreted by many to mean that the patient was an inaccurate judge of depression, whereas the clinical judge was more objective and accurate. Early studies suggesting that the HAM-D was a more conservative measure of treatment effects strengthened this belief. However, recent meta-analytic reviews show that the HAM-D is a much more liberal measure of treatment effects than the BDI, which does not appear to be an overestimate after all. It can still be argued that the HAM-D is more accurate, whether it is liberal or conservative, but the issue has been raised about how blind the HAM-D raters really are and whether they might be seriously biased.

## INTEGRITY OF DOUBLE-BLIND STUDIES

In early studies of drug therapy, single-blind designs were used to compare placebo and drug effects in the patient. Recognition of the clinical evaluator as a source of bias led to the use of double-blind procedures. In fact, it has been found in a meta-analytic review of depression treatment (Steinbrueck, Maxwell, & Howard, 1983) that studies using double-blind procedures had smaller effect sizes than those using single-blind procedures.

The double-blind design has become standard in research on drug therapy. Sometimes a study does not include a placebo control but the double-blind procedure is used to compare two or more drug treatments (e.g., Capponi, Hormazabel, & Schmid-Burgk, 1985; Dunbar, Naarala, & Hijtunen, 1985; World Health Organization, 1986). Typically such studies use psychiatric ratings, particularly the HAM-D, as the main or sole outcome measure. In this type of design, it is not possible to evaluate placebo effects. Instead, they rely on often-cited estimates of antidepressant effect at about 60% to 70% of patients effectively treated, whereas about 30% to 40% improved with placebo (e.g., Stewart et al., 1983).

Another approach to controlling for placebo effects is to have a short period of placebo treatment followed by active treatment (e.g., Goldberg et al., 1986). In the NIMH Collaborative Study (Katz, 1987) there was a 2-week placebo period followed by a 4-week period using two drugs in a double-blind design. It was reported that 4% of the patients improved enough during the placebo phase to be dropped from the study. This figure stands in stark contrast to the 30% to 40% placebo recovery rate reported earlier. Clearly not all the placebo effects were eliminated in this study. It is also interesting that the major result of this study was that it was possible to pick up responders to the drug treatment after only 1 week of treatment using doctors' ratings, including the HAM-D, but not using self-report measures.

Prien and Levine (1984) are very critical of using a placebo washout period as a control for placebo effects. They pointed out that placebo-treated patients often continue to improve after 2 weeks. Along these lines, Quitkin, Rabkin, Ross, and McGrath (1984) found that drug and placebo groups were not reliably different until after 4 weeks. They did find a significant advantage of drugs over placebos by 6 weeks, but it should be noted that they used only the HAM-D and a Clinical Global Impression Scale and not a self-report rating.

The Quitkin, Rabkin, Ross, and McGrath (1984) study also involved an additional design complexity. The placebo-drug comparison was preceded by a 10-day single-blind period during which some unspecified number of patients were dropped. This procedure would tend to attenuate the placebo effect. In a similar study, Spiker and Kupfer (1988) reviewed earlier work in which a 2-week drug-free washout period was used with a 20% spontaneous remission of depressed patients. Following this washout period, they compared placebo- and drug-treated patients, reporting that for nonpsychotic depressed patients there was a 55% responder rate with the drug treatment and only a 13% rate for placebo treatment. There are a number of problems with this design, but it should be noted that the definition of responders was based entirely on a cut-off score on the HAM-D so that conclusions based on this study would be limited by any deficiencies in the HAM-D.

In other studies using a combined washout period plus placebo-drug comparisons, both clinician ratings and self-reports have been used with somewhat inconclusive results with respect to the differential sensitivity of different measures (e.g., Lipman et al., 1986; Richels, Feighner, & Smith, 1985; Stewart et al., 1983). So, too, studies using both types of measures but a placebo control without a placebo washout period show differential but somewhat inconsistent results from different measures (e.g., White et al., 1984). In their meta-analytic review of studies using the HAM-D and the BDI or the Zung, Lambert et al. (1986) raised the interesting possibility that the two types of scales might show differential sensitivity to treatment and control conditions. Unfortunately, they found very few studies that used both the HAM-D and either the BDI or the Zung and also compared drug and placebo treatments, so that a meaningful comparison could not be made. They recommended that such a meta-analysis be performed in the future when more studies of the right kind have been done.

Now there are two issues here. One is the possibility that the HAM-D and the BDI or the Zung might be differentially sensitive to the placebo effect. There seems to be little evidence for this effect although the two measures may differ at times. There is no particular reason to expect that the two types of measures would show a differential placebo effect. If a placebo effect is a *real* decrease in depression due to psychological rather than pharmacological reasons, then the patient should report feeling better and should also show it on interview. The second issue is whether a measure picks up a change in depression that is *not real*. This could happen on the BDI if a patient, for some reason, wanted to appear better than he or she actually feels. The patient could also do this on interview to some extent but might continue to show a sad expression visible to the clinician. So too, the patient could be showing a *real* change in depression but, for some reason, not show it on the BDI but manifest it in interview behavior. Thus, the BDI would be biased by various patient motivations.

On the other hand, the clinician may be motivated, for some reason, to detect a change that is *not real*. The clinician could not distort the BDI but could distort, consciously or unconsciously, the HAM-D or similar ratings. It does not seem unreasonable to assume that psychopharmacological therapists hold strong beliefs about the efficacy of drugs and may be motivated to detect effects that are *not real*. In view of the finding that the HAM-D provides a more generous estimate of drug treatment effects than the BDI or the Zung (Lambert et al., 1986), possible distortions on the part of the clinician become an issue.

However, even if the psychiatrist is consciously or unconsciously motivated to exaggerate the effects of drug therapy, how can he or she accomplish this? After all, such distortions are supposed to be controlled for by the double-blind design. Unless, of course, there is a way around the double-blind design. We now turn to the question of how the integrity of the double-blind design may be threatened.

In an attempt to develop a new method of differentiating true antidepressant drug response from placebo effects, Quitkin, Rabkin, Ross, and Stewart (1984) hypothesized that a true drug response would show a 2-week delay in onset but would then be more persistent in effect. Therefore, weekly ratings were made by a psychiatrist over a 6-week period, using a 7-point Clinical Global Improvement Scale. Now the interesting thing about this procedure is that in addition to making the ratings each week, a decision had to be made about increasing drug dosage based on side effects. If there were no "notable" side effects, the dosage was increased. Therefore, although the global ratings were made double-blind, there was a special interest in side effects that might very well help identify those getting the drugs and those getting the placebos. Actually, almost half the patients were excluded from the final analysis for failure to improve with either drug or placebo. In the remaining cases, there was a tendency for patients treated with drugs to show the hypothesized delay-persistence effect as well as better overall improvement than those given placebos. However, these results are questionable in light of the very strong possibility that the focus on side effects during the evaluation procedure compromised the double-blind design.

The presence of drug side effects represents a clear challenge to the integrity of double-blind studies. It is well known that antidepressant medications produce symptoms such as dizziness, sleepiness, and dry mouth at four or five times the frequency of such symptoms in a placebo-treated group. In addition, other side effects are produced at a lesser frequency and vary with the specific drug and dosage (Rickels et al., 1985; White et al., 1984; World Health Organization, 1986).

In many studies, the treating psychiatrist has to attend to side effects to adjust dosage level and even terminate treatment if necessary (e.g., Dunbar et al., 1985; Klok et al., 1981; Quitkin et al., 1984; Paykel, Hollyman, Freeling, & Sedgwick, 1988; Rickels et al., 1985; White et al., 1984; World Health Organization, 1986). Some of these studies included a side effects checklist (Rickels et al., 1985) or a list of Treatment Emergent Symptoms (White et al., 1984). In the World Health Organization study (1986) a Rating Scale for Side Effects developed earlier by Asberg, Cronholm, Sjokvist, and Tuck (1970) was used. It is difficult to believe that with all this attention paid to side effects the psychiatrists involved were completely blind as to who was being given drugs and who was being given placebo treatment.

The detection of treatment assignment is rarely discussed in the psychopharmacological therapy literature. In one recent study (Sussex Clinical Trials Group, 1985) the investigators were asked to answer the question, "Do you think you know which treatment the patient is on?" Four of the five investigators always said no. One investigator had a few correct guesses. The authors conclude that for "the vast majority of patients, the investigators had no idea as to which treatment was being administered" (p. 85). Yet in this study the investigators used a "Side Effects Inventory" with a 3-point rating scale and asked routinely "have the tablets upset you in any way?"

In another double-blind study, Kleber et al. (1983) asked nurses and patients to try to guess which treatment was being given. The nurses, who also did weekly evaluations, were able to classify patients into drug or placebo treatment correctly at a statistically significant level. The patients showed a nonsignificant trend in the same direction. The psychiatrists were not asked to guess about treatment group.

Wientraub and Aronson (1963) also found that neither resident therapists nor the chief resident could distinguish between those given imipramine and those given atropine in spite of the presence of "obvious clues," including slight differences in the appearance of the two pills, which were picked up by several nurses and patients. Furthermore, they found that both resident therapists and the chief resident tended to assign to the drug group those patients who showed the most improvement. It would seem in this study, as well as others, that there is a strong social demand for psychiatrists to not report an awareness of the treatment given but still allow it to influence judgment.

In a unique experimental study of detecting drug-placebo group assignment, Agnew (1964) administered seconal, benzedrine, and placebo in a repeated crossover design. On the basis of patient symptoms, professionals and other judges were able to identify which treatment the person was getting on any given day. Furthermore, the judges were able to do this even when they had little information about the design of the study. This kind of study needs to be done with antidepressant, antianxiety, and other psychiatric drugs.

Theoretically, both self-report measures, such as the BDI, and clinician ratings, such as the HAM-D, could be influenced by side effects. However, the clinicians are probably more aware of the significance of certain side effects. In view of the finding that the HAM-D overestimates drug treatment effect relative to the BDI (Lambert et al., 1986), it is more likely that clinician ratings are more susceptible to the influence of side effects.

An examination of the items on the HAM-D supports this view. Ordinarily the items are not spelled out, although the HAM-D clearly involves asking about many somatic symptoms. In the World Health Organization study (1986) the actual forms used are reproduced. The HAM-D includes items about sleep disturbances, dry mouth, palpitations, headaches, loss of energy, and fatigability. These very same items appear in the Asberg Rating Scale for Side Effects, also reproduced in the article. Furthermore, Maier et al. (1988) found that in depressed patients, change scores in the Somatic Anxiety subscale of the HAM-A, which is very similar to the comparable scale on the HAM-D, seem to reflect the appearance of new side effects of treatment. Thus, the HAM-D appears to be seriously compromised by side effects.

In summary, double-blind placebo designs were introduced to control for possible biases in clinical judgments about drug treatment effects. On the basis of such studies, the general conclusion has been that antidepressant drugs help about 60% to 70% of patients and placebos about 30% to 40%. Newer studies use a placebo washout period or a combination of both designs. These procedures tend to underestimate placebo effects, particularly when the studies make heavy use of clinical ratings such as the HAM-D, which tends to overestimate drug treatment effects. A major threat to the integrity of the double-blind design is the extensive use made of side effects in regulating dosage. Although several reports conclude that psychiatrists are unaware of treatment-placebo group assignment, it seems likely that there is some awareness, but strong social demands to deny such awareness. Nurses and other observers seem to be able to guess whether patients are on drug or placebo treatment. The HAM-D, and perhaps other psychiatric rating scales, seem to be particularly susceptible to side effect influence because they probe for somatic reactions identical to side effects.

## CONCLUSIONS

The consensus among psychotherapy researchers is that improvement must be evaluated from several vantage points—the most important of which are the patient, the expert clinician, and significant others. Each vantage point has sources of bias and measurement problems, but multiple measures may compensate for these problems. There is general agreement that no one vantage point—such as that of the expert clinician—should be considered more valid than the others.

In contrast to the multiple vantage point approach, the research in the evaluation of psychopharmacological therapy has shown a strong bias in favor of the psychiatrists' or expert clinicians' viewpoint as being the ultimate criterion of status and improvement following the long tradition of clinical medicine. As a result the vast bulk of the literature on drug therapy relies on clinical interviews by the treating psychiatrist as the sole or main source of information. More recently, independent clinical evaluations using better refined scales and patient self-reports have become more widely used. However, only in recent years has the idea of multivantaged measures of equal validity been proposed by drug researchers and has not yet had a real impact on research in this area.

In the area of depression, the most widely used interview measure is the Hamilton Rating Scale for Depression (HAM-D). This scale has questionable inter-rater reliability, concurrent validity, and interval validity. The most widely used self-report, the Beck Depression Inventory (BDI), has relatively good psychometric properties. In spite of this contrast, there is a strong view among drug therapy researchers that the HAM-D has more inherent validity than the BDI. A meta-analysis has shown that, in fact, the HAM-D provides a significantly more generous estimate of the effects of drug therapy than does the BDI.

Although the double-blind designs are supposed to eliminate bias on the part of psychiatrists or other expert clinical evaluators, the integrity of such designs is severely threatened by the clear presence of drug side effects. Although several studies indicate that psychiatrists cannot guess which patients are receiving drugs and which placebos, this seems incredible in view of the findings that nurses and others can guess accurately. Psychiatrists may be, consciously or unconsciously, biased in favor of drug therapy and under social demands not to be aware of patient assignment. The HAM-D seems particularly vulnerable to distortion because many of the details inquired about are the same as symptomatic side effects.

On the basis of these measurement issues, the literature on antidepressant drug therapy must be viewed with some skepticism. At the very least, the widespread belief that about one third of depressed patients improve with placebos and two thirds improve with antidepressive medication needs to be reevaluated. The difference is probably much smaller. In fact, new research needs to establish whether antidepressant drug therapy exceeds a placebo rate at all. These concerns probably apply to antianxiety drug therapy and possibly to drug therapy for other conditions as well.

The new research should adopt the multivantage point of view. Furthermore, much greater use should be made of really objective behavioral and physiological measures. It is doubtful whether the clinical interview can ever be made into an objective measure. Perhaps clinical interviews could be video-audio taped, all references to side effects edited out, and then independent ratings made. Certainly, the deep faith in the clinical interview as representing the ultimate criterion of status and improvement needs to be relinquished.

## REFERENCES

Ackles, P. K. (1986). Evaluating pharmacological-behavioral treatment interactions. In M. Hersen (Ed.), *Pharmacological and behavioral treatment* (pp. 54–86). New York: Wiley.

Agnew, N. McK. (1964). The relative value of self-report and objective tests in assessing the effects of amphetamine. *Journal of Psychiatric Research, 2,* 85–100.

Asberg, M., Cronholm, B., Sjokvist, F., & Tuck, D. (1970). Correlation of subjective side effects with plasma concentrations of nortriptyline. *British Medical Journal, 4,* 18–21.

Ather, S. A., Ankier, S. I., & Middleton, R. S. W. (1985). A double-blind evaluation of trazodone in the treatment of depression in the elderly. *The British Journal of Clinical Practice,* May, 192–199.

Auerbach, A. H. (1983). Assessment of psychotherapy outcome from the viewpoint of expert observer. In M. J. Lambert, E. R. Christensen, & S. S. DeJulio (Eds.), *The assessment of psychotherapy outcome* (pp. 437–568). New York: Wiley.

Bailey, J., & Coppen, A. (1976). A comparison between the Hamilton Rating Scale and the Beck Inventory in the measurement of depression. *British Journal of Psychiatry, 128,* 486–489.

Bech, P., Gram, L. F., Dein, E., Jacobsen, O., Vitger, J., & Bolwig, T. G. (1975). Quantitative rating of depressive states, *Acta Psychiatrica Scandinavia, 51,* 161–170.

Beck, A. T., & Beck, R. W. (1972). Screening depressed patients in family practice: A rapid technique. *Postgraduate Medicine, 52,* 81–85.

Beck, A. T., Rush, A. J., Shaw, B. F., & Emery, G. (1979). *Cognitive therapy of depression.* New York: Guilford.

Beck, A. T., & Steer, R. A. (1984). Internal consistencies of the original and revised Beck Depression Inventory. *Journal of Clinical Psychology, 40,* 1365–1367.

Beck, A. T., Steer, R. A., & Garbin, M. G. (1988). Psychometric properties of the Beck Depression Inventory: Twenty-five years of evaluation. *Clinical Psychology Review, 8,* 77–100.

Beck, A. T., Ward, C. H., Mendelson, M., Mock, J., & Erbaugh, J. (1961). An inventory for measuring depression. *Archives of General Psychiatry, 4,* 561–571.

Beutler, L. E., & Crago, M. (1983). Self-report measures of psychotherapy outcome. In M. J. Lambert, E. R. Christensen, & S. S. DeJulio (Eds.), *The assessment of psychotherapy outcome* (pp. 453–497). New York: Wiley.

Boyle, G. J. (1985). Self-report measures of depression: some psychometric considerations. *British Journal of Clinical Psychology, 24,* 45–59.

Bunney, W. E., & Hamburg, D. A. (1963). Methods of reliable longitudinal observation of behavior. *Archives of General Psychiatry, 9,* 280–294.

Capponi, R., Hormazabel, L., & Schmid-Burgk, W. (1985). Diclofensine and imipramine: A double-blind comparative trial in depressive outpatients. *Neuropsychobiology, 14,* 173–180.

Carr, V., & Smith, J. (1985). Assessment of depression by questionnaire compared to DSM-III diagnosis. *Journal of Affective Disorders, 8,* 167–170.

Carroll, B. J., Fielding, J. M., & Blashki, T. G. (1973). Depression rating scales: A critical review. *Archives of General Psychiatry, 28,* 361–366.

Cicchetti, D. V., & Prusoff, B. A. (1983). Reliability of depression and associated clinical symptoms. *Archives of General Psychiatry, 40,* 987–990.

Davidson, C. V., & Davidson, R. H. (1983). The significant other as data source and data problem in psychotherapy outcome research. In M. J. Lambert, E. R. Christensen, & S. S. DeJulio (Eds.), *The assessment of psychotherapy outcome* (pp. 569–602). New York: Wiley.

Dunbar, G. C., Naarala, M., & Hijtunen, H. (1985). A double-blind group comparison of mianserin and clomipramine in the treatment of mildly depressed psychiatric out-patients. *Acta Psychiatrica Scandinavia, 72,* 60–66.

Edwards, B. C., Lambert, M. J., Moran, P. W., McCully, T., Smith, K. C., & Ellingson, A. G. (1984). A meta-analytic comparison of the Beck Depression Inventory and the Hamilton Rating Scale for Depression as measures of treatment outcome. *British Journal of Clinical Psychology, 23,* 93–99.

Faravelli, C., Albanesi, G., & Poli, E. (1986). Assessment of depression: A comparison of rating scales. *Journal of Affective Disorders, 11,* 245–253.

Fava, G. A., Kellner, R., Lisansky, J., Park, S., Perini, G. I., & Zielezny, M. (1986). Rating depression in normals and depressives: Observer versus self-rating scales. *Journal of Affective Disorders, 11,* 29–33.

Gallagher, D., Breckenridge, J., Steinmetz, J., & Thompson, L. (1983). The Beck Depression Inventory and Research Diagnostic Criteria: Congruence in an older population. *Journal of Consulting and Clinical Psychology, 51,* 945–946.

Gallagher, D., Nies, G., & Thompson, L. W. (1982). Reliability of the Beck Depression Inventory with older adults. *Journal of Consulting and Clinical Psychology, 50,* 152–153.

Garfield, S. L. (1980). *Psychotherapy: An eclectic approach.* New York: Wiley.

Goldberg, S. C., Ettigi, P., Schulz, P. M., Hamer, R. M., Hayes, P. E., & Friedel, R. O. (1986). Alprazolam versus imipramine in depressed out-patients with neurovegetative signs. *Journal of Affective Disorders, 11,* 139–145.

Hamilton, M. (1960). A rating scale for depression. *Journal of Neurology, Neurosurgery, and Psychiatry, 23,* 56–62.

Hamilton, M. (1967). Development of a rating scale for primary depressive illness. *British Journal of Social and Clinical Psychology, 6,* 278–296.

Hammen, C. L. (1980). Depression in college students: Beyond the Beck Depression Inventory. *Journal of Consulting and Clinical Psychology, 48,* 126–128.

Hedlund, J. L., & Vieweg, B. W. (1979). The Hamilton Rating Scale for Depression: A comprehensive review. *Journal of Operational Psychiatry, 10,* 149–165.

Holliman, N. B. & Montross, J. (1984). The effects of depression upon responses to the California Psychological Inventory. *Journal of Clinical Psychology, 40,* 1373–1378.

Hughes, J. R., O'Hara, M. W., & Rehm, L. (1982). Measurement of depression in clinical trials: An overview. *Journal of Clinical Psychiatry, 43,* 85–88.

Katz, M. M. (1987). The multivantaged approach to the measurement of affect and behavior in depression. In A. J. Marsella, R. M. A. Hirschfeld, & M. M. Katz (Eds.), *The measurement of depression* (pp. 297–316). New York: Guilford.

Kerkhofs, M., Hoffmann, G., DeMartelaere, V., Linkowski, P., & Mendlewicz, J. (1985). Sleep EEG recordings in depressive disorders. *Journal of Affective Disorders, 9,* 47–53.

Kleber, H. D., Weissman, M. M., Rounsaville, B. J., Wilber, C. N., Prusoff, B. A., &

Riordan, C. E. (1983). Imipramine as treatment for depression in addicts. *Archives of General Psychiatry, 40,* 649–653.

Klok, C. J., Brouwer, G. J., Van Praag, H. M., & Doogan, D. (1981). Fluvoxamine and cloripramine in depressed patients: A double-blind clinical study. *Acta Psychiatrica Scandinavia, 64,* 1–11.

Knesevich, J. W., Biggs, J. T., Clayton, P. J., & Ziegler, V. E. (1977). Validity of the Hamilton Rating Scale for Depression. *British Journal of Psychiatry, 131,* 49–52.

Lambert, M. J., & Christensen, E. R. (1983). Assessing the effects of psychological treatments: A summary. In M. J. Lambert, E. R. Christensen, S. S. DeJulio (Eds.), *The assessment of psychotherapy outcome* (pp. 629–631). New York: Wiley.

Lambert, M. J., Christensen, E. R., & DeJulio, S. S. (1983) (Eds.), *The assessment of psychotherapy outcome.* New York: Wiley.

Lambert, M. J., Hatch, D. R., Kingston, M. D., & Edwards, B. C. (1986). Zung, Beck, and Hamilton rating scales as measures of treatment outcome: A meta-analytic comparison. *Journal of Consulting and Clinical Psychology, 54,* 54–59.

Lewinsohn, P. M., & Rohde, P. (1987). Psychological measurement and depression. In A. J. Marsella, R. M. A. Hirschfeld, & M. M. Katz (Eds.), *The measurement of depression* (pp. 240–266). New York: Guilford.

Lewinsohn, P. M., & Teri, L. (1982). Selection of depressed and non-depressed subjects on the basis of self-report data. *Journal of Consulting and Clinical Psychology, 50,* 590–591.

Lightfoot, S. L., & Oliver, J. M. (1985). The Beck Inventory: Psychometric properties in university students. *Journal of Personality Assessment, 49,* 434–436.

Lipman, D. S., Covi, L., Rickels, K., McNair, D. M., Downing, R., Kahn, R. J., Lasseter, V. K., & Faden, V. (1986). Imipramine and chlordiazepoxide in depressive and anxiety disorders I. Efficacy in depressed outpatients. *Archives of General Psychiatry, 43,* 68–77.

Maier, W., Buller, R., Philipp, M., & Heuser, I. (1988). The Hamilton Anxiety Scale: Reliability, validity and sensitivity to change in anxiety and depressive disorders. *Journal of Affective Disorders, 14,* 61–88.

Marsella, A. J., Hirschfeld, R. M. A., & Katz, M. M. (Eds.). (1987). *The measurement of depression.* New York: Guilford.

Mazure, C., Nelson, J. C., & Price, L. N. (1986). Reliability and validity of the symptoms of major depressive illness. *Archives of General Psychiatry, 43,* 451–456.

Montgomery, S. A., & Asberg, M. (1979). A new depression scale designed to be sensitive to change. *British Journal of Psychiatry, 134,* 382–389.

Moran, P. W., & Lambert, M. J. (1983). A review of current assessment tools for monitoring changes in depression. In M. S. Lambert, E. R. Christensen, & S. S. DeJulio (Eds.), *The assessment of psychotherapy outcome,* (pp. 263–303). New York: Wiley.

Newman, F. L. (1983). Therapist's evaluation of psychotherapy. In M. J. Lambert, E. R. Christensen, & S. S. DeJulio (Eds.), *The assessment of psychotherapy outcome* (pp. 498–536). New York: Wiley.

Oliver, J. M., & Simmons, M. E. (1985). Affective disorders and depression as measured by the Diagnostic Interview Schedule and the Beck Depression Inventory in an unselected adult population. *Journal of Clinical Psychology, 41,* 469–477.

O'Neil, M. K., Lancee, W. J., & Freeman, S. J. J. (1984). Help-seeking behavior of depressed students. *Social Science and Medicine, 18,* 511–514.

Paykel, E. S. (1985). The Clinical Interview for Depression: Development, reliability, and validity. *Journal of Affective Disorders, 9,* 85–96.

Paykel, E. S., Hollyman, J. A., Freeling, P., & Sedgwick, P. (1988). Predictors of therapeutic benefit from amitriptyline in mild depression: A general practice placebo-controlled trial. *Journal of Affective Disorders, 14,* 83–95.

Paykel, E. S., Prusoff, B. A., Klerman, G. L., & DeMascio, A. (1973). Self-report and clinical interview ratings in depression. *Journal of Nervous and Mental Disease, 156,* 166–182.

Post, R. D., Alford, C. E., Baker, N. J., Franks, R. D., House, R. M., Jackson, A. M., & Petersen, J. L. (1985). Comparison of self-reports and clinicians' ratings of unipolar major depression. *Psychological Reports, 57,* 479–483.

Prien, R. F., Kupfer, D. J., Mansky, P. A., Small, J. G., Tuason, V. B., Voss, C. B., & Johnson, W. E. (1984). Drug therapy in the prevention of recurrences in unipolar and bipolar affective disorders. *Archives of General Psychiatry, 41,* 1096–1104.

Prien, R. F. & Levine, J. (1984). Research and methodological issues for evaluating the therapeutic effectiveness of anti-depressant drugs. *Psychopharmacology Bulletin, 20,* 250–257.

Prusoff, B. A., Klerman, G. L., & Paykel, E. S. (1972). Concordance between clinical assessments and patient's self-report in depression. *Archives of General Psychiatry, 26,* 546–552.

Quitkin, F. M., Rabkin, J. G., Ross, D., & McGrath, P. J. (1984). Duration of anti-depressant drug treatment. *Archives of General Psychiatry, 41,* 238–245.

Quitkin, F. M., Rabkin, J. G., Ross, D., & Stewart, J. W. (1984). Identification of true drug response to anti-depressants. *Archives of General Psychiatry, 41,* 782–786.

Rabkin, J. G. & Klein, D. F. (1987). The clinical measurement of depressive disorders. In A. J. Marsella, R. M. A. Hirschfeld, & M. M. Katz (Eds.), *The measurement of depression* (pp. 30–83). New York: Guilford.

Rehm, L. P. (1987). The measurement of behavioral aspects of depression. In A. J. Marsella, R. M. A. Hirschfeld, & M. M. Katz (Eds.), *The measurement of depression* (pp. 199–239). New York: Guilford.

Reynolds, W. M., & Gould, J. W. (1981). A psychometric investigation of the standard and short form Beck Depression Inventory. *Journal of Consulting and Clinical Psychology, 49,* 306–307.

Rhoades, H. M., & Overall, J. E. (1983). The Hamilton Depression Scale: Factor scoring and profile classification. *Psychopharmacology Bulletin, 19,* 91–96.

Rickels, K., Feighner, J. P., & Smith, W. T. (1985). Alprazolam, amitriptyline, doxepin and placebo in the treatment of depression. *Archives of General Psychiatry, 42,* 134–141.

Rickels, K., Weisman, K. Norstad, N., Singer, M., Stoltz, D., Brown, A., & Danton, J. (1982). Buspirone and diazepam in anxiety: A controlled study. *Journal of Clinical Psychiatry, 43,* 81–86.

Robbins, P. R., & Tanck, R. H. (1984). The Beck Depression Inventory and self-reports of behavior over a ten-day period. *Journal of Personality Research, 48,* 42–45.

Roberts, S., Aronoff, J., Jensen, J., & Lambert, M. J. (1983). Measurement of outcome in anxiety disorders. In M. J. Lambert, E. R. Christensen, & S. S. DeJulio (Eds.), *The assessment of psychotherapy outcome* (pp. 304–355). New York: Wiley.

Rush, A. J. (1987). Measurement of the cognitive aspects of depression. In A. J. Marsella, R. M. A. Hirschfeld, & M. M. Katz (Eds.), *The measurement of depression* (pp. 297–316). New York: Guilford.

Smith, M. L., Glass, G. V., & Miller, T. I. (1980). *The benefits of psychotherapy.* Baltimore: Johns Hopkins.

Spiker, D. G. & Kupfer, D. J. (1988). Placebo response rates in psychotic and non-psychotic depression. *Journal of Affective Disorders, 14,* 21–23.

Steer, R. A., & Beck, A. T. (1985). Modifying the Beck Depression Inventory: Reply to Vredenberg, Krames, & Flett. *Psychological Reports, 57,* 625–626.

Steinbrueck, S. M., Maxwell, S. E., & Howard, G. S. (1983). A meta-analysis of psychotherapy and drug therapy in the treatment of unipolar depression with adults. *Journal of Consulting and Clinical Psychology, 51,* 856–863.

Stewart, J. W., Quitkin, F. M., Liebowitz, M. R., McGrath, P. J., Harrison, W. M. & Klein,

D. F. (1983). Efficacy of desipramine in depressed outpatients. *Archives of General Psychiatry, 40*, 202–207.

Strupp, H. H., & Hadley, S. W. (1977). A tripartite model of mental health and therapeutic outcomes: With special reference to negative effects in psychotherapy. *American Psychologist, 32*, 187–196.

Sussex Clinical Trials Group (1985). Separate and combined anxiolytic and anti-depressant treatment of mixed anxiety/depression. *Acta Psychiatrica Scandinavia, 72*, 81–88.

Ulrich, G., & Harms, K. (1985). A video analysis of the non-verbal behavior of patients before and after treatment. *Journal of Affective Disorders, 9*, 63–67.

Vredenburg, K., Krames, L., & Flett, G. L. (1985a). Re-examining the Beck Depression Inventory: The long and the short of it. *Psychological Reports, 56*, 767–778.

Vredenburg, K., Krames, L. & Flett, G. L. (1985b). Modifying the Beck Depression Inventory: A rejoinder to Steer and Beck. *Psychological Reports, 57*, 903–906.

Waskow, I. E., & Parloff, M. B. (1975). *Psychotherapy change measures.* Rockville, MD: National Institute of Mental Health.

Wechsler, H., Grosser, G. H., & Busfield, B. L. (1963). The depression rating scale. *Archives of General Psychiatry, 9*, 334–343.

Weckowitz, T., Muir, W., & Cropley, A. (1967). A factor analysis of the Beck Inventory of Depression. *Journal of Consulting Psychology, 31*, 193–198.

Weintraub, W., & Aronson, H. (1963). Clinical judgment in psychopharmacological research. *Journal of Neuropsychiatry, 5*, 65–70.

White, K., Razani, J., Cadow, B., Gelfand, R., Palmer, R., Simpson, G., & Sloane, R. B. (1984). Tranylcypromine vs. nortriptyline vs. placebo in depressed outpatients: A controlled trial. *Psychopharmacology, 82*, 258–262.

World Health Organization. (1986). Dose effects of anti-depressant medication in different populations. *Journal of Affective Disorders.* Supplement 2, S1–S67.

# 3 | PHARMACOTHERAPY OF THE ANXIETY DISORDERS

Ronald S. Lipman
*Friends Hospital*

The anxiety disorders, as specified in the Diagnostic and Statistical Manual of Mental Disorders, third edition (DSM-III-R, 1987) include generalized anxiety disorder (GAD), panic disorder (with and without agoraphobia), agoraphobia, social phobia, simple phobia, obsessive-compulsive disorder (OCD), and posttraumatic stress disorder (PTSD). The anxiety disorders can be roughly divided into two major groupings depending on whether the anxiety is primarily stimulus dependent (exogenous) or stimulus independent (endogenous). Panic disorder and GAD are conceptualized as endogenous (Curtis, 1985; Sheehan, 1982). PTSD, agoraphobia, and OCD are more closely allied with the phobic disorders (exogenous) than with the endogenous disorders. This grouping has implications for behavioral approaches to treatment. The anxiety disorders have been found to be very common in epidemiological surveys conducted in this country.

## Epidemiology of the Anxiety Disorders

A 1979 National Survey of Psychotherapeutic Drug Usage employed a modified Hopkins Symptom Checklist (Lipman, Covi, & Shapiro, 1979) to derive DSM-III diagnostic categories (Uhlenhuth, Balter, Mellinger, Cisin, & Clinthorne, 1983). The survey found an annual prevalence rate of 6.4% for GAD, followed by 2.3% for phobias other than agoraphobia/panic, which occurred in 1.2% of the sample ($N = 3161$). All types of anxiety disorders were more frequent in women than in men. The most recent National Institute of Mental Health (NIMH) 1982 Epidemiologic Catchment Area Study Survey

(ECA) found a 6-month prevalence rate of about 9% for the anxiety disorders (Myers et. al., 1984). The anxiety disorders occurred more frequently than depression and substance abuse, which had prevalence rates of about 6%. It should be noted that the ECA study included more than 9,000 respondents from three cities and employed an interview procedure based on DSM-III diagnostic criteria. The prevalence estimate for the anxiety disorders did not include data on GAD or PTSD, so that it clearly underestimates the total frequency of these conditions. One estimate of the lifetime prevalence of the anxiety disorders, excluding transient and situational anxiety conditions, is 13% to 15% (Rickels & Schweizer, 1987). It is also clear that there is considerable comorbidity among the anxiety disorders and between the anxiety disorders and depression and alcoholism. In one comorbidity study, for example, Barlow (1985) found that 80% of patients with the diagnosis of GAD also meet DSM-III criteria for another coexisting anxiety disorder. Along similar lines, some 20% of patients with alcoholism have been found to have an anxiety disorder (Weiss & Rosenberg, 1985) and the overlap of major depressive disorder with GAD and panic disorder is well known to most clinicians (see Curtis, 1985).

The change in criteria for defining the anxiety disorders from DSM-III to DSM-III-R is likely to change the current prevalence rates in the literature and will probably change the extent of comorbidity among disorders. Fyer, Mannuzza, and Endicott (1987) provide a general discussion of the major changes from DSM-III to DSM-III-R. They point out that the change in chronicity required for GAD, from 1 month to 6 months, is likely to greatly diminish the diagnosis of GAD and to increase the comorbidity of GAD and major depressive disorder.

## Use of Psychotropic Medications

Historically, treatment, or at least self-medication of the anxiety disorders, started with the ingestion of alcohol and continued with the use of bromides, opiates and, around the turn of the century, barbiturates such as phenobarbital. These compounds, although somewhat effective, were dangerous in terms of their very sedative nature, high lethality, low range of therapeutic to toxic effects, and high potential for addiction and abuse. The introduction of meprobamate in the fifties and chlordiazepoxide in the early sixties ushered in the more modern era of psychotherapeutic medications. These minor tranquilizers were generally considered to be better able to calm without "clouding the sensorium" and to have significantly less potential for substance abuse and suicidality (Woods, Katz, & Winger, 1987).

Based on data from the National Prescription Audit of Gosselin and Company, Balter and Levine (1973) estimated that 83 million prescriptions for antianxiety agents were written in 1970, accounting for about 39% of the

214 million psychotropic drug prescriptions that year. In a rigorous cross-sectional household survey of American adults aged 18–74, it was found that 15% of some 2,500 respondents had used a minor tranquilizer (12%) or daytime sedative (3%) during the survey year 1970–71 (Mellinger, Balter, Parry, Manheimer, & Cisin, 1974). This was the most frequent class of psychotropic drugs used, followed by stimulants (5%), hypnotics (3%), antidepressants (2%), and major tranquilizers (1%). In this same survey, a modified Hopkins Symptom Checklist was used to classify levels of psychic distress. In this regard, it was reported that the majority of highly distressed persons did not use a psychotherapeutic drug, but the majority of persons who did use a psychotropic drug were classified as high in distress.

The marked acceptance of the benzodiazepine medications diazepam and chlordiazepoxide, was reflected in their first-and third-place status among all drugs prescribed by U.S. physicians (Blackwell, 1973). It should be stressed, however, that these medications were mainly prescribed by general practitioners and internists and that a large aspect of their use was for cardiovascular conditions and for muscle relaxation. In the 1979 National Survey of Psychotherapeutic Drug Usage referred to earlier (Uhlenhuth et al., 1983), it was found that 27% of patients classified as having GAD had taken an antianxiety agent in the past year, whereas 6% had taken a hypnotic, 3% an antipsychotic, 3% a daytime sedative, and 3% an antidepressant medication. About 44% of the antianxiety agent usage was classified as occasional use with 30% of usage being for 4 months or longer. As might be expected from its severity, 59% of agoraphobic patients were taking psychotropic medication. Surprisingly, however, of those taking medication, antidepressants (often the medication of choice, cf. McNair & Kahn, 1981), were taken by only 8% of agoraphobics, whereas antianxiety agents were taken by 55% and antipsychotic agents by 11%. The respondents classified as having an "other phobia" took least medication: 12% antianxiety agents, 6% daytime sedatives, 35% hypnotics, and 1% antidepressants. Weissman (1985) has recently reviewed the epidemiology of the anxiety disorders, including an overview of the prevalence of anxiety disorders in children. In a 1975 survey of some 500 residents of New Haven, she reported that only 25% of persons with a current anxiety disorder had received treatment for their disorder that year. These respondents were, however, high users of health facilities for other than psychiatric treatment. The respective treatment estimates from the Weissman and Uhlenhuth surveys are in close agreement. Weissman also found that persons with panic disorders used more psychotherapeutic medications than other anxiety subgroups, but, again, the minor tranquilizers were the most frequently used drug class.

The pattern of drug usage in this country has been compared with that in other Western European countries (Parry, Balter, Mellinger, Cisin, & Manheimer, 1973). Of interest was the finding that the 15% past year usage

of the minor tranquilizer plus daytime sedative class of drugs in this country
fell in the middle of the national range of drug usage, with Spain and Italy at
the low end of the continuum (10%–11%) and Belgium and France at the
high end (17%). This same article reports that 75% of recent prescription
drug users characterized the effects of these drugs as quite helpful. My sense
of the epidemiological findings regarding the use of drugs for the anxiety
disorders is that there is little evidence to support the hypothesis that "nonpa-
tients" are being treated with psychotropic drugs but much support for the
hypothesis that many adults with anxiety disorders are not receiving treatment
or are not being treated as effectively as they might be, given our understanding
of the relative efficacy of the different classes of psychotherapeutic drugs for
the treatment of the different anxiety disorders. That evidence is reviewed in
the next section of this chapter.

### Establishing Drug Efficacy

It is now well recognized that most psychiatric treatments have both a "specific" and a "nonspecific" treatment component (Shapiro, 1978). This nonspecific component is typically referred to as the placebo effect. When a patient
goes to a therapist for treatment there is the normal expectation that the
patient will receive help, and indeed, almost regardless of the type of treatment
the patient receives—including a "sugar pill"—most anxious patients will
experience some improvement, and roughly 30% will improve significantly
so that further treatment is not needed. An interesting discussion of placebo
effects is provided by Shapiro (1978). Given this nonspecific component of
treatment, it becomes necessary to demonstrate that any treatment, including
psychotropic medication, provides significantly more benefit than would be
expected from just placebo treatment. Although the nature of the placebo
may vary, depending on the nature of the active treatment, in drug trials the
placebo takes the form of a pill or capsule identical in appearance to the
"active" medication. In this way, neither the patient nor the therapist knows
which medication the patient is receiving, and the clinical trial is referred to
as double-blind. This procedure is employed to prevent the bias that might
result from either the patient or the therapist knowing the true nature of the
treatment.

Another procedure employed to prevent bias is the random assignment of
patients to treatment conditions. If random assignment to treatment conditions was not employed, it would probably result in the "best" patients being
assigned to the active treatment condition. Further, because the data from
clinical trials should be evaluated statistically, it becomes necessary to allow
chance factors to operate. In this way, observed differences between treatment
means can be evaluated against differences that would be expected by chance
in a distribution where the true treatment difference was zero. Thus, the key

procedures employed to prevent the results of clinical trials from being biased are random assignment, placebo control, and double-blind conditions. The interested reader is referred to "*Principle and Problems in Establishing the Efficacy of Psychotropic Agents*" for a very thorough discussion of the methodology of psychotropic drug trials (Levine, Schiele, & Bouthilet, 1971). Some investigators and reviewers of drug trials (e.g., Solomon & Hart, 1978) are concerned with whether or not a double-blind study actually remains double-blind. In this regard, Rickels, Lipman, Fisher, Park, and Uhlenhuth (1970) found that physicians were able to reliably distinguish between patients taking meprobamate versus those taking placebo. Although the breaking of the blind may color the perception of improvement on the part of the therapist, the more basic issue, with regard to potential bias, is whether the blind is broken on the basis of side effects or on the basis of clinical improvement. Clearly, an effective medication should result in more improvement than placebo, and the sophisticated clinician should be able to identify the more improved patients. In fact, Rickels et al. (1970) found that physicians initially were only breaking the double blind on the basis of the differential improvement between meprobamate and placebo. It was only after 4 weeks of treatment that side effects (and clinical improvement) had an influence on their medication guesses. Lipman, Park, and Rickels (1966) in another methodologically focused trial with anxious outpatients combined atropine, in a dosage that consistently produced dry mouth, with chlordiazepoxide, in a four-cell design that included placebo, atropine, chlordiazepoxide, and chlordiazepoxide plus atropine. The use of an active placebo, atropine, did not prevent the finding of a significant therapeutic advantage for chlordiazepoxide, relative to both placebo groups. In fact, atropine patients who were told that dry mouth was a good sign that the medication was working effectively did more poorly than those patients who were told that they might experience some dry mouth from the medication but that it was nothing to worry about.

Other criteria the reader should use in evaluating the soundness of a clinical trial include (a) the use of an initial placebo washout procedure, (b) specific criteria for inclusion and exclusion of patients, (c) adequate medication dosage and checks on actual medication compliance, (d) use of rating scales of established sensitivity, (e) use of multiple rater types, (f) adequate sample size, and (g) use of appropriate statistical procedures for evaluating drop-out rates and survivor analyses.

The purpose of the initial placebo washout period is not just to wash out the effects of prior medication the patient may be currently taking, but also to weed out those patients who are likely to deviate from study procedures either by taking nonstudy medication or by missing scheduled appointments. Because most study attrition occurs early, it adds to the precision of the clinical trial to exclude noncompliant patients before they actually enter the double-blind active medication phase of the trial. Another purpose of the washout period is to identify those patients who are sufficiently improved with placebo treatment to no longer require treatment. These patients should be excluded from the trial (and seen outside the study) because they will not provide a test of differential treatment response. Many investigators (cf. for example, Kahn et al., 1986) require that patients maintain the minimum level of symptom severity required for entry into the trial over the placebo washout period in order to be randomly assigned to the active phase of the drug trial.

Sensitivity may also be increased by including patients who are the most appropriate candidates for the drug trial and by excluding those patients who are not very appropriate. For example, many anxious patients have problems with substance abuse. These patients are likely to miss appointments, take nonprescribed medications, and continue taking their drug of choice while in the study. Excluding these patients, and patients who are significantly depressed, will increase the sensitivity of the trial, because minor tranquilizers, which are appropriate for patients with GAD, are contraindicated for depressed patients (Schatzberg & Cole, 1978). If self-rating scales are included in the trial, patients should be literate. Ideally, patients should be carefully diagnosed using a structured or semi-structured interview such as the Structured Clinical Interview for DSM-III-R or the Research Diagnostic Criteria and should have at least a moderate level of anxiety as reflected by such scales as the Hamilton Anxiety Scale, the COVI Anxiety Screen, or the anxiety cluster of the Hopkins Symptom Checklist. A good discussion of such scales is provided by Uhlenhuth (1985).

It should be recognized that the use of inclusion and exclusion criteria to increase sensitivity also decreases the generality of findings. More precise trials are particularly important in the earlier phases of drug evaluation. Because there is typically a great deal of variability in clinical response to drug and placebo, a fairly large sample size is required to detect drug effects, defined as the difference in clinical response between active medication and placebo. Power estimates may be used to estimate the sample size necessary to detect drug-placebo differences, but a general rule of thumb is to use a sample size of at least 25 patients in parallel group designs and a sample size of at least 20 patients in crossover designs. The intensive or multiple crossover design (Chassan, 1979) is typically used with much fewer patients and enables the investigator to determine, for specific patients, whether or not the active medication is better than placebo. Both the crossover design and the multiple crossover design are subject to the potential problem of carry-over effects. When carry-over effects do occur, they present problems in statistical interpretation of study results.

Most careful investigations also monitor medication compliance during the course of the trial. This monitoring should include careful checks on the amount of study medication taken and whether or not the patient has taken other nonauthorized psychotropic drugs. Some (Dunbar & Stunkard, 1979) have estimated that the rate of noncompliance is as high as 30% to 50%. The use of pill counts (i.e., giving the patient more medication than is needed between visits and asking the patient to return unused medication at the next visit) and structured questioning helps to identify patients who have shown major nonadherence (Park & Lipman, 1964; Rickels & Briscol, 1970). A thoughtful review of nonadherence as a problem in clinical trials is provided by Dunbar and Stunkard (1979). In general, patients who take less than two thirds or three quarters of the prescribed medication, either placebo or active medication, should be statistically discounted, as should patients who take more than threshold amounts of other psychotropic medication. All attrition, such as previously described, and patients who do not keep study appointments and/or who prematurely drop out of treatment should be carefully classified with regard to the reasons for deviation, primarily as treatment related (e.g., side effects, failure to improve, improved enough to no longer perceive the need for treatment), or as nontreatment related (e.g., transferred to another office out of state, major physical illness). Nonparametric tests will reveal whether or not treatment-related attrition is disproportionately related to active medication or placebo. It is often found (cf. for example, Downing et al., 1971) that dropouts for failure to improve occur more frequently in placebo conditions, whereas dropouts because of adverse side effects more often occur on active medication. Such information must, of course, be used in interpreting the results of the study. That is, a medication may prove significantly better than placebo for those patients who adhere to protocol, but this result may be true of only a limited proportion of patients who started the trial. Many investigators attempt to deal with the problem of patient attrition by doing analyses on that group of patients who completed the clinical trial with acceptable adherence to protocol (completors) and another series of analyses using an end-point score, which reflects the clinical status of all patients at the last valid visit in the study. End-point analyses thus weigh the data from nonadhering patients. It is hoped that both sets of analyses provide consistent findings and this consistency lends credence to findings of differential drug efficacy.

Another consideration in the consistency of findings relates to ratings of patients and therapists. In the writers' experience, patient self-ratings and therapist ratings typically complement each other (Park, Uhlenhuth, Lipman, Rickels, & Fisher, 1965). Although it is not unusual for physicians (see Uhlenhuth, 1985) or patients to be more likely to detect drug-placebo differences, it is extremely unlikely that patient ratings will favor placebo and clinician ratings will favor drug or vice-versa. When the results of both rater types are in concordance, the validity of findings is enhanced and most investigators now collect both types of data. Some studies also make use of the ratings of an independent clinical evaluator who is not directly involved in treating the patient and who attempts to remain blind to the treatment the patient is receiving. This procedure is particularly useful in studies where both drugs and psychosocial interventions are being evaluated (Lipman & Covi, 1976). Drug effects are usually more difficult to detect in trials where patients are receiving high levels of psychotherapy because of high "placebo" response rates. They are easier to detect in trials where there is little or no psychotherapy and very limited physician contact (Shapiro, 1978). The latter trials are typically conducted by general practitioners.

## THE STIMULUS-DEPENDENT (PHOBIC) DISORDERS

### Simple Phobias

There is general agreement that behavioral methods including in vivo expo-sure and, to a lesser extent, systematic desensitization provide effective treat-ments for simple phobias such as fear of snakes (Curtis, 1985; Klein, Rabkin, & Gorman, 1985; Marks, 1987, p. 518). Because the success of behavioral therapies is well established, there have been relatively few drug studies. In one study, Klein and associates found no advantage for imipramine versus placebo over a 26-week treatment period (Zitrin, Klein, Woerner, & Ross, 1983) in which patients also received either behavior therapy or supportive therapy. Both mixed phobic and agoraphobic patients in the above study did benefit therapeutically from imipramine. Klein attributed this to the presence of panic attacks in these patients. Panic attacks are not characteristic of patients with specific phobias. Specific phobics do experience anticipatory anxiety and phobic avoidance in the presence of the feared stimulus. As would be expected, tolamolol, a beta-blocker, has been shown to decrease the autonomic arousal associated with the feared stimulus. It did not decrease the subjective feeling of anticipatory anxiety or avoidance behavior (Bernadt, Silverstone, & Singleton, 1980). In this same study diazepam, given in a single dose prior to exposure, was found both to decrease anticipatory anxiety and to reduce avoidant behavior. Other studies in press cited by Roy-Byrne and Katon (1987) indicate that both alcohol and naloxone interfere with the beneficial effects of behavioral treatments, probably by blocking the occurrence of anxiety that is a necessary component of the extinction proce-dure. Psychotropic drugs do not seem appropriate for treating patients with simple phobia.

### Social Phobia

The cardinal feature of social phobia is the fear of humiliation or embarrassment while being observed in social situations. Marks and Gelder (1966) originally included patients with specific social fears (such as eating in public) and those with more generalized social anxiety (e.g., initiating conversations or dating).

DSM-III-R excludes patients whose spontaneous panic attacks give rise to generalized social anxiety or to performance anxiety in specific social situations (e.g., public speaking, signing a check in public). It does, however, maintain and sharpen the distinction between more discrete and more generalized social phobias. As we see later, this distinction has an important bearing on treatment outcome (Liebowitz, Gorman, Fyer, & Klein, 1985).

The paucity of controlled pharmacotherapy studies with socially phobic patients has led Leibowitz et al. (1985) to call this a neglected anxiety disorder.

The results of open studies with social phobics suggest the clinical efficacy of the monoamine oxidase inhibitor (MAOI) phenelzine (Liebowitz, Fyer, Gorman, Campeas, & Levin, 1986), the beta-blocker atenolol (Gorman, Liebowitz, Fyer, Campeas, & Klein, 1985) and the recent triazolo-benzodiazepine alprazolam (Lydiard, Laraia, Howell, & Ballenger, 1988). By contrast, two controlled trials that employed beta-blockers failed to find a significant difference between propranolol and placebo (Falloon, Lloyd, & Harpin, 1981) and between atenolol and placebo (Liebowitz et al., 1987). In the former study the sample size was quite small (only 6 patients completed the study in each treatment condition), and all patients received social skills training. The use of social skills training probably enhanced the placebo response and thus made it very difficult to detect drug-placebo differences, particularly with such a small patient sample. The most convincing study to date of the pharmacotherapy of carefully diagnosed social phobic patients is still ongoing but has been verbally reported by Liebowitz and his associates (Liebowitz et al., 1987). Social phobics were initially classified into a generalized social phobic or a discrete social performance anxiety subgroup. After a 1-week single-blind placebo washout period, patients who maintained significant psychopathology were randomly assigned to an 8-week treatment phase with either phenelzine, atenolol, or placebo. Dosage schedules permitted adequate treatment; up to 90 mg/day of phenelzine and up to 100 mg/day of atenolol. Global judgments of clinical response, as rated by a blind evaluator, found phenelzine patients significantly more improved than both atenolol and placebo patients. Atenolol patients did not respond better than placebo controls. One very interesting preliminary finding from this study suggests an interaction between the relative effectiveness of phenelzine and atenolol for the treatment of more generalized versus more discrete socially phobic patients. In this regard, generalized social phobics showed a 79% improvement rate with phenelzine, but discrete phobics evidenced only a 25% rate of improvement. On the other hand, 3 of 5 discrete social phobics showed good improvement with atenolol, whereas only 2 of 13 generalized social phobics showed such meaningful improvement. One by-product of this study was the finding that generalized phobics presented for treatment in a ratio of about 3:1 as compared to more circumscribed social phobics.

A more complete review of mixed anxiety groups that include some social phobics is given by Liebowitz and associates (Liebowitz et al., 1985), and a review of psychosocial treatments of social phobia can be found in several recent publications (Heimberg & Barlow, 1988; Marks, 1987; Ost, Jerremalm, & Johansson, 1980). Many of the reviewed studies suffer from the same problem as many pharmacotherapy studies, that is, the lack of adequate control groups and blind evaluation procedures. For example, Shaw (1979), found social skills training, flooding, and systematic desensitization to be useful therapeutically in the treatment of social phobics. However, the sample size was relatively small, and a "placebo" or wait-group control was not employed. In a better controlled study, Butler, Cullington, Manby, Amies and Gelder (1984) randomly assigned patients to exposure, exposure-plus-anxiety-management training, and a waiting-list control. After 7 weeks, both active treatment groups showed significant improvement but the wait-list control did not. The long-term superiority of the exposure-plus-management group was evidenced by the fact that in the year following treatment none of the combined-treatment group, but 40% of the exposure-alone group, sought additional treatment. In general, it would seem that an effective psychosocial treatment package would consist of the combination of exposure with either social skills training, anxiety management, or cognitive restructuring. Cognitive restructuring would focus on developing more realistic expectations in social situations and would decrease "off-task thinking about failure, humiliation or embarrassment" (Heimberg & Barlow, 1988). In one small N study ($N = 18$) all patients received information about phobias, self-exposure instructions, and assorted anxiolytic medications. Additionally, patients were randomly assigned to (a) no further treatment except monthly appointments, (b) prolonged therapist-assisted in vivo exposure, (c) dynamically oriented supportive psychotherapy, and (d) relaxation training. The patient group with prolonged self-exposure training did better globally and in terms of reduction of phobic behavior than the other groups (Alström, Nordland, Persson, Harding, & Lungquist, 1984).

In the treatment of social phobia, well-designed pharmacotherapy versus psychosocial interventions and combined modality treatment outcome studies are clearly needed. Promising candidates for such studies would be phenelzine, behavioral exposure procedures, and cognitive restructuring approaches. Because treatments for psychiatric disorders rarely interfere with each other but typically either add to overall effectiveness or at least reflect the efficacy of the "best" treatment (Uhlenhuth, Lipman, & Covi, 1969), the combination of pharmacotherapy plus exposure and cognitive restructuring would seem an important regimen for future controlled studies. Such studies should maintain the distinction between generalized versus discrete social phobia and should carefully document the presence or absence of panic attacks. The efficacy of phenelzine in social phobic situations is probably not directly tied to panic reduction per se because Liebowitz et al. (1985) have demonstrated lactate-precipitated panic in only 7% of social phobics as contrasted with roughly 50% of agoraphobic and panic-disordered patients.

Although the limited evidence available (one controlled study) suggests phenelzine may be effective in treating socially phobic patients, it requires a special diet low in tyramine and is associated with troublesome side effects such as orthostatic hypertension, excessive weight gain, and sexual dysfunction (Robinson & Kurtz, 1987). For these reasons, and because psychosocial interventions are most likely to result in sustained improvement, patients with social phobia should preferably be treated with a psychosocial package, when economically and practically feasible. Until phenelzine has been shown in controlled studies to enhance the overall effectiveness of combined psychosocial interventions, it probably should not be used adjunctively.

### Obsessive-Compulsive Disorder

Although the definition of OCD has changed little since DSM-II, the requirement for patient resistance to compulsions has been dropped in going from DSM-III to DSM-III-R. It has been retained, however, with regard to initial resistance to obsessions (Fyer et al., 1987). The lifetime relationship of OCD to major depression has been reported to be as high as 50%, and selected antidepressants have proven modestly effective in treatment outcome studies (Insel & Zohar, 1987; Perse, 1988). One of the most active investigators in this area has suggested that OCD would be better classified with the affective disorders than with the anxiety disorders (Insel, Zahn, & Murphy, 1985).

Obsessions are recurrent thoughts that are experienced by the patient as intrusive, unpleasant, and compelling. The majority of obsessives also have compulsions that are characterized as ritualized behaviors associated with the obsessional thinking. OCD is often the most chronic and debilitating of the anxiety disorders (Roy-Byrne & Katon, 1987) and was not thought to be amenable to treatment with medication until recently (Insel & Zohar, 1987).

The recent literature on the pharmacotherapy of OCD has been reviewed by Marks (1987), Insel and Zohar (1987), Sarwer-Foner (1987), and Perse (1988). There is a general consensus among these reviewers that clomipramine, a potent serotonin reuptake inhibitor available in Europe but not yet approved for marketing in the United States, is effective for the treatment of OCD and that other MAOIs, based on recent open studies, are worthy of controlled trials. Reynynghe de Voxrie (1968) first reported successful open treatment with clomipramine in 67% of 15 OCD patients in the late 1960s. Since then, six double-blind studies have shown that clomipramine, although only moderately effective, was significantly better than placebo and/or other antidepressant medications in reducing OCD symptomatology (see Perse, 1988). This general conclusion has been confirmed by the findings of a meta-analysis of the research literature (Christensen, Hadzi-Pavlovic, Andrews, & Mattick, 1987). Antidepressants, primarily clomipramine, produced appreciable changes in obsessive-compulsive and depressed symptoms in OCD patients.

Two double-blind studies of lithium versus placebo failed to find a significant therapeutic advantage for lithium despite some commonality of biological markers in OCD and affective disorders. In this regard, both decreased REM latency (Insel, Gillin, & Moore, 1982) and a decreased growth hormone response to clonidine (Siever et al., 1983) have been observed in OCD patients. Only a few studies examined the efficacy of the benzodiazepines, but these studies suffered from serious methodological problems and are considered inconclusive. Waxman (1977), for example, compared diazepam, at the low maximum dose of 15 mg/day, with clomipramine, in a 6-week trial in a mixed population of phobics and OCD patients. The data presented does not, however, permit any conclusions regarding the OCD subgroup. Perse (1988) reported that clinically he and his associates have had "minimal success with alprozolam or other anxiolytics" (p. 52). In view of the long-term (several months) medication regimen that seems necessary for most OCD patients (Sarwer-Foner, 1987), the anxiolytics are not good candidates for the treatment of this disorder.

Although clomipramine is recognized as the most promising drug for OCD, it is also recognized that this medication is no panacea. Thus, for example, the mean improvement on ratings of obsessions was only 34% in the study by Insel et al. (1983) and 42% on an OCD scale in the 5-week study by Thoren, Asberg, Cronholm, Jörnestedt, and Träskiman, (1980). To put this finding in perspective, however, it should be noted that placebo response was only 7% in the latter study. Not only is the degree of therapeutic response to clomipramine rather limited, but it has been generally observed that patients relapse when medication is discontinued, even after a continuous 6-month treatment period (Insel, 1983). Sarwer-Foner (1987) has also stressed that OCD patients tend to be difficult to treat with medication because they fear being controlled by others and evidence marked sensitivity to side effects. Although Sarwer-Foner focuses on dry mouth as being most troublesome, a recent report indicates that nearly all of a group of 24 OCD patients, who had normal orgasms prior to treatment with clomipramine, developed total or partial anorgasmia (Monteiro, Noshirvani, Marks, & Lelliott, 1987)! None of 9 placebo controls developed such sexual side effects. This sexual dysfunction was noted within 3 days after starting treatment with clomipramine and reversed within 3 days after treatment was terminated.

There is disagreement among the experts with regard to whether or not the OCD effect of clomipramine is dependent upon the presence and successful treatment of coexisting depression. In this regard, Marks found that the therapeutic advantage for clomipramine was only present in the subgroup of OCD patients who were characterized by high initial depression (Marks, Stern, Mawson Cobb, & McDonald, 1980). In his recent review of the OCD literature, Marks (1987) argued for the view that depression is a prerequisite for a good antiobsessional response to clomipramine and concludes "that there is strong evidence for some link between mood and OCD outcome with antidepressants" (p. 554). Insel and Zohar (1987), on the other hand, report studies by Insel et al. (1983), Thoren et al. (1980), Montgomery (1980), Ananth, Pecknold, Van Den Steen, and Engelsmann (1981), Volavka, Neziroglu, and Yaryura-Tobias (1985), Flarnent et al. (1985) that fail to show a relationship between OCD effects and initial level of depression. Thus, the weight of evidence does not support the view that only significantly depressed OCD patients will profit from antidepressant therapy. A recent quantitative review of this literature using meta-analytic procedures supports this conclusion. In this study, trials were divided into those in which secondary depression was absent or present. The mean effect size for OCD reduction in the subsample of antidepressant drug studies did not significantly change as a result of the presence or absence of secondary depression (Christensen et al., 1987). The correlation between change in OCD scores and depression scores in the many studies cited by Marks (1987) is not seen as central to the argument because most clinicians (and researchers) find that when patients find relief for their target symptoms, other dimensions of psychopathology improve as well.

As Insel and Zohar (1987) have noted, clomipramine has been found more effective than other tricyclic antidepressants and is distinguished from these tricyclics in its high potency for inhibiting serotonin reuptake. Other antidepressant medications that share this mechanism of action in common with clomipramine include zimelidine, fluvoxamine, and fluoxetine (recently marketed in the United States). Interestingly, these latter drugs have all shown promise for the treatment of OCD. In one study, for example, Perse, Greist, Jefferson, Rosenfeld, and Dar (1987) found an 81% improvement rate with fluvoxamine versus a 19% improvement rate with placebo. Carefully diagnosed chronic OCD patients were treated with both medications in a counterbalanced, double-blind, crossover trial. An initial placebo washout period and a 2-week placebo period between medication was employed. The other studies in this series have been reviewed in this article and in articles by Perse (1988) and Charney et al. (1988). A more direct test of the serotonin hypotheses was provided by Charney and his associates (1988). They examined the behavioral and biochemical responses to tryptophan, a serotonin precursor, and m-chlorophenyl-piperazine, a serotonin receptor agonist, in

OCD patients and normals. Partial support for the serotonin hypothesis was found, but primarily in female patients. The authors suggested that it is unlikely that OCD will be explained by a dysfuntion in any single neurotransmitter system.

*Other Somatic Treatments.*    ECT has generally not proved helpful for OCD although an occasional patient does evidence a good response (Perse, 1988). For patients with incapacitating OCD, who have not responded to behavioral and/or somatic treatments, psychosurgery (leucotomy) has been suggested as a reasonable option (see Perse, 1988, p. 53).

*Behavioral Treatments.*    There is some agreement that insight-oriented treatments are not effective in decreasing the core symptoms of OCD but that behavioral techniques involving exposure in vivo and response prevention are highly effective (Foa & Kozak, 1985; Marks, 1987; Perse, 1988). Exposure in vivo consists of bringing the patient into contact with the feared objects (dirt, urine, feces, etc.), whereas response prevention (either through instructions or direct supervision) prevents the patient from carrying out the ritualistic behavior (e.g., washing, checking whether doors and windows have been locked, etc.). This form of therapy works very well with the most common form of OCD; that is, with patients who have obsessions and associated compulsive rituals. Foa and her associates have shown that in vivo exposure mainly affects the anxiety associated with the phobic objects, whereas response prevention mainly decreases compulsive (ritualistic) behavior. She and her colleagues have also demonstrated that prolonged exposure works better than brief exposure and that imaginal exposure combined with in vivo exposure produces a somewhat better result than in vivo exposure along (Foa & Kozak, 1985). The experience of this group has been that from 60% to 85% of OCD patients have been meaningfully improved with the combination of in vivo exposure and response prevention. Marks (1985) also considered behavioral therapy the treatment of first choice for OCD, and in a recent study (Marks et al., 1988) noted that clomipramine may add little to a treatment regimen of exposure plus response prevention. Along these lines, an earlier study by Marks, Stern, Mawson, Cobb, and McDonald (1980), which employed a complicated design involving clomipramine, placebo, relaxation, and in vivo exposure, suggested that clomipramine added little, long term, to the effects of exposure therapy.

Behavioral techniques have not proved very helpful for the treatment of patients with obsessive ruminations although thought-stopping and satiation procedures have been tried (Marks, 1987; Perse, 1988). Most reviewers recognize the difficulty in treating patients with OCD, and there does seem to be a general consensus that drug therapy may serve as a useful adjunct to behavioral treatment or the major modality for patients who refuse to participate in behavioral regimens and/or who fail to respond to such treatments. For the majority of OCD patients, however, behavioral treatment is probably all that is needed.

## Post-Traumatic Stress Disorder (PTSD)

DSM-III-R characterizes PTSD as a cluster of symptoms that develop following an "unusual human experience" such as rape, combat, or a concentration camp internment. The cluster of symptoms are grouped into three areas: (a) reexperiencing of the traumatic situation, (b) persistent avoidance of trauma-related stimuli, and/or general numbing of responsiveness, and (c) a persistent state of hyperarousal. Marks (1987) classified PTSD as a traumatic phobia characterized by irritability, tension, startle, insomnia, nightmares, depression, flashbacks, and fear and avoidance of stimuli associated with the traumatic event. Several studies of patients with PTSD have found a high proportion of other diagnosable DSM-III disorders including other anxiety disorders, depression, and substance abuse (Lipper et al., 1986; Sierles, Chen, McFarland, & Taylor, 1983). The ECA survey (Helzer, Robins, & McEvoy, 1987) of 2,493 respondents also found that PTSD was associated with other adult psychiatric disorders. A history of PTSD was reported by 1% of their sample, with a prevalence of about 3.5% among victims of physical attack and Vietnam veterans who were not wounded. The prevalence rate rose to 20% among Vietnam veterans wounded in combat, and the full syndrome was only currently common in this later group.

Although it is clear the PTSD is characterized by both physiological and neurochemical changes (Blanchard, Kolb, Pallmeyer, & Garardi, 1982; Watson, Hoffman, & Wilson, 1988), there is a very limited pharmacotherapy literature and no double-blind placebo-controlled studies. It is surprising that a disorder with such a clearly biological dimension has not given rise to a larger number of drug trials. Blanchard and colleagues (1982) found that elevated heart rate, in response to an audiotape of combat noises, separated 95% of PTSD cases from controls who also experienced combat but who did not have PTSD. Watson, Hoffman, and Wilson (1988) postulated a basic imbalance between noradrenalin and opiod release in the area of the locus coeruleus in PTSD patients. Basically, in view of the fact that no controlled double-blind studies are now available, one cannot meaningfully draw conclusions about efficacy of any of the drug treatments.[1]

---

[1]A variety of behavioral and psychotherapeutic approaches have been found helpful for PTSD patients. These are reviewed by Ettedgui and Bridges (1985) and Marks (1987, pp. 510–513). In general, exposure in fantasy, fantasy flooding, and desensitization seem to work well.

## THE STIMULUS INDEPENDENT DISORDERS

### Panic Disorder/Agoraphobia

In keeping with the general trend toward diagnostic specificity, DSM-III recognized panic disorder as distinct from GAD (anxiety neurosis). This distinction grew out of early studies by Klein, which he interpreted as showing that imipramine blocked the panic attacks of agoraphobic patients but did not reduce anticipatory or more generalized anxiety (Klein, 1964; Klein & Fink, 1962). In DSM-III, panic disorder was conceptualized either as a primary disorder or as secondary to the occurrence of agoraphobia. By contrast, DSM-III-R placed greater emphasis on the primacy of panic attacks. Panic disorder, defined by the frequency and severity of panic attacks, was classified by itself or with the addition of agoraphobia (fear of public places). Although agoraphobia may occur in the absence of a full-blown panic attack, it is currently thought to be associated with at least some of the major symptoms of the panic attack. These might include such symptoms as heart racing or pounding, shortness of breath, choking, chest pain, smothering sensation, fear of dying or losing control.

The basis for the qualitative distinction between GAD and panic states derives from (a) a purported differential response to psychotropic drugs; (b) family aggregation studies; and (c) the general clinical observation that the occurrence of panic attacks precedes the development of the milder form of anticipatory and/or more generalized anxiety. It was generally thought that whereas panic attacks responded to antidepressant medications, the milder forms of anxiety responded to the benzodiazepines with alprazolam being an exception to the general rule (Ballenger, Rubin, & Dupont, 1985). As we see here, some recent double-blind studies have suggested that response to psychotropic medication does not clearly separate GAD and panic-disordered patients. Thus, GAD patients have been shown to be responsive to imipramine (Kahn et al., 1986), and panic patients have been shown to experience a marked reduction in panic attacks with diazepam (Dunner, Ishiki, Avery, Wilson, & Hyde, 1986; Noyes, Anderson, & Clancy, 1984).

Family aggregation studies have demonstrated an increase in panic disorder and agoraphobia in the families of such patients, whereas the families of GAD patients have not shown an increase in the incidence of GAD (Klerman, 1986; Noyes et al., 1986). In general, a strong genetic etiology is recognized in panic disorder/agoraphobia but is not thought to be present in GAD (Fyer et al., 1987). Torgersen (1983), for example, found a 31% concordance rate for panic disorder in monozygotic twins but a lack of concordance in dizygotic twins. GAD patients, on the other hand, did not show a stronger concordance rate for GAD in monozygotic than in dizygotic twins. Further evidence for the validity of the separation of panic versus GAD is provided by the differential response to yohimbine in these patients (Charney, Woods, Goodman, & Heninger, 1987; D. S. Charney, personal communication, March, 1985).

Unfortunately, the literature on the drug treatment of panic disorders is often interwoven with the drug treatment of agoraphobia where panic attacks are a frequent accompaniment of the patient's fear of public places (Rickels & Schweizer, 1987). It is interesting to note that whereas epidemiological studies clearly document a rather high prevalence (2.9%) of agoraphobia uncomplicated by a history of panic disorder (Weissman & Merikangas, 1986), studies conducted with clinic populations indicate an almost complete comorbidity of agoraphobia and panic (Fyer et al., 1987, p. 1181). In essence, the studies reviewed here do not differentiate agoraphobia and panic with any clarity, and the reader should assume that the studies cited include a majority of patients suffering from both disorders and/or at least the major symptoms of both disorders.

Recent reviews of the panic/agoraphobia literature are in general agreement that (a) exposure procedures are effective particularly with patients who suffer from agoraphobia or from phobic avoidance; (b) imipramine, clomipramine, and phenelzine have been shown effective in placebo-controlled studies and most reviewers think that other tricyclic and MAOI antidepressants are probably effective on the basis of non-placebo-controlled studies; (c) anxiolytics such as chlordiazepoxide and diazepam are probably not very effective or are not as effective as the antidepressants, although only one double-blind trial has found imipramine superior to both chlordiazepoxide and placebo (McNair & Kahn, 1981); (d) based on controlled studies, alprazolam, an atypical benzodiazepine, is probably effective in reducing panic attacks; and (e) the combination of exposure and an effective antidepressant medication is the most effective treatment approach for panic/agoraphobia (Curtis, 1985; Gorman, Liebowitz, & Klein, 1984; Klein et al., 1985; Marks, 1987; Mavissakalian, Michelson, & Dealy, 1983; Noyes, Chaudhry & Domingo, 1986; Rickels & Schweizer, 1987; Roy-Bryne & Katon, 1987; Sheehan, 1982, 1985; Sheehan, Ballenger, & Jacobson, 1980; Telch, Agras, Taylor, Roth, & Gallen, 1985; Zitrin, Klein, & Woerner, 1980). There is also general agreement that patients with agoraphobia who do not experience "full-blown" panic attacks may only require in vivo exposure procedures without medication.

There is a controversy regarding whether or not antidepressant medication, in the absence of exposure procedures, will block spontaneous panic attacks. Klein believes that imipramine blocks the panic attack regardless of exposure procedures. He conceptualized the panic attack—the sudden discrete surge of symptoms of autonomic arousal accompanied by an impending sense of doom—as the core aspect of agoraphobia/panic disorder. Avoidant behaviors and anticipatory anxiety are seen by Klein as secondary developments, following the experience of panic attacks. According to Klein, the role of in vivo exposure is to reduce these secondary aspects of agoraphobia/panic once the panic attack has been successfully blocked by antidepressant medication. Indeed, it has been shown in the laboratory that sodium lactate infusion, which precipitates panic attacks in patients with a history of panic attacks but not in normals (Pitts & McClure, 1967), can be blocked by imipramine or MAOI antidepressants (Gorman, Fyer, Liebowitz, & Klein, 1987, p. 990). This suggests a direct biochemical mechanism of panic blockade. However, a recent study by Telch et al. (1985) raises questions about whether imipramine has a direct panic-blocking effect independent of exposure procedures. In this regard, these investigators randomly assigned 37 agoraphobic patients (severely impaired by spontaneous panic attacks and restricted mobility) to imipramine (up to 300 mg/day) with no exposure, imipramine with exposure, and placebo with exposure. Patients in the imipramine-no exposure condition were given antiexposure instructions during the initial 8 weeks of the study. An evaluation of improvement at 8 weeks revealed that the imipramine-plus-antiexposure group did not experience any reduction in panic attacks and little improvement on phobic indices despite showing significant improvement in anxious and dysphoric mood. The only group that showed a reduction in panic attacks was the group who received both imipramine and exposure to phobic stimuli. Contrary to the position of Marks (1987) that exposure alone is sufficient to eliminate panic attacks, the placebo-plus-exposure group both at 8 weeks, and over the 26 weeks of the study, failed to evidence a reduction in panic attacks. The imipramine-plus-exposure group showed significantly more improvement than did the placebo-plus-exposure group at 26 weeks. The group that initially had imipramine-plus-antiexposure instructions improved when these instructions were changed to instructions "try to venture out into previously feared situations" (p. 327). The improvement in mood and phobic avoidance did not, however, extend to a reduction in panic attacks. It should be noted that these switched patients were not told how to confront phobic situations nor were they given therapist-aided exposure procedures. Apparently, both active ingredients, medication and exposure, are necessary to effect a reduction in panic attacks.

A combined modality study by Mavissakalian et al. (1983) found that imipramine plus programmed in vivo exposure practice resulted in more improvement than did imipramine alone. Although both groups ($N = 9$ per group) experienced a reduction in panic attacks, it is not clear whether the imipramine-alone group actually confronted phobic situations despite the lack of specific instructions to do so.

It seems fair to conclude that those clinical trials that used an adequate dose of antidepressants and that did not specifically employ antiexposure instruction typically found that antidepressant medication resulted in significantly more improvement than placebo (cf. for example, Ballenger, Sheehan, & Jacobson, 1977; Klein, 1964; Klein & Fink, 1962; Mavissakalian & Michelson, 1980; McNair & Kahn, 1981; Sheehan et al., 1980; Telch et al., 1985;

Tyrer, Candy, & Kelly, 1973; Zitrin et al., 1983). Two negative studies (Marks et al., 1983; Solyom, LaPierre, Pecknold, & Morton, 1981) used in vivo exposure conditions but employed rather low dosages of phenelzine (45 mg/day) and imipramine (about 125 mg/day, on average). The Marks et al. study (1983) has been criticized for including patients known to be unresponsive to antidepressants and for data analytic procedures that may have clouded an imipramine effect (see Rickels & Schweizer, 1987, p. 1199).

Recent studies employing the triazolo-benzodiazepine alprazolam have shown a therapeutic advantage for this high potency benzodiazepine, relative to placebo, on panic attacks and associated symptoms (Chouinard, Annable, Fontaine, & Solyom, 1982; Dunner et al., 1986; Sheehan et al., 1984). As might be expected, the therapeutic advantage for alprazolam occurs more quickly (in a week or so) than the more traditional antidepressants. On the other hand, the effects of treatment dissipate quickly when the medication is stopped, and recent discussions among clinicians indicate that many patients have difficulty being removed from medication. At this stage of our knowledge, antidepressant medications, imipramine and phenelzine, are the best studied and should be considered the drugs of choice for the treatment of panic disorders. In general, the treatment regimen should include in vivo exposure (probably therapist assisted and prolonged) plus an antidepressant medication given in adequate dosage (in the range of 150–300 mg/day of imipramine and 45–75 mg/day of phenelzine). With many panic patients it is necessary to start at very low dosages of antidepressant medication and to gradually increase dosage. It is often necessary to continue medication for 6 weeks or longer to ensure the adequacy of the medication trial.

Although it is recognized that the tricyclic antidepressants and MAOIs produce moderate to marked improvement in 60%–75% of panic/agoraphobia patients and that the addition of a behavioral exposure treatment component boosts this improvement rate to about 90% (Ballenger, 1986), it is also clear that many patients cannot tolerate medications and that drop-out rates are frequently high (Noyes et al., 1986). Marks (1983) reported that patient attrition averages about 30% in antidepressant trials with agoraphobic/panic disorder patients.

One recent trend in the agoraphobic/panic disorder literature has been a requestioning of the efficacy of the benzodiazepines for the treatment of panic disorder (e.g., Ballenger, 1986; Noyes et al., 1986; Rickels & Schweizer, 1987). Although there is widespread agreement that alprozolam is effective for panic/agoraphobia, many researches tend to conceptualize alprazolam as "unique" among benzodiazepines. On the other hand, recent studies (Dunner et al., 1986; Noyes et al., 1984) suggest that diazepam may also be effective for the treatment of panic. In fact, no difference in relative efficacy was found between alprazolam and diazepam. Both medications were significantly more effective in reducing panic attacks than was placebo. In one study (Noyes et al., 1984), diazepam was found to significantly reduce the frequency and severity of panic attacks, whereas propranolol was ineffective. The improvement rate of 86% moderate or better improvement with diazepam (33% for propranolol) certainly compares favorably with the improvement rate ranges reported for the antidepressants.

Most researchers are somewhat hesitant to accept the possibility that the benzodiazepines are effective for the treatment of panic because this acceptance would undermine one strong rationale for considering generalized anxiety and panic as separate disorders (Noyes et al., 1986). Further studies with a range of benzodiazepines would be of both clinical and theoretical interest.

A recent study by Charney and associates (Charney et al., 1986) suggests some specificity among the antidepressants used for treating panic disorder/ agoraphobia. In this regard, Charney found that imipramine was effective in treating the frequency of panic attacks and phobic avoidance, whereas trazadone was not effective. These findings support the hypothesis that drugs that are effective for panic/agoraphobia act by altering nonadrenergic functioning. Drugs such as trazadone, which primarily influence serotonergic mechanisms, are less likely to be effective.

The relative efficacy of the MAOIs versus the tricyclic antidepressants has been examined in only one clinical trial (Sheehan et al., 1980). In that study, a slight advantage for phenelzine over imipramine was found on several scales. Both drugs proved significantly more effective than placebo, but relatively low dosages of both drugs were employed. Unfortunately, the proportion of patients who showed significant improvement with each treatment was not reported. Given the dietary restrictions with the MAOIs, imipramine is probably the best choice for treating panic disorder/agoraphobia; certainly it is the best studied of the antidepressants.

Barlow (1986) has recently treated patients with panic attacks by provoking panic attacks with exercise, $CO_2$, and other procedures. The thinking is that patients with panic attacks are not primarily afraid of specific phobic situations such as driving a car or being in the supermarket but, rather, are most fearful of the panic attack itself and the associated sense of impending doom. By inducing the panic attack under controlled conditions, the patient learns that the panic attack will not be the ultimate catastrophic situation, and the physiological cues—for example, racing heart, shortness of breath—that bring on the crescendo of panic gradually extinguish and the panic attack ceases.

A review of nonsomatic treatments for panic disorder makes it clear that behavioral interventions have primarily been targeted to the panic associated with agoraphobia (Dittrich, Houts, & Lichstein, 1983) and that not very much attention has been given to noncontingent panic disorders. Most behaviorists stress the need for further research on interoceptive exposure (such as employed by Barlow) and cognitive restructuring techniques.

Generalized Anxiety Disorder (GAD)

DSM-III-R has modified GAD from its classification in DSM-III as a residual anxiety category of at least 1 month duration. It is now defined by the presence of unrealistic or excessive anxiety about two or more life circumstances (not associated with the focus of other diagnosed anxiety disorders) plus at least 6 of 18 symptoms indicative of motor tension (e.g., feeling shaky, trembling), autonomic hyperactivity (e.g., heart pounding), or excessive vigilance and scanning (e.g., feeling edgy or keyed up). These characteristics must have been present, most of the time, for a period of at least 6 months. It seems that fewer patients will now qualify for the classification of GAD than previously.

The pharmacotherapy of GAD has been the topic of several recent reviews (Greenblatt, Shader, & Abernathy, 1983; Hoehn-Saric & McLeod, 1985; Hollister, 1986; Klein et al., 1985; Rickels & Schweizer, 1987; Woods et al., 1987) that have explored issues of both efficacy and safety. Prior to DSM-III, the pharmacotherapy of GAD was usually reviewed under the rubric of "non-psychotic anxiety" or "neurotic anxiety" (cf. for example, Greenblatt & Shader, 1974, 1978; Rickels, 1981; Roth & Meyers, 1969; Solomon & Hart, 1978). These reviews make it clear that the benzodiazepines are the most frequently prescribed and most frequently studied of the anxiolytics. In 1970–1971 it was found that 15% of a large national sample of respondents had taken a minor tranquilizer/sedative drug and that this usage accounted for 68% of all psychotropic drugs taken that year (Parry et al., 1973). In 1984, Mellinger, Balter, and Uhlenhuth (1984) found that 11% of American adults used an antianxiety agent during the prior year and that benzodiazepines accounted for 84% of that total usage. Roughly 60 million new and refill prescriptions were written for the benzodiazepines with about half of these prescriptions for mental disorders and half for circulatory, digestive, and musculoskeletal problems (Woods et al., 1987).

With regard to efficacy, an early review of the minor tranquilizers (Klein & Davis, 1969) reported 22 double-blind trials in which chlordiazepoxide was compared with placebo: 13 such trials with diazepam and 9 such trials with oxazepam. In all 22 trials chlordiazepoxide was significantly better than placebo, whereas diazepam was significantly better than placebo in 11 of 13 trials and oxazepam in 8 of 9 trials. By contrast to the benzodiazepines, meprobamate proved significantly better than placebo in only 16 of 25 trials and barbiturates exceeded placebo in only 11 of 17 studies. This same relative rank ordering of clinical efficacy was also found in direct comparisons of the benzodiazepines versus the barbiturates (the benzodiazepines were significantly better in 6 of 12 trials) and versus meprobamate (the benzodiazepines were significantly better in 3 of 8 trials). Greenblatt and Shader (1978) reviewed 25 placebo-controlled benzodiazepine trials and found a strong advantage for the benzodiazepines in 18 trials and a slight advantage for the benzodiazepines in 4 trials. In 3 trials no differences were found. All of these studies were short-term, that is, 4 weeks or less. In addition to their therapeutic advantage, the benzodiazepines are known to cause less unwanted drowsiness, to have a low addiction risk at therapeutic dosages (Woods et al., 1987), and to rarely cause serious outcomes in deliberate or accidental over-dosages. Rickels, Case, Downing, and Winokur (1983), for example, found that a large sample ($N = 180$) of anxious outpatients did not develop tolerance with continuous diazepam treatment during a 22-week study period and that only 5% of patients continuously treated with "sedative-benzodiazepines" for up to 8 months developed evidence of withdrawal reactions. These were characterized as neither life threatening nor incapacitating and could be managed by a gradual dose reduction (as opposed to abrupt termination). In an extensive methodological review of 78 studies that compared benzodiazepines with placebo (Solomon & Hart, 1978), it is reported that 56.4% of the studies found a statistically significant advantage for the benzodiazepines. In only one study did placebo actually do better than the active drug, whereas in 26 studies the drug did "slightly better" than placebo. Despite their negative conclusions, this is not a random distribution from a true population distribution in which there was no difference in therapeutic efficacy between the benzodiazepines and placebo. Analogously, the tricyclic antidepressants, which are widely accepted for their efficacy in the treatment of depression, were found to be significantly better than placebo in only 61 of 93 double-blind trials (65.5%) reviewed by Morris and Beck (1974). Conceivably, certain effective medications may not be found to be significantly better than placebo in studies where small samples, insensitive outcome measures, and inadequate drug dosages are employed. We do not know the degree to which such factors account for the findings just mentioned. In any case, despite many negative outcomes the short-term efficacy of the benzodiazepines has been supported by a majority of positive studies.

Klein et al., (1985) cited five recent comparative trials in which patients were specifically selected to fulfill DSM-III criteria for GAD. In two separate studies by Rickels and associates, large samples of GAD patients did significantly better on both alprozolam and diazepam than on placebo. Another three double-blind placebo-controlled trials found both diazepam and buspirone (a non-benzodiazepine anxiolytic) significantly better than placebo on measures of anxiety and global clinical ratings. These trials employed 400 GAD patients (see Klein et al., 1985, for specific references). Other studies by Klein et al. (1985), although not diagnostically specific to GAD, also provide additional support for the efficacy of the benzodiazepines.

It should be recognized that there are eight benzodiazepines currently manufactured in the United States for the treatment of anxiety (additional benzodiazepines are marketed for insomnia and seizure disorders). There does not seem to be any consistent advantage or disadvantage that would guide the selection of a specific benzodiazepine for its anxiolytic properties. Greenblatt and Shader (1978) reviewed 25 trials where one benzodiazepine was compared against another benzodiazepine. In 64% of these trials no differences were found; in the remaining trials only weak (not statistically or clinically meaningful) differences were noted. Thus, consistent differences in efficacy among the benzodiazepines are not apparent.

Five of the benzodiazepines—chlordiazepoxide (the initial prototype), diazepam, prazepam, clorazepate, halazepam—have a long duration of action, whereas alprazolam, oxazepam, and lorazepam have short to intermediate half-lives. Some investigators favor the use of oxazepam and lorazepam with the elderly. Some investigators see an advantage for using alprazolam in patients with a broad spectrum of anxiety, panic, and depressive symptoms. Other clinicians, however, are concerned with a possibly greater risk of dependence with alprazolam (Noyes et al., 1985; Tyrer & Murphy, 1987). Physicians should be aware that some degree (usually mild) of physiological dependence is likely to develop in patients taking a benzodiazepine in therapeutic doses on a regular basis for a period of several months (Covi, Lipman, Patterson, Derogatis, & Uhlenhuth, 1973). However, as Woods et al. (1987) in their exhaustive and well-balanced review point out, even when physiological dependence does develop, patients do not increase their dosage, do not use the drugs recreationally, or engage in other forms of inappropriate use (p. 389). Medication can be discontinued with minimal patient discomfort by a gradual decrease in drug dosage.

Rickels, Case, Downing, and Fridman (1986) indicate that there was a high rate of relapse (63%) in the year following treatment with either 6, 14, or 22 weeks of diazepam. Most patients sought further medical help for their anxiety and most received medication. Rickels et al. propose a conservative drug treatment program in which patients are intermittently treated with benzodiazepines and observed clinically to see how well they function off medication. Although perhaps a third of chronically anxious patients may not require more than 3 to 6 weeks of treatment, most anxious patients will probably require longer periods of treatment. This longer period of treatment should probably employ a "PRN" medication schedule with patients being educated to recognize an increase in the severity of their anxiety symptoms so that if their anxiety does break through, the dosage regimen can be made more regular and higher dosages employed. In this regard, there seems to be a growing concern, particularly among our British colleagues (cf. for example, Tyrer & Murphy, 1987) that even short-term benzodiazepine treatment of GAD patients may result in physical dependence and withdrawal effects upon abrupt termination of treatment. The most persuasive study in this area was carried out by Power, Jerrom, Simpson, and Mitchell (1985). They administered a moderate dose of diazepam (15 mg/day to GAD patients who were drug free for at least 3 weeks and who had no history of long-term or continuous treatment with benzodiazepines. Following a placebo week, patients were randomized to 6 weeks on diazepam or matching placebo. When medications were stopped, the sample of 10 patients on diazepam evidenced more new symptoms and the return of more old symptoms of anxiety than did the 11 placebo patients. Thus, even short-term treatment with diazepam, at a moderate dose, was associated with dependence in GAD patients. Studies such as these have led Tyrer and Murphy (1987) to recommend an intermittent flexible dosage treatment regimen for GAD. They further suggest that if regular treatment is necessary, "it is wise to confine treatment to a few weeks and then to reduce the drug gradually . . . in the same way recommended for long-term use of benzodiazepines" (p. 721).

*Benzodiazepines Versus Major Tranquilizers.* Although most clinicians and reviewers agree that the phenothiazines and haloperidol, in low dosages, are effective for the treatment of anxiety (Greenblatt & Shader, 1978; Rickels & Schweizer, 1987), there is also good consensus that the risks associated with the major tranquilizers, particularly that of tardive dyskinesia, is just too great to warrant their use in more than an occasional patient. Hoehn-Saric and McLeod (1985), for example, state that the neuroleptics should be avoided in nonpsychotic anxiety disorders except in those few rare cases where other effective medications just do not provide relief.

*Benzodiazepines Versus Antidepressants.* In their review of anxiolytics versus antidepressant medication with mixed anxious-depressed patients, Klein et al. (1985) reported eight studies, six of which employed a benzodiazepine. In these six studies the antidepressant and benzodizepine were equally effective for symptoms of anxiety in four trials, but an antidepressant medication was significantly better than diazepam in two trials. Although the reviewers interpret these results as not supporting the superiority of either anxiolytics or antidepressants, they do recognize antidepressants as the "more active drug" (p. 523). Since their review was published, the results of a large-scale NIMH-sponsored collaborative study (Kahn et al., 1986) provided very persuasive data in support of the superiority of the tricyclic antidepressant imipramine versus the benzopiazepine chlordiazepoxide. This study was done concurrently with another study that tested these same drugs in a primarily depressed outpatient sample (Lipman et al., 1986), so that patient samples were clearly separated in terms of anxious versus depressed symptomatology and diagnoses. The study employed 242 carefully diagnosed anxious patients who were randomly assigned, following a 2-week placebo washout period, to 8 weeks of blind treatment with either placebo, imipramine (up to 200 mg/day), or chlordiazepoxide (up to 80 mg/day). Although chlordiazepoxide showed efficacy over the first few weeks of the trial, the therapeutic advantage for imipramine became stronger and more general after the initial 2 weeks. The therapeutic advantage for imipramine was evident both in patient self-ratings and in physician ratings of anxiety, interpersonal sensitivity, and global improvement. The advantage for imipramine was found to be independent of the degree of baseline depression. In view of the global effectiveness of the tricyclic antidepressants across the range of anxiety disorders, this finding for GAD should be taken very seriously, and the drug-of-choice status currently enjoyed by the benzodiazepines should be questioned, particularly for the treatment of chronically anxious GAD patients, who are likely to require more than just a few weeks of treatment.

*Other Medications.* In addition to the benzodiazepines, barbiturates, major tranquilizers, and antidepressant medications, buspirone, a minor tranquilizer unrelated to the benzodiazepines, and beta-blockers, primarily propranolol, have been used and found effective for the treatment of GAD (Noyes, 1985; Rickels & Schweizer, 1987). Noyes (1985) indicated that propranolol proved significantly better than placebo in 4 of 7 studies but that most trials were limited by small sample size, low dosages of medication, and brief treatment periods. Beta-blocking drugs generally were considered to have demonstrated antianxiety effects, based on the response of some 500 patients who participated in 15 controlled trials. However, in 5 of 6 controlled trials, Noyes (1985) found that chlordiazepoxide or diazepam were the more effective drugs, and on balance, he considers the beta-blockers to have a "limited" role in the treatment of anxiety disorders. Because the beta-blocking drugs have a reliable effect on the somatic components of anxiety (e.g., heart rate and tremor), they have been found helpful in stress-related performance situations. Noyes also said that the beta-blockers should be considered in patients prone to benzodiazepine or other substance abuse problems.

Along these same lines, buspirone has proven effective relative to placebo and other benzodiazepines for the treatment of anxiety, and is thought not to potentiate alcohol (Mattila, Aranko, & Seppala, 1982), not to cause physical dependence, or be subject to abuse (Cole, Orzack, Beake, Bird, & Bar-tal, 1982). In two double-blind placebo-controlled studies (Goldberg & Finnerty, 1982; Rickels et al., 1982), buspirone proved significantly better than placebo on measures of anxiety and global improvement but did not differ from diazepam, except in its side effect profile where it was found to be less sedative than diazepam. In fact, most anxious patients who have taken buspirone have not reported adverse effects, and buspirone is not known to interfere with cognitive function (Abramowicz, 1986). Because of its low abuse potential and its lack of interaction with alcohol, buspirone is probably a better choice of anxiolytic than the benzodiazepines for the treatment of GAD patients with a history of alcohol or drug abuse problems. Buspirone takes longer to have an anxiolytic effect than the benzodiazepines and apparently does not produce the more immediate sedative calming effect that benzodiazepine-treated patients have come to expect. For this reason, buspirone does better in naive patients than it does in patients with a history of benzodiazepine treatment (Abramowicz, 1986). Unfortunately, the long-term effectiveness and safety of this recently approved drug have yet to be determined. In fact, very few studies have been done to examine the long-term safety and efficacy of most anxiolytic medications. In one such study, Rickels, Case, Downing and Fridman (1986) reported the results of diazepam treatment with 158 chronically anxious outpatients that lasted for either 6, 14, or 22 weeks followed by placebo substitution and a 1-year follow-up period. Interestingly, maximal improvement was reported after 6 weeks with no further improvement being seen in the 14- and 22-week groups. However, symptom recurrence following placebo substitution was noted in 45% of the 6-week and in 25% of the 22-week diazepam cohorts. Of the 158 patients in the study only 13 evidenced clear-cut withdrawal reactions following placebo substitution. These withdrawal reactions did not include convulsions or psychotic reactions and disappeared within a few weeks. In commenting on the study, these investigators conclude that about half of their chronically anxious patients needed only 6 weeks of treatment to remain symptom free but that many patients require longer treatment periods. In a very interesting national survey on prevalence and characteristics of long-term regular users of anxiolytic medication, Mellinger, Balter, and Uhlenhuth (1984) reported that 15% of adult anxiolytic users took medication on a regular basis for a year or longer. Almost half of this group suffered from a major chronic health problem such as cardiovascular disorder, arthritis, or bursitis, and these regular users also tended to be older and female and had high levels of emotional distress. Most of these long-term users were being monitored by their physician at fairly regular intervals. It is not clear from this study what proportion of anxiolytic drug use was primarily for an anxiety disorder, but other data suggest that only about 25% of respondents who qualify for an anxiety disorder diagnosis actually receive treatment with a psychotropic medication (Uhlenhuth et al., 1983).

*Non somatic Treatments.*    By definition, GAD represents a stimulus independent or endogenous type of anxiety that has been referred to as free-floating or pervasive anxiety (Suinn, 1984). Thus, exposure techniques that have proved therapeutic in the treatment of phobic avoidance, of agoraphobia, and for some types of OCD are not applicable to GAD. Indeed, an NIMH-sponsored conference report (1981) on nonpharmacologic treatments of anxiety indicated that further research was needed in this area. The conference proposed as a treatment package the combination of relaxation therapy (biofeedback) with some form of cognitive restructuring. The thinking underlying this concensus was that biofeedback and relaxation procedures would represent an optimal approach for reducing the physiological symptoms of

GAD, whereas cognitive approaches would be helpful for subjective-"mental" components. Indeed, a recent review of the biofeedback literature found frontal EMG biofeedback training to reduce muscle tension to be helpful. Other biofeedback techniques were either ineffective (heart rate and EEG alpha biofeedback) or insufficiently studied (Rice & Blanchard, 1982). Tarrier and Main (1986) found that applied relaxation training, taught during one session and practiced over a 5-week period, significantly improved the somatic components of GAD relative to a waiting-list control. Although the waiting-list control does not really control for the "placebo" or nonspecific components of treatment, the fact that GAD patients mainly improved in somatic symptomatology and not in "cognitive" domains or depression argues against a nonspecific improvement interpretation of these results. Some form of "attention" placebo would have been helpful. The Tarrier and Main relaxation training method consisted of (a) self-monitoring of anxiety levels; (b) breathing exercises; (c) progressive muscle relaxation, consisting of tension release exercises; and (d) positive mental imagery. A somewhat similar package—anxiety management training—has been developed and tested by Suinn (1984), who has summarized the literature on its efficacy. Over the series of studies cited by Suinn (1984), anxiety management training, which incorporates (a) rationale and relaxation training, (b) guided rehearsal of anxiety provocation and control, (c) identifying anxiety-inducing cues, (d) graduated self-control training, and (e) transfer of training to in vivo situations, has proved helpful in relieving distress associated with the autonomic, somatic, and cognitive symptoms of GAD.

In a wait-group control study, Barlow et al. (1984) found that a combination of EMG biofeedback and relaxation with cognitive interventions resulted in significant improvement in a small sample of both GAD and panic disorder patients. Both patient groups improved somatically and on dimensions of anxiety and panic as measured by self-ratings. A 3-month follow-up evaluation found that the majority of patients maintained their initial improvement, with many continuing to show additional improvement beyond that found over the 14-week treatment phase. Clearly, nonpharmacologic treatments of GAD seems promising and further controlled studies are indicated.

## SUMMARY

Although it seems natural to assume that the anxiolytic medications would be the most effective psychotropic medications for the treatment of the anxiety disorders reviewed in this chapter—simple phobia, social phobia, agoraphobia/panic, OCD, PTSD and GAD—the evidence does not support this assumption. As we have seen, the benzodiazepines are the most frequently prescribed psychotropic medications for the anxiety disorders (Uhlenhuth et al., 1983), but their efficacy, except for the short-term treatment of GAD (Kahn et al., 1986) and alprazolam for the treatment of agoraphobia/panic (Chouinard et al., 1982; Sheehan et al., 1984) is not supported by well-controlled studies. We have evidence to support a moderate level of effectiveness of the antidepressants for the treatment of OCD (Insel & Zohar, 1987) and a relatively greater level of effectiveness for panic/agoraphobia (McNair & Kahn, 1981) and the long-term (beyond 4 weeks) treatment of GAD (Kahn et al., 1986). Although clinicians favor the antidepressants for the treatment of PTSD (Bleich, Siegel, Garb, & Lerer, 1986), controlled studies are absent and the presumed efficacy of the antidepressants must be considered a heuristic hypothesis.

Moreover, we have also seen that the magnitude of treatment effects with the more efficacious antidepressants leaves a good deal of room for improvement, particularly the response of OCD patients to clomipramine (Insel et al., 1983). In general, psychosocial treatments seem to provide a major source of therapeutic effectiveness for treating the various anxiety disorders. They may be a particularly attractive modality for patients who are sensitive to the side effects of psychotropic medications (Foa & Kozak, 1985; Mavissakalian et al., 1983). A consensus favoring the combination of antidepressant medication plus behavioral treatment seems strongest in the panic/agoraphobia area and is, perhaps, weakest for OCD where studies by Marks (Marks, 1985; Marks et al., 1988) suggest that antidepressant medication may not add much to a behavioral regimen. Psychosocial treatments for GAD have not been combined with medications nor have they been evaluated in comparative efficacy studies. Such studies would be most valuable.

Finally, it should again be emphasized that epidemiological studies indicate that only about one in four respondents with a diagnosable anxiety disorder are receiving psychotropic medication (Uhlenhuth et al., 1983; Weissman, 1985). Unfortunately, the most frequently prescribed class of medication—the anxiolytics—are not the most effective for the treatment of the anxiety disorders.

## REFERENCES

Abramowicz, M. (1986). Buspirone: A non-benzodiazepine for anxiety. *The Medical Letter,* 28(728), 117–118.

Alström, J. E., Nordlund, C. L., Persson, G., Harding, M., & Lungquist, C. (1984). Four treatment methods in social phobic patients. *Acta Psychiatrica Scandinavia, 70,* 97–110.

American Psychiatric Association. (1987). *Diagnostic and statistical manual of mental disorders (3rd ed. rev.).* Washington, DC: Author.

Ananth, J., Pecknold, J., Van Den Steen, N., & Engelsmann, F. C. (1981). Double-blind comparative study of clomipramine and amitriptyline in obsessive neurosis. *Progress in Neuro-Psychopharmacology, 5,* 257–262.

Ballenger, J. C. (1986). Pharmacotherapy of the panic disorders. *Journal of Clinical Psychiatry*, 47:6 (Suppl), 27–32.

Ballenger, J. C., Rubin, R., Dupont, R. (1985, April). *Treatment of agoraphobia/panic disorders with alprazolam. Preliminary results from a large multicenter placebo-controlled trial.* Paper presented at the Annual NCDEU Meeting, Key Biscayne, FL.

Ballenger, J. C., Sheehan, D. V., & Jacobson, G. (1977, May). *Antidepressant treatment of severe phobic anxiety.* Paper presented at 130th Annual Meeting of the American Psychiatric Association, Toronto, Canada.

Balter, M. B., & Levine, J. (1973). Character and extent of psychotherapeutic drug usage in the United States. *Proceedings of the Fifth World Congress of Psychiatry*, Mexico, Excerpta Medica.

Barlow, D. H. (1985). The dimensions of anxiety disorders. In A. H. Tuma & J. D. Maser (Eds.), *Anxiety and the anxiety disorders* (pp. 479–500). Hillsdale, NJ: Lawrence Erlbaum Associates.

Barlow, D. H. (1986). Behavioral conception and treatment of panic. *Psychopharmacology Bulletin*, 22, 802–806.

Barlow, D. H., Cohen, A. S., Waddell, M. T., Vermilyec, B. B., Klasko, J. S., Blanchard, E. B., & DiNardo, P. A. (1984). Panic and generalized anxiety disorders: Nature and treatment. *Behavior Therapy*, 15, 431–449.

Bernadt, M. W., Silverstone, T., & Singleton, W. (1980). Behavioral and subjective effects of beta-adrenergic blockage in phobic subjects. *British Journal of Psychiatry*, 111, 535–540.

Blackwell, B. (1973). Psychotropic drugs in use today. The role of diazepam in medical practice. *Journal of the American Medical Association*, 225, 1637–1641.

Blanchard, E. B., Kolb, L. C., Pallmeyer, T. P., & Geraldi, R. J. (1982). The development of a psychophysiological assessment procedure for post-traumatic stress disorder in Vietnam veterans. *Psychiatric Quarterly*, 54, 220–229.

Bleich, A., Siegel, B., Garb, R., & Lerer, B. (1986). Post-traumatic stress disorder following combat exposure: Clinical features and psychopharmacological treatment. *British Journal of Psychiatry*, 149, 365–369.

Butler, G., Cullington, A., Manby, M., Amies, P., & Gelder, M. (1984). Exposure and anxiety management in the treatment of social phobia. *Journal of Consulting and Clinical Psychology*, 52, 642–650.

Charney, D. S., Goodman, W. K., Price, L. H., Woods, S. W., Rasmussen, S. A., & Heininger, G. R. (1988). Serotonin functions in obsessive-compulsive disorder: A comparison of tryptophan and m-chlorophenyl-piperazine in patients and healthy subjects. *Archives of General Psychiatry*, 45, 177–185.

Charney, D. S., Woods, S. W., Goodman, W. K., & Heninger, G. R. (1987). Neurobiological mechanisms of panic anxiety: Biochemical and behavioral correlates of yohimbine-induced panic attacks. *American Journal of Psychiatry*, 144, 1030–1036.

Charney, D. S., Woods, S. W., Goodman, W. K., Rifkin, B., Kinch, M., Aiken, B., Quadrino, L. M., & Heninger, G. R. (1986). Drug treatment of panic disorder: The comparative efficacy of imipramine, alprazolam, and trazodone. *Journal of Clinical Psychiatry*, 47, 580–586.

Chassan, J. B. (1979). *Research design in clinical psychology and psychiatry*. New York: Halsted Press.

Chouinard, G., Annable, L., Fontaine, R., & Solyom, L. (1982). Alprazolam in the treatment of generalized anxiety and panic disorders: A double-blind placebo-controlled study. *Psychopharmacology*, 77, 229–233.

Christensen, H., Hadzi-Pavlovic, D., Andrews, G., & Mattick, R. (1987). Behavior therapy and tricyclic medication in the treatment of obsessive-compulsive disorder: A quantitative review. *Journal of Consulting and Clinical Psychology*, 55, 701–711.

Cole, J. O., Orzack, M. H., Beake, B., Bird, M., & Bar-tal, Y. (1982). Assessment of the abuse liability of buspirone in recreational sedative users. *Journal of Clinical Psychiatry, 43*(12), 69–74.

Covi, L., Lipman, R. S., Patterson, J. H., Derogatis, L. R., & Uhlenhuth, E. H. (1973). Length of treatment with anxiolytic sedatives and response to their sudden withdrawal. *Acta Psychiatrica Scandinavia, 49,* 51–64.

Curtis, G. C. (1985). New findings in anxiety: A synthesis for clinical practice. *Psychiatric Clinics of North America, 8,* 159–175.

Dittrich, J., Houts, A. C., & Lichstein, K. (1983). Panic disorder: Assessment and treatment. *Clinical Psychological Review, 3,* 215–225.

Downing, R. W., Rickels, K., McNair, D. M., Lipman, R. S., Kahn, R. J., Fisher, S., Covi, L., & Smith, V. K. (1981). Description of sample, comparison of anxious and depressed groups, and attrition rates. *Psychopharmacology Bulletin, 17,* 94–96.

Downing, R., Rickels, K., Wittenborn, J. R., & Mattson, N. B. (1971). Interpretation of data from investigations assessing the effectiveness of psychotropic agents. In J. Levine, B. C. Schiele, & C. Bouthilet (Eds.), *Principles and problems in establishing the efficacy of psychotropic agents* (pp. 321–369). Public Health Service Publication No. 2138. Washington, DC: U.S. Government Printing Office.

Dunbar, J. M., & Stunkard, A. J. (1979). Adherence to diet and drug regimen. In R. Levy, B. Rifkind, B. Dennis, & N. Ernst (Eds.), *Nutrition, lipids and heart disease* (pp. 391–423). New York: Raven.

Dunner, P. L., Ishiki, D., Avery, D. H., Wilson, L. G., & Hyde, T. S. (1986). Effect of alprazolam and diazepam on anxiety and panic attacks in panic disorder: A controlled study. *Journal of Clinical Psychiatry, 47,* 458–460.

Ettedgui, E., & Bridges, M. (1985). Posttraumatic stress disorder. *Psychiatric Clinics of North America, 8,* 89–103.

Falloon, I. R. H., Lloyd, G. G., & Harpin, R. E. (1981). Real-life rehearsal with non-professional therapists. *Journal of Nervous and Mental Diseases, 169,* 180–184.

Flament, M. F., Rapoport, J. L., Berg, C. J., Sceery, W., Kilts, C., Mellstrom, B., & Linnoila, M. (1985). Clomipramine treatment of childhood obsessive-compulsive disorder. *Archives of General Psychiatry, 42,* 977–986.

Foa, E. B., & Kozak, M. J. (1985). Treatment of anxiety disorders: Implications for psychopathology. In A. H. Tuma & J. D. Maser (Eds.), *Anxiety and the anxiety disorders* (pp. 421–452). Hillsdale, NJ: Lawrence Erlbaum Associates.

Fyer, A. J., Mannuzza, S., & Endicott, J. (1987). Differential diagnosis and assessment of anxiety: Recent developments. In H. Y. Meltzer (Ed.), *Psychopharmacology: The third generation of progress* (pp. 1177–1191). New York: Raven.

Goldberg, H., & Finnerty, R. (1982). Comparison of buspirone in separate studies. *Journal of Clinical Psychiatry, 43* (12), 87–91.

Gorman, J. M., Fyer, M. R., Liebowitz, M. R., & Klein, D. F. (1987). Pharmacologic provocation of panic attacks. In H. Y. Meltzer (Ed.), *Psychopharmacology: The third generation of progress.* (pp. 985–993). New York: Raven.

Gorman, J. M., Liebowitz, M. R., Fyer, A. J., Campeas, R., & Klein, D. F. (1985). Treatment of social phobia with atenolol. *Journal of Clinical Psychopharmacology, 5,* 298–301.

Gorman, J. M., Liebowitz, M. R., & Klein, D. F. (1984). Panic disorder and agoraphobia. *Current Concepts,* 1–40.

Greenblatt, D. J., & Shader, R. I. (1974). *Benzodiazepines in clinical practice.* New York: Raven.

Greenblatt, D. J. & Shader, R. I. (1978). Pharmacotherapy of anxiety with benzodiazepines and B-adrenergic blockers. In M. A. Lipton, A. DiMascio, & J. F. Killaim (Eds.), *Psychopharmacology: A generation of progress* (pp. 1381–1390). New York: Raven.

Greenblatt, D. J., Shader, R. I., & Abernethy, D. R. (1983). Drug therapy: Current status of benzodiazepines. New England Journal of Medicine, 309, 324–358, 410–416.

Heimberg, R. G., & Barlow, D. H. (1988). Psychosocial treatments for social phobia. Psychosomatics, 29, 27–37.

Helzer, J. E., Robins, L. J., & McEvoy, L. (1987). Post-traumatic stress disorder in the general population: Findings of the epidemiologic catchment area survey. The New England Journal of Medicine, 317 (26), 1630–1634.

Hoehn-Saric, R., & McLeod, D. R. (1985). Generalized anxiety disorder. Psychiatric Clinics of North America, 8, 73–88.

Hollister, L. E. (1986). Pharmacotherapeutic considerations in anxiety disorders. Journal of Clinical Psychiatry, 47, 33–36.

Insel, T. R., Gillin, J. C., & Moore, A. (1982). Sleep in obsessive-compulsive disorder. Archives of General Psychiatry, 39, 1372–1377.

Insel, T. R., Murphy, D. L., Cohen, R. M., Alterman, I., Kilts, C., & Linnoila, M. (1983). Obsessive-compulsive disorder: A double-blind trial of clomipramine and clorgyline. Archives of General Psychiatry, 40, 605–612.

Insel, T. R., Zahn, T., & Murphy, D. L. (1985). Obsessive-compulsive disorder: An anxiety disorder? In A. H. Tuma & J. D. Maser (Eds.), Anxiety and the anxiety disorders (pp. 577–589). Hillsdale, NJ: Lawrence Erlbaum Associates.

Insel, T. R., & Zohar, S. (1987). Psychopharmacologic approaches to obsessive-compulsive disorder. In H. Y. Meltzer (Ed.), Psychopharmacology: The third generation of progress (pp. 1205–1210). New York: Raven Press.

Kahn, R. J., McNair, D. M., Lipman, R. S., Covi, L., Rickels, K., Downing, R., Fisher, S., & Frankenthaler, L. M. (1986). Imipramine and chlordiazepoxide in depressive and anxiety disorders: II. Efficacy in anxious outpatients. Archives of General Psychiatry, 43, 79–85.

Klein, D. F. (1964). Delineation of two drug responsive anxiety syndromes. Psychopharmacologia, 5, 397–408.

Klein, D. F., & Davis, M. (1969). Diagnoses and treatment of psychiatric disorders. Baltimore, Williams & Wilkins.

Klein, D. F., & Fink, M. (1962). Psychiatric reaction patterns to imipramine. American Journal of Psychiatry, 119, 432–438.

Klein, D. F., Rabkin, J. G., & Gorman, J. M. (1985). Etiological and pathophysiological inferences from the pharmacological treatment of anxiety. In A. H. Tuma & J. D. Maser (Eds.), Anxiety and the anxiety disorders (pp. 501–553). Hillsdale, NJ: Lawrence Erlbaum Associates.

Klerman, G. L. (1986). Current trends in clinical research on panic attacks, agoraphobia, and related anxiety disorders. Journal of Clinical Psychiatry, 47, 37–39.

Levine, J., Schiele, B. C., & Bouthilet, L. (1971). Principles and problems in establishing the efficacy of psychotropic agents. Public Health Service, Publication No. 2138.

Liebowitz, M. R., Fyer, A. J., Gorman, J. M., Campeas, R., & Levin, A. (1986). Phenelzine in social phobia. Journal of Clinical Psychopharmacology, 6, 93–98.

Liebowitz, M. R., Gorman, J. M., Fyer, A. J., Campeas, R., Levin, A. P., Sandberg, D., Papp, L., Hollander, E., & Klein, D. (1987, December). MAOI treatment of social phobia. Paper presented at the 26th Annual Meeting of the American Congress of Neuropsychopharmacology, San Juan, Puerto Rico.

Liebowitz, M. R., Gorman, J. M., Fyer, A. J., & Klein, D. F. (1985). Social Phobic: Review of a neglected anxiety disorder. Archives of General Psychiatry, 42, 729–736.

Lipman, R. S., & Covi, L. (1976). Outpatient treatment of neurotic depression: Medication and group psychotherapy. In R. L. Spitzer & D. F. Klein (Eds.), Evaluation of psychological therapies (pp. 178–218). Baltimore: Johns Hopkins.

Lipman, R. S., Covi, L., Rickels, K., McNair, D. M., Downing, R., Kahn, R. J., Lassiter, V. K., & Faden, V. (1986). Imipramine and chlordiazepoxide in depressive and anxiety disorders. I. Efficacy in depressed outpatients. *Archives of General Psychiatry, 43,* 68–77.

Lipman, R. S., Covi, L., & Shapiro, A. K. (1979). The Hopkins Symptom Checklist (HSCL): Factors derived from the HSCL-90. *Journal of Affective Disorders, 1,* 9–24.

Lipman, R. S., Park, L. C., & Rickels, K. (1966). Paradoxical influence of a therapeutic side-effect interpretation. *Archives of General Psychiatry, 15,* 462–474.

Lipper, S., Davidson, J. T., Grady, T. A., Edinger, J. D., Hammett, E. B., Mahorney, S. L., & Cavenar, J. O., Jr. (1986). Preliminary study of carbamazepine in post-traumatic stress disorder. *Psychosomatics, 27,* 849–854.

Lydiard, R. B., Laraia, M. T., Howell, E. G., & Ballenger, J. C. (1988). Alprazolam in the treatment of social phobia. *Journal of Clinical Psychiatry, 49,* 17–19.

Marks, I. M. (1983). Are there anticompulsive or antiphobic drugs? Review of the evidence. *British Journal of Psychiatry, 143,* 338–347.

Marks, I. M. (1985). Behavioral psychotherapy for anxiety disorders. In G. C. Curtis, B. A. Thyer, & J. M. & J. M. Rainey (Eds.), *The psychiatric clinics of North America: Symposium on anxiety disorders* (pp. 25–35). 8,(1), Philadelphia: W. B. Saunders.

Marks, I. M. (1987). *Fears, phobias, and rituals: Panic, anxiety, and their disorders.* New York: Oxford University Press.

Marks, I. M., & Gelder, M. G. (1966). Different ages of onset in varieties of phobias. *American Journal of Psychiatry, 123,* 218–221.

Marks, I. M., Gray, S., Cohen, D., Hill, R., Mawson, D., Ramm, E., & Stern, R. (1983). Imipramine and brief therapist-aided exposure in agoraphobics having self-exposure home-work. *Archives of General Psychiatry, 40,* 153–162.

Marks, I. M., Lelliot, P., Basoglu, M., Noshirvani, H., Monteiro, W., Cohen, D., & Kasvikis, Y. (1988). Clomipramine, self-exposure, and therapist-aided exposure for obsessive-compulsive rituals. *British Journal of Psychiatry, 152,* 522–534.

Marks, I. M., Stern, R. S., Mawson, D., Cobb, J., & Mcdonald, R. (1980). Clomipramine and exposure for obsessive-compulsive rituals. *British Journal of Psychiatry, 136,* 1–25.

Mattila, M. J., Aranko, K., & Seppala, T. (1982). Acute effects of buspirone and alcohol on psychomotor skills, *Journal of Clinical Psychiatry, 43,* (12) 56–60.

Mavissakalian, M., & Michelson, L. (1986). Agoraphobia: Relative and combined effectiveness of therapist-assisted in vivo exposure and imipramine. *Journal of Clinical Psychiatry, 47,* 117–122.

Mavissakalian, M., Michelson, L., & Dealy, R. S. (1983). Pharmacological treatment of agora-phobia: Imipramine versus imipramine with programmed practice. *British Journal of psychiatry, 143,* 348–355.

McNair, D. M., & Kahn, R. J. (1981). Imipramine and chlordiazepoxide for agoraphobia. In D. F. Klein & J. G. Rabkin (Eds.), *Anxiety: New research and changing concepts* (pp. 169–180). Raven: New York.

Mellinger, G. D., Balter, M. B., Parry, H. J., Manheimer, D. I., & Cisin, I. H. (1974). An overview of psychotherapeutic drug use in the United States. In E. Josephson & E. E. Carroll (Eds.), *Drug use: Epidemiological and sociological approaches* (pp. 333–366). New York: Wiley.

Mellinger, G. D., Balter, M. B., & Uhlenhuth, E. H. (1984). Prevalence and correlates of the long-term regular use of anxiolytics. *Journal of the American Medical Association, 251,* 375–379.

Monteiro, W. O., Noshirvani, I., Marks, I. M., & Lelliott, P. T. (1987). Anorgasmia from clomipramine in obsessive-compulsive disorder: A controlled trial. *British Journal of Psychiatry, 151,* 107–112.

Montgomery, S. A. (1980). Clomipramine in obsessional neurosis: A placebo controlled trial. *Pharmaceutical Medicine, 1,* 189–192.

# NEW CIRCULATION PROCEDURE

As of February 1, 2004 **BOOKS will no longer be stamped with a due date.**

- You are responsible for all material checked out on your card and for knowing the due dates. A receipt with book titles and due dates will be printed if requested when the material is charged out.

- You are responsible for returning or renewing materials on time.

- **To view a list of library materials checked out on your account and their due dates, select** My Account **on the library home page under Services or click on the My Account button in** SetonCat. **My Account may be checked anytime from on or off campus.**

- **You may renew books once if they are not overdue. Overdue books must be renewed in person at the Circulation Desk.**

- Overdue notices and statements of fines and fees are sent via email on a regular basis to all patrons with Seton Hall email addresses. You are responsible for checking your email for these notices.

- Please direct questions to the Circulation Desk at 973-761-9435 or send an email to circulation@shu.edu

Morris, J. B., & Beck, A. T. (1974). The efficacy of antidepressant drugs: A review of research (1958–72). *Archives of General Psychiatry, 30,* 667–674.

Myers, J. K., Weissman, M. M., Tishler, G. L., Holzer, C. E., Leaf, P. J., Orvaschel, H., Anthony, J., Boyd, J. H., Burke, J. D., Kramer, M., & Stoltzman, R. (1984). Six-month prevalence of psychiatric disorders in three communities: 1980–1982. *Archives of General Psychiatry, 41,* 959–967.

National Institute of Mental Health. (1981). *Final report of NIMH conference #REP NIMH ER 79-003, Behavioral therapies in the treatment of anxiety disorders: Recommendations for strategies in treatment assessment research.* Bethesda, MD: National Institute of Mental Health.

Noyes, R., Jr. (1985). Beta-adrenergic blocking drugs in anxiety and stress. *Psychiatric Clinics of North America, 8,* 119–132.

Noyes, R., Anderson, D., & Clancy, J. (1984). Diazepam and propranolol in panic disorder and agoraphobia. *Archives of General Psychiatry, 41,* 287–292.

Noyes, R., Jr., Chaudhry, D. R., Domingo, D. V. (1986). Pharmacologic treatment of phobic disorders. *Journal of Clinical Psychiatry, 47,* 445–452.

Noyes, R., Jr., Clancy, J., Coryell, W. H., Crowe, R. R., Chaudhry, D. R., & Domingo, D. V., (1985). A withdrawal syndrome after abrupt discontinuation of alprazolam. *American Journal of Psychiatry, 142,* 114–116.

Noyes, R., Crowe, R. R., Harris, E. L., Hamran, B. J., McChesney, C. M., & Chaudhry, D. R. (1986). Relationship between panic disorder and agoraphobia. *Archives of General Psychiatry, 43,* 227–232.

Ost, L. G., Jerremalm, A. & Johansson, J. (1981). Individual response patterns and the effects of different behavioral methods in the treatment of social phobia. *Behavior Research and Therapeutics, 19,* 1–16.

Park, L. C., & Lipman, R. S. (1964). A comparison of patient dosage deviation reports with pill counts. *Psychopharmacology, 6,* 299–302.

Park, L. C., Uhlenhuth, E. H., Lipman, R. S., Rickels, K., & Fishers, S. (1965). A comparison of doctor and patient improvement ratings in a drug (meprobamate) trial. *British Journal of Psychiatry, 111,* 535–540.

Parry, H. J., Balter, M. B., Mellinger, G. D., Cisin, I. H., & Manheimer, D. I. (1973). National patterns of psychotherapeutic drug use. *Archives of General Psychiatry, 128,* 769–783.

Perse, T. (1988). Obsessive-Compulsive disorder: A treatment review. *Journal of Clinical Psychiatry, 49,* 48–55.

Perse, T. L., Greist, J. H., Jefferson, J. W., Rosenfeld, R., & Dar, R. (1987). Fluvoxamine treatment of obsessive-compulsive disorder. *American Journal of Psychiatry, 144,* 1543–1548.

Pitts, F. N., Jr., & McClure, J. N. (1967). Lactate metabolism in anxiety neurosis. *New England Journal of Medicine, 227,* 1329–1336.

Power, K. G., Jerrom, D. W. A., Simpson, R. J., & Mitchell, M. (1985). Controlled study of withdrawal symptoms and rebound anxiety after six week course of diazepam for generalized anxiety. *British Medical Journal, 290,* 1246–1248.

Reynynghe de Voxrie, G. V. (1968). Anafranil (G34586) in obsession. *Acta Neurologia Belgium, 68,* 787–792.

Rice, K. M., & Blanchard, E. B. (1982). Biofeedback in the treatment of anxiety disorders. *Clinical Psychology Review, 2,* 557–577.

Rickels, K. (1981). Recent advances in anxiolytic therapy. *Journal of Clinical Psychiatry, 42,* 40–43.

Rickels, K., & Briscol, E. (1970). Assessment of dosage deviation in outpatient drug research. *Journal of Clinical Pharmacology, 10,* 153–160.

Rickels, K., Case, G., Downing, R. W., & Fridman, R. (1986). One-year follow-up of anxious patients treated with diazepam. *Journal of Clinical Psychopharmacology, 6,* 32–36.

Rickels, K., Case, G., Downing, R. W., & Winokur, A. (1983). Long-term diazepam therapy and clinical outcome. *Journal of the American Medical Association, 250,* 767–771.

Rickels, K., Lipman, R. S., Fisher, S., Park, L. C., & Uhlenhuth, E. H. (1970). Is a double-blind clinical trial really double-blind? A report of doctors medication guesses. *Psychopharmacologia, 16,* 329–336.

Rickels, K., & Schweizer, E. E. (1987). Current pharmacotherapy of anxiety. In H. Y. Meltzer (Ed.), *Psychopharmacology: The third generation of progress* (pp. 1193–1203). New York: Raven.

Rickels, K., Weisman, K., Norstad, N., Singer, M., Stoltz, D., Brown, A., & Danton, J. (1982). Buspirone and diazepam in anxiety: A controlled study. *Journal of Clinical Psychiatry, 43,* (12) 81–86.

Robinson, D. S., & Kurtz, N. M. (1987). Monoamine oxidase inhibiting drugs: Pharmacologic and therapeutic issues. In H. Y. Meltzer (Ed.), *Psychopharmacology: The third generation of progress* (pp. 1297–1304). New York: Raven.

Roth, M., & Meyers, D. H. (1969). Anxiety neuroses and phobic states. II. Diagnosis and management. *British Medical Journal, 1,* 559–562.

Roy-Byrne, P. P. & Katon, W. (1987). An update on treatment of the anxiety disorders. *Hospital and Community Psychiatry, 38,* 835–843.

Sarwer-Foner, G. J. (1987). The use of psychopharmacology in obsessive-compulsive disorders. *Psychiatric Journal University of Ottawa, 12,* 197–202.

Schatzberg, A. F., & Cole, J. O. (1978). Benzodiazepines in depressive disorders. *Archives of General Psychiatry, 3,* 1359–1365.

Shapiro, A. K. (1978). Placebo effects in medical and psychological therapies. In S. L. Garfield & A. E. Bergen (Eds.), *Handbook of psychotherapy and behavioral change,* 2nd ed., (pp. 369–410). New York: Wiley.

Shaw, P. (1979). A comparison of three behavior therapies in the treatment of social phobia. *British Journal of Psychiatry, 134,* 620–623.

Sheehan, D. V. (1982). Current views on the treatment of panic and phobic disorders. *Drug Therapy,* pp. 1–6.

Sheehan, D. V. (1985). Monoamine oxadise inhibitors and alprazolam in the treatment of panic disorder and agoraphobia. *Psychiatric Clinics of North America, 8,* 49–62.

Sheehan, D. V., Ballenger, J., & Jacobson, G. (1980). The treatment of endogenous anxiety with phobic, hysterical and hypochondriacal symptoms. *Archives of General Psychiatry, 37,* 51–59.

Sheehan, D. V., Coleman, J. H., Greenblatt, D. J., Jones, K. J., Levine, P. H., Orsulak, P. J., Peterson, M., Schildkraut, J. J., Uzogara, E., & Watkins, D. (1984). Some biochemical correlates of panic attacks with agoraphobia and their response to new treatment. *Journal of Clinical Psychopharmacology, 4,* 66–75.

Sierles, F. S., Chen, J. J., McFarland, R. E., & Taylor, M. M. (1983). Post-traumatic stress disorder and concurrent psychiatric illnesses: A preliminary report. *American Journal of Psychiatry, 140,* 1177–1179.

Siever, L. J., Insel, T. R., Jimerson, D. C., Lake, R. C., Uhde, T. W., Aloi, J., & Murphy, D. L. (1983). Growth hormone response to clonidine in obsessive-compulsive patients. *British Journal of Psychiatry, 142,* 184–187.

Solomon, K., & Hart, R. (1978). Pitfalls and prospects in clinical research on antianxiety drugs: benzodiazepines and placebo—A research review. *Journal of Clinical Psychiatry, 39,* 823–831.

Solyom, L., LaPierre, Y., Pecknold, J., & Morton, L. (1981). Phenelzine and exposure in the treatment of phobias. *Biological Psychiatry, 16,* 239–247.

Suinn, R. M. (1984). Generalized anxiety disorder. In S. M. Turner (Ed.), *Behavioral theories and treatment of anxiety* (pp. 279–319). New York: Plenum.

Tarrier, N., & Main, C. J. (1986). Applied relaxation training for generalized anxiety and panic attacks: The efficacy of a learnt coping strategy on subjective reports. *British Journal of Psychiatry, 149*, 330–336.

Telch, M. J., Agras, W. S., Taylor, C. B., Roth, W. T., & Gallen, E. C. (1985). Combined pharmacological and behavioral treatment for agoraphobia. *Behavior Research and Therapy, 23*, 325–335.

Thoren, P., Asberg, M., Cronholm, R., Jornestedt, R. N., & Traskiman, L. (1980). Clomipramine treatment of obsessive-compulsive disorder. *Archives of General Psychiatry, 37*, 1281–1285.

Torgersen, S. (1983). Genetic factors in anxiety disorders. *Archives of General Psychiatry, 40*, 1085–1092.

Tyrer, P., Candy, J., & Kelly, D. (1973). Phenelzine in phobic anxiety: A controlled trial. *Psychopharmacologia, 32*, 237–254.

Tyrer, P., & Murphy, S. (1987). The place of benzodiazepines in psychiatric practice. *British Journal of Psychiatry, 151*, 719–723.

Uhlenhuth, E. H. (1985). The measurement of anxiety: Reply to Finney. In A. H. Tuma & J. D. Maser (Eds.), *Anxiety and the anxiety disorders* (pp. 675–679). Hillsdale, NJ: Lawrence Erlbaum Associates.

Uhlenhuth, E. H., Balter, M. B., Mellinger, G. D., Cisin, I. H., & Clinthorne, J. (1983). Symptom checklist syndromes in the general population: Correlations with psychotherapeutic drug use. *Archives of General Psychiatry, 40*, 1167–1173.

Uhlenhuth, E. H., Lipman, R. S., & Covi, L. (1969). Combined pharmacotherapy and psychotherapy: Controlled studies. *Journal of Nervous and Mental Disorders, 148*, 52–64.

Volavka, J., Neziroglu, F. & Yarywra-Tobias, J. A. (1985). Clomipramine and imipramine in obsessive-compulsive disorder. *Psychiatry Research, 14*, 85–93.

Watson, I. P. B., Hoffman, L., & Wilson, G. V. (1988). The neuropsychiatry of post-traumatic stress disorder. *British Journal of Psychiatry, 52*, 164–173.

Waxman, D. (1977). A clinical trial of clomipramine and diazepam in the treatment of phobic and obsessional illness. *Journal of International Medical Research, 5*, 99–110.

Weiss, K. J., & Rosenberg, D. J. (1985). Prevalence of anxiety disorder among alcoholics. *Journal of Clinical Psychiatry, 46*, 3–5.

Weissman, M. M. (1985). The epidemiology of anxiety disorders: Rates, risks and familial patterns. In A. H. Tuma & J. D. Maser (Eds.), *Anxiety and the anxiety disorders*. Hillsdale, NJ: Erlbaum.

Weissman, M. M., & Merikangas, K. R. (1986). The epidemiology of anxiety and panic disorders: An update. *Journal of Clinical Psychiatry, 47*, (6) (Suppl.), 11–17.

Woods, J. H., Katz, J. L., & Winger, G. (1987). Abuse liability of benzodiazepines. *Pharmacological Reviews, 39*, 251–419.

Zitrin, C. M., Klein, D. F., & Woerner, M. G. (1980). Treatment of agoraphobia with group exposure in vivo and imipramine. *Archives of General Psychiatry, 37*, 63–72.

Zitrin, C. M., Klein, D. F., Woerner, M. G., & Ross, D. C. (1983). Treatment of phobias: I. Comparison of imipramine hydrochloride and placebo. *Archives of General Psychiatry, 40*, 125–138.

# 4 PSYCHOTHERAPY VERSUS MEDICATION FOR SCHIZOPHRENIA: EMPIRICAL COMPARISONS

Bertram P. Karon
*Michigan State University*

It is taken as axiomatic these days in most settings that schizophrenic patients must be treated with medication, and recent research efforts on psychosocial interventions have tended to focus on them solely as adjuncts to medication. Thus, in the 1987 *Special Report* of the NIMH *Schizophrenia Bulletin,* in the article on treatment (Kane, 1987), psychotherapy is dismissed as of no value in itself, not worthy even of further research, and, if supportive in nature, of minor value as an adjunct to medication. It is assumed that medication is the indispensable treatment of choice, and May's (1968) research is cited as definitive.

Even Goldstein (1987) in his review of psychosocial issues summarized the studies on family interventions, as an adjunct to medication, as consistently being of greater value than medication alone, but had nothing to say about such treatments as alternatives to medication.

These views are not new. Cole and Davis (1969) reviewed the then available evidence and concluded that although there were double-blind studies where "antipsychotic" medication was no better than the placebo, the bulk of such studies showed these medications to be more helpful, particularly at doses greater than 500 mg of chlorpromazine, or its equivalent. (Of, course, none of these studies used active placebos, and the side effects of "antipsychotic" medication are so gross that neither patients nor doctors are apt to be ignorant for long as to whether the patient is receiving an active medication.) As to interaction of medication and social therapies, they concluded: "drug therapy combined with social therapies can often be a more effective treatment mode then either drug or social therapy" (p.502).

Lipton and Burnett (1979) in their survey of the literature on medication noted that "The dramatic and relatively rapid benefits of the neuroleptic drugs when compared with psychological treatments generated the opinion, which prevailed by the end of the 1960's, that treatment of schizophrenia without medication was unjustifiable" (p. 344). They cited the May (1968) study as the best evidence and noted that although the experience of the therapists in that study have been questioned, Grinspoon, Ewalt, and Shader (1972) used "highly trained psychotherapists with similar results" (p. 344). They then cited later reviews of the relevant literature by May (1974b, 1975) that dismissed conflicting findings as flawed, but which found no flaws in May's research and its conclusions.

Lipton and Burnett cited Hogarty's research (Hogarty, Goldberg, Schooler, Ulrich, & the Collaborative Study Group, 1974a) on major role therapy (psychosocial and vocational rehabilitation) as demonstrating that social treatment improves the quality of life, and should be added to maintenance drug treatment. Even then 30% of the patients will relapse by 18 months. Lipton and Burnett did note that in an NIMH study of young schizophrenic patients (Gunderson, 1977), 30% recovered within the first month without medication, and that a similar figure—30% recoveries—is generally found with placebo controls in studies evaluating neuroleptic drugs, but they did not feel that it was possible to know who those 30% of patients will be. They also recognize the Soteria House data (Mosher & Menn, 1976) that unmedicated young schizophrenics in that setting do better than medicated patients treated through the hospital and community mental health center. Nonetheless, they reject the idea of the treatment of schizophrenics without drugs, but concluded that "certainly the evidence is very strong that drugs alone are insufficient for the optimal management of the schizophrenic patient" (p. 346).

Despite the relabeling of major tranquilizers as "antipsychotic" medication as if they were as specific and efficacious for psychosis as vitamin C is for scurvy, there is a nagging awareness among professionals that patients are not really functioning that well on medication, that something seems to be lacking. There are still reports os subgroups of patients (e.g., Rappaport, Hopkins, Hall, Belleza, & Silverman, 1978) who do better on placebos in blind studies.

Patients caught in the treatment system and maintained on medication do not seem to return to independent living, and they seem to follow a downward, if erratic, course. Professional and semi-professional mental health workers try to explain this to themselves as the natural history of the disorder, but studies published in the last 15 years clearly demonstrate that this is not so (cf. M. Bleuler, 1978; Ciompi, 1980; Harding, Brooks, Ashikagawa, Strauss, & Breier, 1987a, 1987b; Harding, Zubin, & Strauss, 1987; Huber, Gross, & Schuttler, 1975).

Cohorts of patients in Switzerland, starting in 1900 and continuing to more recent cohorts, followed for 40 years, show long-term trends toward improvement, with 60% apparently improved and living outside hospitals and approximately 30% completely recovered. More recent studies by independent investigators in Switzerland, Germany, and the United States have similar outcomes. Nor is there a typical course of the disorder, but many "typical" courses, how many depending on how one chooses to classify. Nor do differing diagnostic schemes, for example, DSM-III, make any major difference in these findings (Harding et al., 1987b, Harding, Zubin, & Strauss, 1987).

There is also increasing evidence for tardive dyskinesia (Breggin, 1983), a behavioral syndrome of mouth and tongue movements caused by irreversible brain damage, due to chronic use of "antipsychotic" medication. Although articles still are being published in psychiatric journals denying that any such syndrome exists or that it is causally connected with these medications, most professionals (and even manufacturers) now acknowledge this as a serious problem. Other possible syndromes due to the medications, "akinesia," "supersensitivity psychosis," and "tardive dementia" have been described, and possible underlying mechanisms postulated (Goldberg, 1985; Jones, 1985), as well as articles denying their existence (e.g., Mukherjee & Bilder, 1985).

Unfortunately, there has been a tendency to try to resolve the controversy as if it were purely a political or economic dispute, and not a scientific one.

When a psychiatrist (Dr. Peter Breggin) acknowledged on a television interview ("Oprah Winfrey Show," April 2, 1987) that patients' concerns about tardive dyskinesia were justified, that this was a serious problem, and that patients should seek out professionals who are interested in helping the patients understand themselves, and not professionals who are interested in only medicating, an attempt was made to silence him. The American Psychiatric Association had a transcript of the telecast made (as indicated on the transcript) and given to the National Association for the Mentally Ill, an organization of families of schizophrenics, who filed charges with the Medical and Chirurgical Faculty (The Medical Licensing Board) of Maryland to revoke Dr. Breggin's medical license for making these statements on television. In a later telecast ("Oprah Winfrey Show," August 17, 1987) while the hearing was pending, the President-elect of the American Psychiatric Association (Dr. Paul Fink) chided Dr. Breggin and stated that tardive dyskinesia was not a major problem. Dr. Breggin pointed out that Dr. Fink knew that the American Psychiatric Association's own Committee on Tardive Dyskinesia had placed the figure at 40%, for patients who continue to take their medication for long periods. (Schizophrenic patients and their families are told they must take "antipsychotic medication" for the rest of their lives. Dr. Fink himself on that broadcast had said that he tells patients that it is "like diabetes"; if you go off your medication, you are going to have problems.)

Dr. Fink characterized Dr. Breggin's statement as "outrageous," as an "overstatement," and stated that the American Psychiatric Association's committee report had never said 40%. When Dr. Breggin produced a copy of the report, Dr. Fink replied that Dr. Breggin had not specified long-term use (which he had) and "This is not a court of law!" But the facts should be important.

After articles appeared in the *New York Times* (Goleman, 1987), the *Baltimore Sun*, and other newspapers about the attempted punishment of Dr. Breggin, the Medical and Chirurgical Faculty dismissed the charges as without merit, which one hopes they would have done without the publicity ("Psychiatrist is cleared," 1987).

Even more controversial than tardive dyskinesia are the concepts of supersensitivity psychosis (Chouinard & Jones, 1980) or tardive psychosis (Breggin, 1983)—psychotic symptoms due to neurological changes induced by the medication, which appear when the medication is withdrawn. Thus, the discovery that there were excess dopamine receptors in the brains of schizophrenic patients led to another highly publicized "breakthrough" in the biological causation of schizophrenia, especially because it was well known that "antipsychotic" medications block dopamine receptors. But when it was discovered that the excess dopamine receptors were the result of the brain's adaption to the medication (Porceddu, Giorgi, Ongini, Mele, & Biggio, 1986; Porceddu, Ongini, & Biggio, 1985), interest in the behavioral effects of those excess receptors disappeared. Such an established physical change in the brain adds credence to the concept of tardive psychosis. But the existence of tardive psychosis calls into question research designs that withdraw medication and find disordered functioning, which improves when medication is resumed.

It is of interest that in Kane's (1987) summary of the studies of the effectiveness of maintenance medication compared with a placebo, the duration of the medication is only 9 to 12 months for all but two studies, one of which is for 24 months, and one for 48, with the difference between the effectiveness of active medication and of placebo decreasing with time. It is possible that one factor may well be neurological changes or damage with long-term maintenance medication.

Nonetheless it is reasonable to accept the common clinical experience, as well as the usual inference from placebo trials, that medication is useful in the short run in improving immediate clinical status for most schizophrenic patients.

Obviously, schizophrenic symptoms are terrible to live with, for both the patient and those in touch with the patient. On the other hand, the probability of permanent neurological damage and recent suggestions of a possibly higher death rate for those who take antipsychotic medication suggest further research into alternative treatment is certainly in order.

The question of the relative merits of psychotherapy versus medication has not been examined in a systematic study recently, but six major American controlled studies have been carried out. It is instructive to review them because their findings are usually mis-cited in order to justify current practice.

Before 1960, as in psychoanalysis and psychoanalytic therapy in general, so too for the psychoanalytic therapy of schizophrenics, there were many published case histories and ample clinical experience concerning the successful treatment of individual cases, but there were no studies of psychotherapy with schizophrenic patients that made any serious attempts at combining a control group of matched or randomized patients treated by different methods and a systematic comparable evaluation of out-come for all patients. Since 1960, the six major American studies were the Pennsylvania study (Bookhammer, Myers, Schober, & Piotrowski, 1966); the Wisconsin project (Rogers, Gendlin, Kiesler, & Truax, 1967); the California project (May, 1968); the Massachusetts project (Grinspoon et al., 1972); the Illinois project (Paul & Lentz, 1977); and the Michigan project (Karon & Vandenbos, 1981).


## THE PENNSYLVANIA STUDY

This was the first attempt systematically to compare a sample of schizophrenic patients receiving a specific form of psychotherapy with a sample of schizophrenic patients receiving routine hospital treatment. The form of treatment was "direct analysis" (Rosen, 1953), a form of psychoanalytic psychotherapy. As described, it is a dramatic, intensive technique intended to establish a strong parental transference and employing interpretations of unconscious content to foster the transference, interfere with the psychotic defenses, and bring the basic issues of early development into consciousness and into the therapist–patient relationship so that a sounder reintegration can occur. In addition to the therapy hours, patients are given considerable individual attention in humane surroundings by cooperative attendants. Unfortunately, the technique, as practiced in the study (Brody, 1959), was fundamentally different. There was more emphasis on intimidation and producing compliant behavior than on making the unconscious conscious, as earlier formulations had suggested. The primary affect involvement of the therapist was described as being with the audience rather than with the patient. (The therapy sessions were conducted in front of an audience of psychiatrists, psychologists, and/or attendants.) At the time it was fashionable to note with approval that the technique actually used bore little relation to most psychoanalytic papers on therapeutic technique with such patients, including Rosen's own writings, and to attribute this to his "intuitive" technical skill. In fact, intimidation will frequently produce immediate behavioral improvement in front of an audience in patients who are already frightened (as are schizophrenics), but it has little to do with what most psychotherapists mean by psychotherapy, and we would not expect long-lasting gains.

Although a number of books (e.g., Brody, 1959; Scheflen, 1961) were written on the basis of the project, the data representing the comparison of the treatment with the control patients were only briefly and separately reported (Bookhammer et al., 1966). Ultimately, two different "comparison" samples were chosen—a matched, concurrently selected sample and a retrospectively selected "random" control group. Both control groups were treated with psychotropic drugs; the psychotherapy patients were not. All three groups consisted of young first-admission patients. A clinical team rated patients as "improved" or "unimproved" and did so after a 5-year follow-up. The reason for the brevity of the outcome report seems to be the lack of significant difference.

The crudity of the criterion, and, most important, the discrepancy between the techniques described in earlier writings and those employed on the project all contributed to obscuring the scientific implications. Nonetheless, a tentative conclusion can be arrived at that this psychotherapeutic technique, as used in the project, crude as it was, without medication seemed to be about equal in effectiveness with psychotropic medication. The importance of the study is that it was a first attempt at rigorous evaluation of psychotherapy, as compared to medication, with schizophrenic patients.

## THE WISCONSIN PROJECT

In this project, an attempt was made to assess the elements of therapeutic relationships as well as outcome (Rogers et al., 1967). The relationships between the client-centered therapy "relationship elements" (warmth, empathy, and genuineness) and treatment outcome were explored. The researchers were building on a body of research, frequently ignored, that had already demonstrated client-centered therapy to be of value to neurotic patients (e.g., Rogers, 1951); however, the project was daring in that not only had these techniques not been investigated with respect to schizophrenic patients, they had actually not been employed with such patients, and the experienced therapists were requiring themselves to develop a new expertise as well as to evaluate it.

It was not merely a test of client-centered therapy, however, There was an attempt to recruit a group of therapists who represented diverse therapeutic orientations, but this was only partially successful. Although there was considerable variation in orientation, the client-centered point of view was overrepresented (Rogers et al., 1967, p. 33).

The design involved the selection of a stratified sample of 16 "more chronic" schizophrenic patients, 16 "more acute" schizophrenic patients, and 16 "normals" functioning outside of the hospital. Subjects, within each "severity" category, were selected in pairs, being matched according to socioeconomic status, age, and sex. For these matched pairs, assignment was made to psychotherapy or hospital control by flip of a coin.

The hospital control subjects received the usual hospital treatment including medication, milieu therapy, and in some cases group therapy. The experimental subjects were seen in twice-a-week treatment for up to 2 1/2 years. Patients were evaluated by a variety of instruments, ratings of behavior and symptoms, and interviews. The evaluations were made at 3- or 6-month intervals, depending on the instrument. In addition, the therapy sessions were recorded on tape and rated using the Rogerian process (relationship) scales. In addition to the therapist warmth, genuineness, and empathy scales, a new variable—"experiencing" (by the patient)—was evaluated because it seemed meaningful.

Overall findings were not impressive. On most measures, the differences between experimental and control patients were not significant. Two significant findings were that those who received psychotherapy showed a decreased need to "deny" experience, and greater appropriateness on the Thematic Apperception Test. The psychotherapy patients also had a better rate of release, and spent less time in the hospital in the year after treatment. Although these differences reached only the .10 level of significance, they are striking. In the year after the termination of therapy, psychotherapy patients spent an average of 117 days in the hospital, and control patients spent an average of 219 days. That even a difference of this magnitude falls short of statistical significance illustrates the weakness of small-sample research.

The most interesting findings had to do with the relationship between therapists and patients. Schizophrenic patients initially saw their therapist as low on the Rogerian "relationship variables" of "warmth, empathy, and genuineness," regardless of the level of the therapist on these relationship variables as seen by independent raters. Only slowly over therapy did they perceive somewhat more warmth, empathy, and genuineness in their therapist. Level of patient "experiencing" (as opposed to talking about things without being involved) was positively related to the patient's perception of these relationship conditions. The level of both patient "experiencing" and perceived relationship conditions was positively associated with many objective measures of outcome. Higher levels of these process measures were associated with a significant decrease in schizophrenic pathology and symptoms, and with a better record of remaining out of the hospital. Poor therapeutic relationship and experiencing were associated with worse outcome and longer stays in the hospital. These results were statistically significant.

This was the first major study that has shown with a control group that psychotherapy had an effect on the outcome. Moreover, it demonstrated that the quality of the therapeutic relationship with a schizophrenic patient impacts directly on the outcome of treatment. It also documented the pessimism with which such patients approach the therapeutic situation, and the necessity for the therapist to be active in creating a therapeutic alliance, although that was not the terminology used by Rogers et al. (1967) in describing this fact.

The differences between the control group and the experimental group were contaminated and minimized by the fact that some of the control-group patients did receive group therapy and some of the experimental patients did receive medication. These contaminants were not controlled, or documented and quantified, thus tending to obscure the differences between patients receiving psychotherapy and those receiving medication as the primary mode of treatment.

These researchers performed a valuable service in making clear the complexity of doing meaningful research with any degree of rigor, and the complexity of the psychotherapeutic relationship. They, for the first time, attempted either to control or to study the quality (i.e., to use different language, pay attention to "quality control") of the psychotherapy. They make clear the difficult problem of balancing rigorous design with keeping the research relevant to the phenomena supposedly studied. They also document the unpredicted difficulties added by medication-oriented members of the hospital staff who ought to have been neutral with respect to the outcome of the research, but clearly were not. That is a finding that will be replicated by any psychotherapeutically oriented researcher who attempts research in a medication-oriented setting. These researchers made clear the importance of evaluating patients at regular chronological intervals, but also the realistic difficulty of carrying out such a design.

## THE CALIFORNIA STUDY

May and his associates at Camarillo State Hospital attempted a controlled study of five methods of treating schizophrenic patients (May, 1968). These treatment methods were (a) psychotherapy without medication, (b) psychotherapy with medication, (c) medication alone, (d) ECT, and (e) milieu therapy. Forty-one psychiatrists and residents having between 6 months and 6 years of "experience" were used as therapists. To control for personality factors, each psychiatrist practiced each of the five methods.

Patients were reported to be assigned randomly to the five treatments and those treated were only first-admission, clearly schizophrenic patients between the ages of 16 and 45, without organicity, who were in the middle third on severity of the disorder. This eliminated the very sick as well as the not very sick. Somehow this led to a largely lower middle-class White population of above-average intelligence, surprising for patients supposedly selected representatively from a state hospital schizophrenic population. Two hundred twenty-eight patients were used. On the average, patients in psychotherapy were seen twice a week until discharged or declared a treatment failure. Total time in psychotherapy ranged from 7 to 87 hours, with a mean of 49 hours. Superficially, the study seems very rigorous.

The therapists in May's study were not only inexperienced in general, but particularly inexperienced in administering psychotherapy with schizophrenic patients. Therapists ranged considerably in their aptitude, personality type, and experience in living. All therapists were required to practice all five methods, without special recompense, despite any reservations about them (and some physicians seemed to have reservations about each form of treatment). Although the therapists are reported to have volunteered, one of the investigators later (A. H. Tuma, personal communication, 1966) in discussing research design, as NIMH grant administrator for the Michigan project, suggested that it was not necessary to pay psychiatric residents to work on a psychotherapy research project, just require them to participate in order to finish their residency "like we did."

The psychotherapy provided was supervised by what were initially reported as highly experienced and prestigious psychoanalysts; however, all but one of them had little or no experience in treating schizophrenic patients beyond what they had received in their own residency. Some of them did not feel it was even appropriate to attempt psychotherapy with such patients (Wexler, 1975). The quality and frequency of supervision also varied. The quality control of the psychotherapy provided on May's study thus was doubtful at best.

A battery of objective psychologic instruments was used to evaluate outcome. In addition, hospitalization data were collected, ward behavior was rated, and an independent research team rated improvement from the ward records. Cost data were also collected as a major feature of the research. Patients who refused the pretreatment testing were included in the study, even though they were included in the study, even though they were not included in the data analyses of outcomes on tests they had refused initially, as well as on tests refused at outcome. The post-treatment evaluations were conducted on the day of discharge, rather than at a regular time interval from the inception of treatment. This procedure introduced a bias against the psychotherapy group. Because discharge meant termination of psychotherapy, as continued psychotherapy with the same therapist or any therapist was not a part of the research design, the day of discharge was traumatic for patients receiving psychotherapy, particularly if the relationship had been meaningful and helpful.

The authors' conclusions were that medication was the treatment of choice, that improvement on their criteria up to day of discharge showed an advantage to patients receiving medication over those not receiving medication, and that all other differences were trivial. Their book and most of their subsequent discussions in the literature have been based on the predischarge functioning and day-of-discharge evaluations. Unfortunately, as is well known, medication is particularly effective in improving ward adjustment, but ward adjustment is not highly correlated with real-world functioning. Much of the discussion of these authors is devoted to money spent on treatment and the argument that medication is cost-effective in the short run, that is, while in the hospital.

They do note greater insight in patients receiving psychotherapy, but minimize the importance of such differences. Whenever they admit some benefit from psychotherapy, it is as frosting on the cake, an adjunct to the prime treatment—medication.

For a long time they did not publish follow-up data, although they had gathered it. In their published follow-up, reporting hospitalization data up to 5 years (May, Tuma, Yale, Potepan, & Dixon, 1976, 1981), the differences after release from the initial hospitalization are not statistically significant. It should be recalled that this is a study with large numbers of subjects so that even small real differences should be statistically significant, but by 4 years from initial hospitalization less than half their sample is included in the data. Variability must have been high, because differences in mean hospitalization as high as 200 versus 600 days were not statistically significant.

It is noteworthy that the difference between the medication and no treatment (so-called milieu) decreases with time. It is also noteworthy that the apparent effectiveness of ECT as compared to other treatments increases with time. This raises the question as to how much of the findings are due to selective, as well as massive, dropout, because patients who have received an unpleasant treatment like ECT are likely to attempt to avoid (or lie to) the hospital and the research personnel who might schedule them for another course of treatment if they were thought to be ill. Indeed, even maintenance antipsychotic medication is more often than not perceived by the patient as unpleasant, which leads to the well-known compliance problems (Boczowski, Zeichner, & DeSanto, 1985; Breggin, 1983) of avoidance of treatment or lying.

May avoided the difficulties encountered by the Wisconsin group and the Michigan project in dealing with hospital personnel covertly inimical to the project.

In the Camarillo study (May, 1968) the principal investigator took charge of the admission service, and had veto power on the research wards. Deliberate personal contact with the treatment staff was supplemented by weekly meetings with the nurses and progress reviews of the physicians cases. . . . Put bluntly, the most sophisticated design will get you nowhere if the head nurse and ward physicians are not on your side. And even then it helps to have muscle in the administrative hierarchy! (May, 1974a, p. 127)

The efficiency of such authority is obvious, but one has to wonder whether the staff would have dared not to find or report what they thought the man in charge wanted them to find, and whether the evaluations could possibly have been blind.

## THE MASSACHUSETTS STUDY

Grinspoon et al. (1972) rigorously evaluated the efficacy of medication in the treatment of schizophrenic patients and did an admirable job. Twenty experimental subjects were selected from among 41 single males who had been hospitalized for over 3 years in Boston State Hospital. Random design was attempted, but "experimental" patients who refused, or whose families refused to change hospitals, were reassigned to the control group. The control group remained in the state hospital on phenothiazines. The experimental patients were transferred to a new and unfamiliar setting—the Massachusetts Mental Health Center. All patients started on placebos in the new setting. Thirteen weeks later half of these patients ($n = 10$) were randomly selected to receive phenothiazine and the other half continued to receive the placebo. Medication was clearly more effective than placebos in terms of ward adjustment measures.

In evaluating psychotherapy, the control group was not so carefully matched. The experimental patients were all nominally in individual psychotherapy, twice a week for over 2 years, with analytically oriented senior staff members supposedly favorable toward the psychotherapy of schizophrenic patients, but the most experienced member of the treatment staff (E. Semrad, personal communication, 1974) expressed skepticism that the patients were really involved in a psychotherapeutic process. Only one patient was reported to develop a "therapeutic alliance" with his therapist. In other words, only one patient felt the therapist and he were on the same side.

This study is often cited as evidence that even experienced therapists are ineffective with schizophrenic patients, but although all of the psychotherapists were senior staff and "experienced," many were not experienced with schizophrenic individuals, particularly chronic schizophrenic patients, nor were they experienced with the resistances characteristic of low socioeconomic patients and the ethnic subcultures (e.g., the lower socioeconomic Boston Irish and Boston Italian subcultures). One third of the therapists "found themselves for the first time in their life in a long-term therapy relationship with a resistant patient" (Grinspoon et al., 1972, p. 259). Although distinguished (and presumably experienced), all participated without pay. They were asked and felt they could not refuse. It is stated that half of them reported this was not a problem. Presumably it was for the other half. Psychotherapy is too difficult a skill to practice against one's will. Those therapists experienced with chronic schizophrenic patients felt that twice a week was not sufficient time to work in their accustomed manner.

The easiest control would have been for each therapist to treat two patients blindly, one receiving placebo and the other medication. The next best procedure would have been to randomize rigorously assignment of therapists as well as assignment of patients to medication of placebo conditions. Neither of these procedures would have posed serious practical difficulties, and their omission is therefore notable. But the most serious problem was the lack of quality control of the psychotherapy.

Furthermore, an examination of the patients suggests that they were habituated to Boston State Hospital. As Braginsky, Braginsky, and Ring (1969) have noted, a chronic hospital population develops a way of life with satisfactions. These satisfactions were disrupted for psychotherapy patients only, by transfer to the middle-class Mental Health Research Center. Moreover, at least 11 of the 20 patients selected for therapy had a history of ECT or insulin comas (5 were reported as having had ECT alone, 2 had insulin comas alone, and 4 had both), and hence were probably brain damaged. Psychotherapists experienced with treating schizophrenic patients have doubts about attempting psychotherapy with patients who have previously had ECT or insulin comas. It is not that treatment is impossible; it is just that treatment has been made much less effective. No serious study of psychotherapy would include such patients, particularly when there was such a small number of patients.

The measures of improvement emphasized were behavioral ratings by nurses, ward residents, patients' families, and the therapists. These ratings showed slight improvement for the patients receiving medication as compared to those receiving placebos, or to themselves when not on medication. No appreciable effect of psychotherapy was credited.

It was reported, however, that more of the psychotherapy patients (68% vs. 37%) were able to live outside the hospital, a finding the authors do not value. The investigators thought that the patients' lives outside the hospital were not good enough to warrant being considered better than they were when they were living in a hospital. Noteworthy is the absence of direct measures of the thought disorder, and of rigorous comprehensive blind clinical evaluations.

## ILLINOIS PROJECT

The Illinois Project (Paul & Lentz, 1977), although not a study of individual psychotherapy, evaluated psychosocial treatment and has relevant implications. Chronic "hard-core" hospitalized schizophrenic patients were randomly assigned (28 per group) to routine treatment (medication within a state hospital) or one of two psychosocial treatments (milieu therapy or social learning treatment). To keep the wards full, additional patients were assigned as others were discharged.

The psychosocial treatments were specified in detail. The milieu therapy consisted primarily of encouraging social interactions, and was a very active form of treatment, much more active than what was referred to as milieu therapy in the California Study. The social learning treatment consisted of rewarding the acquisition of skills and independent behavior.

It was noteworthy that great pains were taken to train the staff and to check whether the staff involved in the psychosocial treatments were carrying out the specified treatments appropriately.

The major findings were:

1. Both psychosocial treatments had an effect in initially improving the patients and maintaining them.

2. The social learning treatment was more effective in the long run than either milieu treatment or medication.

3. The major advantages were in release rates (social learning, almost 95%; milieu, about 67%; and medication control/comparison, around 45%). Regardless of treatment condition, patients out of the hospital functioned equally well (or badly) and had comparable rehospitalization rates, but it must be emphasized that almost twice as many social-learning patients were released as compared to patients treated with medication. The psychosocial treatments also showed advantages in terms of ward adjustment; however, no measure of the thought disorder was obtained.

4. The social learning and intensive milieu treatments were cost-effective as compared to the medication controls. The per case operational costs were 16.9% and 15.8% less than routine treatment with medication. When the additional treatment capacity of the social-learning staff (because of discharges) is taken into account, the savings become 32.6%. both treatment approaches saved strikingly more than routine hospital care in terms of reduced need for continuous hospitalization. (Nonetheless, a later administrative decision terminated the programs as part of an "economy" drive, and returned patients to treatment by medication.)

5. When a randomized placebo design of patients on psychosocial wards was used (Paul & Lentz, 1977; Paul, Tobias, & Holly, 1972), it was found that medication was not only of no additional value if the patients were involved in either of the active psychosocial treatments; it actually interfered with improvement. Subsequently, 85% of the patients on psychosocial treatments were withdrawn from medication, and patients not on medication did better in the 3-year follow-up of the social-learning, milieu, and traditionally treated controls.

6. The milieu therapy was initially successful but tended to founder when sanctions (e.g., isolation) for violence were discontinued. Promoting interaction was not therapeutic when patients did not feel physically secure.

Thus, chronic hospitalized schizophrenic patients benefit from planned meaningful human intervention to a greater extent than from medication, and this is reflected in the ability to live outside the hospital. It casts doubt on the "proven" worth of medication as the treatment of choice, and it illustrates the tendency for administrative decisions to be made on political rather than evidential bases. The popularity not of the "medical" model but more narrowly the "medication" model as a justification for treatment to be determined by medically trained, but psychologically and psychotherapeutically naive, institutionally designated "psychiatrists" (who in some cases have never even completed a residency in psychiatry) is called into question.

## THE MICHIGAN PROJECT (Karon & Vandenbos, 1981)

The design called for the selection of clearly schizophrenic patients to be assigned on the basis of a random number table to one of three treatments: (a) psychotherapy without medication, (b) psychotherapy with adjunctive medication, and (c) routine hospital treatment consisting primarily of phenothiazines. Criteria were: (1) unquestionably schizophrenic; (2) onset of blatant psychotic symptoms within 3 months prior to admission; (3) first admission; (4) no history of ECT or insulin shock treatment; (5) no organic brain damage; and (6) no history of alcoholism or drug addiction. (Criteria 2 and 3 were not met, as described later.)

The selection and assignment of patients were made by independent research personnel not connected with treatment. Selection was made by the same criteria and the same research personnel throughout. The intent to obtain acutely ill but clearly schizophrenic patients (with no organic pathologic condition or previous hospitalization) required more adequate case histories and more thorough medical examinations before selection than the routine hospital procedure required. If a patient was discharged before the assessment was complete (2 weeks), that patient was replaced as a potential project patient by another patient who was still hospitalized.

Suitable patients were selected in sets of three, and randomly assigned to the three groups: psychotherapy without medication, psychotherapy with medication, and hospital comparison. Assignment between experienced and inexperienced therapists and among inexperienced therapists was on a rotation basis. Supervisors did not select which patient they would work with. It was necessary that the cases chosen in the first weeks be assigned to the supervisors, so that their work could be observed by the inexperienced therapists, via closed-circuit TV, and discussed. Because of the schedules and commitments of the inexperienced therapists, it was necessary that they begin to be assigned by the third set of patients. Hence, the supervisors treated the psychotherapy patients selected in the first two sets and in the last two sets of patients chronologically. Any differences in patient characteristics reflected possible week-to-week fluctuation in admissions (although they were well within the bounds to be expected from random variation).

Thirty-six patients were studied. The small number was necessary in order to be careful about gathering data on the patients, including careful, detailed, and blind rigorous outcome evaluations, as well as to obtain greater than usual quality control of the psychotherapy provided.

The patients were primarily poor, inner-city, and Black. They tended not to trust authorities, particularly White authorities. The selection of patients took place about 12 months before the Detroit riot of 1967. In their world, information is to be divulged to authorities only if it cannot be used to punish the informant or his friends. They do not expect help simply for being emotionally ill; they are hospitalized primarily because they have disturbed or frightened someone else. Bizarre behavior and emotional suffering are accepted by the patients and their families as part of a painful world rather than as illness to be alleviated. Hence, they tend to have been ill for a long time (by middle-class standards) before hospitalization. According to an independent study conducted in the same city (Dunham, 1965), the median time between onset of blatant psychotic symptoms and the first presentation to treatment was 34.5 months! The emphasis on the patients being clearly schizophrenic, and the attempt to get a rigorous baseline of independent measurements, led paradoxically to selection of a more severely impaired chronic population, resistant to treatment. The utility of a randomized control group in psychotherapy research is illustrated by the fact that the patients were more severely and chronically ill than was intended, but this difference applied equally to treatment and control groups. In the initial phase of the project, the treatment staff was disappointed in the apparently slow response to treatment as compared to previous experiences with "acute" patients. It was only after the 6-month data were gathered, and the control group found to be functioning even less well, that they became aware they were dealing with a chronic population.

Some patients had had previous hospitalization, which neither the patient nor the relatives had revealed. Initial screening revealed no previous psychiatric hospitalization among project patients, but, by the end of the project, it was established that at least one third of the patients had been previously hospitalized (Group A = 4, Group B = 2, Group C = 5). Of those previously hospitalized, length of previous hospitalization ranged from 7 to 72 days, with a mean of 23.7 days. The patients and their families reasoned (correctly) that a previous history of hospitalization leads to worse treatment not only by hospitals, but by employers, social agencies, and people in general. The severity of illness of these patients is also shown by their pretreatment scores on the Drasgow-Feldman Visual-Verbal Test (VVT); 29 of the 35 patients initially scored at or below the norms for schizophrenic patients hospitalized continually for 3 or more years.

Despite the attempt at careful medical screening, medical problems were also not ruled out. Four dramatic instances occurred.

Two patients died of embolisms (both diagnosed as catatonic). The first of these died before randomization had occurred, so that a new patient was selected, and that set of three randomized. The other patient lapsed into silence and died after therapy began. Additional information on this last patient (which had been suppressed by patient and family) became known just before her death: She was a long-standing drug addict, had been hospitalized as well as jailed for several years, and had undergone a long course of ECT. Any one of these factors would have made her data ineligible for inclusion in the analyses.

Another patient (a female, in Group A, treated by Karon) was eventually diagnosed as suffering from multiple sclerosis as well as schizophrenia. This patient initially had been cleared by both the neurology and internal medicine services before being selected for the project. This patient was *included* in the data, although analyses excluding this patient were run, and the findings were not materially altered.

Another patient (a male, in Group A, treated by a trainee), whose social history stated, "No history of drug addiction," began to produce material suggesting an organic pathologic condition. It was only after 10 months of treatment that the patient and family developed sufficient trust in the therapist to reveal the heavy and varied drug history confirming toxic impairment. This patient was *excluded* from the data analyses, in light of the inappropriate selection for the project.

Three of the initially selected patients are not *included* in the final analyses: the patient who died, the organic patient just described, and a third patient because of staff interference with the treatment. Analyses including the two living (but excluded) patients have been run; their inclusion does not materially alter the findings.

*Group A* used a psychoanalytic psychotherapy *without* medication. In this group, psychotherapy sessions were held 5 days a week until discharge (if discharge was in 2 to 8 weeks) and, for the most part, once per week thereafter. Four patients were treated by an experienced therapist (Karon), and the remaining eight patients were treated by five inexperienced therapists (three graduate students in clinical psychology and two residents in psychiatry) under his supervision.

Three patients in this nonmedication group received medication for very brief periods of time (in no case more than 2 weeks during 20 months of treatment) upon the demand of the ward staff as an alternative to mechanical restraints.

Two of these cases, however, do *not* appear in the final data; one because of evidence of an organic pathologic condition, and one because of staff interference with the treatment. Data analysis deleting the third patient would only increase the apparent effectiveness of psychotherapy.

*Group B* utilized an "ego-analytic" psychotherapy, *using adjunctive medication* (phenothiazines). The dosages were between 50 and 200 mg of chlorpromazine (Thorazine)—or its equivalent—two or three times a day, and generally tended to be decreased or eliminated at discharge. In this group, psychotherapy was initiated three times per week, for at least 20 sessions, and eventually reduced in frequency to one session per week. Four patients were treated by an experienced therapist (Tierney), and the remaining eight patients were treated by five inexperienced therapists (two graduate students in clinical psychology and three residents in psychiatry) under his supervision.

In both *Groups A and B*, all therapists, both supervisors and trainees, were White, reflecting the ethnic composition of the hospital's professional staff and of the graduate students and medical students in clinical training at that time. This was a bias we were aware of and would have preferred to address, but minority therapists were unavailable in those training programs. Fortunately, the situation has since changed. In general, this should be a bias against psychotherapy, particularly in the 1960s, and indeed, was. The Detroit riot occurred during the 12-month evaluations. Black patients felt guilty about having a close relationship with a White person.

Heterogeneity of professions among both supervisors and students was intentional, and intended to minimize professional jealousies as a contaminating factor. It was successful for project personnel, but unsuccessful in reducing interprofessional jealousy on the part of nonproject hospital personnel.

"Experienced therapist," as used here, meant approximately 10 years of experience (not merely doing psychotherapy, but specifically treating schizophrenic patients) and familiarity with patients of the relevant ethnic subculture, predominantly the Detroit Black subculture.

Psychotherapy was maintained whether the patient was on an inpatient or outpatient basis, and the same therapist treated the patient on an inpatient and outpatient basis.

In order to make attendance economically feasible, payment for transportation and baby-sitting expenses was available, $5 per session.

*Group C,* the hospital comparison, utilized phenothiazines as the primary treatment. This is treatment as currently practiced at good public institutions and considered to be the treatment of choice by the majority of the staff of the hospital. The patient/resident ratio was 8:1. Psychiatric residents, under close supervision of senior staff psychiatrists familiar with this patient population, were permitted by the research design to adjust medication and dosage level for each patient individually in terms of their and their supervisor's clinical judgment of the optimal dosage for the patient at that time. Dosage levels typically were approximately 400 mg of chlorpromazine (or its equivalent), varying at different times in treatment from a high of 1,400 mg daily to a low of 100 mg. The dose was decreased somewhat at discharge, but was recommended by the physician for indefinite use. Interviews were used primarily to adjust medication levels, assess whether discharge or transfer was most appropriate, and provide minimal support.

If, after a few weeks, the patients in Group C did not respond to the point of discharge, they were transferred to a state hospital, where treatment by medication was continued but with a higher patient/physician ratio (30–50:1). This is still a low patient/staff ratio for a state hospital and sufficient for adequate drug treatment. All other services were, in fact, better staffed than DPI (Detroit Psychiatric Institute). The transfer practice between DPI and the state hospital was routine and usual practice. In light of the regular relationship between the hospitals, the transfer of the patient and his records occurred simultaneously in one day. Medication was uninterrupted. The state hospital was better equipped with auxiliary services (occupational therapy, vocational rehabilitation services, recreational therapy, social services, etc.). DPI was organized as a 2-week stay hospital, and fully developed auxiliary services did not seem as imperative. The availability of the project psychotherapists made retention in DPI necessary if psychotherapy were to continue on an inpatient basis for Groups A and B. Thus, psychotherapy patients were relatively deprived in the availability of auxiliary services.

Treatment (medication) continuity was maintained in Group C; however, patient-physician continuity was not maintained, either when the patient changed institutions or inpatient/outpatient status. Most institutions that emphasize medication as the primary treatment modality do not typically maintain continuity of physicians because it is not generally believed to be central to the efficacy of the treatment.

These procedures were followed with the comparison group because it seemed the most appropriate control group—patients treated with care but in the usual way.

Patients were evaluated at 6 months, 12 months, and 20 months (end of treatment phase) after the inception of treatment, irrespective of whether they were in or out of the hospital, or were cooperating with or resisting the treatment.

Each examination included a battery of intellectual tests, projective tests, and a clinical status interview. Hospitalization data were, of course, maintained. Intellectual tests were the Thorndike-Gallup Vocabulary Test (TGV), the Porteus Mazes (PM), Wechsler Adult Intelligence Scale (WAIS), and the Feldman-Drasgow Visual-Verbal Test (VVT). The patients were also administered a Rorschach and the Thematic Apperception Test (TAT). A clinical status interview was conducted by an experienced psychoanalytic psychiatrist who was familiar with the hospital's patient population, and recorded on tape. The Rorschach protocols, TAT protocols, and Clinical Status Interviews were reduced to quantitative data, using a scaling technique.

Each evaluation was carried out by personnel not otherwise connected with treatment or ward operations, who did not know to which treatment group the patients belonged, except as the patient might spontaneously reveal it. Because a good clinical status interview is not likely to leave the interviewer "blind," these interviews were recorded on tape, and references to treatment deleted from the tapes before being rated blindly with regard to clinical status. Discharge was not entirely blind, but was determined by ward chiefs who were not members of the project treatment staff or the research team. The ward chief's decision was made on the basis of the nursing reports of ward behavior, the therapist's recommendation (which was generally to delay), and the ward chief's own evaluation. The ward chief's concern was primarily to alleviate the shortage of beds on the ward by discharging any patient as early as such a decision could be made responsibly. The ward chiefs were *not* biased in favor of the project. If anything, they were biased against the project, the outside investigator, and the use of nonmedical psychotherapists.

Patients were reimbursed for their time and travel expenses when they returned for examinations subsequent to the initial one. This helped to account for the fact that *all* patients were evaluated at the end of the treatment phase of the project.

Hospitalization data were routinely collected from DPI, various State Hospitals, and other area general hospitals with psychiatric units. In addition, at each evaluation, the patients were questioned regarding hospitalization as a double check. Hospitalization data were collected for the 2 years beyond the end of the treatment phase of the project. In other words, hospitalization data were gathered for a total of 44 months.

The findings after 6 months are instructive. If one were to include only the two groups of patients of inexperienced therapists, medication seemed to account for all of the improvement. This is strikingly similar in design and findings to the California findings.

But the patients of the supervisors, as compared to the hospital comparisons, showed an improvement in the thought disorder on both the WAIS and the VVT, and a reduction in days hospitalized. Even in a period as short as 6 months, psychotherapy with or without adjunctive medication was of demonstrable value to schizophrenic patients as compared to medication alone.

By the 12-month evaluations the patients of inexperienced therapists were functioning better than the medication group, and the trends were more striking by 20 months.

At the end of 20 months, the period during which psychotherapy was

made available to these patients, the patients had received an average of
70 sessions of psychotherapy. On all criteria patients in all three groups
tended to show improvement, but psychotherapy was more effective than
medication.

The patients of experienced therapists manifested a balanced improvement across all outcome measures. They were hospitalized less than the
medication-treated controls (Group C), were functioning better than
the controls according to blind clinical evaluation, and showed greater
improvement in the thought disorder as directly measured. Clearly, appropriately trained and relevantly experienced psychotherapists were effective in
the psychotherapy of schizophrenic patients, whether or not adjunctive
medication was used.

For the inexperienced therapists, there was an imbalance across criteria,
depending on whether adjunctive medication was used. If adjunctive
medication was not used, the patients were functioning at a higher level
according to blind clinical evaluations, and greatly decreased thought
disorder, directly measured, compared to Group C. If adjunctive medication
was used, improvement on these measures was comparable to medication
alone, but time in the hospital was greatly reduced. On no measure was
either psychotherapy group worse than medication alone, even though the
therapists were inexperienced, although relevantly motivated and with
experienced supervisors. (If the hospitalization data were not statistically
corrected for significant covariates, the patients receiving psychotherapy
alone by inexperienced therapists would have had more days in the hospital
than medication alone, but even this disappears in the follow-up data, as
described later.)

The measure designed specifically to reflect the schizophrenic thought
disorder, the VVT, yielded the most striking differences ($p < .001$). Patients
of the supervisor and trainees in Group A, receiving psychoanalytic therapy
without medication, not only showed more improvement in the thought
disorder than Group C (receiving medication alone), but also more improvement in the thought disorder than both subgroups (supervisor and trainees,
respectively) of Group B, receiving medication as well as psychoanalytic
therapy. All three groups are improved over their pretreatment means, but
those patients treated without medication showed the most dramatic improvement. Changes in the thought disorder produced by medication alone were
not comparable to the changes produced by psychotherapy, and although
psychotherapy in addition to medication does produce greater improvement
in the thought disorder, it does not have the same potency as psychotherapy
without medication.

However, the patients treated by the experienced therapist with adjunctive
medication showed nearly as much improvement in the thought disorder as
those treated without medication. That is because he told the patients that

the medication did not cure anything, that it merely made it possible to work together, but only their understanding would cure them, and he reduced the medication as rapidly as the patients could tolerate it. The data indicated that that was an extremely effective way to work. But the inexperienced therapists were seduced by the behavioral control that medication produces, and tended not to reduce the level of medication. This diminished effect on the thought disorder of psychotherapy, when accompanied by medication, may in part be a function of the diminished affective reactions of the patient on medication. Although diminishing affective reaction, particularly of fear and anger, is useful in maintaining behavioral control, it interferes with one aspect of what is specifically therapeutic in psychotherapy (e.g., Alexander & French, 1946; Krystal, 1975).

The apparent lack of affect of schizophrenic patients is really a chronic terror state, which overrides other affects. Because of its chronicity, the patient may not even have it labeled as "fear." ("You're wrong, Doctor. I am not afraid. I just can't live outside a hospital. I can't survive, and I can't feel anything, and I mustn't talk.")

One of the therapeutic actions of medication is to reduce the massiveness of that anxiety. This, in some cases, may provide the appearance of increased affect. The adjunctive use of medication at the beginning of treatment may be necessary for some patients and/or therapists, but the importance of decreasing medication was underlined by the thought disorder finding. Although it is usual to hear lip service paid to the idea of decreasing medication, in practice, medication is usually maintained forever for schizophrenic patients (at least insofar as people other than the patient make the decision).

The use of medication with schizophrenic patients not only reduces anxiety for the patients, but also often reduces the therapist's anxiety. The inexperienced and uncertain therapist has a "treatment" that makes an obvious difference in a short period of time. Maxwell Jones has described this well; in his pioneer therapeutic community, psychiatrists prescribed less and less medication the longer they were there. This was not related to changes in the kinds of patients treated, but to decreases in the professional's own anxiety (Jones, 1953).

Psychotherapy, particularly with schizophrenic patients, arouses anxiety in the novice therapist because of the issues with which it deals; it also arouses feelings of inadequacy because it is an incompletely mastered complex skill, because these patients are so difficult, and because the feedback from these patients rarely indicates that they appreciate or are being helped by the therapist.

Is it any wonder that so many therapists get seduced by the medication and the immediate behavioral improvement it provides? This may have unfortunate long-term consequences for their professional development. Never having to master their anxiety about having to handle difficult situations psychotherapeutically, they never learn the potency of psychotherapeutic work. They never learn really to do psychotherapy with such patients. Consequently, they may carry throughout their professional careers the belief that what they offer to patients in psychotherapy is barely useful (and, unfortunately, they may well be correct—for they have never mastered their anxiety and never learned their supposed professional skills). This may lead to obsessive defenses—a ritualized approach to psychotherapy or an obsessive search for the "ideal" drug.

Medication is better than no treatment at all, certainly, in the short run; and it may even be better than treatment provided by inappropriately trained and unmotivated therapists. As an adjunct to psychotherapy, it may be helpful to some psychotherapists in the beginning of treatment, or as an adjunct to weather a particularly upsetting crisis. Whether or not, and to what extent, medication is employed will always be a clinical decision based on the importance to the therapist at a given time of change in behavioral control versus change in the thought disorder.

Follow-up hospitalization data were collected 2 years after the termination of the treatment phase of the project, not only from the public hospitals where patients had been previously hospitalized, but also from private and possibly relevant psychiatric hospitals in the metropolitan area. Luckily, these patients tended to confine their geographic mobility to the Detroit area, and hence were not likely to be hospitalized outside this metropolitan region.

The pooled psychotherapy patients had an average of 56.4 days of hospitalization, and the controls had 99.8 days. Patients who had received psychotherapy spent roughly half as much time in the hospital during the follow-up 2 years as did those who had received primarily medication therapy. Indeed, patients who did *not* receive psychotherapy had a 2 to 1 chance of being rehospitalized. That probability was exactly *reversed* for the patients receiving psychotherapy; they had a 2 to 1 probability of *not* being rehospitalized.

In both psychotherapy groups, patients of experienced therapists did better in the long run than those of the inexperienced therapists. Moreover, the patients of experienced therapists have spent *much* less time in the hospital than the comparisons (Group C). There did not seem to be a large *differential* impact on long-term hospitalization between the patients of the two experienced therapists (despite differences in adjunctive use of medication). Differential utilization of medication was more critical when the treatment was conducted by inexperienced therapists.

Patients of the inexperienced therapists *not* using medication (Group A) showed a marked reduction in hospitalization during the follow-up period as compared to Group C, whereas the patients of the inexperienced therapists using medication (Group B) were hospitalized essentially as long as the comparison group in the follow-up period (but much less in the total 44 months).

The long-term follow-up hospitalization data seemed to reflect the change in the thought disorder during therapy. Scores attained on the 20-month, end of therapy, administration of the VVT (Feldman-Drasgow Visual-Verbal Test, 1951) are the outcome that best predicts long-term rehospitalization, much more so than initial length of hospitalization during the treatment phase. These findings suggest that the immediate change in the thought disorder is more closely related to the long-run ability to function outside of the hospital than are the short-term behavioral criteria (e.g., docility) usually related to ward adjustment and to hospital discharge. This is in keeping with Eugen Bleuler's (1950) classic observations that the thought disorder is a primary symptom, and others are secondary. It is also in keeping with Cancro's (1968, 1969) findings that severity of the thought disorder was highly predictive of prognosis.

A striking similarity emerges across studies. In the Michigan follow-up data, the patients receiving psychotherapy were hospitalized less than those on medication alone. Those patients who received psychotherapy with medication were the intermediate group in long-term hospitalization.

This is consistent with the frequently overlooked findings of both the Wisconsin and Massachusetts studies. In the Wisconsin project, psychotherapy patients spent an average of 117 days in the hospital during the year after termination of therapy, whereas the control (medication) patients spent an average of 219 days in the hospital in the same period. In the Massachusetts study, 68% of the psychotherapy patients were able to live outside of the hospital, whereas only 37% of the control (medication only) patients were able to do so.

Thus, the medication-alone group was certainly improved over its pretreatment level, but compared to the other treatment groups, it did not look impressive.

In the Michigan study, cost-benefit data were analyzed, because this was a major emphasis in the California study, and of governmental and insurance decision makers. Making the questionable, but conservative, assumption that every hour of psychotherapy and of supervision, and of incidental payments to poor patients for transportation and baby-sitting, had to be an additional cost over existing budgets, it was found that adding psychotherapy was certainly cost-effective in the long run (44 months), that psychotherapy was cheaper than medication, that experienced therapists were cheaper than trainees, and that psychologists were cheaper than psychiatrists (even when salary differentials were equated, because of lesser tendency in this study to rely on medication), and that these differences would presumably get greater as time went by, since it was the longer term data (20–44 months) where the advantages of having had psychotherapy were more striking. In addition, 75% of the patients treated by medication needed welfare payments as opposed to only 33% of the patients who had received psychotherapy. The differences in clinical status and ability to think logically were mirrored by increased ability to be economically self-sufficient.

However, if there were no long-term follow-up data, if the ability to be economically self-sufficient were not examined, and if one confined cost-benefit data to hospital costs in the first 6 months, the conclusions would be exactly the opposite—medication would be cheaper than psychotherapy, inexperienced therapists would be cheaper than experienced ones, and psychiatrists would be cheaper than psychologists (because of their greater reliance on medication in this study). Unfortunately, government agencies, hospital administrators, and insurance company executives are apt to be more concerned with short-term than long-term savings; in the long run the administrators expect to have different responsibilities.

## BASIC ISSUES IN PSYCHOTHERAPY RESEARCH WITH SCHIZOPHRENIC PATIENTS

Six major American controlled studies have been undertaken. Unfortunately, their results conflict. Because no study is without flaw, it is useful to specify the differing conditions under which differing results have been obtained.

The Pennsylvania and Wisconsin studies successively served to clarify the problems involved in this research area, but drew no strong conclusions about treatment. The Massachusetts study (Grinspoon et al., 1972) and the Illinois study (Paul & Lentz, 1977) worked with chronically hospitalized patients.

The Massachusetts study, using primarily patients previously receiving ECT and insulin coma therapy and therefore probably unsuitable for psychotherapy, receiving psychotherapy from "experienced" therapists inexperienced in the treatment of schizophrenics, and unpaid for their time, showed little benefit from psychotherapy, except an increased ability to live outside the hospital, while medication clearly improved ward adjustment. The Illinois study showed that a carefully executed behavioral approach increased discharge and ability to live outside the hospital, and was less effective when medication was maintained.

Most instructive is the comparison of the California and Michigan studies. The California study had been presented and accepted as a conclusive one. The May (1968) book (which included no follow-up data) was nonetheless described in the preface as "the definitive study" that would "never" have to be repeated. This book concluded that medication was the treatment of choice, from both a cost and a clinical perspective, and that psychotherapy made no appreciable difference. Follow-up data (May et al., 1976, 1981), when finally published, found no statistically significant differences between treatments. But Kane (1987) was typical in accepting their conclusion as definitive. The Michigan findings suggest a contrary conclusion.

## STRENGTHS AND WEAKNESSES OF THE CALIFORNIA AND MICHIGAN STATE STUDIES

Some of the strengths of the California study were the large number of subjects, the study of five treatment modalities, and the attempted control for the personality of the therapist. Some of the weaknesses were the lack of attention to relevant experience of the therapists, the apparent lack of attention to *relevant* training for the therapists, gross discontinuity (termination) of the psychotherapy at discharge from the hospital, inconsistent timing of evaluations, contaminated criteria of outcome, and idiosyncratic data analyses (including, among other things, procedures that eliminated the sickest patients from consideration).

Some of the strengths of the Michigan study were the careful attention to relevant training and experience of the therapists, carefully blind evaluations, evaluations at regular chronological intervals, and no deletion of patients for being too sick. Some of the weaknesses are the small sample size, discontinuity of patient–doctor relationship in drug-alone treatment, and a number of uncontrollable external circumstances, such as the hospital staff bias against psychotherapy and for medication, and the Detroit riot near the hospital during the middle of the project, which made Black patients feel guilty about getting help from White therapists. The latter circumstances are important biases, but ones that worked in the direction of minimizing the effects of psychotherapy.

It has been objected (May & Tuma, 1970; Tuma & May, 1975) that the evaluations on the Michigan study were not blind, that the techniques of data analysis were inappropriate, that the experience of nonmedical therapists cannot be considered experience, that arbitrary scores were assigned to untestable patients at the various outcome evaluations, and that patients were included who should have been deleted because of organic impairments and/or utilization of medication.

None of these objections are factually correct.

They have also objected that there were not a large number of cases in the study, nor were there a large number of therapists, that the experienced therapists supervised the inexperienced therapists, that the assignment of patients to therapists was not random (although assignment to treatment groups was random), and that these findings conflict with other studies.

These objections are facts.

The number of cases and the number of therapists had to be small so that whether the patients really were appropriate and the therapists were practicing psychoanalytic therapy could be carefully checked. Any number of observations of the wrong patients treated haphazardly would be of little scientific value. That there were only two experienced therapists, who also were the supervisors, was necessary to be sure that the experienced therapists really had something to teach and were known to their professional colleagues to be clinically effective. The assignment of patients to each treatment group was rigorously randomized, but within the psychotherapy groups it was not random. The first two cases in each group had to be assigned to the experienced therapists so that the student therapists could observe the treatment of these cases and discuss them as part of their training. Cases were assigned on the basis of the therapists' schedules after that; however, selection of cases was made on the same basis throughout the project by people who did not know to which treatment group the subjects would be assigned, let alone which therapists.

That these findings conflict with those of other studies in the literature is understandable inasmuch as there are some aspects of this project that are unusual, although they ought not to be. First of all, the therapists wanted to practice psychotherapy with schizophrenic patients; there were no reluctant therapists. The student therapists wanted to work with their particular supervisors and viewed them as people from whom they thought they could learn. The experienced therapists (who were also the supervisors) had over 10 years experience, not only in working with schizophrenic patients, but also in working with poor people and Black people (80% of the patients were Black). The same therapist worked with the patient on an inpatient and outpatient basis. Any understanding of psychotherapy that takes the concept of transference seriously would utilize such a procedure.

It may be worth noting that other studies have not shown psychotherapy to be effective with schizophrenic patients because either (a) they used unwilling therapists (and therapy is not likely to be effective if the therapist does not want to do it); (b) they used supervisors who had little experience or interest in doing psychotherapy with schizophrenic patients, and it is axiomatic that people cannot teach what they do not know; (c) they had therapists inexperienced in doing psychotherapy with schizophrenia, and people do not generally do well that which they have never done before; (d) they used therapists who were not familiar with patients of the socioeconomic class or of the ethnic subgroup of the patients; (e) they examined the patients on the day of termination of psychotherapy, discharge, and other irregular intervals; (f) they have not measured the thought disorder with any degree of care; (g) they base their conclusions on ward behavior, not real-world functioning; (h) they did not do long-term follow-up of the patients; or (i) they have done all of these. Under such conditions of poor quality control of psychotherapy and inappropriate evaluation, psychotherapy is not effective.

## PSYCHOTHERAPY QUALITY CONTROL

Evident in the last paragraph is the issue of the general lack of attention to quality control of the psychotherapy provided in psychotherapy research projects, and particularly in research on the psychotherapy of schizophrenic patients. In every reasonably rigorous study on the effectiveness of psychotherapy with schizophrenic patients, where psychotherapy has been reported as unhelpful, quality control of *relevant* training, experience, and motivation has not been maintained. For example, the Massachusetts study (Grinspoon et al., 1972) appears to have very rigorous controls. It does have rigorous controls for the medication versus no medication comparison, but not very comparable controls for the psychotherapy versus no psychotherapy comparison. Moreover, the therapists were not working in their usual way (e.g., frequency of session) or with economic and ethnic subgroups with which they were therapeutically familiar. "Experienced" therapists referred to experience doing some kind of psychoanalytic treatment, not experience in working with resistant schizophrenic patients. One third of the "senior experienced" therapists found themselves "for the first time in their life in a long-term therapy relationship with a resistant patient" (Grinspoon et al., 1972, p. 259). The therapists were *not* paid for their time. It is reported that "half of these therapists felt this to be no problem." Presumably, the other half did.

The California project and the Michigan State project differed considerably in the attention paid to the control of the quality of the psychotherapy being provided. How different the concept of relevant training and experience was on the two projects is reflected by the fact that there were no psychologists as therapists in the California project (in a hospital where May helped set policy), and that these investigators (May, 1974a; May & Tuma, 1970) emphasize the value of the experience of treating "physical (and emotional) disorders in medical school and during internship" (May, 1974a, p. 129), whereas the Michigan investigators consider experience in treating neurotic patients by psychotherapy only partially relevant. Nowhere do the California investigators emphasize the importance of understanding sociocultural factors as they influence therapeutic technique with schizophrenic patients.

It is of interest that in both the California and Massachusetts studies, only psychiatrists were used as therapists, and in both studies psychotherapy was not effective. A mystique concerning the medical degree and its value seems to obscure the need for specifically relevant training. The phrase "fully trained psychiatrist" is used to describe someone who has "never treated a resistant patient" in continuing psychotherapy. This use of language is not objectionable, unless it is taken to imply competence at skills never acquired. It is interesting to note that the Wisconsin project, the Illinois project, and the Michigan State project used psychologists (as well as psychiatrists) as therapists

and found psychotherapy potent. This may reflect, not some equally mysterious mystique about the PhD., but an underlying variable—a concern with
the processes called psychotherapy, and a belief that whatever the process, it
can be and must be learned and cannot be assumed simply by professional
affiliation.

Let us consider some of the specific details of the psychotherapy provided
on the California project and on the Michigan State project:

1. *Experience of therapists.* The Michigan State project used both experienced and inexperienced therapists. The experienced therapists had over
10 years of relevant experience in doing psychotherapy with schizophrenic
patients, and in doing psychotherapy with lower class and ethnic groups
similar to the project patient population. The California project used only
inexperienced "medical" therapists who had "very, very little experience with
psychotherapy of schizophrenia" (Wexler, 1975, p. 432).

2. *Experience of supervisors.* The Michigan State project utilized two
relevantly experienced and relevantly trained supervisors with over 10 years
experience with patients of the socioeconomic and ethnic subgroup of schizophrenic patients. Not only were they experienced in doing psychotherapy
with schizophrenic patients, they were experienced at working in the way the
project required, that is, working with difficult patients without medication
or with adjunctive medication. Even this difference raises differential problems, and like all problems in psychotherapy, one cannot teach appropriate
techniques to others unless one has first learned them oneself. The California
project used supervisors who were "distinguished" psychoanalysts, but whose
training and experiences with schizophrenic patients was highly variable, and
in some cases essentially nonexistent. They were experts in this area by
designation, not by training or experience.

3. *Knowledge of patient population.* Knowledge of the characteristics and
consequent specific resistances of people of a given socioeconomic, ethnic,
and subcultural background is at least as important as knowledge of the specific
psychopathology being treated. The two supervisors in the Michigan State
project were better acquainted with poor and with Black patients than are
most psychotherapists. It is not clear how familiar the supervisors of psychotherapy in the California project were with patients of the socioeconomic and
subcultural background of the patients, even though these patients were not
so low in the socioeconomic hierarchy as were the Michigan patients.

4. *Training of inexperienced therapists.* Learning a complex skill is difficult.
In the early phases of the Michigan State project, careful attention was
paid to training. In addition to didactic reading material, the inexperienced
therapists observed, and later discussed, the psychotherapy of the experienced
therapist working with schizophrenic patients. The initial sessions of the

inexperienced therapist were also observed and discussed by the supervisors and other trainees. In the later phases of the project, conventional supervision sessions were held. It is unclear what special attention was given to the kind and amount of psychotherapy training in the California project. Apparently it consisted of supervisory hours on project patients in addition to whatever training was usual in the residency; however, Wexler (1975) noted that there was tremendous variation in the quality, frequency, and intensity of the supervision. Training and supervision of the therapists was not a closely attended to matter in the California project.

   5. *Motivation of therapists.*   In the Michigan State project, the inexperienced therapists were truly volunteers. The trainees wanted to learn to practice psychotherapy with schizophrenic patients, and chose their supervisors as someone whose training they valued. Trainees were paid for the extra difficulty and time invested in learning psychotherapy with schizophrenic patients and treating the project patients. In the California project, all therapists were required, as part of their residency, to practice five finds of therapy. Participation was required, and no special recompense was given for the extra work and effort involved. It was a well-intended but confounding "control" to have each therapist practice each treatment. The intent was to control for the personality of the therapist, but it ignored the roles of motivation, interest, and needed skills. Certain treatments such as ECT or drugs require little or no personal involvement with the patient and are usually reported by psychiatric residents as feeling continuous with their previous medical training. Psychotherapy and psychosocial treatments raise entirely new issues and perspectives that require considerable new learning and a complex personal involvement with patients that seems discontinuous with previous training. These differences provoke anxiety, and schizophrenic patients in particular provoke anxiety in their supposed therapists. The frank discussion (Grinspoon et al., 1972) of countertransference reactions to schizophrenic patients by "senior staff members" (who were to a large extent really inexperienced therapists with schizophrenic patients) illustrated how demanding this work really is. For the psychiatric resident to face this work without his old friend, medication, is to make him feel naked in the face of the enemy. An experienced and kind supervisor can be helpful in facing such situations.

   Thus, there are major questions about the quality of the psychotherapy provided in the California project.

   The California project did answer the question: "Is psychotherapy provided by inappropriately trained but medically qualified psychiatric residents of much use?" The answer seems to be no.

   The Michigan Project asked the question: "Is psychotherapy provided by appropriately trained professional (psychiatrists *and* psychologists) useful?" The answer seems to be yes. Both experienced and inexperienced psychiatrists and psychologists produced improvement in their patients not achieved through routine medication-only treatment.

The fact that the trainees in the Michigan State Psychotherapy Project really did learn to do psychotherapy effectively, as evidenced by the actual progress of their patients during the project, clearly indicated that psychotherapy with schizophrenic patients is a skill that is both teachable and learnable.


## RESEARCH DESIGN ISSUES

Because of their apparently discrepant findings it is worth examining their research designs in some detail.

*Patient Population and Selection.*   In both the California project and the Michigan State project, the patients were drawn from a public hospital and on clinical examination were considered clearly schizophrenic. Nonetheless, there were striking differences between the patients selected in the two projects in demographic characteristics as well as severity of pathology. The California project managed to select in an "unbiased" manner an unusual set of patients. The "average" California patient was high school educated, with above average IQ, employed predominantly as a skilled laborer (or as a housewife). In other words, the patients were at least lower middle class. By contrast, the "average" patient of the Michigan State project was a high school dropout, with below average IQ, and was employed as an unskilled laborer (or receiving public assistance). In other words, the patients were lower class, poor, and predominantly Black.

The sociologic data have been unequivocal that the typical schizophrenic population is predominantly poor and lower class. For example, Hollingshead and Redlich (1958) reported schizophrenic patients as 12 times more frequent among people from the lowest socioeconomic class (on a five-class basis) than in the highest. Aside from the proportion being Black, which will vary with geographic and urban location, the demographic characteristics of the patients of the Michigan State project were consistent with those reported of schizophrenic patients treated at public hospitals in the United States, whereas the patients of the California project seem to have been, at least inadvertently, subject to some kind of economic screening. This may be the result of the California project intentionally choosing as a treatment population of the "middle third" in severity (i.e., neither the very sick nor the relatively well). It is not clear why this should exclude the poor so effectively.

An additional screening on the basis of severity of symptoms occurs in the California project, even though it is never described as such. The data were analyzed only in terms of patients who took both the pretest and posttest, thus excluding the sicker patients. It is a practically easier, but hardly comprehensive, procedure of investigation that leads to conclusions applicable only to those patients well enough and cooperative enough to take elaborate testing before treatment. No such limitation makes sense if we are talking about the treatment of schizophrenia. The Michigan State sample was biased toward the severest cases, since these were the cases where the diagnosis was the most clear-cut.

*Number of Cases.* The California project had a large sample. There were 228 patients, or some subset depending on which comparison or publication cited. The Michigan State project had a modest sample. There was a total of 36 original patients, one of whom died within the 1st month of treatment. A large sample permits subtle differences to be statistically significant. A small sample permits only striking differences to be statistically significant.

It was possible to do more careful data-gathering on the patients, including carefully detailed and more rigorously blind outcome evaluations, to locate and assess all living patients, and to obtain greater quality control of psychotherapy with a small sample. Because many of the characteristics of the patient population became clear only after repeated follow-ups, less careful work, as is unfortunately necessary with a large sample, would be more misleading. Accuracy of inference is obviously affected not only by the number of cases, but even more by any systematic (planned or unintentional) bias in selecting cases.

*Randomization.* Both studies attempted randomization. In the Michigan State project, suitable patients were selected in sets of 3, and randomly assigned to the three groups. Patient selection and assignment was done in 4 months in the same manner with the same criteria by research personnel not involved in treatment or supervision. In the California project, assignment to treatment groups was also random, but not assignment to therapist. Patients were selected over a 2-year time span.

Assignment between experienced and inexperienced therapists, and among inexperienced therapists, on the Michigan State project was on a rotation basis, because of training demands and the schedules and commitment of the inexperienced therapists. Supervisors had no role in the selection of their patients. Any differences in patient characteristics reflected possible week-to-week fluctuation in admissions (although they were well within the bounds to be expected from random variation). All therapists treated whatever patients were assigned to them. In the California project, a disqualifying condition for the assignment of a psychotherapy case was assignment to a resident in his first 6 months. Seventeen percent of the psychotherapy cases were randomly assigned to such disqualified residents and had to be reassigned.

*Continuity of Treatment.*   Both studies had problems with the continuity of treatment. The California project interrupted psychotherapy on day of discharge from the hospital and did not routinely provide follow-up psychotherapy with either the same or different therapists. Medication, however, was maintained after discharge. The Michigan State project maintained continuity of psychotherapy, and even of psychotherapists, up to one year of hospitalization or up to 20 months of total treatment. The same psychotherapist had the patient both as an inpatient and as an outpatient; however, there was a discontinuity of treatment setting (but not treatment) for the medication-only patients.

This represents a real difference in the two studies, undoubtedly reflecting differences in the values and interests of the investigators. In the California project, careful attention was paid to maintaining continuity of medication, but not of psychotherapy. Undoubtedly, this reflects a genuine concern that the drug treatment be given under optimal conditions. In the Michigan State study, continuity of psychotherapy was maintained, but not as much attention to continuity of prescriber within drug treatment. Continuity of drug treatment was maintained, but the transfer of hospital (if prolonged hospitalization was necessary) meant that a new psychiatrist was in charge of medication, even if the hospital was in other ways better equipped. Being more centrally concerned with quality control of the psychotherapy, the Michigan investigators took account of the fact that psychotherapy is a relationship in which transference factors are an essential therapeutic tool, and any interference with these factors is a disturbance of the therapeutic process. The relationship is undoubtedly a factor in all medical treatment, including the drug treatment of schizophrenia (Shapiro, 1971), but it is not emphasized in the literature, or in clinical discussion by competent medication-oriented psychiatrists. It is not generally believed that changing the prescriber while maintaining the medication and dosage interferes with treatment. Therefore, such stringent care was not undertaken, although it would have been a nice control to have maintained.

*Drug Dosage.*   Both studies permitted psychiatrists to adjust medication and dosage level for each patient individually, in terms of their judgment of the optimal dosage for the patient at that time. Neither study held medication at a fixed arbitrary level, but allowed it to vary in accordance with good clinical practice.

In the California project, medication was reported in terms of average total dosage. For the medication-alone group, it was males, 4.02-g trifluoperazine (Stelazine); females, 3.19g. For the medication and psychotherapy group, it was males, 3.71 g; females, 2.2 g. The maximum daily dosages ranged from 20 to 120 mg for the medication-alone group, and they ranged from 4 to 120 mg for the psychotherapy with medication group.

In the Michigan project, dosage levels typically were approximately 400 mg of chlorpromazine (Thorazine) daily, varying at different times from a low of 100 mg to a high of 1,400 mg daily. It would be inappropriate to label the psychotherapy without medication as contaminated by drug usage. Although three patients in that group did receive medication briefly, two were deleted for other research reasons, as described earlier, and deleting the third "contaminated" patient would have increased the apparent effectiveness of psychotherapy.

The medication-alone group in the Michigan project and the medication-alone group in the California project were hospitalized the same length of time. This would suggest comparability of the medication and of the clinical judgment of the medication-oriented psychiatrists in charge of such treatment. If anything, the comparison between the use of medication in the two projects would favor the clinical effectiveness of the prescribing psychiatrists in the Michigan project, because these patients had a worse prognosis. But the real difference between the two projects is that this level of clinical effectiveness represents the best group in the California project, and the least benefited group in the Michigan State project.

*Untestable Patients.*    In any investigation of schizophrenic patients, there will be some patients who cannot be tested. This is particularly the case before treatment begins. One should be suspicious of any research data on schizophrenic patients that does not report such difficulties.

The way this problem is dealt with influences the conclusions that can be drawn. There are four options for dealing with this: (a) replace untestable patients with testable ones; (b) exclude from data analysis those untestable patients; (c) medicate to whatever point is necessary for testing; (d) use "untestable" as a score on the pretesting, attempting a theoretically meaningful way of quantifying this latter option, with built-in statistical checks on its appropriateness.

Before choosing any of these options, it is assumed that one will use experienced, benign examiners who will go to considerable trouble and are effective in getting cooperation from very resistant patients. Certainly that was the procedure on the Michigan project. It was possible to test patients who were refusing to talk to their therapists and the ward staff. You cannot get such cooperation if you use inexperienced examiners or experienced examiners who are inexperienced in testing schizophrenic patients. Nonetheless, there will always be some patients who are initially untestable.

The California project excluded the most severely disturbed one third of their acute patients routinely. Despite this, they had patients who were untestable, even in the middle range of patients. They excluded from data analysis patients who refused pretreatment testing. Obviously, they also had to exclude any patient who refused post-testing. Their procedures were simple and straightforward, but they introduced systematic bias against including sick patients.

The Michigan project handled the problem of *initially* untestable patients using the fourth option. Theoretically determined initial scores were assigned, and checked for appropriateness (with respect to determining regressions), so that no patient need be excluded from data analysis simply for being initially untestable. Obviously, if patients were untestable at later evaluations, they could not be included in the data analyses for that particular test. But patients took all intellectual tests at the end of treatment, which reflected two things: the care and perseverance of the evaluation and research staff, and that patients were, in all groups, less sick at the end of the project than at the beginning.

This illustrated a very basic difference in the approaches of the two projects. In the California project, larger numbers of subjects were depended on to make generalization possible, but systematic biases were not considered. In the Michigan State project, the number of cases was small, but careful attention was paid to quality control of evaluations as well as of treatments. It was strongly felt that no study of treatment with schizophrenic patients should exclude patients because they are too sick.

*Timing of Evaluations.*    The California project and Michigan State project differed in the timing of evaluations. Of course, both projects tested patients before treatment, although with somewhat different success. The California project used a variable interval post-treatment evaluation schedule determined by the discharge of the patient from the hospital. The Michigan State project utilized a fixed interval outcome evaluation schedule, evaluating the patients 6, 12, and 20 months after they had begun treatment, whether or not they were continuing or resisting treatment. After all, continuation of treatment is itself a treatment effect, which may represent either health or sickness.

The California study, insofar as it draws conclusions from evaluations, which it tended not to, drew them from evaluations made on the day of discharge. This is another bias against the psychotherapy group, because this was also the day of termination of psychotherapy in that project, and the day of termination of psychotherapy is well known to be a time of crisis, particularly if the psychotherapy was meaningful.

The California project was really conceptualized and hence designed as a study of in-hospital treatment of schizophrenic patients, as if a mental hospital were comparable to a surgical ward where processes not continuous with life occur. That project reflects a mystique about the mental hospital that implies a special potency independent of the treatment process.

The Michigan project saw the hospital as an adjunctive facility where the same therapeutic processes do or do not occur as could occur in other settings. The hospital setting has advantages and disadvantages, and these can be specified. Indeed, in private practice, other settings are commonly used to provide support, protection, supervision, or availability to treatment. Medication is not more or less effective in the hospital, nor is psychotherapy. The Michigan project was a study of the treatment of schizophrenic patients in its complete sense, that is, both inpatient and outpatient, and it was evaluated as such.

*Nature of Evaluations.* There were differences in the nature of the outcome evaluations on the two projects. First, the Michigan project made extraordinary efforts to locate and get cooperation with the evaluation, lest a systematic bias be introduced. Second, the specific measures used to measure the thought disorder differed in their sensitivity. The Michigan State project included a number of intellectual tests known to reflect psychopathologic impairment, including one specifically designed and validated as measuring schizophrenic thought disorders (the VVT). The California project used fewer and more general measures, relying primarily on ward adjustment ratings, or disguised ward adjustment, such as the Menninger Health-Sickness rating scale (rated by independent professionals, but based on the written record of ward observations recorded by personnel primarily concerned with ward adjustment). In fact, the measures used in the California project were all considered by the Michigan State project but rejected because the literature on their validity was discouraging, or because they were too diffuse and insensitive to disturbances that were specifically schizophrenic.

*Blindness of Evaluations.* The California project and Michigan State project differed in terms of the "blindness" of the evaluations. The California project used primarily criteria that are likely to be "contaminated" by knowledge of the patient's treatment and the value system of the evaluators, for example, discharge, ward behavior, and therapist reports. The "independent" team of psychoanalysts making clinical ratings relied heavily on narrative accounts of the patient that were prepared by personnel (nurses, therapists, and social workers) fully cognizant of the treatment the patient had received, in addition to their own interviews. It is not clear whether the psychologic tests were given and evaluated blindly. The issue of blindness on the California project is particularly relevant, given May's (1974a) description of the iron-handed authority he had over all hospital personnel.

In the Michigan project, particular care was taken to ensure the blindness of the clinical ratings. The psychiatrist who conducted the clinical status interviews and the psychologist administering the Rorschach, the Thematic Apperception Test (TAT), and the intellectual tests were not informed as to which treatment group the patient belonged. Of course, a good clinical status interview is not likely to leave the interviewer blind; these interviews were recorded on tape, and references to treatment were deleted from the tapes before being rated blindly with regard to clinical status by independent judges. Separate independent raters also blindly rated the Rorschach and TAT. Discharge was not entirely blind, but it was determined by ward chiefs not involved in the research, and probably biased against psychotherapy. Follow-up rehospitalization data were entirely blind.

*Statistical Methods.*   Both studies used analyses of variance and covariance. The California project chose to report the majority of their findings in terms of analysis of variance, because they report covariates to be basically not significant. The Michigan project chose to report its findings in terms of analysis of covariance and analysis of variance when covariates were not relevant.

The California project's use of statistics, however, is more creative than convincing. Many of their procedures are questionable for regression effects and for possible biased selection of subsets of the data. Comparisons are made for subsets of as few as two thirds of the cases, because the sicker patients who would not take some test either pretreatment or post-treatment are excluded from analysis. It must be remembered that the project was already using a restrictive range of the middle third of severity. In addition, the procedure of "winsorizing," deleting the patients (on whom they have data) who are doing best and those who are doing the worst in each group, leads to ignoring 20 cases in their data when winsorizing once, and 40 cases when winsorizing twice.

The particular subset of patients used by the California project varies almost with each test of significance. It would be necessary for the analyses to be rigorous to check each time that the distributions of the samples *actually used* are within the limits of random variation on relevant background characteristics. There is no evidence such tests of significance were routinely carried out.

Moreover, when they utilize analyses of covariance, it is in an unusual way (Forsythe, Engleman, Jennrich, & May, 1973). Regression coefficients were determined only from 44 control patients, which means that fewer coefficients were found to be statistically significant than if the total sample were used. In addition, a new "stopping rule" was invented specifically for this study, which justified stopping earlier, that is taking into account fewer covariates than more conventional statistical procedures, even if the total sample had been used. Thus, the procedures must result in the conclusion that fewer background characteristics need be taken into account, and that taking these into account is less important and makes less difference than more traditional statistical procedures. Given that even in a rigorously randomized design some differences in background characteristics and prognoses must occur by chance, their statistical analyses seem intended not to discover these differences or take them into account. It would be interesting to see if more conventional regression analyses would change their findings in any major way.

The Michigan project used analysis of covariance. This allowed for correction for possibly relevant background variables after a multiple regression procedure determined which of the many possibly relevant background variables need to be taken into account. In recent years, the severe limitations of covariance analysis (Campbell, 1970) have become clear; however, these data meet these most recent stringent standards. Matching, difference scores, and analysis of variance (as used in the California project) are subject to more serious errors and regression effects as Campbell, among others, has made clear. Moreover, the $F$ test, as used in the Michigan State project, is not invalidated by minor violations and certain known kinds of major violations of normality assumptions, particularly where the small sample size will permit only large effects to be significant. Analysis of covariance was used because it was most appropriate for that situation, that is, most sensitive and least biased. Interestingly enough, analysis of variance yields essentially the same results with the data of the Michigan State project, except for one comparison between the Supervisor B and B trainees on one variable.

## CONCLUSION FROM THE COMPARISON
## OF THE CALIFORNIA AND MICHIGAN STUDY

No study is perfect. Moreover, no two studies are identical. It would be inappropriate simply to discard *apparently* conflicting data. A careful scrutiny reveals differing conditions under which meaningfully different results have occurred, which are consistent not only with each other, but with clinical experience.

The California and the Michigan State projects differed in the questions they were attempting to answer and differed in how they attempted to gather data to answer those questions. The California study was aimed at evaluating specifically in-hospital treatment provided by untrained residents. The Michigan State project was concerned with the total course of treatment in and out of the hospital, provided by relevantly trained professionals. It was as much an assessment of the effectiveness of training as it was of the effectiveness of treatment. The projects differed, therefore, in terms of the quality control of the psychotherapy as well as of the outcome evaluations. In both cases, the Michigan State Psychotherapy Project was more attentive to these issues.

The current data suggest the following: medication seems more helpful for schizophrenic patients than no treatment at all, especially in the short run; psychotherapy for schizophrenic patients by average inexperienced (but medically qualified) therapists is not of much help. If careful quality control of what it is that is called psychotherapy is maintained, psychotherapy is helpful for schizophrenic patients.

Researchers need to strive for the greatest rigor possible, consistent with being sure the phenomenon being studied is the one intended; in this case, that "psychotherapy" is psychotherapy, and the "experience" and "training" are relevant experience and training. As Gendlin (1973) has stated, "just because two people are talking in a room and one is called a doctor and the other labeled a patient, it does not mean that any psychotherapy is occurring."

## RECENT STUDIES

A recent American study (Gunderson et al., 1984; Stanton et al., 1984) is sometimes cited as if it were relevant to the issue of psychotherapy versus medication for schizophrenic patients. But it was a comparison of two types of psychotherapy (exploratory, insight-oriented vs. reality-adaptive, supportive) while the patients were maintained on medication. There were no patients treated only by medication, and there were no patients treated only by psychotherapy, nor were there differences in dosage levels. In general, there was not much difference between the effects of the two approaches, with some differences in ego functioning favoring the insight-oriented (EIO) group, and rehospitalization and employment data tending to favor the reality adaptive, supportive (RAS) approach. But the large drop-out rate (only 31% of the patients remained in either treatment to the end of the study, and only 76% of these permitted themselves to be evaluated) raises questions about even these conclusions.

One can reasonably raise the question whether the insistence of the therapists on maintaining medication may have had something to do with the lack of continuing cooperation by the bulk of patients (Karon, 1984), because clinical experience leads to the conclusion that more than half of patients eventually discontinue medication because of its unpleasantness (Irwin, Weitzel, & Morgan, 1971; Seltzer, Roncari, & Garfinkel, 1980; VanPutten, 1974), and lie about it for fear of rehospitalization or forced administration. The lie is rarely discovered unless the patient is rehospitalized. Even in studies where the patients know they are being monitored (e.g., Boczkowski et al., 1985), there is poor agreement between actual pill count and self-reported or significant others' reports of compliance, with actual intake being lower than that reported, or believed by the significant other.

An interesting subsequent finding of this comparative study was that the existence of a therapeutic alliance, in either EIO or RAS therapy, predicted favorable outcome (Frank, 1985). This is enlightening given the report in the Grinspoon et al. (1972) study that only one of those therapists ever had a patient who formed a therapeutic alliance.

Two European studies, however, help to clarify the meaning of the available research on psychotherapy versus medication. In both of these studies patients were not randomly assigned to treatment, but matched retrospectively as carefully as possible with controls selected from a larger pool of patients on characteristics other than response to treatment.

Schindler (1980) compared 116 patients treated by "bifocal family therapy," carried out by therapists very familiar with this technique with similar patients treated by pharmacotherapy. Patients were followed for a minimum of 10 years. On the criteria of work record, partner relationships, relationship with children, social isolation, and invalidism either at home or in the hospital, the patients receiving psychotherapy were clearly superior.

Sjostrom and Sandin (1981) reported on a 6-year follow-up of 12 patients given individual psychotherapy, as opposed to matched controls treated only by pharmacotherapy in the same hospital. The patients were maintained on medication, but the medication was greatly reduced for the psychotherapy patients; over half of the patients receiving psychotherapy were entirely off medication in the last year of the study as compared to only one of the controls, and the dosage levels for psychotherapy patients on medication were very small compared to the controls. Medication had been adjusted according to the best clinical judgment of the treating psychiatrist. The patients receiving psychotherapy were found to be functioning at a much higher level at the end of the study. Although the difference in over all hospitalization data was not statistically significant, it favored the patients who had received psychotherapy. Most importantly, time in the hospital for the psychotherapy patients was much greater for the first 2 years, but this shifted with time, and was much greater for the medication-only patients in the last year of followup, underscoring the importance of longer term follow-ups in comparing psychotherapy and medication.

An intensive psychosocial residential milieu (Soteria House) for young first-admission schizophrenics, without medication during or after their residential treatment, was found to lead to lower relapse rates than controls on standard neuroleptic treatment (Matthews, Roper, Mosher, & Menn, 1979; Mosher & Menn, 1976; Mosher, Menn, & Matthews, 1975). The patients were not medicated for the first 6 weeks, and only 10% were eventually placed on maintenance medication; nonetheless the Soteria House patients did much better than their medication-treated controls.

Gunderson's (1979) review of the literature on individual psychotherapy noted that Hogarty et al. (1974a) reported that their psychosocial treatment was not helpful or was even noxious in the absence of medication, which they attributed to its being overstimulating. On the other hand, Gunderson noted that there is evidence that major tranquilizers can interfere with learning (Paul et al., 1972), and that long-term follow-ups of patients treated by intensive psychotherapy at Yale Psychiatric Institute (Rubenstein, 1972) and at Michael Reese (Kayton, 1975) show surprisingly favorable outcomes, despite the severity of illness, although the absence of rigorous controls makes inference uncertain. Gunderson concluded that psychotherapy may not be the treatment of choice for short-term goals, but it may be in the long run, particularly if the patients are well chosen, although how they should be chosen is not clear. Matching of patient and therapist so that a therapeutic alliance is possible is an important consideration in that it was found (Gunderson, 1978) empirically to predict improvement.

Usually unnoticed by reviewers is that the findings of Hogarty et al. (1974a, 1974b) that the optimal treatment was maintenance medication plus their kind of psychosocial intervention was to a large extent due to the female patients. The difference in recidivism rate for drugs versus placebo is much smaller for men than for women, and Hogarty et al. (1974b) report that when not relapsed male patients treated by placebo were better adjusted than those treated with medication, especially if they did not receive this kind of psychosocial intervention. However, the more recent finding by Hogarty et al. (1986) was that utilizing family interventions with medication seems more consistently valuable than their previous approach.

Revere, Rodeffer, Dawson, and Bigelow (1983) found that even schizophrenics who have been chronically institutionalized (mean hospitalization of 15 years), despite medication in this era of rapid discharge, responded when Warm Intrusive Therapy (their form of psychoanalytic group therapy) was added to the treatment. Five out of seven experimental patients obtained employment, or discharge, or both. Patients also showed statistically significant improvement on the Rorschach, TAT, and Brief Psychiatric Rating Scale. Control patients did not show such improvement. Interestingly enough, relationships with ward staff was rated as decreased, but ability to function in the outside world obviously improved, once more demonstrating the lack of correlation between ward adjustment and real-world functioning.

But available studies, in addition to the Michigan Study, cast doubt on the indispensability of medication. Thus, Hamilton, Hordern, Waldrop, and Lofft (1963) had found that an intensive milieu without drugs was as effective as medication for chronic patients, and that medication added to an intensive milieu made no difference. As mentioned above, in the social learning and in the intensive milieu of Paul and Lentz (1977; Paul et al., 1972) chronic hospitalized patients randomly and blindly placed on placebos did better than those maintained on neuroleptic medication, both immediately and in the 3-year follow-up. Carpenter, McGlashan, and Strauss (1977) in a 4-month intensive milieu with individual and group psychotherapy found no difference between nonchronic patients treated with and without drugs. Both medicated and unmedicated patients in this setting did better than patients treated in the usual short stay and maintenance medication at community hospitals. Rappaport et al. (1978) assigned nonchronic patients in an intensive hospital milieu randomly and blindly to drugs or placebos. In a 3-year follow-up patients given placebos had lower rates of recidivism and higher levels of social functioning. Patients originally assigned to drugs who stopped taking them did worse than those who had never been treated with medication at all.

## CONCLUSIONS

The view that schizophrenics must be treated by medication is at best an overgeneralization. Judiciously used, medication can be useful, depending upon the patient, the therapist, and the setting, and the type of other treatment available. Medication certainly seems to be of benefit in the short run for most patients, especially in the absence of effective psychosocial treatment. Patients usually become less frightened and frightening. They also generally become less angry. They may lose some of their dramatic "positive" symptoms, like hallucinations, which were generated to cope with their terror. In other cases, the hallucinations and delusions remain, but the patients are not as troubled by them. They take orders better, and comply with other people's demands better. They tend not to frighten ward staff, relatives, and others. Violent patients usually become manageable, although sometimes only by dosage levels that leave the patient barely awake. The ward staff, treating physician, and family do not feel powerless. Patients are spared some of the destructive things that other people, out of fear, often used to do to schizophrenic patients, both in and out of hospitals.

Sometimes the patients are able to resume ordinary life. More often, they function marginally, but are not seen as troubling to others. So-called negative symptoms, for example, lack of initiative, self-direction, motivation for growth, seem to remain, or even increase. The thought disorder typically diminishes, but does not disappear. Nonetheless, the patient is usually dischargeable from the hospital. But the board and care home in the community has replaced chronic hospitalization for many medication-treated schizophrenics.

Roth (1986) estimated that for 35% of schizophrenic patients "drugs made little or no lasting impression" (p. 169). According to Lipton and Burnett (1979), approximately 30% of medicated patients are rehospitalized within a year despite continued medication, and of the 60% of acute schizophrenics treated with medication who are considered "socially recovered" at the end of 5 years, less than half (30%) are employed at any time during the first 5 years. In the Michigan study, 75% of the patients treated with medication without psychotherapy required and received welfare benefits during the first 20 months after inception of treatment, as compared to only 33% of the randomly assigned patients receiving psychotherapy (with or without medication); 67% of the patients treated with medication, but without psychotherapy, were rehospitalized during the follow-up period (20–44 months), as opposed to 33% of those who received psychotherapy. However, a number of different psychosocial treatments have been demonstrated to add to the overall effectiveness of medication on most criteria, both in terms of life adjustment and in terms of symptoms.

Of course, psychosocial treatments, even without medication, are also useful to most schizophrenic patients in the short run. How useful depends on the type of treatment and the experience of the therapists. Approximately 10% to 15% of patients suffer from misdiagnosed organic conditions that do not respond well to either psychotherapy or neuroleptic medication. In the Michigan study approximately 75% of the schizophrenic patients treated only with psychotherapy were able to be discharged within 8 weeks (most within 2 to 4 weeks) and function out of the hospital.

However, it is the longer term view of medication that is more questionable. Evidence of serious neurological consequences in the long run continues to accumulate, strongly suggesting the need to consider alternate treatments with lesser side effects.

At the very least, psychosocial treatments permit lower dosage levels, decreasing risk. Further they improve the overall level of functioning of medication-treated patients. But the conclusion that schizophrenic patients must be treated with medication, whatever else is done, is based on poorly designed studies, the most serious flaw of which is the absence of psychotherapists experienced in the treatment of schizophrenic patients by psychotherapy. Labeling therapists without such experience and training as "experienced" does not substitute for *relevant* training and experience. The Michigan study using individual psychoanalytic psychotherapy, the Illinois study using intensive milieus, especially behavioral treatment, the Soteria House milieu study, and the Schindler family therapy study all indicate that appropriate and careful use of psychosocial treatment is more effective in the long run than medication as currently used.

The clinical implication of the Michigan study still seems to be valid that the optimal treatment for a schizophrenic is psychotherapy, from a competent therapist, without medication, if the patient, the therapist, and the setting can tolerate it. (Hospitals and families vary as to what behaviors they consider tolerable.) But if any one of those three requires it, medication should be used. However, if medication is used, it should be seen as a temporary adjunct, to be withdrawn as the patient can tolerate it, and the withdrawal should be a planned part of the treatment. Such an approach minimizes the danger of side effects. Similar conclusions seem warranted for other forms of psychosocial treatment.

Unfortunately, political and economic factors and a concentration on short-term cost-effectiveness, rather than the scientific findings, currently seem to dictate the type of treatment. The data seem to clearly indicate the value of psychosocial treatments, including individual psychotherapy, as opposed to medication. One can repeat specifically with respect to the psychoanalytic therapy of schizophrenia, as well as other psychosocial treatments, Freud's comment about psychoanalysis, that, in Mark Twain's words, "The reports of my death are greatly exaggerated."

## REFERENCES

Alexander, F., & French, T. M. (1946). *Psychoanalytic therapy.* New York: Ronald Press.

Bleuler, E. (1950). *Dementia praecox, or The group of the schizophrenias* (English translation). New York: International Universities Press. (Original work Published 1911)

Bleuler, M. (1978). The schizophrenic disorders: *Long term patient and family studies.* (S. M. Clemens, Trans.) New Haven: Yale. (Original work published 1972)

Boczowski, J. A., Zeichner, A., & DeSanto, N. (1985). Neuroleptic compliance among chronic schizophrenic outpatients: An intervention outcome report. *Journal of Consulting and Clinical Psychology, 53,* 666–671.

Bookhammer, R. S., Myers, R. W., Schober, C. C., & Piotrowski, Z. A. (1966). A five-year clinical follow-up study of schizophrenics treated by Rosen's "direct analysis" compared with controls. *American Journal of Psychiatry, 123,* 602–604.

Braginsky, B., Braginsky, D., & Ring, K. (1969). *Methods of madness: The mental hospital as a last resort.* New York: Holt, Rinehart & Winston.

Breggin, P. R. (1983). *Psychiatric drugs: Hazards to the brain.* New York: Springer.

Brody, M. W. (1959). *Observations on direct analysis.* New York: Vantage Press.

Campbell, D. T. (1970, June). *Experimental and quasi-experimental designs for psychotherapy research.* Address presented at the Society for Psychotherapy Research, Chicago.

Cancro, R. (1968). Thought disorder and schizophrenia. *Diseases of the Nervous System, 29,* 846–849.

Cancro, R. (1969). Clinical prediction of outcome in schizophrenia. *Comprehensive Psychiatry, 10,* 349–354.

Carpenter, W. T., McGlashan, T. H., & Strauss, J. S. (1977). The treatment of acute schizophrenia without drugs: An investigation of some current assumptions. *American Journal of Psychiatry, 134,* 14–20.

Chouinard, G., & Jones, B. (1980). Neuroleptic induced supersensitivity psychosis: Clinical and pharmacological characteristics. *American Journal of Psychiatry, 137,* 16–21.

Ciompi, L. (1980). Catamnesic long-term study on the course of life and aging of schizophrenics. *Schizophrenia Bulletin 6,* 606–617.

Cole, J. O., & Davis, J. M. (1969). Antipsychotic drugs. In L. Bellak & L. Loeb (Eds.), *The schizophrenic syndrome* (pp. 478–568). New York: Grune & Stratton.

Dunham, H. W. (1965). *Community and schizophrenia: An epidemiological analysis. (Lafayette Clinic Monographs in Psychiatry,* No. 1) Detroit: Wayne State University Press.

Feldman, M. J., & Drasgow, J. (1951). A visual-verbal test for schizophrenia. *Psychiatric Quarterly Supplement, 25,* 55–64.

Forsythe, A. B., Engleman, L., Jennrich, R., & May, P. R. A. (1973). A stopping rule for variable selection in multiple regression. *Journal of the American Statistical Association, 68,* 75–77.

Frank, A. F. (1985, June). *The therapeutic alliance.* Paper delivered at the Society for Psychotherapy Research meeting, Wellesley, MA.

Gendlin, E. T. (1973, August). *Discussion of "Psychotherapy is effective with schizophrenics."* Symposium, American Psychological Association Convention, Montreal.

Goldberg, E. (1985). Akinesia, tardive dysmentia, and frontal lobe disorder in schizophrenia. *Schizophrenia Bulletin, 11,* 255–263.

Goldstein, M. J. (1987). Psychosocial issues. *Schizophrenia Bulletin, 13,* 157–172.

Goleman, D. (1987, September 22). Free expression or irresponsibility? Psychiatrist faces a hearing today. *New York Times,* p. C3.

Grinspoon, L., Ewalt, J. R., and Shader, R. I. (1972). *Schizophrenia, pharmacotherapy, and psychotherapy.* Baltimore: William & Wilkins.

Gunderson, J. G. (1977). Drugs and psychosocial treatment of schizophrenia revisited. *Journal of Continuing Education in Psychiatry, 38,* 25–40.

Gunderson, J. G. (1978). Patient therapist matching: A research evaluation. *American Journal of Psychiatry, 135,* 1193–1197.

Gunderson, J. G. (1979). Individual psychotherapy. In L. Bellak (Ed.), *Disorders of the schizophrenic syndrome* (pp. 364–398). New York: Basic Books.

Gunderson, J. G., Frank, A. F., Katz, H. M., Vanicelli, M. L., Frosch, J. P., & Knapp, P. H. (1984). Effects of psychotherapy in schizophrenia: II. Comparative outcome of two forms of treatment. *Schizophrenia Bulletin, 10,* 564–598.

Hamilton, M., Hordern, A., Waldrop, F. N., & Lofft, J. (1963). A controlled trial on the value of prochlorperazine, trifluoperazine, and intensive group treatment. *British Journal of Psychiatry, 109,* 510–522.

Harding, C. M., Brooks, G. W., Ashikagawa, T., Strauss, J. S., & Breier, A. (1987a). Aging and social functioning in once chronic schizophrenics 22–62 years after first admission: The Vermont story. In G. Hudgins & N. Miller (Eds.), *Schizophrenia, paranoia, and schizophreniform disorders in later life* (pp. 74–82). New York: Guilford Press.

Harding, C. M., Brooks, G. W., Ashikagawa, T., Strauss, J. S., & Breier, A. (1987b). The Vermont longitudinal study of persons with severe mental illness, II: Long term outcome of subjects who retrospectively met DSM-III criteria for schizophrenia. *American Journal of Psychiatry, 144,* 718–726.

Harding, C. M., Zubin, J., & Strauss, J. S. (1987). Chronicity in schizophrenia: Fact, partial fact, or artifact? *Hospital and Community Psychiatry, 38,* 477–486.

Hogarty, G. E., Anderson, C. M., Reiss, D. J., Kornblith, S. J., Greenwald, D. P., Javana, C. D., & Madonia, M. J. (1986). Family psychoeducation, social skills training, and maintenance medication in the aftercare treatment of schizophrenia. *Archives of General Psychiatry, 43,* 633–642.

Hogarty, G. E., Goldberg, S. C., Schooler, N. R., Ulrich, R. F., & the Collaborative Study Group. (1974a). Drug and sociotherapy in the aftercare of schizophrenic patients. II. Two year relapse rates. *Archives of General Psychiatry, 31,* 603–608.

Hogarty, G. E., Goldberg, S. C., Schooler, N. R., Ulrich, R. F., & the Collaborative Study Group. (1974b). Drug and sociotherapy in the aftercare of schizophrenic patients. III. Adjustment of non-relapsed patients. *Archives of General Psychiatry, 31,* 609–625.

Hollingshead, A. B., & Redlich, F. C. (1958). *Social class and mental illness.* New York: Wiley.

Huber, G., Gross, G., & Schuttler, R. (1975). A long term follow-up study of schizophrenia: Psychiatric course of illness and prognosis. *Acta Psychiatrica Scandinavia, 52,* 49–57.

Irwin, D. S., Weitzel, W. D., & Morgan, D. W. (1971). Phenothiazine intake and staff attitudes. *American Journal of Psychiatry, 127,* 67–71.

Jones, M. (1953). *The therapeutic community.* New York: Basic Books.

Jones, B. J. (1985). Tardive dysmentia: Further comments. *Schizophrenia Bulletin, 11,* 187–189.

Kane, J. M. (1987). Treatment of schizophrenia. *Schizophrenia Bulletin, 13,* 133–157.

Karon, B. P. (1984). The fear of reducing medication and where have all the patients gone? *Schizophrenia Bulletin, 10,* 613–617.

Karon, B. P., & VandenBos, G. R. (1981). *Psychotherapy of schizophrenia: The treatment of choice.* New York: Aronson.

Kayton, B. P. (1975). Clinical features of improved schizophrenics. In J. G. Gunderson & L. R. Mosher (Eds.), *Psychotherapy of schizophrenia* (pp. 361–395). New York: Aronson.

Krystal, H. (1975). Affect tolerance. In J. Frosch & N. Ross (Eds.), *Annual of psychoanalysis* (Vol. 3, pp. 179–220). New York: International Universities Press.

Lipton, M. A., & Burnett, G. B. (1979). Pharmacological treatment of schizophrenia. In L. Bellak (Ed.), *Disorders of the schizophrenic syndrome* (pp. 320–352). New York: Basic Books.

Matthews, S. M., Roper, M. T., Mosher, L. R., & Menn, A. Z. (1979). A non-neuroleptic treatment for schizophrenia: Analysis of the two year postdischarge risk of relapse. *Schizophrenia Bulletin, 5*, 322–333.

May, P. R. A. (1968). *Treatment of schizophrenia: A Comparative study of five treatment methods.* New York: Science House.

May, P. R. A. (1974a) Psychotherapy research in schizophrenia—another view of present reality. *Schizophrenia Bulletin, 9*, 126–132.

May, P. R. A. (1974b). Treatment of schizophrenia. I. A critique of reviews of the literature. *Comparative Psychiatry, 15*, 179–185.

May, P. R. A. (1975). Schizophrenia: Overview of treatment methods. In A. M. Freedman, H. I. Kaplan, & B. J. Sadok (Eds.), *Comprehensive textbook of psychiatry* (pp. 923–938). Baltimore: William & Wilkins.

May, P. R. A., & Tuma, H. H. (1970). Methodological problems in psychotherapy research: Observations of the Karon-VandenBos study of psychotherapy and drugs in schizophrenia. *British Journal of Psychiatry, 117*, 569–650.

May, P. R. A., Tuma, H. H., Yale, C., Potepan, R. & Dixon, W. J. (1976). Schizophrenia: A follow-up study of results of treatment. *Archives of General Psychiatry, 33*, 481–486.

May, P. R., Tuma, H. H., Yale, C., Potepan, R., and Dixon, W. J. (1981). Schizophrenia: A follow-up of the results of five forms of treatment. *Archives of General Psychiatry, 38*, 776–784.

Mosher, L. R., & Menn, A. Z. (1976). Dinosaur or astronaut? One year follow-up data from the soteria project. *American Journal of Psychiatry, 133*, 919–920.

Mosher, L. R., Menn, A. Z., & Matthews, S. M. (1975). Soteria: Evaluation of a home-based treatment for schizophrenia. *American Journal of Orthopsychiatry, 45*, 455–467.

Mukherjee, S., & Bilder, R. M. (1985). Commentary. *Schizophrenia Bulletin, 11*, 189–190.

Paul, G. L., & Lentz, R. J. (1977). *Psychosocial treatment of chronic mental patients: Milieu vs. social learning programs.* Cambridge, MA: Harvard University Press.

Paul, G. L., Tobias, L. L., & Holly, B. L. (1972). Maintenance psychotropic drugs in the presence of active treatment programs. *Archives of General Psychiatry, 27*, 106–115.

Porceddu, M. L., Giorgi, O., Ongini, E., Mele, S., & Biggio, G. (1986). ³H-SCH 23390 binding sites in the rat substantia nigra: evidence for a presynaptic location and innervation by dopamine. *Life Sciences, 39*, 321-328.

Porceddu, M. L., Ongini, E., & Biggio, G. (1985). ³H-SCH 23390 binding sites increase after chronic blockage of D-1 dopamine receptors. *European Journal of Pharmacology, 118*, 367–380.

Psychiatrist is cleared in ethics case. (1987, October 13). *New York Times*, p. C8.

Rappaport, M., Hopkins, H. K., Hall, K., Belleza, T., & Silverman, J. (1978). Are there schizophrenics for whom phenothiazines may be unnecessary or contra-indicated? *International Pharmaco-psychiatry, 13*, 100–109.

Revere, V. L., Rodeffer, C. J., Dawson, S. D., & Bigelow, L. B. (1983). Modifying psychotherapeutic techniques to meet the needs of chronic schizophrenics. *Hospital & Community Psychiatry, 34*(4), 361–362.

Rogers, C. R. (1951). *Client-centered therapy.* Boston: Houghton Mifflin.

Rogers, C. R., Gendlin, E. T., Kiesler, D. J., & Truax, C. B. (1967). *The therapeutic relationship and its impact: A study of psychotherapy with schizophrenics.* Madison, WI: University of Wisconsin Press.

Rosen, J. N. (1953). *Direct analysis.* New York: Grune & Stratton.

Roth, M. (1986). Diagnosis and prognosis of schizophrenia. In G. D. Burrows, T. R. Norman, & G. Rubenstein (Eds.), *Handbook of studies of schizophrenia Part 1: Epidemiology, aetiology, and clinical features* (pp. 169–182). Amsterdam: Elsevier.

Rubenstein, R. (1972, April). *Mechanisms for survival after psychosis and hospitalization.* Paper presented at the annual meeting of the American Psychoanalytic Assocation, Dallas, TX.

Scheflen, A. E. (1961). *A psychotherapy of schizophrenia: Direct analysis.* Springfield, IL: Thomas.

Schindler, R. (1980). Die Veranderung psychotischer Langzeitverlaufe nach Psychotherapie [The change of long-term progress of psychotics after psychotherapy]. *Psychiatria Clinica, 13,* 206–216.

Seltzer, A., Roncari, I., & Garfinkel, P. (1980). Effect of patient education on patient compliance. *Canadian Journal of Psychiatry, 25,* 638–645.

Shapiro, A. K. (1971). Placebo effects in medicine, psychotherapy, and psychoanalysis. In A. Bergin & S. Garfield (Eds.), *Handbook of psychotherapy and behavior change* (pp. 439–473). New York: Wiley.

Sjostrom, R., & Sandin, B. (1981, September). *Effects of psychotherapy in schizophrenia: A retrospective study.* Paper presented at the First European Conference of Psychotherapy Research, Trier, Federal Republic of Germany; Psychiatric Research Center, Ulleracher Hospital S-750, 17 Uppsala, Sweden.

Stanton, A. H., Gunderson, J. G., Knapp, P. H., Frank, A. F., Vannicelli, M. L., Schnitzer, R., and Rosenthal, R. (1984). Effects of psychotherapy in schizophrenia: I. Design and implementation of a controlled study. *Schizophrenia Bulletin, 10,* 520–563.

Tuma, A. H., & May, P. R. A. (1975). Psychotherapy, drugs, and therapist experience in the treatment of schizophrenia: A critique of the Michigan state project. *Psychotherapy: Theory, Research, and Practice, 12,* 138–142.

Van Putten, T. (1974). Why do schizophrenic patients refuse to take their drugs? *Archives of General Psychiatry, 31,* 67-72.

Wexler, N. (1975). Comment on the five treatment comparative study. In J. G. Gunderson & S. R. Mosher (Eds.), *Psychotherapy of schizophrenia* (pp. 431–433). New York: Aronson.

# 5

# ATTENTION DEFICIT DISORDER: THE EMPEROR'S CLOTHES, ANIMAL "PHARM," AND OTHER FICTION

Diane McGuinness
*University of South Florida*

## THE SOUND OF ONE HAND CLAPPING

It is difficult to write a conventional chapter on the topic of pharmacological intervention in Attention Deficit Disorder (ADD) or Hyperactivity. This is because two decades of research have not provided any support for the validity of ADD or ADDH, the diagnostic categories established in the Diagnostic and Statistical Manual of Mental Disorders, DSM-III (American Psychiatric Association, 1980). Given this fact, why does the diagnosis persist, or perhaps more important, how did the diagnosis originate in the first place? These questions are the focus of this chapter, but first it is important to understand the scope of the problem. It is currently fashionable to treat approximately one third of all elementary-school boys as an abnormal population because they are fidgety, inattentive, and unamenable to adult control. The most common treatment for this "disorder" is the prescription of stimulant medication that acts in the short term to reduce the problematic symptoms, creating the impression that the child is better able to "pay attention," and hence process information more efficiently. The introduction of pharmacological interventions for childhood behavioral problems has meant that the search for a medical diagnosis, rather than therapy, has become the central issue in ADD research.

Establishing valid diagnoses has been an intractible problem in psychiatry because there are no consistent physiological or biochemical indicators for any diagnostic category, even for the psychoses. Although personal histories and reports by family and friends are critical in identifying extreme non-normal groups, as in the case of schizophrenia, the same approach when applied to behaviors that are part of a normal continuum is largely unworkable as a diagnostic strategy, particularly in the case of ADD. There are a number of obvious reasons for this. For example, parents and teachers are asked to rate a particular child on a questionnaire as the central part of the diagnostic procedure. The average layman has no clinical training and no knowledge of behavioral norms in childhood, even assuming these norms existed. Any good clinician knows that a person's perceptions are often more real than reality. For a parent or teacher to describe a child as being "inattentive" or "hyperactive" tells us as much, or more, about the adult (their tolerance, their disciplinary skill, etc.) as it does about the child.

The history of the transition from the old-fashioned view that naughty, disruptive, and inappropriate behaviors are "symptoms" of an underlying psychological problem (such as family difficulties, learning problems, etc.) to the view that these same behaviors constitute a medical "syndrome" is difficult to unravel. One clue concerns the demarcation of treatment specialization between the medical profession (psychiatrists and pediatricians) and nonmedical clinicians and case workers. In the DSM-I (1952) children referred for psychiatric assessment fit into two major categories: schizophrenia and "adjustment disorder." The latter included the two poles of extreme neuroses: withdrawn/depressive and conduct disorder/agressive. All other childhood behavior problems fell under the province of the school system, the courts, the clinical psychologist, the social worker, or the church minister. What has occurred since 1952 is a broadening of the second diagnostic classification to include the vast middle ground of childhood behavior problems. This in turn has led to finer and finer distinctions, each accompanied by a set of largely invalid diagnostic criteria. As Hinshaw (1987) noted in his outstanding review of the problem, the DSM-III contains 65 pages on childhood and adolescent disorders, which include "many unreliable classifications that have received little or no empirical support" . . .

Coupled with the process of subsuming childhood behavior problems under a psychiatric umbrella is the inevitable administration of pharmacological agents to perfectly healthy children, the medical practitioner's intervention of choice. This wholesale transfer of care turns out to have created a double-edged sword. If the major form of treatment is drugs, this means that a host of childhood behavior problems become classified as medical problems. Children who were previously "clients" are now called "patients" and can be given drugs despite the fact that they have no definable disease. This leads to a kind of mind warp or malady of circular reasoning: Behavior is altered by drugs. Drug use requires a diagnosis. A diagnosis implies a disease or disorder, therefore: "behavioral problems" = "disease." In formal logic: A causes B,

$A = C$, $C = D$, therefore $B = D$ (a type of syllogism known mainly to those with medical training). A corollary axiom completes the reasoning: As behavior cannot cause diseases, therefore the disease must cause the behavior. This topsy-turvy point of view is impregnable to any amount of research or reasoning. The final irony is that it is legally inadmissible to give children stimulant medication *without* a diagnosis, making it virtually impossible to carry out double-blind drug studies using non-ADD controls.

The sequence of precipitating factors leading to this state of affairs is unknown, but one thing is clear: the discovery of a "suitable drug" established the necessity for a diagnosis. Obviously, the most critical event was the discovery that certain pharmacological agents have "paradoxical" effects on children. The amphetamines and other forms of stimulant medication, although acting to increase energy drive in adults, often produce the reverse effect in children, reducing motor activity and restlessness. This paradoxical effect was reported as long ago as 1937 by Bradley, but did not appear to spark any interest until a paper by Laufer, Denhoff, and Solomons in 1957 outlined a "hyperkinetic behavior syndrome" and advocated "a favorable response to amphetamine," as the criterion for a diagnosis. The reasons why this paper made an impact and Bradley's did not remain a mystery. It could have something to do with a more permissive attitude to drugs. It might relate to an escalating divorce rate and increased stress on the child, plus the reduced ability and opportunity for many single mothers to discipline their children. Another important factor is the media where the number of newspaper and magazine articles and TV coverage expanded enormously from the early 1960s. Last but not least, there were the marketing efforts of the drug companies and the generous profits derived from the escalating sales of stimulant drugs. The production of Ritalin (methylphenidate) has doubled in the last 5 years. The spin-off of all the aforementioned is that medical practitioners who deal with early childhood problems experienced a rapid upswing in patient load, and for those who administer stimulant medication, a flock of adoring parents who express their wonderment at the doctor's ability to "cure" their naughty, disruptive children.

By the end of the 1957 to 1966 period, the Department of Health, Education and Welfare gave its formal blessing to the "diagnosis," calling it "Minimal Brain Damage." During that decade, research efforts tended to become divided into two independent factions, the first, represented by researchers with a background in neurology, psychiatry, or pediatrics, and the other, the experimental psychologist, each differing fundamentally in his or her approach to research on behavior. Medically trained researchers generally begin with a disease model, and the questions that guide research are very different from the questions posed to understand normal behavioral variation. First and foremost, a disease has a cause., often a unique and physical cause. In treatment, one can either reply on the body's natural defenses and prescribe rest, or treat the disease with drugs or through surgical intervention. Certain drugs can cure, but many drugs merely reduce the symptoms of the disease, arresting further development or producing a greater ability to cope with the symptoms. If you observe that badly behaved children can be controlled by drugs, then it is but one step to infer, in this one-dimensional world view, that the drugs are relieving the symptoms of some unknown disease or disorder. This means that the major question of interest in research is to define or classify the disease, the greatest focus of effort in medical research on ADD.

This is understandable, given the fact that medical students spend many years being indoctrinated with this philosophy. However, serious problems emerge when medical research strategies are applied to children with deviant behavioral patterns. Clinical research in medicine relies on two major forms of research design. The first is correlational, in which patterns of behavior, lifestyle, diet, and so forth, are correlated with the onset of the disease process at some later stage. Although researchers are aware that correlations provide no information on causality, this fact is often ignored by practitioners, as for example, in the problem of the hidden variable. Something hidden may be responsible for the lifestyle *and* the disease, such as the fact that personality traits (Type A behavior) may produce the behaviors that in turn predispose someone to cardiovascular disease. To my knowledge, this issue has rarely been addressed in medical research on ADD or hyperactivity. This is the question whether something "hidden" may be causing the behavior, that is, something *other than* a "disease," or brain disorder.

The second major form of medical research is experimental and largely confined to drug research designs, which have some highly restricted properties. In well-controlled research the intervention is measured in absolute terms by the amount of the drug administered, with an objective outcome in terms of physical and physiological indicators. In the absence of objective indicators, the researcher must rely on the patient's reports of symptoms. However, drug research almost never has to account for a host of intervening variables that are of central concern to the psychologist, such as family patterns of deviance, personality, learning deficiencies, intelligence, and so forth. Behavior is multiply caused, and for that reason psychological research is multivariate. Drug research is univariate: one cause (the drug) and one outcome as represented by the physical change in some measure.

These differences in approach have implications for how one thinks about the research problem, with the result that medical students become biased toward a disease model and a univariate cause/effect mode of thought. Furthermore, the lack of training in multivariate research designs makes it difficult for medical practitioners to understand the psychological literature, especially as it is often couched in inscrutable jargon. This is compounded by the fact that there is a long history of disdain for nonmedically trained clinicians and researchers by medical practitioners. These factors create the situation in which most research on ADD and hyperactivity carried out by psychologists is unknown to psychiatrists and especially to pediatricians. There is even a suspicion that psychologists have an axe to grind because, as one pediatrician put it: "psychologists don't believe in drugs, so any research they carry out is bound to be suspect." This typical remark indicates a singular lack of understanding of the scientific method, implying that psychologists are incapable of being objective, and that a belief in drugs is different in kind than nonbelief. (For a detailed exploration of this problem, see Kingsbury, 1987.)

Because of these and other factors, the past 25 years have seen a dramatic shift in therapeutic intervention from behavioral to drug-oriented regimes. As is seen later, an overwhelming number of overactive, energetic, and disruptive children are being referred for drug treatment to psychiatrists and pediatricians, and drugs are often the only form of intervention, despite lip service to the contrary. Parents, seduced by media hype and brochures from drug manufacturers, find that drugs are not only an inexpensive and less time-consuming form of treatment, but more important, take the onus off them by attributing the child's difficult behavior to causes beyond their control. This is reinforced by the instant reduction in problematic behavior produced by stimulant medication. One pediatrician described the drug outcome as "like a miracle." Because this miraculous substitute for learning self-discipline and self-control is seen to be beneficial, more and more parents and teachers rush children to doctors for an instant cure. The problems that cause the symptoms of fidgety, inattentive, disruptive behavior in the first place, such as serious learning problems, family and emotional problems, are often not dealt with at all, as follow-on studies have shown. Drugs do not help children read or do math, teach a child how to control his behavior, or teach sensitivity to others; they don't stop Dad's drinking, and what is more, do not even provide improvement in attentional control as currently believed. Children *appear* to be more "attentive" at home and in the classroom, but objective studies indicate that this has virtually no impact on the learning process.

The past 25 years has led to a phenomenon almost unique in medical history. Methodologically rigorous research (reviewed later) indicates that ADD and hyperactivity as "syndromes" simply do not exist. We have invented a disease, given it medical sanction, and now must disown it. The major question is how we go about destroying the monster we have created. It is not easy to do this and still save face, another reason why physicians and many researchers with years of funding and an academic reputation to protect are so reluctant to believe the data.

This chapter addresses four fundamental issues that are critical in understanding the scope of the problem. The first issue concerns the "diagnostic" instruments and their construction. Due to the lack of any valid diagnosis, variability in "attention" and "activity level" are ascertained by pen-and-paper questionnaires that lack constructional (internal) validity, much less external validity. These are filled out by people with no clinical training, that is, parents and teachers. Thus, the initial diagnosis is based on opinion, and opinion varies with a number of factors, not the least of which is the adult's "tolerance for annoying behavior." Despite a wide range of test instruments available (Hinshaw, 1987, reviewed over 60), far and away the most commonly used test, the Conners Scale, is also the most poorly designed in terms of both internal and external validity.

The second and perhaps most important problem is overinclusion. Due to the lack of any valid diagnosis, the cutoff point for inclusion or exclusion in the "syndrome" is completely arbitrary. It can be based on the judgment of the physician or that of the person who designed the test instrument. Neither is a valid procedure, because the tests are not based on any objective norms of childhood "activity levels" or "attentional span," and so there is no means for making even a *statistical* judgment, much less a valid judgment.

The third section presents the evidence from laboratory-controlled studies on comparisons between ADD or hyperactive children and normal controls on a variety of attentional tasks. If, as the DSM-III alleges, attentional problems are at the heart of the ADD syndrome, then controlled tests that manipulate the variable of attention ought to show profound differences between groups.

Last but not least is the intervention process itself. What is the evidence that drugs alone or in combination with behavioral techniques solve the problems that led to the disruptive behaviors? There are a number of studies in the literature that assess the improvement in behavior and in academic performance by comparing behavioral strategies alone or in combination with a drug regime. Finally, a more difficult question to answer: do physicians provide the necessary clinical support in setting outcomes and goals against which they can evaluate a drug regime? Further, do these goals have anything to do with the initial precipitating causes of the behavioral disturbance?

## BELL, BOOK, AND CANDLE

Laufer et al. (1957), described a hyperkinetic syndrome that included hyperactivity, problems in the control of attention, inability to delay gratification, irritability, explosiveness, and poor school performance. They noted that these problems were symptomatic of children with obvious neurological deficits, like epilepsy, cerebral palsy, or mental retardation. They made the assumption that because children with brain dysfunction exhibited these behaviors, the behaviors would be indicative of children with brain dysfunction, a kind of rationale in which the disease and its symptoms are considered to be mutually inclusive. However, when normal children who exhibited many of these behavioral problems were given a neurological work-up and an electroencephalogram, no differences could be found between them and a control group. These disappointing results did not modify their reasoning. Instead they concluded that an appropriate neurological measure had not yet been discovered, and until this time, the best diagnosis for the "syndrome" was a "favorable response to amphetamine."

Since 1957, in several controlled laboratory studies using more sophisticated techniques, no evidence has been found for any type of brain damage or abnormality in otherwise normal children with problematic behavior. For this reason, the diagnosis of "minimal brain damage" (see Clements, 1966) has been discarded. It has also been found that hyperactivity, the major presenting symptom of the "hyperkinetic syndrome," is a poor diagnostic criterion. Objective measurements have shown that activity level is extremely context dependent, with so-called hyperactive children exhibiting fidgety and disruptive behavior in one situation, but relatively little activity in another, such as the psychiatrist's clinic. It is this singular fact that has made it impossible to establish any norms for levels of activity in childhood. (The research on physiological indicators of brain damage and on activity levels has been extensively reviewed by McGuinness, in a chapter called "Hyperactivity: A Diagnosis in Search of Patient," 1985.)

Without a neurological indicator or a valid measure of activity level, the one remaining symptom of the "hyperkinetic syndrome" is a problem with attentional control. It is for this reason that there has been a shift in diagnosis in the current DSM manual from "hyperactivity" (DSM-II) to attention deficit disorder (DSM-III). ADD may or may not be accompanied by hyperactivity, according to the manual. This is merely an exercise in semantics for two very obvious reasons. First, the identical test instrument is still the major diagnostic tool (the Conners Scale), whether the "syndrome" is called "hyperactivity" or "ADD." Secondly, not only has research failed to demonstrate any objective validity for neurological signs, or activity levels, as correlates for a diagnosis of ADD/hyperactivity, but there has been a consistent failure to find attentional problems in children diagnosed ADD as noted later. Furthermore, these word games have not dissuaded most psychiatrists and pediatricians from the implicit belief that ADD is the result of some form of brain damage or neurologic anomaly, because every patient is viewed through the lens of a disease-model. If a child is supposed to have trouble paying attention, and attention is regulated by the brain (not the heart or liver), then the child must have something wrong with his brain.

Because attempts to discover neurological and physiological indices of hyperactivity or ADD have largely been abandoned, the diagnosis has come to depend exclusively on questionnaire data. Two major reviews are available on problems arising from this approach. Hinshaw (1987) extensively reviewed the factor analytic studies on childhood behavioral dimensions, and McGuinness (1985) reviewed the various questionnaires utilized as the major and often the only diagnostic instruments for ADD and hyperactivity. The highlights from these reviews are presented here.

In contrast to the psychoses, classification and diagnosis of ADD and hyperactivity must deal with behaviors that are distributed on a continuum in the population as a whole. The general defining criterion is one of having too much of a particular behavior compared to a normal population, rather than exhibiting behaviors that can be classified into a discrete category, such as schizophrenia. As a general rule, the psychiatric orientation is toward defining independent constructs, whereas psychologists focus more on continuous dimensions, using statistical cutoffs in standard deviations as a criterion of deviancy. This is because, historically, the major province of psychiatry was centered on the psychoses, presumed to be non-normally distributed. Psychology, traditionally, has been more concerned with behavioral variation in normal populations. It is argued here that this psychiatric bias, which leads to viewing ADD as a construct instead of an extreme of normal variation, has exacerbated the problem of overinclusion. This bias has also had a profound effect on the development and use of diagnostic tests for ADD and hyperactivity.

Most of the efforts to obtain satisfactory measuring instruments for childhood behavior disorders suffer from the same basic flaws. Almost all are based on questionnaire or survey information most typically obtained from classroom teachers or parents. Few efforts have been made to collect objective data in the form of observational ratings or via instrumentation. Also, despite the fact that much lip service has been paid to the variability in deviant behaviors due to situation specificity, little work has been done to control for variation of target behaviors in more than one context or situation. (For some notable exceptions, see Rapoport, Donnelly, Zametkin, & Carrougher, 1986; Schachar, Rutter, & Smith 1981.)

Questionnaire construction has been determined largely by the clinical descriptions of a range of common problems brought to the attention of the clinician by parents. Initially, there were two major categories of behaviors that were contraindicative of adequate social adjustment. Children were described as either anxious/depressed and withdrawn, or acting out and aggressive, reflecting the global dimensions: "internalizing/externalizing." These extreme behaviors were seen as a response to the children's inability to cope with events in their lives. It is largely through attempts to refine these broad constructs into narrow-band syndromes (like ADD) that much of the problem as arisen.

Hinshaw's review essentially pinpoints the difficulty of separating specific behaviors such as "attentional problems," "hyperactivity," and so forth, from these two basic categories or from each other. In an assessment of all major factor analytic studies since 1970 with $N = 100$ or greater, he found consistent evidence for the emergence of separate factors for conduct problems/aggression and attention deficits/hyperactivity. However, although there are high factor loadings on question items pertaining to these dimensions, intercorrelations between factors indicate that there is also considerable overlap between them and also with other factors such as anxiety, academic problems, social withdrawal, and so forth. It is clear from these correlations that children can exhibit a variety of behavioral problems, none of which are truly independent. These narrow band factors do not constitute a "syndrome." As is illustrated in the next section, some children are hyperactive and inattentive, some hyperactive and aggressive, some all three, some only one, and so forth.

Hinshaw's review points to a number of problems with the internal validity of behavioral questionnaires, and as he noted, this is quite independent of the problem of *external* validity of any of these constructs, which would require verification through objective measurement. Most revealing is his finding that the Conners scale is perhaps the weakest instrument available, a point also raised by McGuinness (1985). The Conners scale is the most frequently used scale for diagnosing ADD in the United States. The current version of the Conners scale (Goyette, Conners, & Ulrich, 1978) produced three factors for teacher ratings: conduct problems, hyperactivity, and inattentive-passive, and four factors for parent ratings: conduct problems, learning disabilities, anxiety-withdrawal, and impulsive/hyperactive. (It is important to note the complete absence of any factor of "attention," in this scale. Despite this, the Conners scale is the major diagnostic tool for *Attentional* Deficit Disorder!) Correlations between the individual items on the teacher's scale are far too high to indicate the independence of the factors, ranging from .49 to .68. Strong correlations are found on the parent scale between conduct problems and hyperactivity (.55). Other research using the Conners scale has produced even higher correlations between factors. Trites and Laprade (1983) report correlations for their sample of .84 between hyperactivity and conduct disorder.

If the full-scale Conners is invalid on constructional grounds, it is not surprising that the abbreviated version, the most widely used screening instrument, is even less valid. Several authors report that many items on the abbreviated Conners Teacher Rating Scale (ATRS) confound hyperactivity with aggressivity (Edelbrock, Greenbaum, & Conover, 1985; Loney & Milich, 1982; Ullmann, Sleator, & Sprague, 1985). Thus, children selected by the ATRS for ADD/hyperactivity are likely to be highly aggressive. A major reason for this problem is that the scale construction of the abbreviated form completely ignores the factor structure of the parent instrument. Thus, for example, items included in the abbreviated scale were selected from Factors I, II, IV, and V from the Parent's scale (conduct disorder, learning problems, hyperactivity, and anxiety, respectively) plus Factor III from the Teacher's scale (hyperactivity). (For a more extensive analysis of this problem, see McGuinness, 1985.)

If the Conners scale is particularly weak, other test instruments also suffer from similar problems. This is because there are no operational definitions for any of the terms employed, and hence no means of establishing objective data. Some studies have made an attempt to go beyond the questionnaire format and include information on social factors and objective scores of academic performance. These studies are of particular interest because they indicate the strong influence of academic, psychosocial, and familial factors on childhood behavioral problems. They also point up the more important fact that searching for a "syndrome" as if it were a unique manifestation or inherent property of the child, independent from his family or environment, is astonishingly naive. Reports from Loney's laboratory (Loney, Kramer, & Milich, 1981; Milich & Loney, 1979; Paternite & Loney, 1980) indicate that aggression is associated with socioeconomic status, family hostility, and delinquency, whereas hyperactivity is related to academic achievement problems. Family variables, especially alcoholism, were also found to be highly related to childhood aggression by Steward, deBlois, and Cummings (1980). A further study by August and Steward (1983) showed that children with conduct disorder and hyperactive symptoms were considerably more likely to come from a family with a highly deviant profile, including antisocial personality, substance abuse, and hysteria. McGee, Williams, and Silva (1985) found that poor control of attention was strongly related to academic problems, lower intelligence, plus speech difficulties and poor motor coordination.

The studies just mentioned highlight a central problem in the assessment and diagnosis of ADD and hyperactivity. This is the inappropriateness of the medical-disease model when applied to childhood behavior problems. The implication of this approach is that it is the child who "has" the disorder, rather than the family, the teacher, or the school system. Parents, prompted by physicians and teachers, typically express this belief with expressions like, "My child has ADD," or "is hyperactive," as if this were a unique property of the child and totally independent of family or social dynamics. Drugs are administered to the child, and not to the parents or teachers. The data indicate the reverse, that the child's behavior is often a reaction to learning or family problems, and not the cause of the problems. The direction of causality is inferred from the unlikely possibility of the child's behavior playing a causal role in a parent's alcoholism, or being solely responsible for a hostile family environment. And it is far more likely that low IQ and/or poor academic skills produce fidgety, inattentive symptoms, than the reverse.

## CHICKEN LITTLE

One third of normal American schoolboys are now considered to constitute an "abnormal" group, a problem of overinclusion without historical precedent. The lack of any valid diagnosis for ADD coupled with the arbitrary nature of current diagnostic practices has led to a bandwagon phenomenon that can only be described as a national disaster.

In 1985, McGuinness published a review of the literature on hyperactivity and attention deficit disorder as part of a book dealing with a range of so-called learning disabilities. At that time we lacked large-scale demographic studies that could firmly establish the scope of the problem. However, we did have enough information to determine that the vast majority were males, with estimates ranging as high as 90%. In that review, a best guess concerning the number of children classified as ADD and/or hyperactive was between 10% and 15% of the total population. This meant that with the correction for sex ratios, the proportion of boys meeting the criteria for diagnosis rose to nearly double that figure, or 18% of schoolboys. As McGuinness pointed out, hyperactivity is only one end of the bipolar measure of deviance. You cannot have hyper-anything unless you also have "hypo," by definition. Hyper means "too much," and hypo "too little" of something. Thus, to be a valid procedure, if 18% (less than one standard deviation from the mean) is adopted as a cutoff value at the *hyper*active end of a bipolar dimension of activity, this must be balanced by an equal cutoff at the *hypo*active end. If this valid statistical procedure was adopted, it would lead to a situation in which 36% of all schoolboys would be considered to be abnormal or deviant, making a nonsense of the word normal.

Actually, the situation turns out to be much worse. Since this book appeared, two large surveys on normative U.S. samples have been published. Both surveys put the incidence for ADD/hyperactivity/conduct problems in boys at approximately 33%, and this value does not include measures of the opposite hypoactive, indistractible, passive, and so forth, pole of deviance. In the first study by Satin, Winsberg, Monetti, Sverd, and Foss (1985), 1,077 households were surveyed using the Conners scale. A group of normal boys aged 6–9 years were interviewed and diagnosed by two psychiatrists. The major purpose of this survey was to determine whether questionnaire data alone would provide as valid a diagnostic criterion as a clinical assessment. In the second survey, Goldstein (1987) reported on the test results for 7,119 boys and girls in the age range 6–11. These data include both cognitive and attentional/behavioral measures. Both surveys are extremely important in revealing much more than they intended about the problems surrounding the diagnosis of ADD and hyperactivity. For this reason they are presented in some detail.

Satin et al.'s stated goal was to identify children in the population at large
who represent "untreated cases." Thus, the study begins with an unstated bias
that reflects an implicit assumption that there is a valid medical diagnosis
called ADDH, and that they are providing a service by locating all children
who would fit this "diagnosis," in case they had escaped the notice of their
parents and/or teachers.

To set about this task, they contacted 1,077 households either by mail or
by phone and obtained scores on the abbreviated form of the Conners Teacher
Rating Scale. From these households they obtained scores on 1,884 children
between the ages of 2 and 13. The Conners scale scores are illustrated in Fig.
5.1. This figure represents the mean scores for boys and girls living in eastern
Long Island, New York. The figure is very revealing.

First, it indicates the overwhelming sex differences across the age range in
the behaviors tapped by the Conners scale in such behaviors as fidgetiness,
impulsivity, conduct and learning problems, and so on. It also shows a strong
developmental shift in these behaviors as the child matures. Lastly, judging
from the noisiness of the curves despite very large sample sizes, there appears
to be a huge amount of variance within each age group. This variance, of

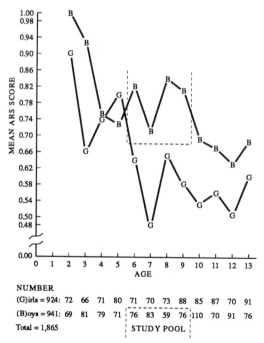

FIG. 5.1.   Age-sex specific means on the Conners' Abbreviated Rating Scale
(ARS). Reprinted with permission from Satin et al. (1985).

course, is the result of the fact that these are not objective data. They reflect the parents' opinion about the normality or otherwise of a hodgepodge of indicators of their child's behavior. It is clear from the plateau in the slope of the boys' scores at ages 6–9 that parents generally hold the opinion that their boys are more disruptive, poorer scholars, and less amenable to discipline than they should be for their age. This opinion could also reflect reality, if there were objective data available, that boys between 6 an 9 years actually do exhibit fairly stable levels of high activity, distractibility, and immunity to adult control. Whichever way one chooses to interpret these findings, either of these interpretations is "true." The opinions held by parents are true opinions, and objective measures, should they support these opinions, may also be true. There is no reason to suggest that there is anything "abnormal" about these results. Despite this, the authors decreed that boys in the age range 6–9 years represented a "high-risk" group, and it was this group that they selected for further psychiatric assessment. Their reasoning is never made clear. Ultimately, 94 boys in the 6–9 year age range were randomly selected for further evaluation.

On what information was this evaluation based? The authors quite rightly pointed out that abbreviated Connors Scale scores and full-scale scores that parents and teachers subsequently completed should not be revealed to the psychiatrists, otherwise the psychiatric evaluation would not be an independent assessment, which was the goal of the study. To solve this problem they asked the parents to fill out a different questionnaire: The Werry-Weiss-Peters scale. This is a hyperactivity scale with questions on fidgetiness, restlessness, talkativeness, and attention seeking. These questionnaire data were submitted to the psychiatrists because they were unable to make a "diagnosis" without this information. As the authors stated: "The WWPAS was made available to the diagnosticians because of the *necessity* for standardized parent behavioral reports for *valid* ADDH diagnosis." And further: "Diagnoses were made only if the psychiatrists *believed* that the symptoms were sufficiently severe to warrant treatment or careful follow-up" (italics added). Reading between the verbiage: The psychiatrists were unable to make any diagnosis without being told how by the parents.

Despite a wealth of identical information, the two psychiatrists, working independently of one another, agreed on only 69% of the cases, an inter-rater reliability figure so low that it would prohibit publication in any journal of experimental psychology. Thus, despite the same test scores from the parents and extensive interview information, the psychiatrists differed in their opinion of what was "severe" or not "severe." Undaunted by this poor result, the authors eliminated all discrepancies by asking the two doctors to resolve their differences and agree on a diagnosis.

The results: 33% of all of this normative sample of schoolboys were found to be abnormal. Twenty-four percent were classified as ADDH, and the remainder were given other DSM-III diagnoses. When teachers were asked to rate the same children on the same test instrument as the parents, they were found to disagree with parents most of the time. In fact, only 8% of all children in the sample were found to exhibit deviant behaviors both at home and at school (an agreement rate of 25%), a result that could be considered the only valid finding of the study. Teacher ratings were also less likely to predict the final psychiatric diagnosis, which is opposite to the DSM-III manual recommendation that teacher ratings be considered more valid than parent ratings. The discrepancy, of course, must have something to do with the fact that parents' interviews and not the teachers' were part of the psychiatrists' diagnostic material.

Finally, in an assessment of a variety of additional survey information, it was found that the diagnosis ADDH was highly related to intelligence and to socioeconomic indicators. Boys who received a diagnosis (either ADDH or other) were found to have significantly lower IQ scores, worse reading and math scores, more gestation or delivery problems, and parents with a lower education level who were less likely to be in professional occupations. Thus, the boys diagnosed as ADDH were of lower ability and hence developmentally delayed compared to the remainder of the sample.

Suppose it was suggested that the following scenario was the best way to discover which children needed help.

1. Begin with an invalid test instrument, preferably one that does not measure the target behavior (in this case "attention").
2. Find two psychiatrists who disagree 31% of the time on how to interpret the test results.
3. Use the same invalid instrument to show how parents and teachers disagree with each other and with psychiatrists 75% of the time about the severity of the child's behavior.
4. Choose those children who are of lower IQ and have poorer academic skills for their age.
5. Use a cutoff for "deviance" of 33%.
6. On the basis of all the above, give these children a diagnosis for a psychiatric disorder (preferably ADD) and (if you're so inclined) promptly administer drugs.

Would you agree with this approach? The authors found no difficulty.

They conclude that "the observed ADDH prevalence rate of 24% is surprisingly high" (p. 763). Then after much verbal gymnastics in discarding the discrepancies in the data, they continue: "Since low SES and education are associated with both ADDH diagnosis and nonparticipation, the true prevalence rate for the area should be *even higher* than the one observed"

(p. 763 italics added). And further: "Finally, it is possible that the diagnoses are valid, the sample is representative and that the observed prevalence is close to the true prevalence"—because—"Six to nine year old boys were chosen for this study because they are a relatively high risk group" (p. 763) (a tautology by any other name).

This paper is the product of people working in one of our top institutions. The work has been supported by NIH and state grants. If they cannot think rationally about the problem and give us better guidance, then how can the average parent stand against the wave?

The second study is more cautious, adhering to a straightforward report of the data with fewer unwarranted assumptions. Subjects were 7,119 children throughout the United States chosen to represent a broad and well-founded demographic sample. All were Caucasian and between the ages of 6 and 11, with an IQ of 70 or above. The behavioral measures were teacher ratings on three major criteria: Attentiveness (defined as the ability to pay attention or maintain sustained attention), hyperactivity (defined as ratings on motoric control and restlessness), and aggressivity (defined as the amount and necessity for disciplinary action). The teacher ratings were made using a Guttman-type scale with four phrases to indicate the level of severe/not severe for each behavioral indicator. Each phrase included the words "as most children of the same age." In addition, a number of cognitive measures were taken, including tests from the Wechsler and the Wide Range Achievement Test battery.

The initial results are remarkably similar to the New York study. Overall, 33% of the boys were scored as being at the top rank of very inattentive, excessively hyperactive or aggressive, or any combination thereof. By contrast, only 15% of the girls were scored high on these dimensions. What do these figures tell us? If the teachers were completely objective in their ratings, and were able to determine accurately how children of either sex should behave for their sex and age group, one would expect to find a normal distribution. This would place approximately 68% of the children in ranks 2 plus 3, and about 15%-16% in each outer ranks 1 and 4. These outer ranks would represent children scoring outside one standard deviation from the mean. This normal distribution was found for the girls. However, teachers in the United States appear to regard normal behavior for boys as more abnormal or more extreme than it really is.

The study also broke down these behavioral categories in more detail and this table is presented here.

These scores are very informative. First, the most common complaint for both sexes is attentional control. For the boys, teacher ratings of attentional problems alone and in combination with hyperactivity and aggression account for 28.1% of the total population. For the girls this figure is 14%, about half. Looking at aggressivity alone and in combination with other problems, high levels are reported in 8% of the boys, but only 1.8% of the girls. Hyperactivity

TABLE 5.1
Percentages of Children with Low Attentiveness
Hyperactivity and Aggressivity

| Group | Boys | Girls |
|---|---|---|
|  | N=2616 | N=2418 |
| Comparison | 66.70 | 84.53 |
| Low attentive | 18.73 | 11.70 |
| Hyperactive | 1.51 | 0.67 |
| Aggressive | 2.43 | 0.54 |
| Low attentive/hyperactive | 5.01 | 1.32 |
| Low attentive/aggressive | 0.38 | 0.04 |
| Hyperactive/aggressive | 1.26 | 0.29 |
| Low attentive/hyperactive/aggressive | 3.98 | 0.91 |
| Total | 100.00 | 100.00 |
| All low attentive | 28.10 | 13.97 |
| All hyperactive | 11.76 | 3.19 |
| All aggressive | 8.05 | 1.78 |

Note: Table reprinted with permission from Goldstein (1987).

alone and in combination with other problems is reported for 11.8% of the boys, but only 3.2% of the girls, a male/female ratio of about 4 to 1. One further important fact to emerge from these data is that hyperactivity alone, excluding problems of attention and aggressive behavior, is exceedingly rare: reported in only 1.5% of the boys and .67% of the girls.

In the comparison between children who had high scores on the measures of deviance and those who did not, there was a very clear indication of lowered cognitive ability. However, this cognitive deficit was almost exclusively found in those children who were rated poorly on attention, whether or not they had other contributing problems. The girls and the boys both showed the same trend. By contrast, those children who were described as "hyperactive" or "aggressive" only, performed normally on all cognitive measures.

Now the main question arises as to the direction of causality. Do problems in the classroom, such as difficulty with reading and math, lead to the inability to maintain attention to the task? This is the common interpretation in most studies that manipulate attention or motivation experimentally. It has been found repeatedly that as task difficulty increases and competency is exceeded, the ability to maintain attention decreases. This general principle is a variant of the classic Yerkes-Dodson Law, or the inverted U arousal/efficiency function (see Kahneman, 1973, for review). However, despite the cause/effect problem, Goldstein concluded as follows: "The findings affirm the central role of attention in the development of academic disability in the school-aged child"

(p. 218). "The findings of the present study demonstrate that in the sphere of cognitive development, attentiveness is the critical variable. Inattentive children are doing less well on measures of intellectual and academic performance." Goldstein added that the child with ADD plus hyperactivity may suffer greater disability than a child with ADD and no hyperactivity, in spite of the fact that he began his paper with a stern criticism of his colleagues for failing to produce a valid diagnosis.

Taken together, both studies indicate that it is common, in the United States, to view about one third of boys of elementary school age as a non-normal group. This figure is quite extraordinary. It is over three times the figure for access to special education services for both sexes as allowed by school districts in the United States. But, the diagnosis of ADD is considerably more serious because it is considered a psychiatric disorder. Formerly, psychiatric diagnoses were either reserved for extreme (non-normally distributed) patient groups, or clinical cutoffs for normally distributed behaviors ranged around two standard deviations from the mean, or about 1% of the population. One third of all school boys is not statistically abnormal by any stretch of the imagination. And, as noted earlier, this value does not even tap the opposite pole of deviancy: passive, overattentive, obsessive, and indistractible.

Part of the fault for this state of affairs must originate in the unrealistic view of adults (mainly female) of what male behavior should be like in early childhood. Coupled with this is a singular lack of many of psychiatrists or physicians engaged in research on ADD and hyperactivity to view their own data objectively, thus compounding the problem. There is now so much machinery in motion to promote a diagnosis of deviance for perfectly normal behavior that it seems almost impossible to slow it down, much less bring it to a halt.

## THE EMPEROR'S CLOTHES

One of the major purposes of separating attentional factors from hyperactivity per se in DSM-III was to provide a more limited set of criteria. This shift in emphasis and terminology occurred because, as noted earlier, a number of studies indicated that hyperactivity alone is not a useful prognostic indicator for a variety of measures such as school performance, delinquency, social adjustment, and so on, (Minde et al., 1971; Weiss, Kruger, Danielson, & Elman, 1975; Weiss, Minde, Werry, Douglas, & Nemeth, 1971). However, if a lack of attentional control is at the heart of various behavior problems exhibited by school children, then laboratory studies using well-matched controls ought to produce clear evidence of group differences in a variety of attentional tasks.

There are several attentional control systems in the brain that operate to allow both the efficient monitoring of the environment and the exclusion of distracting signals during intense concentration (McGuinness & Pribram, 1980; Pribram & McGuinness, 1975). As well, there is an additional concept of "span," which is related both to the maturity of the nervous system and to competency. In short, there is no such thing as "attention," uniformly manifest in all situations, but a variety of aptitudes that allow one to pay attention to certain events and ignore others and to shift attention efficiently between tasks. These different forms of attention have various names in cognitive psychology.

1. Short-term memory or span of apprehension. Holding items in awareness for a brief period.
2. Sustained attention. The amount of time someone can attend to the same type of material or event.
3. Focused attention. The amount of detail that can be monitored or encoded during concentration on a task.
4. Selective attention. The ability to attend to certain features of the environment and ignore others.
5. Distractibility. The degree to which irrelevant environmental stimuli interrupt ongoing behavior and thought.
6. Flexible noticing order. The ability to shift attention rapidly to another set of events or sequence of actions when it is appropriate.
7. Habituation. The speed at which the nervous system codes new information is reflected by rapid waning of attention to a repeated stimulus.

All of these types of attentional control are highly influenced by three major factors. These are the maturity of the nervous system, interest in the event or stimulus, and competence in the required task. For these reasons, it is often difficult to determine the extent to which motivation plays a part in studies on attention, because motivation reflects both interest and competency.

In the studies reviewed in this section, the descriptor ADD is used, whether or not the authors describe the population as "hyperactive." This is because in almost all cases, the children are selected on the basis of the same questionnaire (usually the Conners) that is used interchangeably for the two categories.

A number of studies have investigated focused and sustained attention in children diagnosed as ADD. One series of experiments investigated children's performance on the Matching Familiar Figures Test, which is believed to measure the cognitive styles of "reflective" or "impulsive." Impulsivity can be defined as the inability or unwillingness to maintain attention sufficiently to make correct choices, and is measured by the speed of response and error scores. In general, children classified as ADD were found to be impulsive, but they did not differ from other non-ADD children also classified as impulsive (Campbell, 1973; Campbell, Douglas, & Morgenstern, 1971; Kroener, 1975). Focused attention is also required in a variety of rather boring, repetitive tasks frequently used to test ADD children. These are reaction-time tasks, in which a child pays attention to a signal or to some aspect of a set of signals, and is required to make rapid and accurate responses. ADD children make more errors of commission and are more variable in their response times than control groups. However, this deficit is not apparent at the beginning of the trials and disappears entirely if the children are paid for their correct responses (Cohen, 1970; Cohen & Douglas, 1972; Sykes, Douglas, & Morgenstern, 1973). These findings strongly suggest that ADD children are not motivated to persist in boring, repetitive tasks, although they are perfectly capable of doing so if they want to. When extra cognitive demands, such as adding a memory load, or complex strategies, were added to reaction time tasks, the ADD children generally did better than the control group (Kroener, 1975; Sykes et al., 1973).

Another type of speeded task requires the subject to withhold a highly practiced response and substitute a novel response. This requires not only response inhibition, but flexible attentional control. Such a task is the Stroop Test, in which subjects have to repress a habitual response by reading the name of a color printed in another color, such as the word "brown" written in green, or to name the color of the letters, for example, say "green" instead of "brown." There are no differences between ADD children's ability to do this task and a control group (Campbell, Douglas, & Morgenstern, 1971; Cohen, Douglas, & Morgenstern, 1971).

Distractibility, one of the alleged hallmarks of the ADD child, has been investigated in several studies. These studies present the child with a vigilance task or a set of problems and then bombard him with extraneous distracting stimuli. Essentially no differences in performance have been found with respect to changes from baseline measures in ADD children and their controls (Campbell et al., 1971; Sykes, Douglas, Weiss, & Minde, 1971). In a more complex version of this approach, Bremer and Stern (1976) required their ADD and control subjects to read passages for comprehension while they were intermittently bombarded with loud noises and flashing lights. The ADD children did look up more often, but this in no way disturbed their performance, which was identical to the control group. Furthermore, the authors found that the ADD children did not look up more frequently than the control group in the nondistraction condition.

Studies that require sustained attention during a problem-solving task have also shown no differences between ADD children and their controls, indicating that not only are they not deficient in attentional control but are equal to other children in highly complex cognitive problem-solving skills (Dykman, Ackerman, & Oglesby, 1979; Freiberg & Douglas, 1969). In both studies, however, the ADD groups were significantly different from controls in their willingness to persist in the task under partial reward conditions and in their estimation of the length of time they had been engaged in the task. ADD/hyperactive children, as distinct from normal controls and children with learning problems, estimate time on repetitive tasks to be much longer than it really is.

These studies, carried out in laboratory settings, away from the classroom that the child appears to find problematic, and providing the necessary control over IQ, reading level, and so forth, show that when ADD children are matched for initial ability with a control group, their performance is essentially identical. What differences do appear seem to reflect their unwillingness to persist in tasks they do not prefer. Sykes et al. (1973) summarized their results with the remarks that ADD children appear to perform just like other children on all tasks in which they are in control of the situation (for example, on internally paced tasks) but fail to do well in tasks controlled by someone else. When this occurs, they appear to experience frustration accompanied by a distortion of the sense of time. It appears that this lack of amenability to adult control and the desire to exert self-control may be at the core of the problem many of these children experience with adults, rather than an inability to maintain attention. It is clear from the data that if ADD children have problems of maintaining attention to a task, this deficit cannot be demonstrated in controlled laboratory conditions.

## ANIMAL "PHARM"

The flurry of activity in the attempt to develop a rigorous test instrument for classification of children into aggressive, hyperactive, or attentional deficit disorder categories has one central aim: that of determining which children are candidates for drug treatment. In the absence of a pharmacological intervention, all of this would be unnecessary. Children with behavior problems would be treated as they have been treated for decades, on an individual basis, employing techniques of behavior modification, through provision of individual and/or family therapy, or through special education.

Advocates of drug intervention claim that stimulant medication is the treatment of choice because it has the immediate impact of reducing hyperactive behavior and appears to increase focused attention. This enables teachers, parents, therapists, and so on, to deal with the child's problems because he/she is more receptive to instruction and advice, hence more amenable to control by an adult. This is not a totally invalid point of view (especially in extreme cases) if indeed some positive consequences and no negative ones were obtained for the child as well.

As an initial precaution it should be ascertained that no side effects occur as a result of a drug regime. Generally speaking, most professionals are careful to warn against side effects and monitor this through verbal reports from the parents. However, side effects can easily go unobserved unless routine check-ups are carried out. Stimulant medication has a marked effect on the cardiovascular system, chronically elevating basal heart rate. Skin temperature is also lowered, and there is an abnormal effect on the sympathetic nervous system as indicated by pronounced changes in basal skin conductance (Cohen et al., 1971; Porges, Walter, Korb, & Sprague, 1975; Zahn, Abate, Little, & Wender, 1975). Parents have reported weight loss and sleeplessness in their children.

Side effects may be less of a problem than long-term effects of the drug. So far there are no follow-up studies in the literature on the physiological and neurological impact of a long-term drug regime. The amphetamines interact with dopamine and norepinephrine. The consequences of a prolonged use of amphetamines could produce subsequent changes in the production and action of these two neurotransmitters. Dopamine is implicated in Parkinson's disease, and it is the major transmitter in the basal ganglia and frontal lobes, areas that regulate postural and attentional set and the temporal organization of behavior (McGuinness & Pribram, 1980; Pribram & McGuinness, 1975). Norepinephrine functions in the control of focused attention, and its output is correlated with task difficulty, thus serving a major function in the neurochemistry of effortful cognitive processing and stress (Whybrow, 1984). These effects are related to optimal cognitive functioning and well-being and would be very difficult to measure or to monitor over a long time period. Aside from these considerations, prolonged use of amphetamines has been found to produce addiction in adults, and their use is highly controlled for that reason.

Assuming that none of these considerations is a worry to either the parents or the doctor, what effect, if any, takes place in the short term? Do drugs make the child learn more efficiently? Do they make the child happier and more able to cope? Is there any evidence that drugs alone or in combination with behavioral techniques are more successful than behavioral techniques alone?

## Academic Performance

Studies on the impact of a drug regime on school performance have generally indicated that academic skills do not improve merely by taking drugs. Unfortunately, due to problems of diagnosis and the lack of construct validity in the scales used to select children for treatment, these populations contain children with a wide variety of problems ranging from learning disabilities to conduct disorder. However, despite this difficulty, if the drugs were able to produce enhanced attention and if this, combined with reduced motoric output, correlated with increased performance in the classroom, some effects should be noted. At least this is the claim in the marketing material of many drug companies that is distributed to doctors and in turn to parents.

For example, the following excerpt is by Silver, a psychiatrist at Rutgers Medical School, and is found in a brochure produced by the drug manufacturer Ciba-Geigy: "The medication . . . appears to help the nervous system compensate for the deficits resulting in a decrease in motor behavior, a decrease in distractibility, or an increase in attention span. The medication will not cure learning disabilities, it will only make your child more able to learn." (Note the inference that learning disabilities is a disease amenable to "cure" and that being more able to learn has nothing to do with "learning disabilities.")

In an article in a magazine called *Drug Therapy* alongside various advertisements from companies such as Sandoz, Jellinek, a psychiatrist at Harvard Medical school, wrote (1981a): "Barkley's review of over 110 medication trials indicates that a high percentage of subjects 'improve' but notes that many studies do not define the nature of this improvement. Many studies report that after children take medication, their behavior improves and they attend to tasks better and are less impulsive. Other studies note that after being given medication, children perform better in laboratory learning tests" (p. 79). Apart from the Barkley paper, no references are cited in support of these conclusions. What is more critical, however, is that Barkley is misrepresented, because he and his colleague Cunningham found no evidence for any academic benefits of a drug regime in two reviews published in 1976 and 1978. (These reviews are discussed later.)

In the same issue of *Drug Therapy*, Jellinek (1981b) provided "A Drug Therapy Guide for Parents." The guide is supposed to clear up misconceptions that parents might have about hyperactivity, "a complex disorder that doctors are only beginning to understand." (This arouses interest in the reader because it is difficult to see how misconceptions can be cleared up about something that no one understands. This lack of understanding, however, does not prevent the prescription of drugs.) The gist of the message is that it is the child who has the problem due to some abnormality of his nervous system, making him have little or no voluntary control over his behavior. The paper states that if all else fails, then drugs are the obvious next step. "These stimulants improve the hyperactive child's ability to concentrate, and, therefore, he is better able to focus on schoolwork and other activities. It has not been shown that these medications improve your child's achievement in school over months and years" (p. 86). (This last sentence not only contradicts the one in front of it, but the comments cited in the preceding paragraph that appeared in the same magazine.) Next Jellinek informed the parents that the drugs may be highly addictive: "You may be alarmed about reports emphasizing the dangers of children becoming 'hooked on stimulating drugs.' Although this is undoubtedly a serious possibility to consider, there has been no evidence thus far to suggest that addiction to stimulating drugs is a problem among hyperactive children" (p. 86). (Does this mean that the evidence is negative or that there simply isn't any? Whichever is true this statement is scarcely comforting.)

The purpose of these quotes is to illustrate the seriousness of the problem when psychiatrists from prestigious Medical Schools lend their names and support to printed material either directly or indirectly involved with marketing efforts of drug companies. It also illustrates a singular lack of aptitude on the part of members of the psychiatric community to deal logically with the problem as a whole.

In general, the gist of these remarks is that drugs are supposed to make a child more alert and attentive to school work. We have already seen in the preceding section that if children diagnosed ADD are matched to children of equal ability, *no differences on any measure of attention can be found.* Therefore, if you put the ADD children on a drug that enhances attention, they should be superior to other children of their age and ability. That is, improvement in attentional control ought to lead to greater information processing. At least this is what everyone believes to be the consequence of paying attention. However, there is a considerable difference between the appearance of being attentive and efficient information processing. Mentally retarded children can attend obsessively to the same object for hours at a time. This is no guarantee they will learn anything about it. Thus, the claim that attentional factors are altered by the drug is completely irrelevant, unless other indices of increased performance can be demonstrated. Objective data, unlike the comments cited above, indicate that the appearance of being "attentive" induced by stimulant medication has little impact on learning in general, and no impact on acquiring new or missing skills.

In a 2-year follow-up study of boys between the ages of 8 and 10, Rapoport and her colleagues (Quinn & Rapoport, 1975; Riddle & Rapoport, 1976) followed boys who were diagnosed hyperactive and who were divided into drug and placebo groups. There was no evidence of any difference between the groups either at the 1-year or 2-year assessment, on tests of reading, spelling, or math. Other similar studies using longer follow-up periods of 4 and 5 years have indicated that neither the amount of drug dose nor the length of time the drug was administered had any impact on objective scores of achievement (Charles & Schain, 1981; Minde et al., 1971).

In an extensive review of the data on academic outcomes following a drug regime, Thorley (1984) could find no evidence that stimulant medication had any impact whatsoever on school performance. The children on a drug regime continued to show evidence of poor academic skills and poor social adjustment, despite taking drugs. However, studies reviewed by Thorley indicated that hyperactive young adults did not exhibit any greater degree of serious pathology, such as psychoses, criminal behavior, or drug abuse, than their peers.

Barkley and Cunningham (1978) reviewed a large number of short- and long-term studies on the impact of a drug regime on academic performance. In 17 short-term studies (ranging from 2 weeks to 6 months) they found no improvement in a wide variety of reading, spelling, and math tests in most (82%) of the 52 test indices that were reported. Some improvement was noted in the remaining 18%, but these effects were inconsistent, even within the same experiment. Long-term studies fared no better, and overall no impact of a drug regime was noted. In a previous review, Barkley (1976) reported that a wide variety of tests are completely unaffected by a drug regime: IQ (Wechsler and PMA), Wide Range Achievement tests and other reading tests, Tests of psycholinguistic abilities, Goodenough Draw-a-man, and Bender Gestalt. As Barkley and Cunningham noted: "The data surveyed point to a significant discrepancy between objective measures and the subjective opinions of teachers and parents on achievement performance" (p. 90). One might comment, also, on a significant discrepancy between the subjective opinions of *doctors* and objective performance criteria.

Although stimulant medication does improve performance on repetitive and boring tasks, most research indicates that drugs will not make it possible for a child to develop or expand academic skills, especially those he or she does not already possess. Despite a wealth of evidence on this topic, researchers continue to search for cognitive tasks that will show *some* impact of a drug regime. For example, a series of tasks were provided for children diagnosed ADD in a highly controlled laboratory setting (Douglas, 1985). The tasks included basic arithmetic, spelling, creating words from a 10-letter stimulus word, and paired-associate learning. It was found that children on methylphenidate performed better on paired-associated learning and completed more arithmetic problems with slightly greater accuracy than in the off-drug condition (87% vs. 80%). Spelling (which was generally poor) did not improve on drugs, even with practice, nor did the word discovery task.

Although Douglas argued in her conclusions that the previous negative results on the academic efficacy of drugs were due to "insensitive assessment techniques," this kind of remark is a red herring. The same results could have been obtained if it had been argued that the stimulant drug makes a child more compliant and able to endure performance in boring repetitive tasks. Paired-associate learning has nothing to do with academic success, and the number of arithmetic problems completed in a specific amount of time tells us nothing about a child's overall mathematical competence, which is what academic achievement tests measure.

In an extensive assessment of the impact of stimulant medication on a wide variety of behaviors, Kavale (1982) attempted through the use of meta-analysis to combine the data from a number of different studies using stimulant medication. In Kavale's assessment he selected only studies with a control group: either placebo, no-drug, or different-drug. There were 135 studies that fit these criteria. Meta-analysis is a statistical manipulation in which the data from a pool of studies using similar dependent variables are combined to produce a greatly enlarged N. The technique reduces to one global mean in standard deviation units. This value represents a shift in a dependent variable for the experimental groups in comparison to a control condition or group.

Meta-analysis results in what is essentially a $z$ score, called an "effect size" ($\overline{ES}$), represented in standard deviation units. The formula is:

$$\overline{ES} = \frac{\overline{X}_E - \overline{X}_C}{SD_C}, \text{ (the } z\text{-score formula).}$$

Usually, the normal curve is represented in standard deviation units with an $\overline{X}$ of 0. However, the $\overline{ES}$ value is the *mean change in standard deviation units*, from a control to the experimental group, so the $\overline{ES}$ is never zero, but some positive or negative value. In addition, standard deviations (of standard deviations) are also provided by the meta-analysis technique. This can result in a situation in which the standard deviations are considerably larger than the mean, and often make interpretation confusing or difficult. Kavale chooses to base his conclusions on the mean shift in percentiles, which partially gets around the problem, but does not solve it. The essential difficulty for meta-analysis is that as $\overline{ES}$ is comparable to $z$ scores, the $z$ scores need to be approximately 1.65 to be significant at the $p = .05$ level, $\overline{ES}$ values are rarely, if ever, that large, making $\overline{ES}$ difficult to assess. The highest value reported by Kavale is $\overline{ES} = .945$, cited for comparisons using the Frostig test of visual perception. Behavioral measures, such as activity levels, had $\overline{ES}$ values ranging from .118 to .886; cognitive measures ranged from .367 to .467, and physiological indicators combined value was $\overline{ES} = -.275$. The problem of how to interpret these values remains throughout the following discussion.

Before assessing the results for the cognitive measures in more detail, it is important to reveal one of the major findings of the survey. This is the fact that certain groups of researchers under certain conditions produced far larger (significantly so) effect sizes than others. Kavale carried out only pairwise comparisons between categories of experimenter, subject and design variables, and so forth, so that it is not possible to determine the extent of their additive effects. Nevertheless, to maximize the "positive" impact of stimulant medication, adopt the following procedures:

1. The senior investigator is an MD.
2. The funding is from an undisclosed or unspecified source (e.g., drug companies).
3. The research is conducted in a clinic.
4. Global rating scales are employed, especially those that are easy to bias.
5. The experimental design employs a random or nonrandom placement of subjects into drug and placebo groups.

6. The child is diagnosed as exhibiting signs of neurological problems and/or hyperactivity specifically, not in conjunction with any other behavior problems.

To minimize getting any drug effects, the protocol is the opposite.

1. The senior investigator is a PhD.
2. The funding is from a Government agency with peer review procedures.
3. The research is conducted either in the field (the classroom) or the laboratory.
4. Objective measures are employed, which are difficult to bias.
5. The control group is matched to the experimental group in age, sex, ability, and SES.
6. The child exhibits a behavior disorder, or learning disabilities or mental retardation, in conjunction with symptoms of "hyperactivity."

In every case, there was a highly significant difference between the ES values produced in these comparisons. It remains to be determined what the precise impact would be if all of these variables were considered simultaneously. One must keep all of these factors in mind, plus the problem of the lack of valid diagnostic criteria for the selection of subjects in the first place, when assessing the following results. The comparison of studies using cognitive measures showed the smallest ESs of the three categories investigated. Performance on the WISC was seen to improve marginally. Full IQ scores shifted in the position direction ($\overline{ES}$ = .453, SD = .511). The greatest gain on any subtest was in digit span (.446) and the least in block design (.067). Subtest scores were not provided for the verbal subscales, though verbal IQ was enhanced overall ($\overline{ES}$ = .412, SD = .534).

Achievement test performance showed shifts from about one third to one half of a standard deviation. $\overline{ES}$ values ranged from .094 to .628. More studies employed the Wide Range achievement subtests than any other achievement test battery. Eleven studies that investigated reading ability on or off stimulant medication produced a total effect size of .322, with a very high standard deviation of .711. Ten studies investigating performance on the WRAT arithmetic subtest showed no effect of the drug whatsoever ($\overline{ES}$ = .094, SD = .761). Once again the variance is large. Spelling on the WRAT improved only modestly with drugs ($\overline{ES}$ = .365, SD = .698). Studies employing other achievement test batteries fared marginally better with higher $\overline{ES}$ values and lower standard deviations. Six studies that employed the Iowa Test of Basic Skills produced a combined $\overline{ES}$ of .628 and an SD of .378, the best result of all the achievement test findings.

It is worth commenting that the two tasks reported by Douglas to be critical markers for drug effects, arithmetic and paired-associate learning, were not tasks that produced any noticeable effect sizes in Kavale's assessment. Performance on arithmetic was completely unaffected by drugs in 10 studies, suggesting that what Douglas had been measuring was something other than aptitude. Altogether, 15 studies on paired-associate learning produced an unremarkable $\overline{ES}$ value of only .196, despite the fact that this is supposed to be "*the* marker" for drug effects on ADD. In fact, short-term memory showed far greater improvement ($\overline{ES}$ = .617), and this is supported by the higher ES values obtained in digit span on the WISC.

Several studies were combined into a category called "attention." Because these studies utilize a variety of dependent variables, it is impossible to determine what was being influenced to produce minor improvements in performance. However, performance on vigilance tasks, especially the Continuous Performance Task, showed the greatest impact of stimulant medication. $\overline{ES}$ value was .558. Reaction time performance fared less well, with an overall $\overline{ES}$ value of .345.

Although the Frostig Test and the Bender Visual-Motor Gestalt are classified as "drawing" or "copying" tasks, they also require sustained focal attention for efficient performance. It is of some interest that these two tests produced the highest $\overline{ES}$ values of all the cognitive and attentional tasks reviewed (.945 and .606). It is obviously of considerable interest that if one wants to discover what the stimulant drugs are really doing, these two tasks are the ideal candidates for further research. The possibilities range from compliance, to slowed motor performance (speed/accuracy trade-off), to enhanced fine-motor control, to regulation of saccadic eye movements. It would be of some interest to pursue this question, that is, assuming these results are genuine and can be replicated under the circumstances outlined above.

Despite the fact that Kavale has performed a very important and useful task in bringing all these studies together, several precautions must be kept in mind in evaluating these results. First, it is extremely important that the dependent variables are *identical* across studies, and the test or task administered in as similar fashion as possible. This is a major stumbling block in many meta-analysis surveys, which often end up combining apples and oranges. Second, a meta-analysis does not solve the problem of diagnosis in determining who is selected for drug treatment, nor individual differences in reaction to drugs, nor the variation in drug dose levels from one study to another. These issues are quite separate to those already described, in which certain key factors could predispose the results going in favor or against positive drug effects. Last, there is the great difficulty of interpretation of the $\overline{ES}$ statistic, and the inability to determine absolute significance levels in any conventional way.

It is quite obvious from a variety of studies that the stimulant drugs are doing *something* that makes a child stick longer with a task he or she may not prefer. Whether that "something" is basically increased compliance (a sapping of the energy to exert willpower against an adult, for example, "mind control") or, as Douglas suggests, an enhancement of attentional control to sustain and organize effort, is a point well worth debating. But as noted earlier, neither position necessarily predicts any improvement in academic ability, at least ability that would be sustained over months and years. If academic ability was truly enhanced by drugs, we should surely know it after several decades of longitudinal research, which, despite meta-analysis, shows essentially no improvement over time with stimulant medication.

In dramatic contrast to the lack of any impact of a drug regime on academic performance is the high success rate reported with remediation in conjunction with behavior modification techniques. To be effective, however, these techniques must be specific to academic deficiencies or learning problems and be implemented through the cooperative efforts of both the parents and teachers. It is not sufficient for children who have problems in the classroom merely to be asked to "behave," and "sit still." Children, especially those who resist adult control, need to have a reason to be in the classroom. They need to be given tangible goals that they can achieve, and to feel some sense of satisfaction in achieving them. Drugs cannot possibly provide these goals or the necessary skills and structure.

Studies carried out by O'Leary and his colleagues (Friedling & O'Leary, 1979; O'Leary, 1981; O'Leary & O'Leary, 1977) and by others (Allyon, Layman, & Kandel, 1975) have shown that when the appropriate behavioral modification approach is adopted, children on stimulant drugs can stop medication entirely while academic skills and behavior continue to improve. O'Leary has found that behavioral control accompanies the new-found success in academic performance. This supports the suggestion made earlier that the learning difficulties produce the attentional problems rather than the reverse. These findings are in contrast to the poor results found with behavioral modification (with or without drugs) when learning problems are ignored (see McGuinness, 1985, for a detailed review of these studies).

## Behavioral, Social, and Emotional Factors

Drugs undoubtedly reduce fidgety behavior, and they do so in most children whether or not they are considered normal or "hyperactive" (Rapoport et al., 1980; Sostek, Buchsbaum, & Rapoport, 1980). But drugs should not be used, as seems to be the case today, as a substitute for discipline and learning self-control. However, in some extreme cases, drugs may provide a valuable tool in helping youngsters to calm down sufficiently to be able to deal meaningfully with their lives. Hyperactivity is a well-known consequence of a number of neurological problems, such as lead and chemical poisoning, minor brain damage, and parkinsonism (McGuinness, 1985). But children with these deficiencies constitute a very small proportion of the population, estimated at less than

1%. Goldstein (1987) found that approximately 1% of the more than 7,000 children tested were considered hyperactive with no other presenting symptoms.

The problem arises in diagnoses of these extreme cases, in that a variety of situational and temperamental factors can also lead to excessive activity and lack of behavioral control. This makes it difficult to disentangle cause-effect relationships when a child becomes hyperactive in response to environmental or social factors. If a child is frustrated and becomes aggressive, this automatically changes activity level. Similarly, one reaction to failure at academic pursuits is to fidget, wander aimlessly around the room, or call out to the teacher and students. The same behavior can occur if the student is bored. In such cases, it seems far more reasonable to deal with the child's problems and frustrations than to prescribe drugs.

The fact that drugs reduce motor behavior does not necessarily imply any change in attention span or information-processing ability. Although there is a high correlation between motor activity and sustained attention (see Obrist, Howard, Hennis, & Murrell, 1973), this is not necessarily an equivalent relationship. In order to maintain attention to a task, motor behavior must be reduced. However, merely reducing motor behavior does not guarantee that attention will be improved.

What might prove of interest are parental reports or objective observations on improvements in compliance, a major complaint of parents, and an aspect of the ADD child's behavior pattern that emerged from the laboratory studies on attention. There is evidence that negative behaviors diminish with stimulant medication in structured environments supervised by adults (Abikoff & Gittelman, 1985; Rapoport, Quinn, Bradbard, Riddle, & Brooks, 1974; Whalen, Henker, Collins, Finck, & Dotemoto, 1979). However, the evidence is equivocal when negative behaviors in nonstructured environments, such as spontaneous social play, are considered. Whalen et al. (1987) found that children on 3 mg and on 6 mg of dextroamphetamine reduced negative interactions with other children during free-play, with no increase in solitary play. However, the control condition in which the negative behaviors were observed was a drug-free period during the mid-point of the study. Because of rebound effects, and because the authors had no initial drug-free baseline, the increase in negative behaviors may not reflect a typical off-drug state. Other studies have not confirmed this result. Barkley (1985) and Cunningham, Siegel, and Offord (1985) could find no evidence of drugs reducing negative behaviors in social play, and there is also evidence for medication-induced dysphoria (Gittelman-Klein, Klein, Katz, Saraf, & Pollack, 1976; Whalen & Henker, 1984).

Reports from the children themselves concerning how they view the drug regime and their own behavior are few and far between. In general, studies indicate that children on a long drug treatment program feel worthless and have extremely low self-esteem as indicated by follow-up studies (Charles & Schain, 1984; Hoy, Weiss, Minde, & Cohen, 1978; Thorley, 1984; Hechtman, Perlman, Hoplins, & Wener, 1979). In a series of extensive interviews with youngsters on stimulant medication for a number of years, Whalen and Henker (1976) reported that the children come to view the drugs as a crutch and feel helpless in controlling their own behavior without them. Equally serious is the problem of attribution, as indicated by the common belief that their normal off-drug behavior is not their fault.

In a report on over 872 children diagnosed ADD in Germany (Eichlseder, 1985), comments from the children were revealing. All children, according to this report, began to complain about the drug regime by the end of the first year. The general tenor of these complaints was that they felt "unhappy" on the drug. This statement was often made in the reverse, that they wished they could be happy and carefree like they were before. Sometimes this was explained by statements that suggested the children felt a greater sense of obligation, or greater awareness, which they resented. On the other hand, these remarks may reflect a loss of spontaneity and exuberance that masked an awareness of obligations for chores and duties. In other words, the drugs erased the joyful "oblivion" of childhood, and the children expressed sadness about this. These comments were selected by Eichlseder for inclusion in his paper and would appear to represent a reasonably accurate assessment, as he expresses great support for the use of stimulant medication for children with behavior problems. It would be of considerable interest to discover whether these reactions were created by the distress of being labeled and placed on a drug regime, or by the drug itself. However, more important is the information that most children in the long-term drug group, ostensibly considered to have neurologic and psychiatric problems (hence the diagnosis ADD), were, prior to a drug regime, generally happy and carefree. This is the first evidence that we have to indicate that although parents and teachers may find an ADD child's behavior problematic, this behavior may not be a problem to the child.

So far, the data strongly support the conclusion that an extended drug regime is of greater benefit to the teacher and parent, and of little social or emotional benefit to the child. In fact, the reverse appears to be the case.

THE PIED PIPER

In drug brochures and publications aimed at parents, the stated objectives of physicians are that the child be thoroughly tested, provided with any necessary remedial help, given therapy, and so forth, prior to entering upon a drug program. In conversation with pediatricians and psychiatrists, what happens in practice is usually quite different. Parents who have children with deviant and difficult behaviors more typically seek advice from their family physician or pediatrician. Often they are not told of other courses of action prior to putting their child on drugs. Whether or not the child receives drugs is determined by that particular physician's knowledge and/or attitudes about stimulant medication. Nevertheless, for the most part the management of children diagnosed as ADD or hyperactive is carried out by the family doctor, or through referrals to another doctor who "specializes" in ADD and hyperactivity. To gain some insight as to what transpires in this process, the paper by Eichlseder (1985) published in the American Academy of Pediatrics (presumably meeting with their approval) is reviewed in some detail. This paper is especially relevant because it is a longitudinal study of a very large group of children.

Eichlseder is a pediatrician in Munich, West Germany, who has reported on his experience with 1,000 children (787 boys and 213 girls) treated for ADD or hyperactivity over a period of 10 years. The account is unscientific and often vague, but it is, nevertheless, sincere and extremely revealing. The first question that arises is, how did Eichlseder find so many ADD children in his practice? Actually, he did not. This population was attracted by his reputation for diagnosing and treating ADD, and his numerous articles on the topic published in parents' magazines. Clearly, he writes persuasively about his point of view, and parents seem eager to follow his advice, especially the upper middle-class parents. Scarcely any of the children had fathers who were blue-collar worker or unskilled laborers.

The children typically had symptoms corresponding to the DSM-III descriptors, plus academic problems and/or conduct problems, indicating that parents are being misled into seeking drug therapy for their child's learning disabilities and conduct disorders. The behavior most affected by the action of the drug: activity level, was the behavior that bothered the parents the least. As Eichlseder remarked: "Hyperactivity per se, albeit frustrating for the surrounding adults, rarely was a reason to seek help."

The diagnoses consisted of an intensive case history, a routine physical exam, and a neurologic exam, plus two psychomotor tasks that were subsequently found to be of little value. As he noted: "it is the clinical symptomatology and the associated problems that demand alleviation, that are most salient in pediatric practice" (p. 177). Of the 1,000 children, 872 were treated with stimulant medication (10mg/day) for a period longer than 6 months. Of those not treated, only 14 were considered not severe enough for treatment (14 out of 1,000 is 1.4%). Parents refused medication initially in 30 cases and the children themselves in 4 cases. In other words, Eichlseder's "diagnosis" selected as candidates for drug therapy nearly 100% of the patients who sought treatment. It might be wondered why it was necessary to take any case histories or carry out any medical examinations, unless, perhaps, there was some intention to provide help for the children's learning and conduct problems.

Not all of the patients seen remain in the program. Eighty children were discontinued from medical intervention because of noncooperation from the child, the parent, or the teacher. A further 137 experience no benefits and/ or intolerable side effects. These consisted of sleeplessness, weight loss, and symptoms of Tourette Syndrome. Many parents in this group complained that their child had a changed personality which some described as "depressed," but which appeared to reflect an abnormal degree of passivity or disinterest. One mother noted: "The fire in his eyes disappeared." Of the remainder who stayed on drug treatment, many of whom are still continuing treatment, Eichlseder considered these children as "successes," and those not on drugs as "failures." The average period of time each child remains on drugs is about 5 years, despite the fact that all children pleaded to be taken off drugs by the end of the first year.

When it came to providing any additional therapy or counseling, this was not of any concern initially because: "medication brought such a dramatic change in behavior that no additional measures were necessary." At least, this was the case for the early months and sometimes for up to 1 or even 2 years. After this early period of euphoria, however, things began to go downhill. Eichlseder reported that the social behavior began to wane on drug treatment. Apparently, behavior deteriorated to such an extent that "many children developed traits that needed additional environmental management and counseling as well as specific behavioral interventions." Some of these counseling techniques were provided by Eichlseder himself and consisted of token reinforcement, rewards, punishments, extinction, and time out. Eichlseder discusses in some detail the necessity to increase dosages and change from one drug to another as the beneficial effects evaporate.

Reading between the lines, the scenario goes something like this: Parents who can't (won't) discipline their children put them on a drug regime that provides them with a brief respite of up to 1 year. During this time, physiological tolerance (indicative of addiction) and psychological adjustments to the drug occur, and the child's behavior slowly returns to its previous undisciplined state. At this point, the dose is increased, the drug is changed, and/or behavioral techniques are introduced. Meanwhile, as much as 2 years are lost in training the parents how to control their children and in training the child how to achieve self-discipline, not to mention the inevitable decline in academic skills in children with learning problems.

Of the various learning difficulties noted at intake no further mention is made, except a comment that those children who have serious problems in academic subjects will continue to exhibit the same deficiencies, despite the medication. However, later in his concluding remarks, he said the opposite: "The outcome of treatment with these cerebral stimulants appears to be a chemically mediated advancement of the academic and the social learning process. The newly acquired control of impulsivity and new attentional capabilities lead to higher achievement in all realms of daily life and make available a repertoire of social skills that are necessary for a happy childhood and adolescence" (p. 183).

Eichlseder has no data to support this statement. Furthermore, with an initial population of 1,000 children, what a wonderful opportunity for a well-controlled study of children on and off stimulant medication. The children who were withdrawn from the medication in early months would provide an excellent control group. However, Eichlseder, like everyone else who "believes in drugs," is not remotely interested in whether they really work, or demonstrating to anyone that they do. In fact, many times in the course of the article he complains that parents asked for their children to be taken off drugs because he suspects that they were influenced by "psychologists," whose data must be familiar to Eichlseder, because he is well aware the drugs have no impact on academic performance: "Thus in judging our therapeutic efforts, we should not count grades and repeated classes, but value the child's acceptance of medication as indicative of his or her desire to sustain better performance and good behavior. . . . When one considers the resistance of some parents and children to medication, continued desire for treatment becomes an even more meaningful indicator of success" (p. 182).

Orwell could not possibly have put it better!

## CONCLUSIONS

The preceding section illustrates very well the problems outlined in this chapter, the absence of any valid diagnostic procedure, the problem of over inclusion, the failure of drug therapy to promote any academic, social, or emotional well-being for the child, and the continuing animosity that has developed between the medical and nonmedical communities over this issue, plus the apparent futility of dislodging the medical practitioner from his point of view because of the initial impact of stimulant drugs on behavior. Writing chapters in learned volumes, read by those committed to the same point of view, will not make an ounce of difference. Many of the points raised in this chapter were raised over a decade ago by Adelman and Campos (1977) and continue to be raised by those who exhibit a genuine concern for the welfare of children. The data consistently fail to support any benefits from stimulant medication. This is not to say that such benefits might not be found. However, it is up to the medical profession who employ the drugs to find them, and up to them to be aware of the research done in the field. Stimulant medication is a drastic invasion of the body and nervous system. People who employ drugs, especially to modify behavior, must convince the scientific and lay communities that these drugs have no harmful effects either physiologically or psychologically, and that in addition they provide positive benefits to the child as well as to parents and teachers. So far, the medical profession has utterly failed in this responsibility.

Whereas the medical practitioner must take the major share of the blame for the problem of overinclusion and for the excessive prescription of drugs, the academic and research communities are not entirely without blame. ADD or ADDH is "big business." This is as true for research laboratories in universities as it is for the drug companies, the family pediatrician, and the psychiatrist. Scores of research psychologists earn their living from government grants to study ADD. The eighties seem to have marked a watershed in the ability of these creative talents to dream up ever more trivial research projects and tasks. Some of these people even take a stand against what was discovered in their very own laboratories in the preceding decade. It may be a painful admission to recognize that one has spent 10 or 20 years studying something that doesn't exist, but when considering the accumulated amount of human suffering, the substitution of medication for otherwise remediable behavioral problems, then it is time to stop and think.

## REFERENCES

Abikoff, H., & Gittelman, R. (1985). The normalizing effects of methylphenidate on the classroom behavior of ADDH children. *Journal of Abnormal Child Psychology, 13,* 33–44.

Adelman, H. S. & Compas, B. E. (1977). Stimulant drugs and learning problems. *The Journal of Special Education, 11,* 377–416.

Allyon, T., Layman, D., & Kandel, H. J. (1975). A behavioral educational alternative to drug control of hyperactive children. *Journal of Applied Behavioral Analysis, 8,* 137–146.

American Psychiatric Association. (1952). *Diagnostic and statistical manual of mental disorders* (1st ed.). Washington, DC: Author.

American Psychiatric Association. (1980). *Diagnostic and statistical manual of mental disorders* (3rd ed.). Washington, DC: Author.

August, G. J., & Steward, M. A. (1983). Familial subtypes of childhood hyperactivity. *journal of Nervous and Mental Disease, 171,* 362–368.

Barkley, R. A. (1976). Predicting the response of hyperactive children to stimulant drugs: A review. *Journal of Abnormal Child Psychology, 4,* 327–348.

Barkley, R. A. (1985). The social behavior of hyperactive children: Developmental changes, drug effects, and situational variation. In R. McMahon & R. Peters (Eds.), *Childhood disorders* (pp. 218–243). New York: Brunner/Mazel.

Barkley, R. A., & Cunningham, C. E. (1978). Do stimulant drugs improve the academic performance of hyperkinetic children? *Clinical Pediatrics, 17,* 85–92.

Bradley, C. (1937). The behavior of children receiving benzedrine. *American Journal of Psychiatry, 94,* 579–585.

Bremer, D. A., & Stern, J. A. (1976). Attention and distractibility during reading in hyperactive boys. *Journal of Abnormal Child Psychology, 4,* 381–387.

Campbell, S. B. (1973). Mother-child interaction in reflective, impulsive and hyperactive children. *Developmental Psychology, 8,* 341–349.

Campbell, S. B., Douglas, V. I., & Morgenstern, G. (1971). Cognitive styles in hyperactive children and the effect of methylphenidate. *Journal of Child Psychology and Psychiatry, 12,* 55–67.

Charles, L., & Schain, R. (1981). A four-year follow-up study on the effects of methylphenidate on the behavior and academic achievement of hyperactive children. *Journal of Abnormal Child Psychology, 9,* 495–505.

Clements, S. D. (1966). Task force one: Minimal brain dysfunction in children. *National Institute of Neurological Diseases and Blindness Monograph 3.* Washington DC: US Department of Health, Education and Welfare.

Cohen, N. J. (1970). *Physiological concomitants of attention in hyperactive children.* Unpublished doctoral dissertation, McGill University, Montreal.

Cohen, N. J., & Douglas, V. I. (1972). Characteristics of the orienting response in hyperactive and normal children. *Psychophysiology, 9,* 238–245.

Cohen, N. J., Douglas, V. I., & Morgenstern, G. (1971). The effect of methylphenidate on attentive behavior and autonomic activity in hyperactive children. *Psychopharmacologia, 22,* 282–294.

Cunningham, C. E., Siegel, L. S. & Offord, D. R. (1985). A developmental dose-response analysis of the effects of methylphenidate on the peer interactions of attention deficit disordered boys. *Journal of Child Psychology and Psychiatry, 26,* 955–971.

Douglas, V. I., Barr, R. G., O'Neill, M. E., & Britton, B. G. (1986). Short term effects of methylphenidate on the cognitive, learning and academic performance of children with attention deficit disorder in the laboratory and the classroom. *Journal of Child Psychology and Psychiatry, 27,* 191–211.

Dykman, R. A., Ackerman, P. T. & Oglesby M. (1979). Selective and sustained attention in hyperactive, learning-disable and normal boys. *Journal of Nervous and Mental Diseases, 167,* 288–297.

Edelbrock, C., Greenbaum, R. & Conover, N. C. (1985). Reliability and concurrent relations between the teacher version of the child Behavior Profile: I. Boys aged 6-11. *Journal of Consulting and Clinical Psychology, 13,* 295–304.

Eichlseder, W. (1985). Ten years experience with 1,000 hyperactive children in a private practice. *The American Academy of Pediatrics, 76,* 176–184.

Freiberg, V., & Douglas, V. I. (1969). Concept learning in hyperactive and normal children. *Journal of Abnormal Psychology, 74,* 388–395.

Friedling, C., & O'Leary;, S. G. (1979). Teaching self-instruction to hyperactive children; A replication. *Journal of Applied Behavioral Analysis, 12,* 211–219.

Gittelman-Klein, R., Klein, D. F., Katz, S., Saraf, K. & Pollack, E. (1976). Comparative effects of methylphenidate and thioridazine in hyperkinetic children: Clinical results. *Archives of General Psychiatry, 33,* 1217–1231.

Goldstein, H. S. (1987). Cognitive development in low attentive, hyperactive and aggressive 6 through 11 year-old children. *The American Academy of Child and Adolescent Psychiatry, 26,* 214–218.

Goyette, C. H., Conners, C. K., & Ulrich, R. F. (1978). Normative data on revised Conners' parent and teacher rating scales. *Journal of Abnormal Child Psychology, 6,* 221–236.

Hinshaw, S. P. (1987). On the distinction between attentional deficits/hyperactivity and conduct problems/aggression in child psychopathology. *Psychological Bulletin, 101,* 443–463.

Hoy, E., Weiss, G., Minde, K., & Cohen, N. (1978). The hyperactive child at adolescence: Cognitive, emotional and social functioning. *Journal of Abnormal Child Psychology, 6,* 311–324.

Jellinek, M. S. (1981a, October). Current perspectives on hyperactivity. *Drug Therapy,* 77–81.

Jellinek, M. S. (1981b, October). A drug therapy guide for parents. *Drug Therapy,* 83–86.

Kahneman, D. (1973). *Attention and effort.* Englewood Cliffs, NJ: Prentice-Hall.

Kavale, K. (1982). The efficacy of stimulant drug treatment for hyperactivity: A meta-analysis. *Journal of Learning Disabilities, 15,* 280–289.

Kingsbury, S. J. (1987). Cognitive differences between clinical psychologists and psychiatrists. *American Psychologist, 42,* 152–156.

Kroener, S. (1975). Concept attainment in normal and hyperactive boys as a function of stimulus complexity and type of instruction. *Dissertation Abstracts International, 36,* 1913.

Laufer, M. W., Denhoff, E., & Solomons, G. (1957). Hyperkinetic impulse disorder in children's behavior problems. *Psychosomatic Medicine, 19,* 38–49.

Loney, J., Kramer, J., & Milich, R. S. (1981). The hyperactive child grows up: Predictors of symptoms, delinquency, and achievement at follow-up. In K. D. Gadow & J. Loney (Eds.), *Psychosocial aspects of drug treatment for hyperactivity* (pp. 381–415. Boulder: Westview Press.

Loney, J., & Milich, R. S. (1982). Hyperactivity, inattention and aggression in clinical practice. In M. Wolraich & D. Routh (Eds.), *Advances in developmental and behavioral pediatrics* (pp. 113–147. Greenwich: JAI Press.

McGee, R., Williams, S., & Silva, P. A. (1985). Factor structure and correlates of inattention, hyperactivity, and antisocial behavior in a large sample of 9-year-old children from the general population. *Journal of Consulting and Clinical Psychology, 53,* 480–490.

McGuinness, D. (1985). *When children don't learn.* New York: Basic books.

McGuinness, D., & Pribram, K. H. (1980). The neuropsychology of attention: Emotional and motivational controls. In M. Wittrock (Ed.), *The brain and psychology* (pp. 95–139). New York: Academic Press.

Milich, R., & Loney, J. (1979). The role of hyperactive and aggressive symptomatology in predicting adolescent outcome among hyperactive children. *Journal of Pediatric Psychology, 4,* 93–112.

Minde, K., Lewin, D., Weiss, G., Lavigneur, H., Douglas, V., & Sykes, e. (1971). The hyperactive child in elementary school. *Exceptional Children, 38,* 215–221.

Obrist, P. A., Howard, J. L., Hennis, H. S., & Murrell, D. J. (1973). Cardiac-somatic changes during simple reaction time tasks: A developmental study. *Journal of Experimental Child Psychology, 16,* 346–362.

O'Leary, K. D. (1981). Assessment of hyperactivity: Observational and rating methodologies. In S. A. Miller (Ed.), *Nutrition and behavior* (pp. 291–297). Philadelphia: Franklin Institute Press.

O'Leary, K. D., & O'Leary, S. G. (1977). *Classroom management: The successful use of behavior modification.* New York: Pergamon Press.

Paternite, C. E., & Loney, J. (1980). Childhood hyperkinesis: Relationships between symptomatology and home environment. In C. K. Whalen & B. Henker (Eds.), *Hyperactive children: The social ecology of identification and treatment* (pp. 105–141). New York: Academic Press.

Porges, S. W., Walter, G. F., Korb, R. J., & Sprague, R. L. (1975). The influences of methylphenidate on heart rate and behavioral measures of attention in hyperactive children. *Child Development, 46,* 727–733.

Pribram, K. H., & McGuinness, d. (1975). Arousal, activation and effort in the control of attention. *Psychological Review, 82,* 116–149.

Quinn, P. O., & Rapoport, J. L. (1975). One-year follow-up of boys treated with imipramine and methylphenidate. *American Journal of Psychiatry, 132,* 241–245.

Rapoport, J. L., Buchsbaum, M., Zahn, T., Ludlow, C. Weingartner, E., & Mikkelse, E. (1980). Dextroamphetamine: Cognitive and behavioral effects in normal and hyperactive children and normal adult men. *Archives of General Psychiatry, 37,* 933–946.

Rapoport, J. L. Donnelly, M., Zametkin, A., & Carrougher, J. (1986). Situational hyperactivity in a U.S. clinical setting. *Journal of Child Psychology and Psychiatry, 27,* 639–646.

Rapoport, J. L., Quinn, P. O., Bradbard, G., Riddle, K. D., & Brooks, E. (1974). Imipramine and methylphenidate treatments of hyperactive boys. *Archives of General Psychiatry, 30,* 789–793.

Riddle, D., & Rapoport, J. L. (1976). A 2-year follow-up of 72 hyperactive boys. *Journal of Nervous and Mental Diseases, 126,* 126–134.

Satin, M. S., Winsberg, B. G., Monetti, C. H., Sverd, J. N., & Foss, D. A. (1985). A central population screen for attention deficit disorder with hyperactivity. *The American Academy of Child Psychiatry, 24,* 756–764.

Schachar, R., Rutter, M., & Smith, A. (1981). The characteristics of situationally and pervasively hyperactive children: Implications for syndrome definition. *Journal of Child Psychology and Psychiatry, 22,* 379–392.

Sostek, A. J., Buchsbaum, M. S., & Rapoport, J. L. (1980). Effects of amphetamine on vigilance performance in normal and hyperactive children. *Journal of Abnormal Child Psychology, 8,* 491–500.

Stewart, M. A., deBlois, C. S., & Cummings, C. (1980). Psychiatric disorder in the parents of hyperactive boys and those with conduct disorder. *Journal of Child Psychology and Psychiatry 21,* 283–292.

Sykes, D. H., Douglas, V. I., & Morgenstern, G. (1973). sustained attention in hyperactive children. *Journal of Child Psychology and Psychiatry, 14,* 213–221.

Sykes, D. H. Douglas, V. I., Weiss, G., & Minde, K. (1971). Attention in the hyperactive child and the effect of methylphenidate (Ritalin). *Journal of Child Psychology and Psychiatry, 12,* 129–139.

Thorley, G. (1984). Review of follow-up and follow-back studies of childhood hyperactivity. *Psychological Bulletin, 96,* 116–132.

Trites, R. L., & Laprade, K. (1983). Evidence for an independent syndrome of hyperactivity. *Journal of Child Psychology and Psychiatry, 24,* 573–586.

Ullmann, R. K., Sleator, E. K., & Sprague, R. L. (1985). A change of mind: The Conners abbreviated rating scales reconsidered. *Journal of Abnormal Child Psychology, 13,* 553–565.

Weiss, G. Hechtman, L. Perlman, T. Hoplins, J., & Wener, A. (1979). Hyperactives as young adults: A controlled, prospective ten year follow-up of 75 children. *Archives of General Psychiatry, 6,* 675–681.

Weiss, G., Kruger, E., Danielson, V., & Elman, M. (1975). Effects of long-term treatment of hyperactive children with methylphenidate. *Canadian Medical Association Journal, 112,* 159–165.

Weiss, G., Minde, K., Werry, J. S., Douglas, V., & Nemeth, E. (1971). Studies on the hyperactive child: VIII. Five-Year follow-up. *Archives of General Psychiatry, 24,* 409–414.

Whalen, C. K., & Henker, B. (1976). Psychostimulants and children: A review and analysis. *Psychological Bulletin, 83,* 1113–1130.

Whalen, C. K., & Henker, B. (1984). Hyperactivity and the attention deficit disorders: Expanding frontiers. *Pediatric Clinics of North America, 31,* 397–427.

Whalen, C. K., Henker, B., Collins, B. E., Finck, D., & Dotemoto, S. (1979). A social ecology of hyperactive boys: Medication effects in structured classroom environments. *Journal of Applied Behavioral analysis, 12,* 65–81.

Whalen, C. K., Henker, B., Swanson, J. M., Granger, D., Kliewer, W., & Spencer, J. (1987), natural social behaviors in hyperactive children: Dose effects of methylphenidate. *Journal of Consulting and Clinical Psychology, 55,* 187–193.

Whybrow, P. (1984). Contributions from neuroendocrinology. In K. R. Scherer & P. Ekman (Eds.), *Approaches to emotion* (pp. 59–70). Hillsdale, NJ: Lawrence Erlbaum Associates.

Zahn, T., P., Abate, F., Little, B., & Wender, P. (1975). Minimal brain dysfunction, stimulant drugs, and autonomic nervous system action. *Archives of General Psychiatry, 32,* 381–387.

# 6 | THE CLINICAL IMPACT OF THE SIDE EFFECTS OF PSYCHOTROPIC DRUGS

Mantosh J. Dewan
Marvin Koss
*State University of New York Health Science Center
and Veterans Administration Medical Center*

*Cumulative side effects took their toll on my perception and when I could no longer tell the difference between my brother Morris and two soft-boiled eggs, I was discharged.*
—Woody Allen (1980)

It is well known that all medications, including psychopharmacological agents, produce their own side effects (SEs) and that if there are SEs to be gotten, Woody Allen's unfortunate characters will certainly suffer them all! What is less certain is the true impact that these SEs have on patients in general and on the clinical outcome of the disorder for which they are being treated.

Selected studies suggest that SEs in fact have a profound clinical impact. Side effects from psychotropics may occur in up to 100% of patients treated and lead to drug discontinuation in about 5%–10%. Side effects may cause 7.5% of all admissions to an acute psychiatric unit (Hermesh, Shalev, & Munitz, 1985), and perhaps 20% to psychogeriatric units (Learoyd, 1972). They may also cause irreversible neurological damage, and even death. More specifically, there appears to be ongoing concern regarding the toxic potential of each of the three major kinds of psychotropics (antipsychotics [AP], antidepressants [AD], and antianxiety agents [AA]). Antipsychotics can cause irreversible neurological damage in the form of tardive dyskinesia (TD) in a high percentage of chronic users. It has recently been suggested that informed consent forms, similar to those used for medical and surgical procedures but not indicated for drug therapy, be required from patients at risk for TD, and

189

that a warning label—such as on cigarette packs—be put on all AP bottles. Concern over serious SEs has prompted a newly marketed AD to be withdrawn literally weeks after it was introduced. There is such great concern about the widespread abuse and addictive potential of one of the most commonly prescribed kinds of drugs, the AA benzodiazepines, that New York State legislated the use of triplicate prescriptions for them, equating them with highly addictive drugs such as morphine and codeine.

However, others have chastised the "alarmists," noting that, from their review of the literature and in their practice, they do not find this amount or degree of SEs and conclude that psychotropics are both safe and effective (Ananth, 1987; Baldessarini & Cohen, 1986); and so the debate carries on.

This chapter, after an overview of general issues, focuses on the following questions: (a) What are the common and particularly dangerous SEs? How often do they occur? (b) What variables influence the appearance and/or reporting of these SEs? and (c) Overall, how seriously do SEs impact on the treatment process?

## A GENERAL OVERVIEW AND CRITIQUE

Despite persistent concerns about the safety of psychotropics, their SEs appear to be an understudied area, lacking systematic, sophisticated, and comprehensive coverage. A computerized literature search followed by the tracking of selected cross-references and the scanning of relevant journals and texts turned up an enormous volume of scientific data that, however, generally addressed the SEs of these drugs only peripherally. It is striking that, except in some instances, the numerous factors essential to the study of SEs were not clearly addressed. As expected, SEs were not the focus of the vast majority of these studies and so were reported only as incidental findings that were not adequately described or analyzed in relation to our specific questions. However, it should be added that the initial thrust toward proving the efficacy of psychotropics in various disorders (which spawned many excellent symptom and outcome rating scales) appears to be shifting toward keener detection and systematic evaluation of SEs, accompanied by the development of comprehensive SE rating scales (e.g., Grohmann et al., 1984; Levine & Schooler, 1986; Lingjaerde, Ahlfors, Bech, Dencker, & Elgen, 1987).

Space limitations prevent us from reporting every study we found and from critiquing the scientific merits of those we did include. Instead, we provide a more generic review of the contextual complexity in which SEs appear.

All medications, and particularly the AP and AD drugs, have multiple pharmacological actions and therefore produce a varied range of SEs in addition to their therapeutic effect. Generally, these SEs are adverse to the therapeutic enterprise and therefore unwanted, but some may be very useful.

One system (Vestergaard, 1983) classifies these unwanted pharmacological properties into two types. "Type A reactions" tend to be predictable and occur with high frequency and low mortality. They are dose dependent and therefore easily treated by simply lowering the dose (e.g., AD sedation) or the addition of another drug (e.g., extrapyramidal SEs). Most SEs occur within the therapeutic range; however, some occur at below therapeutic levels (e.g., AD-related hypotension) or above therapeutic levels (e.g., some types of AD cardiotoxicity). In contrast, "Type B reactions" are infrequent, and unpredictable, because they are unrelated to the known activity of the drug. Because they are not dose dependent, their treatment generally requires the drug to be stopped. Examples include drug allergies and neuroleptic malignant syndrome.

## FACTORS AFFECTING SIDE EFFECTS

The wide variation in reported appearance of SEs in the literature is attributable to numerous factors. Whereas some relate to the drug itself and how it is prescribed, most are extraneous factors related to such things as study design and patient characteristics.

### Drug Factors

The specific drug chosen to represent any of the broad psychotropic categories will have a major impact on the SE findings, because within each class a specific drug may have a high potential for a particular SE, whereas another may have a very low incidence. Within the AP group, chlorpromazine frequently causes marked hypotension and weight gain whereas molindone rarely causes hypotension and may actually decrease weight. Similarly in the AD group, nortriptyline causes markedly less hypotension than does amitriptyline. It is therefore important not to generalize for a whole class, for example, "antidepressant," from findings pertaining to a single drug.

The amount of drug prescribed will influence the occurrence of SEs. Generally, the higher the dose the greater the probability (and severity) of SEs. However, there is a crucial problem in comparing drug levels across drugs. Dose equivalents for different AP drugs cannot be defined with precision because reported potencies for a single drug may, as noted in the literature (Baldessarini, 1984, 1985a; Bernstein, 1988; Davis, 1985; Hollister, 1988; Mason & Granacher, 1980; Sederer, 1986; Tomb, 1988) have a 500% variance. This is a problem that appears more often with the high-potency drugs, for example, the reported dose that equals the therapeutic efficacy of 100 mg of chlorpromazine for fluphenazine or haloperidol ranges from 1 mg to 5 mg. Therefore, informed comparison amongst APs is difficult and raises questions about the efficacy and SEs literature. It is surprising that this issue has never before been adequately addressed. There are also treatment implications, because vagueness with respect to what quantity of a more potent drug is equivalent to a less potent one can lead to prescribing excessive amounts of the more potent one without apparent good justification (Baldessarini, Katz, & Cotton, 1984). With ADs and AAs, there is considerable agreement about comparable dose potency although an equivalent "therapeutic dosage range" is used instead of potency (e.g., 100–300 mg/d for the ADs desipramine and imipramine, and 2–40 mg/d for the AA diazepam).

Drug dosages are rough and removed measures of the activity of a drug at a specific brain site. Blood levels of the drug, although still remote to the site of action, are a step closer. Could they be a correlate of SEs? In a review of AP plasma levels, Baldessarini, Cohen, and Teicher (1988) found a lack of correlation between plasma levels of the drug and clinical response. Significantly, poor response was associated with both very high and very low doses and plasma levels; in fact, high levels carry the additional risk of increased SEs. Interestingly, this supports the report that APs, and haloperidol in particular, may have a "therapeutic window" with a proposed range of 2 to 12ng/mL (Van Putten, Marder, Mintz, & Poland, 1988). Noting that levels at and above the upper "therapeutic" end are known to be associated with serious extrapyramidal effects, Baldessarini et al. (1988) theorize that maximal therapeutic effects occur at doses that cause only minimal SEs, "whereas even moderate SEs are associated with less than optimal improvement" (p. 84). It may well be that unwanted SEs bear a more direct and closer relationship to plasma levels than do clinical effects. An identical conclusion has been drawn for the anxiolytics (Lader, 1984).

For ADs (the tricyclics, in particular) evidence is accumulating that SEs are related to plasma levels of these drugs. There are often considerable interindividual discrepancies between oral dose levels and plasma levels. Certainly, attempts to correlate oral dose levels with SEs and therapeutic effects can be frustrated in view of interindividual variations in plasma level of as much as 20-fold on the same oral dose.

The appearance of SEs also depends on the time of day the drug is administered. Hypotension with ADs can be avoided by prescribing multiple divided doses, whereas daytime sedation and extrapyramidal symptoms can be minimized by ordering most or all of the drug at bedtime. This was illustrated by Prien and Cole (1968), who put half of their sample of patients on chlorpromazine 500 mg four times a day and half on 600 mg in the morning and 1,400 mg at bedtime for a fixed total of 2,000 mg per day. Whereas the drug was equally effective in both groups, 10% of the first group terminated the protocol due to intolerable SEs. The latter group showed a 0% drop-out rate, and reported a significantly lower rate of SEs and a lower need for antiparkinson medication.

Rapid increase in dosage will lead to a higher incidence of SEs since tolerance and accommodation to the drug cannot develop adequately. Because some SEs develop after weeks or even months, the length of the study and the timing of SE data collection are important factors. Lack of attention to these factors will affect SE measurement.

## Methodological Distorting Factors

There are numerous methodological problems in the study of SEs. First, it is recognized that placebos produce a wide range of SEs, with headaches and anxiety being two of the most common. It is important, therefore, that both efficacy and SE studies report "true effects," which is the drug effect (or SE) minus the placebo effect (or SE). Second, some signs or symptoms that resemble drug SEs appear spontaneously in the general population. For instance, Emil Kraepelin described patients with a TD-like movement disorder years before the advent of neuroleptics. Therefore the incidence of a symptom in a carefully matched control group or in the general population must be taken into account. Third, there is the need to establish a causal relationship of the SE to the drug because SEs may resemble symptoms of the very condition being treated. For example, in a schizophrenic patient, it is often difficult to distinguish increasing agitation from akathisia (inability to sit still) or negative symptoms from akinesia (decreased mobility). A partial solution is obtained by doing a pre-drug screen for the SEs to be studied, thereby arriving at "treatment-emergent SEs." Fourth, it has been shown that differences in the method of diagnosis and data collection of SEs lead to widely discrepant results. For instance, in a study of patients on antihypertensive medications, the frequency of impotence is 10% when patients are left to report it on their own initiative, 26% when they are questioned about this, and as high as 47% when patients fill out a questionnaire in private (DeLeo & Magni, 1983). However, critics note that questionnaires or checklists may suggest complaints and thereby inflate the reported incidence. On the other hand, it is also feared that both patients and doctors vastly underassess the frequency of SEs because some are mistaken for symptoms of the disease itself (e.g., akathisia for agitation, akinesia for withdrawal/negative symptoms), as SEs and disease symptoms are difficult to differentiate accurately and objectively (Van Putten & Marder, 1987).

What does measurement of an SE involve? Is it a SE's presence or severity, or both? Also, how is a SE determined to be present? For instance, with orthostatic hypotension, is ANY drop in blood pressure a positive finding, or only if it is $> 10$ mm Hg, or only if it causes clinical symptoms such as dizziness, falls, or fractures? Clearly the "incidence" and the clinical impact of SEs will vary markedly according to the criteria used. Asymptomatic or mild SEs have no clinical impact whatsoever but may contribute to a drug's "high incidence of SEs."

Even when a standard scale is used, there remains the issue of investigator unreliability, as shown by Rhoades and Overall (1984). They studied patients who had each been rated independently by several investigators on the same standard SE scale on relatively unambiguous measures such as rigidity, tremor, dystonia, akathisia, dry mouth, constipation, blurred vision, and nasal congestion. Their analysis revealed "a highly significant difference ($p < .001$) among the 12 investigators in their average levels of SE reporting" (p. 85). In fact, this considerable unreliability contributed as much to the variance as did the differences between the drugs themselves.

How closely do results from research protocols parallel the clinical situation? Rabkin, Quitkin, McGrath, Harrison, and Tricamo (1985) have argued that "participation in a study protocol limited some options for SE management usually available in clinical practice. Consequently, more severe SEs may have had the opportunity to have developed in this sample than would have appeared in open treatment" (p. 8). Certainly, study protocols usually do not allow for the choosing of the individually most appropriate medication (e.g., the least hypotensive for an older subject) or altering the dose level to allow for tolerance and the minimizing of SEs; or switching to another class of drug if a particular SE did occur; or for the medication to be given at different times during the day. Relatively rigid research protocols will tend to inflate the incidence, severity, and drop-out rates due to SEs. However, we believe that many clinical situations do not allow for much flexibility either. For example, newly admitted severely agitated psychotic patients are routinely treated with high doses of APs resulting in rapid control and significant SEs. It should also be emphasized that, in the clinical context, a symptom reported as a SE may not be an adverse reaction but in fact useful: a sedating AD that could cause unwanted drowsiness in one patient may be the drug of choice in another who suffers from marked insomnia (Rosenbaum, 1984).

## Patient/Population Factors

Having examined some drug, methodological, and investigator influences, we were eager to learn if there were particular patient factors that influence the probability of developing SEs.

## Age

The elderly, differentially more susceptible to SEs (Friedel, 1978), are at higher risk for AP-related parkinsonism, weight gain, and tardive dyskinesia (TD); also for sedation from any of the psychotropics. The risk of AD-induced hypotension is not greater but is of concern because the consequences in the elderly (e.g., falls leading to fractures) are more serious. Learoyd (1972) suggested that at least 20% of the admissions to a psychogeriatric unit are caused by unmanageable SEs from psychotropics. Younger patients are at particular risk for AP-related dystonias and neuroleptic malignant syndrome.

## Sex

Among bipolar patients, ADs are more likely to cause women to switch from depression to mania. The best studied differences occur with AP use where men are at higher risk for dystonia (disordered muscle tone) and neuroleptic malignant syndrome, whereas women suffer more parkinsonism, akathisia, obesity, and TD. Seeman (1983) elegantly tied in age and sex effects and noted that AP "dose requirements in psychotic women seem to rise in the 40s when estrogen levels begin to fall" (p. 127). The antidopaminergic estrogens also help explain gender differences in AP SEs. Women's relative immunity to AP-induced dystonias (seen most always in young males) is attributed to the protection afforded by "an estrogen induced accommodation of dopamine-acetylcholine balance. Women's higher risk for TD in older age can be conceptualized as supersensitivity due to postmenopausal estrogen withdrawal" (p. 127).

Women predominate among users of psychoactive drugs, yet are poorly studied. Although they share some SEs with males, others are specific to women. However, all SEs may have special meaning to women. A few speculative points may be considered. Mogul (1985) suggested that giving or not giving medications to a woman patient has special meaning focused on control and dependency. She also alerted us to the possibility that psychotropics, by disrupting or stopping the menstrual cycle, threaten women's sense of order and control. Such cessation also raises pregnancy and menopause fantasies, as does AP-induced galactorrhea (milk from the breast), which can be embarrassing and is often hidden from the prescribing doctor. If a patient is pregnant and inadvertently takes drugs during the first trimester, anxiety and guilt over possible damage to the baby are inevitable and can be used to rationalize her decision to abort the baby about whom she may be conflicted.

## Diagnosis

Although the focus is on the drug being studied, the underlying disorder for which it is being used may affect the SEs seen. Brain damage and affective disorders predispose a patient to AP-related TD and neuroleptic malignant syndrome. Medically ill patients are prone to neuroleptic malignant syndrome on APs and delirium with ADs. Intriguingly, depression itself may be a risk factor for AD-induced orthostatic hypotension, which possibly could be a biological marker for depression (Glassman et al., 1983). Glassman et al.

reported that hypotension occurs in a much higher percentage of depressed patients on ADs than in nondepressed cardiac patients on the same drug. That shows a rare patient-drug-diagnosis-SE interaction rather than the more common paradigm, patient-drug-SE.

## Personality Factors

Personality variables were not addressed in the vast majority of studies. Levinson, Malen, Hogben, and Smith (1978) confirmed Klein and Rosen's (1973) findings and demonstrated that premorbid social competence significantly predicted the relative increase in extrapyramidal SEs per unit dosage of chlorpromazine. Thus, premorbid asocial schizophrenics had an increased susceptibility to drug-induced motor phenomena.

The characteristics of patients who are likely to complain of SEs are not well defined (Shapiro, 1971). However, it has been demonstrated that patients who have difficulty openly expressing their feelings (particularly negative ones) may be expressing their hostility indirectly when they complain about their SEs (Downing & Rickels, 1967). As Gutheil (1982) noted, the doctor may be deeply identified with the medication he prescribes and "telling a doctor that his pills aren't working is like telling a mother her baby is ugly!" (p. 328). It is difficult to imagine that hostility would not play a significant role in the behavior of patients who are involuntarily held by, yet dependent on, their doctor.

Another personality factor was described by Sarwer-Foner (1960). He showed that normals and patients, if they were both more action oriented and displayed a high need for control of their milieu, tended to react paradoxically to sedating medications by becoming increasingly agitated and confused, thereby requiring larger amounts of drug before sedation eventually occurred.

## Class Differences

This is another entirely neglected area. The single study we found related to the differentiation between sedative and anxiolytic effects. Hesbacher et al. (1970a, 1970b) used barbiturates and AAs in doses that made patients comparably sedated and found that although diazepam had superior antianxiety properties for middle-class private patients, there was no such difference with reference to a lower class population that clearly identified sedation as treatment.

## Ethnicity and Race

An elegant review by Lin, Poland, and Lesser (1986) notes that Asian patients improve on less than half the AP dose required by Europeans and Americans, even when equated for body weight (Lin & Finder, 1983). Asians exhibited extrapyramidal symptoms at lower doses and had a 52% higher plasma level than non-Asian U.S. patients on equal amounts of drug/kg body weight (Potkin, Shen, & Pardes, 1984).

Asians and Hispanics also respond to, and suffer SEs at, lower doses of ADs. Marcos and Cancro (1982) showed that even though Hispanics were three times more likely to suffer SEs and to drop out, their improvement rates were comparable to that of the Anglo group.

In general, pharmacokinetic studies of ADs in different ethnic groups have revealed inconsistent results. However, on comparable doses, one study (Ziegler & Biggs, 1977) found that Blacks achieved twice the AD blood level of, and improved more rapidly than, Whites. In a small study, 20% of Blacks and 5% of Whites suffered a delirium that was independent of age and plasma level, suggesting an intrinsically greater sensitivity to this SE in Blacks. (Livingston, Zucker, Isenberg, & Wetzel, 1983)

Lin et al.'s (1986) review of the scanty data on the AA benzodiazepines suggests that in Asians, these drugs are metabolized at a slower rate, are more likely to build up after chronic use, and are more likely to cause behavioral toxicity.

In summary, there are significant ethnicity and race-related differences in therapeutic dose, blood levels, and incidence of SEs that have important clinical application in our "melting pot culture." These are rarely addressed as confounding variables in research studies.


## SIDE EFFECTS OF ANTIPSYCHOTIC MEDICATIONS

Contrary to the tradition in medical nomenclature, antipsychotics (APs) are one of the rare drug classes named for their SEs (neuroleptics) as well as their main therapeutic action (antipsychotic). In fact, when first introduced, clinicians would medicate patients until SEs were produced in the belief that neuroleptic and antipsychotic activity were closely related processes. Not only has this been shown to be untrue (Cole & Clyde, 1961), but it has been suggested that the pendulum may have swung too far in the other direction. Mason and Granacher (1980) reported that inadequate doses of medications are a common cause of treatment failure and that some physicians prescribe low doses because they "may be fearful of SEs and their ability to handle them" (p. 41).

Within the accepted therapeutic dose range for APs, what percentage of patients have at least one SE? Hansell and Willis (1977) encouraged their patients to fully discuss their SEs and found an incidence of "over two-thirds" in a sample of 575 outpatients. In a cross-sectional study of 2,391 Scandinavian patients (1,259 men, 1,132 women) by Lingjaerde et al. (1987), both patients and their physicians rated SEs. Physicians found 72% to have SEs whereas 63% of the patients reported that they had SEs. More detailed ratings of these SEs (into mild, moderate, and severe categories) resulted in physicians classifying 48% of the patients in a "mild" category, 20% in a "moderate" category, and 4% in a "severe" category. The corresponding values for patients' ratings of their own SEs were 39%, 21%, and 5% respectively.

## Central Nervous System Effects

Central nervous system effects consist of two types: the early onset acute extrapyramidal disorders that are reversible, and the late onset, often irreversible tardive dyskinesia.

### The Acute Extrapyramidal Disorders

Extrapyramidal Symptons (EPS) consist of dystonias, parkinsonism, and akathisia and are the most frequently encountered SEs. Ayd (1961) reported an overall incidence of 38.9% during the treatment with APs of 3,775 patients. Cole and Clyde (1961) reviewed 23 articles covering 1,423 patients treated with thioridazine and report an incidence of just 3%. Their analysis of six of these articles showed that the use of fluphenazine in 504 patients resulted in 183 (36%) of them suffering EPS, confirming that high-potency APs are particularly likely to cause EPS, and thus emphasizing one probable reason for the wide variance in reported incidence of SEs.

*Dystonia and Dyskinesia.* *Dystonia* refers to the sudden onset of bizarre, uncoordinated, involuntary turning or twisting movements produced by massive and sustained muscle spasms. Predominately affected are the head and neck, with the most common presentation being the spasm of the tongue and mouth leading to difficulty in speaking and swallowing. *Dyskinesia* refers to coordinated, involuntary, stereotyped, rhythmic movements.

Dystonias and dyskinesias usually develop within an hour to 5 days after starting or raising the dose of APs. More males than females experience dystonias and dyskinesias (Klein, Gittelman, Quitkin, & Rifkin, 1980) with younger males being at greatest risk. The incidence of dystonia and dyskinesia has been variously reported as 1.3% (Galbrecht & Klett, 1968), 2.3% (Ayd, 1961), and even approximately 10% (Kaplan & Sadock, 1988). As noted, high-potency APs are more likely to produce dystonia. The landmark NIMH Collaborative study (1964) of 463 patients found an incidence of 6.6% with the use of fluphenazine, 1.1% with thioridazine, 0% with placebo, and a dropout rate due to dystonia of 0.5%. Another AP, thiothixene, caused 9.8% dystonia in 276 patients included in 10 studies (Ban, 1978). Even though dystonias can be quickly treated and result in a negligible dropout rate (NIMH, 1964), it has been posited that their frightful nature may lead to noncompliance (Mason & Granacher, 1980).

*Parkinsonism.* The signs of drug-induced parkinsonism are identical to those of Parkinson's disease. The first signs are usually a reduction in facial movements (masked facies), followed by a reduction in arm movements, muscular rigidity, postural instability (one of the more troublesome signs), tremor (seen at rest but disappears when performing voluntary movements), pin-rolling movements of the hand, shuffling gait, difficulty starting and stopping movements, loss of associated movements, hypersalivation, and drooling. The initial akinetic presentation (diminished motor and psychic spontaneity) is notoriously difficult to distinguish from the negative signs of schizophrenia or from post-psychotic depression and therefore "often goes unrecognized" (Van Putten & Marder, 1987, p. 15).

The frequency of drug-induced parkinsonism is greater among women then men by about twice (Kaplan & Sadock, 1988), as well as in the elderly, and in patients who have a relative with parkinsonism. This SE appears within 5 to 20 days of initiating therapy, with some degree of "tolerance" seeming to develop as, unlike antipsychotic effects, the parkinsonism tends to disappear after the first few months (Herrington & Lader, 1981).

A review by Herrington and Lader (1981) concludes that at moderate doses, parkinsonism occurs in about 15%–25% of patients. Specific large studies report an incidence of 15.4% (Ayd, 1961) and 8.9% (Galbrecht & Klett, 1968). The NIMH Collaborative Study (1964) reports a differential rate among the three subclasses of phenothiazine APs for "facial rigidity" of 12.5% for chlorpromazine, 8.8% for thioridazine, 14.3% for fluphenazine, and 5.4% for placebo, with a drop-out rate of 0.5%. Ban's (1978) review of 13 studies indicates an incidence of 21.3% in 385 patients on thiothixene. Parkinsonism is easily treated by the addition of antiparkinson agents and rarely leads to AP discontinuation. However, while antiparkinson agents decrease one SE, their addition increases the incidence of other SEs, particularly anticholinergic SEs.

*Akathisia.* Akathisia refers to a subjective desire to be in constant motion rather than to any specific motor pattern. The subjective feeling of muscle discomfort, often in the inner abdominal area, precedes the onset of overt motor restlessness. Patients may shuffle or tap their feet when seated, march in place if standing, and pace ceaselessly. This is often accompanied by fidgeting, chewing and lip movements, and finger movements. It is of vast clinical concern that akathisia is frequently misdiagnosed as agitation (and a sign of the underlying psychotic condition), resulting in an increase in medication, and a worsening of the drug-induced akathisia.

Akathisia usually occurs within 5 to 40 days of beginning therapy, is more likely to be produced by high-potency drugs, and is more frequent in females. The reported incidence of akathisia ranges from 5% to 75% (Ayd, 1961; NIMH, 1964; Galbrecht & Klett, 1968; Van Putten, May, & Marder, 1984).

The NIMH Collaborative Study (1964) shows a differential rate of 5.7% for chlorpromazine, 5.5% for thioridazine, 12.1% for fluphenazine, and 4.1% for placebo. No patients dropped out because of akathisia. Ban's (1978) review of 1,170 patients in 41 studies using thiothixene reveals an incidence of 18.9%. However, in one study when patients were specifically asked about akathisia by physicians "sensitive" to this condition, it was found in 76% of patients who had been on haloperidol for a week and in 63% of patients on thiothixene for a month (Van Putten et al., 1984). Akathisia may respond quickly to a dose reduction, or to the addition of antiparkinson or AA agents. However, it is often treatment resistant and may require a change to another AP that is less likely to produce akathisia. Akathisia, in the extreme case, can drive people to suicide or to homicide (Van Putten & Marder, 1987) and was found to contribute to 3.4% of all acute psychiatric admissions in one study (Hermesh et al., 1985).

*Tardive Dyskinesia*

Tardive Dyskinesia (TD) is a late-developing, rarely before 6 months (Kaplan & Sadock, 1988), potentially reversible, neurological syndrome consisting primarily of abnormal, involuntary, stereotyped, rhythmic movements of the face. These include spasms of the eyelids (blepharospasms), puckering of the mouth, licking, smacking, and constant tremor of the lips. The tongue darts or pushes out the cheek. Less commonly, and later, other parts are involved, for example, choreoathetoid movements of the extremities, ballistic movements of the arms. Breathing, eating, and talking may be compromised. Fine vermicular movements of the tongue may be an early sign. Because movements can be voluntarily suppressed, patients should be observed when distracted. Patients are characteristically indifferent to their condition. A significant percentage, perhaps 50%, of patients with TD claim to be not only undisturbed but also unaware of their persistent involuntary movements and continue to deny awareness even after they have been informed by their physicians (Alexopoulos, 1979; DeVeaugh-Geiss, 1979; Munetz & Roth, 1985). However, a malignant form of TD seen in younger patients may be both painful and distressing to them (Gerlach & Casey, 1988).

Tardive dyskinesia is probably caused equally by all antipsychotics and is more common in women and the elderly. Other risk factors suggested, but not established, are brain damage, the presence of an affective component, use of antiparkinson drugs, drug-free holidays (Gardos & Cole, 1983), and higher steady-state levels of a neuroleptic (Yesavage, Tanke, & Sheikh, 1987). Interestingly, TD-like movements were reported in 5% of pre-AP era schizophrenics and in 18% of elderly retirees, particularly women (Bourgeois,

Bouilh, Tignol, & Yesavage, 1980) and can also occur secondary to other drug treatment, for example, L-dopa.

A review of 34,555 patients in 56 studies revealed a 20% incidence of TD, with a trend toward higher rates in more recent studies that used standardized rating scales (Kane & Smith, 1982). The incidence reportedly increased by "approximately 3% to 4% per year after 4 to 5 years of treatment" (Kane, Woerner, & Lieberman, 1984, p. 99); and approximately 50% to 60% of chronically institutionalized patients have this syndrome. The magnitude of this problem is enormous: it has been approximated that 1% (Uhlenhuth, Balter, Mellinger, Cisin, & Clinthorne, 1983) of the 178 million adults (U.S. Bureau of the Census, 1986) in the United States take APs. If even 20% of them develop TD, then 0.2% of this population (or about 360,000 people) already suffer from TD and more may be at risk as the population ages. However, TD is reversible to some (disputed) degree with discontinuation or reduction of APs. Early signs of TD commonly remit within 6 weeks (Quitkin, Rifkin, Gochfeld, & Klein, 1977). In established cases, about a third to half may remit within 2 years, and some improvement may continue even beyond 5 years after AP withdrawal (Gardos & Cole, 1983). This still leaves a substantial number of patients with "this deeply troubling iatrogenic disorder" (Dean, 1987, p. 261) that has no known treatment.

## Sedation

Patients commonly report difficulty awakening in the morning and complain of daytime drowsiness during the first few days of AP treatment before they develop tolerance. Klein et al. (1980) noted that the total daily dose given as a single bedtime dose alleviates daytime drowsiness but not difficulty awakening in the morning. This difficulty responds quickly to the patient being gotten out of bed and active. The Klein et al. review indicates drowsiness to be variously reported as 2% to 92%. The NIMH Collaborative Study (1964) found that it was the most frequently reported SE: 53.4% for patients on chlorpromazine, 51.6% on thioridazine, 36.3% on fluphenazine, and 9.5% on placebo. The VA study (Galbrecht & Klett, 1968) reports a lower incidence of 23%, 17%, and 12% respectively for these same three active drugs, a surprising result because the VA patients were on higher doses and sedation is dose related.

## Cardiovascular Effects

The most common cardiovascular SE, orthostatic hypotension, is a fall in blood pressure that occurs when rising from a lying or sitting position to a standing one. Orthostatic hypotension may be asymptomatic or accompanied by symptoms such as light-headedness, dizziness, weakness, unsteady gait, syncope, or falls. It usually appears during the first 5 days of treatment and tolerance develops rapidly, thereby seldom remaining a significant problem. The NIMH Collaborative Study (1964) found that patients complaining of symptoms of hypotension (syncope, dizziness, faintness, weakness) ranged from 12.1% on fluphenazine to about 25% each for both chlorpromazine and thioridazine, with a drop-out rate of 0.25%. Galbrecht and Klett (1968), despite using higher doses, report lower occurrences of dizziness, fainting, and weakness, 5% for thioridazine and fluphenazine, 12% for chlorpromazine, and 7.3% for the entire sample of 297 patients. Of patients on thiothixene 12.2% to 16.9% report these symptoms (Ban, 1978).

## Anticholinergic Effects

Anticholinergic SEs are usually mild and easy to manage. Dry mouth was reported in the VA study (Galbrecht & Klett, 1968) as 12% overall, 12% for chlorpromazine, 17% for thioridazine, and 8% for fluphenazine. The NIMH Collaborative Study (1964) reported rates of 25%, 30.8%, and 18.7% respectively, with placebo being 5.4%. For thiothixene, it is 13.9% (Ban, 1978). Dry mouth is usually mild and lasts for the first few days until tolerance develops.

Other anticholinergic symptoms are constipation, which occurs in 20% to 33% of patients; urinary hesitancy in 2% to 9%; and blurred vision in 4% to 8% (Galbrecht & Klett, 1968; NIMH Collaborative Study, 1964). Paralytic ileus and urinary retention rarely occur.

## Weight Gain

Patients treated with APs tend to gain excessive weight. This compounds the fact that psychotic patients will gain weight in the early part of hospitalization even if they are not on any medications (Gordon, Law, Hohman, & Groth, 1960). It comes as no surprise then that 40% of VA and state hospital patients were found to be overweight. Gopalaswamy and Morgan (1985) studied inpatients and found 15% of the men and 36% of the women to be obese as compared to 6% and 8% respectively in the general population. Overweight was more common among the older women and among the more intelligent women. The men did not show such associations. Obesity was not associated with social class, marital status, psychiatric diagnosis, diet, or level of activity. Patients receiving two or more psychotropics were more often obese than patients receiving only one. Bernstein (1987) cited chlorpromazine as most likely to induce weight gain (up to 9 lb over 12 weeks), with other phenothiazines being roughly half as likely, and haloperidol being least likely. Another AP, thiothixene, caused an average weight gain of 2 to 11 lb in 26.6% of 500 patients in

17 studies (Ban, 1978). Weight gain is speculated to be particularly damaging to female patients' self-esteem and recovery (Mogul, 1985).

## Neuroleptic Malignant Syndrome

The neuroleptic malignant syndrome has gained close attention. It is an idiosyncratic, potentially fatal complication of AP treatment with core features of hyperthermia, rigidity, fluctuating levels of consciousness, and autonomic instability (e.g., tachycardia, hypertension, diaphoresis) accompanied by laboratory changes reflecting abnormal blood, liver and muscle function (Abbott & Loizou, 1986; Delay & Deniker, 1968; Guze & Baxter, 1985; Pope, Keck, & McElroy, 1986).

When it occurs, this syndrome starts 3–9 days after initiating treatment with neuroleptics (Pearlman, 1986), develops over a 1–3 day period (Guze & Baxter, 1985), and lasts 5–10 days, or up to 3 weeks when the patient has received depot AP medication (Abbott & Loizou, 1986). It can end with recovery, neurological sequelae (e.g., dementia, parkinsonian signs), or death (Guze & Baxter, 1985; Pope et al., 1986). Pearlman (1986) found a mortality rate of 22% for cases reported before 1980 and of 4% from 1980 to 1986. In one study, about 0.2% of roughly 500 patients receiving APs, or 14.3% of the subgroup that developed this syndrome, died (Pope et al., 1986). A higher mortality rate of 38% reported with depot AP versus 14% with oral APs (Caroff, 1980) was not confirmed in a review by Pearlman (1986).

Neuroleptic malignant syndrome occurs more frequently in younger patients, with 80% under the age of 40 years in one review (Abbott & Loizou, 1986). It is also 1.4 to 2.0 times more common in males than females (Abbott & Loizou, 1986; Pearlman, 1986). No relationships to socioeconomic, educational, or psychological factors have been reported; but patients with affective disorders (Addonizio, Susman, & Roth, 1986; Pearlman, 1986; Pope et al., 1986), organic brain damage (Abbott & Loizou, 1986; Pearlman, 1986), and medical illnesses (e.g., neurological disorders, malnutrition) may be at higher risk (Sternberg, 1986).

The estimated incidence of the neuroleptic malignant syndrome ranges from 0% (0/425 patients) and 0.2% (3/1500 over a 6-year period) (Abbott & Loizou, 1986) to 1.4% (Pope et al., 1986). Addonizio et al. (1986) examined the records of young male patients, who are believed to be at highest risk, and found that 2.4% developed the full syndrome whereas 9.8% had a milder variant.

Early detection, prompt discontinuation of the AP drug, and aggressive medical treatment are essential to prevent the mortality (4%–22%) associated with this syndrome. Wide recognition of the neuroleptic malignant syndrome is primarily responsible for the dramatic decrease in death rate, from 22% until 1980 and down to 4% since then.

Teratogenicity

The evidence about the teratogenicity of antipsychotics is not adequate to draw firm conclusions, because much of it does not consider other factors influencing birth defects, for example, use of illicit drugs, alcohol, and other medications. In addition, the "data appears to suggest that the psychotic population as a whole may represent a group with high neonatal risk independent of drug exposure" (Elia, Katz, & Simpson, 1987, p. 556).

Though most studies have not shown evidence of teratogenicity, the fact that increased congenital anomalies have been found in a large study of women receiving prochlorperazine (as an anti-emetic) is sufficient to warrant caution in the use of antipsychotics, especially during the first trimester (Elia et al., 1987).

Perinatal effects in infants born to mothers taking phenothiazines have been described, including EPS in a few cases (Elia et al., 1987).

## SIDE EFFECTS OF ANTIDEPRESSANT MEDICATIONS

The antidepressants (ADs) are comprised of the tricyclic ADs and a heterogenous group of newer drugs, which together are referred to as the heterocyclic ADs. In addition, there are the less commonly prescribed monoamine oxidase inhibitors (MAOIs), for example, phenelzine and tranylcypromine. Although sharing many SEs in common, there are differences between the major groups (heterocyclic ADs vs. MAOIs), as well as within groups. For the most part the differences are in the relative propensity (and degree) to which they cause certain SEs. There are also some SEs that are particular to a group of ADs (e.g., hypertensive crises are caused by MAOIs but not heterocyclic ADs), or to a particular AD within a group (e.g., among the heterocyclic ADs, trazadone alone causes bradycardia and priapism). For the most part we focus on the tricyclic ADs, because they are the most frequently prescribed and best studied.

The Boston Collaborative Drug Surveillance Program (1972) reported that 15.4% of patients on ADs had adverse reactions, 4.6% (of all patients) had major adverse reactions, and 0.4% had a potentially lethal adverse reaction. They report the following frequency of SEs: drowsiness in 6.1%, anticholinergic effects in 2.7%, psychotic symptoms in 1.5%, extrapyramidal signs in 1.2%, increased depression in 0.4%, and headache in 0.4%. Patients on ADs did not have a greater frequency of cardiac complications than controls.

## Sedation

Sedation or drowsiness is one of the more commonly occurring SEs of ADs (Klein et al., 1980). It varies among ADs (Hollister, 1983), with amitriptyline, doxepin, and trazadone causing more drowsiness (Berger, 1977) and nortriptyline and protriptyline causing less drowsiness (Cole & Davis, 1975). Protriptyline is reported as causing stimulation in some patients (Akiskal, 1986). Sedation is a dose-related effect. It is also one that diminishes with time. In a study (Bryant, Fisher, & Kluge, 1987) of amitriptyline SEs, complaints of sedation occurred in 15.6% of short-term (2 weeks or less) and 0% of long-term (average of 227 days) patients. Klein et al. (1980) reported a frequency for sedation of 0%–20% for imipramine and amitriptyline and 0%–15% for nortriptyline, based on a review of several studies. Sedation did not lead to drug discontinuation or dose reduction in any patients in a study of desipramine (Nelson, Jatlow, Boch, Quinlam, & Bowers, 1982), nor in a study of medically ill patients receiving ADs (Popkin, Callies, & Mackenzie, 1985). Gwirtsman, Ahles, Halaris, DeMet, and Hill (1983) found a 4% dropout rate due to excessive sedation in elderly patients receiving maprotiline or doxepin.

Available data suggest that though common, sedation is not a troublesome SE likely to limit the use of ADs.

## Anticholinergic Side Effects

A number of SEs of tricyclic ADs are due to the anticholinergic properties of these drugs (along with some adrenergic contribution) (Van der Kolk, Shader, & Greenblatt, 1978). These include the commonly occurring SEs of dry mouth, constipation, blurred vision, sweating, and urinary hesitancy, as well as the less frequent, but more serious, urinary retention, paralytic ileus, and exacerbation of narrow angle glaucoma (Baldessarini, 1985b; Hollister, 1983). The clinical occurrence of anticholinergic SEs varies among the ADs, generally paralleling their affinity for muscarinic acetylcholine receptors (Snyder & Yamamura, 1977). Amitriptyline is the most potent, desipramine the least, and doxepin, nortriptyline, and imipramine fall in between.

The frequency of anticholinergic SEs, based on several representative studies, is reported by Klein et al. (1980). Dry mouth, the most common of these, occurs in 20%–40% of patients on amitriptyline or imipramine and 15%–25% on nortriptyline. This effect is dose dependent (Szabadi, Grazner, & Bradshaw, 1980). Assessment of the frequency of this SE is complicated by the decrease in salivary secretion found in untreated depressed patients (Noble & Lader, 1971). Other anticholinergic SEs (constipation, urinary retention, disturbed vision and sweating) occur in 5%–30% of patients on amitriptyline or imipramine and in 0%–10% on nortriptyline. A study by Rickels et al. (1987), while reporting similar percentages for these SEs for imipramine, is of interest because it also reports the frequency of these SEs in patients on a placebo. Dry mouth occurs in 19.5% of patients on imipramine and 7.1% of those on placebo. Constipation, blurred vision, and sweating occur in 5.4%–8.7% of patients on imipramine and 0.8%–2.9% on placebo. All differences in frequency of occurrence between imipramine and placebo are statistically significant.

Anticholinergic SEs are said to decrease in incidence and severity with time. Bryant et al. (1987) examined this issue in a study comparing short- and long-term SEs of amitriptyline. Their results challenge this common impression for some of the anticholinergic SEs. Dry mouth, again, was the most common, reported by 18% of the short-term and only 12.5% of the long-term patients, with the severity also being less. Constipation, although reported as less severe, remained at the same incidence (about 5%) in both these groups. Blurred vision and difficulty urinating occurred in a greater percentage of long-term patients. Comparing short- to long-term patients, the incidence was 2.2% versus 7.5% for blurred vision and 2.2% versus 5.0% for urinary difficulties. The latter SE was also more severe in the long-term patients.

Though anticholinergic SEs occur frequently, they rarely lead to discontinuation of treatment with ADs. In a study (Nelson et al., 1982) of the incidence of SEs of desipramine that interrupted treatment, 3.6% of patients developed anticholingeric SEs of this severity. In medically ill patients treated with ADs (Popkin et al., 1985), 6% of patients had the drug discontinued because of anticholinergic SEs, indicating that this population may be at higher risk.

## Delirium and Confusional States

Delirium and confusional states are serious SEs of ADs. A retrospective study (Davies, Tucker, Harrow, & Detre, 1971) reported an incidence of 13% overall and 35% in patients older than 40 years. Prospective studies (Meyers & Mei-Tal, 1983; Nelson et al., 1982; Schmidt et al., 1987) report an incidence of delirium of 6%–7%, which is further supported by a retrospective study (Preskorn & Simpson, 1982) reporting an incidence of 6%. This SE usually results in a decrease or discontinuation of the AD. Though the study by Davies et al. (1971) suggested a higher incidence in older patients, subsequent studies have found no relationship to age (Meyers & Mei-Tal, 1983; Preskorn & Simpson, 1982). Concurrent medical illness appears to increase the incidence of delirium. Popkin et al. (1985) found that delirium led to discontinuation of the AD in 16% of patients with medical illnesses. In their study it was the most common cause of medication discontinuation, accounting for half the cases. In contrast, a recent efficacy study (Rush et al., 1985) reports no delirium in a group of 24 patients on amitriptyline.

Clearly, delirium is an important problem in the use of ADs, but perhaps it should be considered a toxic effect from excessive medication rather than a SE. Studies have demonstrated a clear relationship to high plasma levels of ADs in adults (Meador-Woodruff, Akil, Wisner-Carlson, & Grunhaus, 1988; Preskorn & Simpson, 1982) as well as in children (Preskorn, Weller, Jerkovich, Hughes, & Weller, 1988). Delirium occurred only in those patients with plasma levels well above the therapeutic range. Amitriptyline was more likely to cause delirium than imipramine and desipramine.

## Orthostatic Hypotension

Though also occurring with APs, orthostatic hypotension is a more serious problem with ADs. It involves a fall in blood pressure that occurs when rising from a lying or sitting position to a standing one. It may be asymptomatic or accompanied by symptoms such as dizziness, light-headedness, ataxia (unsteady gait), syncope or falls. As a result of falls, lacerations, bruises, and bone fractures have occurred, and as a result of decreased blood pressure, angina, myocardial infarction and transient ischemic attacks could occur (Glassman, Giardina, Perel, & Davies, 1979; Jarvik, Read, Mintz, & Neshkes, 1983; Marshall & Forker, 1982; Schneider, Sloane, Staples, & Bender, 1986; Tesar et al., 1987).

The reported incidence of AD-induced orthostatic hypotension varies from 0% to 100% (Tesar et al., 1987), depending on the ADs used, patients studied, and whether orthostatic hypotension or its consequences are examined. The ADs most studied are imipramine and nortriptyline, with more limited data available on others.

Although Hayes, Born, and Rosenbaum (1977) report that 100% of the 19 depressed inpatients on imipramine or clomipramine they studied had "striking orthostatic hypotension sometime during the first 2 weeks of treatment" (p. 510), only 11% had severe orthostatic hypotension (i.e., were unable to walk) and in only 5.3% (1 patient) was the medication discontinued. Other studies with imipramine report clinically significant orthostatic hypotension in 6% to 20% of patients (Glassman et al., 1979; Roose et al., 1987). In the Glassman et al. (1979) study, in which orthostatic hypotension led to changes in treatment in 20% of inpatients, they report falls, ataxia, or both in 14% of the total (30% of these resulted in fractures or lacerations requiring suturing) and severe, prolonged dizziness leading to modification or discontinuation of the treatment in 6%. In contrast, Tesar et al. (1987), studying outpatients receiving various ADs (mostly imipramine and desipramine), found only 7% of patients developed symptomatic orthostatic hypotension that resulted in inadequate dosing, syncope, or drug discontinuation. Though

4% had syncopal episodes, no injuries were sustained. Tesar et al. (1987) attributed this better outcome to the health and younger age of this outpatient population. Symptomatic orthostatic hypotension requiring dose reduction or discontinuation has been reported in 7.1% of patients on desipramine (Nelson et al., 1982) and 0% on nortriptyline (Glassman et al., 1979; Roose et al., 1987; Schneider et al., 1986; Tesar et al., 1987).

Cardiac disease is an important factor that increases the risk of clinically significant orthostatic hypotension. Congestive heart failure (Glassman et al., 1983) and conduction disease (Roose et al., 1987) increase the risk, but a history of myocardial infarction does not (Veith et al., 1982). Orthostatic hypotension requiring medication discontinuance in patients on imipramine occurs in 47% of patients with congestive heart failure (Glassman et al., 1983), and in 32% of patients with conduction disease (Roose et al., 1987). Discontinuation with nortriptyline occurs in only 5% of patients with conduction disease (Roose et al., 1987). Age and sex do not appear to be risk factors for orthostatic hypotension, though the consequences may be more serious in the elderly (Glassman et al., 1979). The concurrent use of blood pressure lowering medications appears to increase the risk (Tesar et al., 1987). In addition, the degree of pretreatment orthostatic blood pressure drop is the best predictor of orthostatic hypotension during treatment (Glassman et al., 1979).

Although orthostatic hypotension is clearly a significant SE of ADs, limiting treatment in up to almost 50% of patients with congestive heart failure and conduction disease when imipramine is used, it can be minimized with the use of nortriptyline. In the absence of cardiac illness, clinically significant orthostatic hypotension occurs in 0% to 20% of patients, largely depending on the AD used.

As with the heterocyclic ADs, orthostatic hypotension occurs with the use of MAOIs. Nies and Robinson (1982) report that orthostatic hypotension occurs in 40% of patients on phenelzine, and dizziness, a common symptom, occurs in 5%–10%. Klein et al. (1980) report dizziness in 0%–25% of patients on phenelzine and 5%–20% on tranylcypromine, based on data from a number of studies. Rabkin, Quitkin, Harrison, Tricamo, and McGrath (1984) report severe orthostatic hypotension (with patients passing out and/or having repeated falls) in 11% of patients on phenelzine and 14% of patients on tranylcypromine compared to 9% on imipramine and 0% on placebo. No age or sex relationships were found (Rabkin et al., 1984). Not all patients with orthostatic hypotension required discontinuation of the drug. Tesar et al. (1987) report an incidence of 21% of clinically significant orthostatic hypotension (dose reduction in 14% and discontinuation in 7%). In a study by Kronig, Roose, Walsh, Woodring, and Glassman (1983) 14% of patients had changes in treatment because of orthostatic hypotension. The majority (about 70%) developed severe orthostatic hypotension in the first 2 months. Unlike tricyclic ADs, orthostatic hypotension caused by MAOIs diminished after a month on medication (Kronig et al., 1983).

It has been suggested that depression itself may put patients at higher risk for AD-induced orthostatic hypotension (Glassman et al., 1983). More cardiac patients who are treated with imipramine for depression experience clinically significant orthostatic hypotension than nondepressed patients treated with imipramine for arrhythmias. It has also been found that patients with a pretreatment drop in systolic blood pressure with postural changes of greater than 10 mm Hg have a higher likelihood of responding to AD treatment than those who show a lesser change (Davidson & Turnbull, 1986; Jarvik et al., 1983; Schneider et al., 1986). These findings suggesting a greater tendency for depressed patients to have orthostatic hypotension are consistent with evidence of noradrenergic dysregulation in depression (Rudorfer, Ross, Linnoila, Sherer, & Potter, 1985).

## Heart Rate–Tachycardia

Increased heart rate or tachycardia and the accompanying symptom of palpitations are often mentioned SEs of ADs, especially the tricyclics (Baldessarini, 1985b; Hollister, 1983; Luchins, 1983). If it occurred to a significant degree, it could theoretically create a hazard for patients with coronary artery disease and angina by increasing the heart's demand for oxygen. However, studies have found that on the average most ADs cause only a small increase in heart rate (Burckhardt, Raeder, Muller, Imhof, & Neubauer, 1987; Reed et al., 1980; Smith, Chojnacki, Hu, & Mann, 1980). In addition, tricyclic ADs may cause a small decrease in heart rate in perhaps as many as 50% of patients (Reed et al., 1980; Smith et al., 1980). Phenelzine has also been shown to cause a small decrease (7 beats/min) in heart rate (McGrath et al., 1987). The various ADs differ as to the occurrence of changes in heart rate (Glassman & Bigger, 1981; Hayes, Gerner, Fairbanks, Moran, & Waltuch, 1983). In overdoses tachycardia is quite frequent, occurring in 30%–71% of patients (Langou, VanDyke, Tahan, & Cohen, 1980; Marshall & Forker, 1982). In conclusion, it appears that changes in heart rate and tachycardia are not a clinically significant SE in most patients on ADs at therapeutic dose levels (Glassman & Bigger, 1981; Nelson et al., 1982).

## EKG Effects

A number of effects on the EKG are reported with tricyclic AD treatment. The typical changes are increases in P-R interval, QRS and QTc and decrease in T wave amplitude (Baldessarini, 1985b; Glassman & Bigger, 1981). These reflect the quinidine-like slowing of conduction within the heart, especially distal to the bundle of His (Risch, Groom, & Janowsky, 1981). At therapeutic doses, in most cases, these changes are of no clinical significance, the exception being patients with preexisting conduction disease (Glassman & Bigger, 1981; Roose et al., 1987).

## Sudden Death (Cardiac)

Evidence from the Boston Collaborative Drug Surveillance Program (1972) found no evidence for inpatients receiving ADs to be at greater risk of sudden death than a control group. This report indicated a frequency of sudden death of 0.4% in patients on ADs and 0.3% in those not on ADs. This study involved patients admitted to the hospital for medical or psychiatric illnesses. The patients received a number of different ADs, with most on amitriptyline, at relatively low doses (mean daily dose of amitriptyline was 71 mg).

## Sexual Dysfunction

Available data on sexual SEs of ADs are quite limited. They consist for the most part of case reports, small studies, and information obtained from pharmaceutical firms (Mitchell & Popkin, 1983). Sexual dysfunction attributed to ADs include changes in sexual desire, erectile dysfunction and impotence, ejaculatory problems (including painful or delayed ejaculation), orgasmic dysfunction in women, and with trazadone, priapism (DeLeo & Magni, 1983; Mitchell & Popkin, 1983). On the positive side, phenelzine may increase spermatogenesis (DeLeo & Magni, 1983) and a MAOI (isocarboxazid) was reported to successfully treat 6 patients with premature ejaculation (Mitchell & Popkin, 1983).

A double-blind controlled study by Harrison and colleagues (1986) evaluated the effect of imipramine and phenelzine on sexual function in 82 depressed patients. Of their initial sample, 10% were excluded from the study because of pretreatment sexual dysfunction. Patients were randomly assigned to one of three groups: placebo, imipramine (200–300 mg/d), or phenelzine (60–90 mg/d). Then, following a 10-day placebo wash-out period, they were treated for 6 weeks. A questionnaire, in which patients rated items pertaining to sexual interest, ability, and frequency, was used to assess sexual functioning. The study found that both medications caused a statistically significant decrease in sexual functioning compared to placebo. The frequency of decreased sexual functioning was 30% in the imipramine group, 40% with phenelzine, and 6% with placebo. Improved sexual functioning occurred in 15% of patients on imipramine, 4% on phenelzine, and 9% on placebo. Patients with sexual dysfunction had a higher mean imipramine/desipramine plasma level than those with no dysfunction.

Klein et al. (1980) report increased sexual desire in 0%–20% of patients on phenelzine and decreased sexual desire in 0%–10%. Nies and Robinson

(1982) cite an estimated frequency of "impaired sexual response" in 20% of men and perhaps 5% of women taking phenelzine. In Rabkin and colleagues' (1985) study of clinically significant SEs they found impotence or anorgasmia in 22% of patients on phenelzine and 2% on tranylcypromine. This made sexual dysfunction the most common SE of phenelzine in their study.

Sexual dysfunction may decrease or remit with time, perhaps after only a few weeks (Harrison et al., 1986; Rabkin et al., 1985). In contrast, Evans, Davidson, and Ratt (1982) reported a 14% incidence of sexual dysfunction emerging after 3–6 months of treatment.

## Induction of Manic/Hypomanic Episodes

Clinically, ADs (including MAOIs) seem to precipitate a "switch" from depression to mania or hypomania in patients treated for depression, especially bipolar patients (Baldessarini, 1985b; Wehr & Goodwin, 1987). In some cases ADs have been considered the cause of rapid cycling in bipolar patients. Some studies suggest a switch rate among patients on ADs of about 8% for unipolars and 33% for bipolars, but other studies yield widely divergent figures (Angst, 1987; Lewis & Winokur, 1987; Wehr & Goodwin, 1987). Unipolars primarily switch to hypomania (Wehr & Goodwin, 1987).

Unfortunately, the scientific data for these observations are far from conclusive. Available data are derived from drug efficacy studies not designed to address this question or come from studies that are retrospective, have skewed samples, or lack control groups. A number of the studies do not adequately distinguish between drug-induced switching and the inherent course of bipolar affective disorder. Nevertheless, in a recent critical review of the literature on this subject Wehr and Goodwin (1987) concluded that "the available evidence suggests that ADs can precipitate mania and hypomania in bipolar patients" (p. 1409). The actual incidence awaits further study.

## Suicide

The prevalence of suicide and suicidal attempts has been shown to decrease with increasing doses of ADs, occurring in about 30% of patients at low doses or with no treatment and in 0.5% at high doses (Baldessarini, 1985b).

## Weight Gain

A number of studies have reported weight gain with heterocyclic ADs (Bernstein, 1987). Average weight gains of about 3–13 lb were found in patients on amitriptyline, nortriptyline, and imipramine for periods up to 9 months. Carbohydrate craving was reported by 73%–87% of patients (compared to 29%, in patients who had the medication discontinued). Interestingly, in 6 normal volunteers given 100 mg/d of amitriptyline for 28 days, no weight gain was found. Studies report no average weight gain with desipramine and fluoxetine. In fact, these ADs resulted in weight loss (greater for fluoxetine than desipramine). In the reported study of desipramine, weight loss occurred in 77%, weight gain in 19%, and no change in weight in 3%. In a study (Levitt, Joffee, Esche, & Sherret, 1987) of desipramine's effect on weight in depressed patients, comparing responders to nonresponders, there was a statistically significant weight gain of about 2 lb in responders at 8 weeks but no statistically significant change in the nonresponders. This suggests weight gain is related to improvement in depression and not to the administration of desipramine.

Weight gain is not commonly mentioned as a problem with MAOIs. Yet Nies and Robinson (1982) report an estimated frequency of overeating and weight gain in 10%–15% of patients on phenelzine. Rabkin and colleagues (1985) report significant weight gain as occurring in 8% of patients on phenelzine but in none of the patients receiving tranylcypromine or imipramine. Of patients with this SE, 82% were females.

## Hypertensive Crises—"Tyramine-Cheese Reactions"

Though infrequent, hypertensive crises constitute the most serious and significant SE of MAOIs. This does not occur with heterocyclic ADs. The relationship between dietary intake of food, in particular cheese, and the occurrence of hypertensive crises was first suggested by Blackwell (1963). This was soon followed by Asatoor, Levi, and Milne (1963) suggesting that it was the tyramine in cheese that was responsible for the reaction. Subsequently it has been found that the reaction is caused by the interaction between MAOIs and foods containing tyramine (e.g., cheeses, yeast products, pickled herring, etc.) as well as medications containing sympathomimetic agents (e.g., amphetamines, decongestants) (Baldessarini, 1985b).

The reaction can cause severe headaches and other symptoms of elevated blood pressure (e.g., palpitations, sweating, pallor, nausea, chest pain, apprehension). In severe cases it can result in intracranial bleeding and even death (Baldessarini, 1985b; Klein et al., 1980).

Blackwell, Marley, Price, and Taylor (1967) estimate that the incidence of hypertensive crises in patients taking MAOIs is 4.3%, with a relative incidence of 8% for tranylcypromine and 1.5% for phenelzine. They give incidences reported between 1961 and 1964 as ranging from 0.28% to 20% of patients treated with tranylcypromine, with a mean of 9.9%. They state that with the recognition of the syndrome, its cause, and the need for dietary restrictions, the frequency has declined. Blackwell et al. (1967) found no relationship between age, sex, personality, or predisposition to headache and the occurrence of hypertensive crises.

According to Klein et al. (1980) in a group of about 22,000 patients on MAOIs, 2.1% developed paroxysmal headaches and about 0.3% more serious hypertensive syndromes. They note that the "estimated risk in a patient being treated with MAOIs is about 2% for headaches, 0.3%–0.5% for hypertensive crises, and less than 0.001% for death" (p. 463).

Teratogenicity

Evidence for teratogenic effects of tricyclic ADs consists of case reports and retrospective studies. Though these suggest a relationship to congenital abnormalities (birth defects) "the small number of cases and the concomitant use of other medication in the study population prevent any definite conclusions" (Elia et al., 1987, p. 549).

No evidence is available on the effects of MAOI use during pregnancy.

## SIDE EFFECTS OF ANTIANXIETY AND HYPNOTIC DRUGS

One of the most frequently used class of drugs in the world, the benzodiazepines are by far the most widely prescribed antianxiety (AA) drugs today, which is considered a tribute to their efficacy and remarkable safety. Other AAs like the dangerous barbiturates are obsolete, and drugs like meprobamate and hydroxyzine are infrequently prescribed. Comprehensive surveys of the general population revealed that about 10% (Mellinger & Balter, 1981) to 22% (Parry, Balter, Mellinger, Cisin, & Manheimer, 1973; Uhlenhuth, Balter, & Lipman, 1978) used benzodiazepines at least once in the past year; and of this group 15%–20% still took them after 6 months (Williams, Murray, & Clare, 1982), 2.4% had used them every day of the past year, and 0.7% had used them for 7 years or more (Petursson & Lader, 1984). There are twice as many women users as men. AAs are most often used in the 50–64-year age range, but less frequently in the elderly (Mellinger & Balter, 1981). Severe SEs are essentially unknown. The frequent but mild and easy to manage SEs have been described as an "inconvenience." Adverse effects occur at higher plasma levels and are dose related, but blood levels are not related to the clinical efficacy of anxiolytics (Lader, 1984).

The specific SEs of the benzodiazepines are now reviewed.

Sedation

The most common SE, drowsiness, is a transient phenomenon that is observed for a day or two after initiating the anxiolytic or raising its dose. Although sedation occurs in every age group, it is more likely in the elderly (Pitts, Fann, Sajadi, & Snyder, 1983) and less likely in chronic smokers (Boston

Collaborative Drug Surveillance Program, 1973). It was found by Svenson and Hamilton (1966) to occur in 3.9% of 17,935 patients given chlordiazepoxide in 287 studies. Recent drug company advertisements give figures of 15.9% sedation in 3,500 anxious patients treated with lorazepam, and 14% in 1,003 patients on triazolam versus 6.4% on placebo. Other signs of central nervous system depression such as ataxia (3.9%), muscular weakness (0.3%), and dysarthria (0.2%) may also be seen (Svenson & Hamilton, 1966).

In general, long-acting benzodiazepines (e.g., diazepam, flurazepam) are more likely than short-acting agents (e.g., oxazepam, triazolam) to produce cumulative sedation, which may affect psychomotor and intellectual function. Although it is important to warn the patient about this, cumulative sedation is offset by tolerance, and so, SEs are mild even on high doses.

## Behavioral Toxicity

"Behavioral toxicity" with signs of central nervous system excitation, rather than depression, was reported in 0.2%–0.3% of 4,709 patients treated with anxiolytics (Greenblatt, 1976). Patients displayed "paradoxical" psychomotor hyperactivity, hostility, irritability, rage reactions, or strange behavior. Whereas this reaction has been seen as paradoxical by many, others have hypothesized that in patients with poor impulse control or with aggressive tendencies, the anxiolytic disinhibits sufficient hostility to result in a rage reaction, and thus, in these patients this is a predictable response (DiMascio, Shader, & Giller, 1970).

## Dependence and Withdrawal

It has been convincingly established that all benzodiazepines can cause psychological and physical dependence, which is an issue of great concern. In an influential monograph, Marks (1985) noted that numerous studies show that subjects consistently choose barbiturates and amphetamines over benzodiazepines; some even prefer placebos over them. On the streets, they are not a primary drug of abuse. In the clinical situation, studies (Bush, Spector, & Rabin, 1984; Tessler, Stokes, & Pietras, 1978) indicate that patients actually consume far fewer tranquilizers than prescribed and that "few patients take benzodiazepines on a continuous basis" (Marks, 1985, p. 72), usually preferring lower doses on an "as needed" basis. When AAs were available on demand to patients, there was no evidence of increased intake. In fact, use very closely followed the level of anxiety and tended to decrease with time (Balmer, Battegay, & Von Marschall, 1981; Winstead, Anderson, Eilers, Backwell, & Zaremba, 1974). These data are consistent with an unusual feature of the benzodiazepines, namely, although long-term use carries a substantial risk of dependence, "classic" dependence does not occur in that tolerance (i.e., the need for ever-increasing doses to meet the same demand) does not develop.

Marks (1985) also pointed out that AAs are excellent and remarkably safe drugs compared to the barbiturates they replaced and that morbidity from chronic AA use is "infinitely" (p. 70) less than from alcohol or tobacco.

But what of the high dependence potential even with a few months of use at therapeutic levels and the almost universal withdrawal symptoms associated with even gradual tapering? Initially it was reported that abrupt discontinuation after long stretches on high doses would lead to withdrawal symptoms, including severe ones like psychosis and seizures. It is now confirmed that withdrawal occurs even with gradual reduction of therapeutic doses in up to half the patients. More specifically, the risk of withdrawal has been estimated as "virtually nil" for use less than 4 months, and "relatively small" under a year, after which it "rises steeply." It is 5%–10% after 6 months and 25%–45% after 2–4 years of AA use (Marks, 1985).

Withdrawal symptoms may be varied and include confusion, clouded sensorium, heightened sensory perception, dysosmia, paresthesias, muscle cramps, muscle twitch, blurred vision, diarrhea, decreased appetite, and weight loss (Pecknold, Swinson, Kuch, & Lewis, 1988). Tachycardia, hypertension, tremulousness, sweating, dysphoria, depression, agitation, insomnia, and nausea have also been reported. Withdrawal symptoms are more rapid in onset and more severe after stopping relatively short-acting benzodiazepines, particularly alprazolam (Browne & Hauge, 1986). It is therefore recommended that these drugs be tapered over 4 weeks, and perhaps 8 weeks with alprazolam (Pecknold et al., 1988). In a recently reported, large, multicenter study of 525 anxious patients treated with an average of 5.7 mg of alprazolam per day for 8 weeks, tapering led to 35% of the patients exhibiting rebound (i.e., recurrence of the original symptoms of the disorder but with greater severity) and 35% experiencing a "distinct, transient" but not severe withdrawal that lasted a week (Pecknold et al., 1988). In an earlier study, Tyrer, Owen, and Dowling (1983) found that 45% of their patients who had been on continuous therapy for an average of 4 years reported two or more withdrawal symptoms when their AAs were tapered. In contrast, 22% of the patients had withdrawal symptoms on steady doses of AAs when they thought they were being withdrawn.

## Overdose

Despite their widespread use, anxiolytics are remarkably unlikely to cause death by overdose. We could find only 3 documented cases where benzodiazepines were solely responsible. Finkle, McCloskey, and Goodman (1979) studied 1,239 cases sent to the medical examiner and found 941 where drugs were reported as the cause of death. Benzodiazepines in combination with alcohol were

responsible for 51 (4.1%) fatalities. In just over half of the fatalities benzodiazepines were found in therapeutic range and did not contribute toward death.
Benzodiazepines alone were deemed solely responsible for death by overdose in
only 2 (0.16%) cases. Prescott (1983) found only 1 (0.01%) of 8,000 cases over
20 years to be linked solely to benzodiazepine use.

## Teratogenicity

Though several retrospective studies suggested a significant association between benzodiazepine exposure during the first trimester of pregnancy and
oral clefts and cleft palate in the offspring, subsequent studies have not
confirmed this relationship. Overall the evidence suggests no significant risk
for birth defects in children whose mothers took benzodiazepines during the
first trimester of pregnancy, with the exception of a suggestion that infants
may be at greater risk of inguinal hernias (Elia et al., 1987). Concern has
been expressed about the continuous use of benzodiazepines during pregnancy,
because it may accumulate in fetal tissue and lead to muscle hypotonia,
hyperbilirubinemia, hypothermia, and withdrawal at birth (Elia et al., 1987).

## CONCLUSIONS

It is clear from our review that Woody Allen's pathetic character is not the
exception; the majority of patients on psychotropics suffer SEs. In fact it is
probably true that a patient is as—or more—likely to have an SE than a
clinical response! However when considering the impact of SEs, the severity
of symptoms is more important than their frequency. Most patients suffer mild
SEs that are of statistical but not clinical significance. Some suffer additional
misery due to SEs like delirium, akathisia, or AA withdrawal; these are usually
transient phenomena measurable in days, with no known permanent sequelae.
Serious complications, such as neuroleptic malignant syndrome and hip fractures from orthostatic-hypotension-induced falls, that have an associated risk
of chronic disability or even death occur in a fraction of these patients. Finally
there is the distressingly large group of patients who have neurological damage
(TD) that is irreversible in a substantial percentage of cases. Psychotropic
SEs, besides causing personal anguish, also levy a fiscal penalty. When outpatients suffer unmanageable SEs, costly hospitalizations result. Unreplicated
studies done outside the United States indicate that SEs cause 7.5% of all
general psychiatric and 20% of psychogeriatric admissions (Hermesh et al.,
1985; Learoyd, 1972), considerably adding to the cost of psychiatric care.
However, the Boston Collaborative Study (Miller, 1974) found that only
3.7% of 7,017 admissions over 3 years were due to SEs from a host of drugs,
and of these, all psychotropics combined were responsible for just 3% (or 3
patients per year). This U.S. study suggests a substantially lesser problem,

which would nevertheless cost additional monies nationwide. The treatment of SEs suffered by inpatients may also increase costs by prolonging hospital stays. One study (Schmidt et al., 1987) found that patients who developed delirium stayed twice as long as those who did not (95 days vs. 45 days). This ratio suggests that the cost of treating serious SEs of psychotropic drugs may also add substantial amounts to the health bill.

The widely varying incidence rates and often conflicting data make a more precise evaluation of the impact of SEs difficult. The limitations of the available information on SEs must be emphasized. Unfortunately, much of the data on SEs are not derived from well-designed studies. The numerous difficulties inherent in studying SEs must also be considered. The patient must identify a symptom being experienced as a SE related to the medication and report it, or a physician must detect an observable SE. The symptom has to be established as a SE and distinguished from symptoms of the illness being treated or from incidental intercurrent causes. Even with carefully developed algorithms, reliably determining if a treatment emergent symptom is a drug SE can be a stumbling block (Grohmann, Dirschedl, Scherer, Schmidt, & Wunderlich, 1985). Many of the reported SEs of ADs, for example, have been found to occur in untreated depressed patients and these must be distinguished from the true SEs (Busfield, Schneller, & Capra, 1962; Letemendia & Harris, 1959; Mathew, Weinman, & Claghorn, 1980; Rabkin et al., 1984). This points to the importance of a placebo control group or the establishment of pretreatment rates of "side effects" in determining accurately the incidences of true SEs. Without measures to determine only true SEs, the incidence of SEs may be overestimated. This might be balanced by the likely underestimation of incidence resulting from the common use of patient reports and symptom checklists. Checklists, of course, limit results to only those SEs included. That even significant and obvious SEs may not be acknowledged or reported by patients is demonstrated in the case of TD (Alexopoulos, 1979). Even studies that measure the incidence of SEs by their readily recognized, "objective" consequences, such as drug discontinuation, are dependent on subjective factors such as the physician's judgment or the patient's tolerance of the distress SEs cause. For the most part, studies reporting on the incidence of SEs do not give information on their magnitude or severity, without which the significance of these cannot be determined. When a measure of severity is included, interesting and important information can emerge. For instance, Schmidt et al. (1984) found that the AD amitriptyline caused SEs in 62%–79% of patients, leading to discontinuation in 10%–16%, whereas another AD, doxepin, caused SEs in more patients (96%) but led to discontinuation in fewer patients (4%).

Two other factors need to be considered in understanding the variations in reported incidence of SEs. First, the incidence of a SE may vary among drugs within a class of medications. For example, AD-induced orthostatic hypotension is reported in 6%–20% of patients on imipramine and 0% on nortriptyline (Glassman et al., 1979; Roose et al., 1987; Schneider et al., 1986; Tesar et al., 1987). Secondly, the patient population studied can affect the incidence of a SE. Incidence can be affected by whether inpatients or outpatients, medically ill or healthy patients are studied. It should be noted that most studies involve hospitalized patients, whereas most medications are prescribed to outpatients. Caution is needed in generalizing from data on one drug to the entire class and from one patient population to another.

How do the different classes within the psychotropic group compare amongst themselves, and, are the concerns raised at the head of this chapter regarding their toxicity justified?

Of the three psychotropic classes, APs are the most likely to produce serious SEs, followed by ADs, and AAs. As a rough estimate, over a 1 year period 1% of the adult population in the United States, that is, 1.78 million people, take APs (Uhlenhuth et al., 1983). Overall, 60%–75% of patients on APs get SEs, and about 5% have to discontinue that AP medication. Antipsychotics are of concern primarily due to their potential for causing TD and neuroleptic malignant syndrome. Yet, it is remarkable that even after years of wide recognition of these disorders, it is not known precisely how many people suffer from them. Therefore, we attempted to estimate these figures by constructing a best- and worst-case scenario, recognizing that they would be rather crude estimates because some essential data are still unknown. We constructed the best-case scenario for TD by modifying Gerlach and Casey's (1988) calculations. They use a 15% prevalence rate of TD from which they subtract 5% for spontaneously occurring abnormal TD-like movements in the general population to arrive at a true drug-induced prevalence of 10%. Because this is a point prevalence figure, an annual incidence rate of 3% is added to it in order to roughly approximate the annual prevalence rate (not yet reported for TD), which would therefore be 13%. Using 1986 U.S. census figures, that would amount to roughly 230,000 people who suffered TD at any time during that year. Gerlach and Casey argue that TD would remit in 60% of these patients, even in those who have to continue APs (although judiciously and on a lower dose). Thus the remaining 40% (approximately 90,000 people) or about 5% of all patients on APs suffered permanent TD that year. A worst-case scenario was similarly constructed. A 25% prevalence rate of drug-induced TD was assumed and 5% was added to approximate the annual prevalence rate, which would therefore be 30%. Of the remaining 70% of patients without manifest TD, a third, that is, an additional 23%, could manifest "emergent" TD when their AP drugs are withdrawn (Kane, Woerner, & Lieberman, 1988). Thus a total of 53% (or approximately 945,000 people) could have had TD in 1986. Because a prospective study found that stable remission may occur in only 33% of patients with TD (Kane, Woerner, Borenstein, Wegner, & Lieberman, 1986), irreversible or recurring

TD may be predicted in 35% of all patients on APs, that is, approximately 625,000 people in 1986. Our estimates that 90,000 to 625,000 people suffer irreversible TD in a given year underscore the seriousness and enormity of this problem. We must reiterate, however, that these numbers are extremely tentative due to two major factors. First, we calculated the population "at risk" based on the annual prevalence of all AP users, which does not specify the proportion of chronic users who are truly at risk for TD. Second, the corresponding figure needed for accuracy, the annual prevalence rate for TD in the general population, is not known. We therefore roughly estimated this rate by summing point prevalence and annual incidence rates that were, however, from studies of selected cohorts and not from the general population. Although both these factors may have tended to exaggerate the totals, several findings by Gardos et al. (1988) could make the worst-case scenario, which estimates prevalence for just one year, even more grim. They reported that TD may improve for 4 years, plateau for the next 2, and then worsen in year 7. Thus, in a group of patients on APs, some with and others without TD, there is an increased prevalence of TD over time. This means that, over the years, the number of new cases of TD developing in the previously unaffected group is greater than the number of TD cases that are remitting.

Of all inpatients on APs, 0.2%–2.4% suffer neuroleptic malignant syndrome and about 4% of this group die (Addonizio et al., 1986; Pearlman, 1986). This yields an estimated mortality rate of 0.008%–0.096% in the total population at risk. Pope et al. (1986) conservatively estimate, at an incidence rate of 2.4%, that the cases of neuroleptic malignant syndrome in this country number in the thousands per year. This figure may be as high as 43,000 (i.e., 2.4% of the population exposed to APs, which is 1% of adults or 1.78 million) or as low as 3,560 patients if the incidence of 0.2% is used. The corresponding number of deaths at a 4% rate are 140 and 1,700 respectively. However, there are two important caveats. First, the total numbers at risk for neuroleptic malignant syndrome, that is, those initiating AP treatment, are certainly lower than the total number of patients exposed to an AP, which is the figure used in our calculations. Second, it has not been established that the incidence rates, derived from inpatient studies, are applicable to the population at large. Reports indicate that outpatients may not suffer from equivalent rates of neuroleptic malignant syndrome because this SE is not found in studies of outpatients nor is it a cause of admissions to the hospital (Hermesh et al., 1985; Miller, 1974). Both these considerations would reduce the above numbers (of cases and deaths) and thus these should be considered the approximate range of worst-case scenarios. This combination of TD and neuroleptic malignant syndrome resulting from AP use produces a much higher rate of morbidity and mortality than the other psychotropics. Therefore concern regarding AP SEs appears justified.

It has been estimated that about 2% of the adult population (i.e., 3.5

million people) had 35 million prescriptions filled for ADs in 1986. Fifty-five percent of these patients took ADs for less than 4 months (Baum, Kennedy, Knepp, Faich, & Anello, 1987; Uhlenhuth et al., 1983). Overall, up to 95% of inpatients and 40% of outpatients receiving ADs experience SEs (Bryant et al., 1987; Schmidt et al., 1984). Major adverse reactions, typically requiring drug discontinuation, may occur in 5%–18% (Schmidt et al., 1984; Nelson et al., 1982; Rabkin et al., 1984), with higher rates for patients on MAOIs (Rabkin et al., 1984) and those hospitalized with medical illnesses (Popkin et al., 1985). The most common and serious SEs are delirium, orthostatic hypotension, sexual dysfunction, and with MAOIs, hypertensive crises. Delirium occurs in approximately 6%–7% of inpatients (Meyers & Mei-Tai, 1983; Nelson et al., 1982; Preskorn & Simpson, 1982). Though based on a small sample, among Blacks it may be as high as 22% (Livingston et al., 1983). The incidence among outpatients is probably much lower. In a number of studies of outpatients (Bryant et al., 1987; Rabkin et al., 1984; Rickels et al., 1987) no delirium was reported.

Symptomatic and clinically significant orthostatic hypotension occurs in 0%–20% (Glassman et al., 1979; Roose et al., 1987; Schneider et al., 1986; Tesar et al., 1987) of patients, depending on age, health, and the particular AD they are receiving, with higher rates in patients with certain cardiac diseases. These patients can experience significant dizziness, ataxia, fainting, and falls. As a consequence, up to 4% of inpatients on ADs may sustain a serious injury such as lacerations or a hip fracture; such injuries were not reported for outpatients (Glassman et al., 1979; Tesar et al., 1987). Based on the ratio of AD prescriptions filled in 1986 (Baum et al., 1987), we estimate that 60,000 patients took MAOIs. About 2%–4% (or 1,200–2,400 patients) may have suffered a hypertensive crisis, and it is suggested that less than 0.001% (Klein et al., 1980) or, at most, 1 patient may have died.

Sexual dysfunction, including anorgasmia and impotence, may occur in 5%–30% of patients on tricyclic ADs and 20%–40% of those on MAOIs, at least during the initial period of treatment (Harrison et al., 1986; Klein et al., 1980; Rabkin et al., 1985). Sexual dysfunction has not been identified as a SE leading to drug discontinuation (Nelson et al., 1982; Popkin et al., 1985; Schmidt et al., 1984). However, the expected psychological distress associated with it and its impact on treatment with ADs have not yet been investigated.

A remarkably large number of adult Americans take AA drugs, with estimates ranging from 10% (17.8 million) to 22% (39 million) (Mellinger & Balter, 1981; Parry et al., 1973; Uhlenhuth et al., 1978). Of this group, 2.4% (or 430,000 to 940,000 people) had taken AAs every day for a year (Petursson & Lader, 1984). Sixty-one million prescriptions for AAs were filled in 1986 (Baum et al., 1987). With the use of AAs, perhaps 15% of all patients were found to suffer some SE, and in about 1% this caused drug discontinuation (Grohmann et al., 1984). It is ironic that the psychotropic drug with the least troublesome SE profile is also the one often classified as the most dangerous because of its addictive potential. The literature indicates that benzodiazepine AAs have a definite dependence liability in long-term users and that 25%–45% will have withdrawal symptoms (Marks 1985; Tyrer et al., 1983). However, the evidence also suggests that AAs are not a primary drug of abuse; do not require ever-increasing doses, because tolerance does not develop; are typically used for a short period (80%–85% of users stop within 6 months); have much less mortality than the barbiturates they replaced; and have infinitely less morbidity than either alcohol or tobacco; and that, unless the drug is stopped suddenly, withdrawal symptoms are generally not serious (Marks, 1985). Judging by SEs alone, it would appear that the attention being paid to the alleged dangers and abuse potential of AAs is exaggerated and patients would be better served if this energy were diverted in a constructive way toward the psychotropics with the most troublesome SEs, the APs.

Having addressed each class of psychotropics individually, we must emphasize that the incidence of SEs increases when patients receive two or more of these drugs together. For instance, Schimdt et al. (1987) found that the incidence of toxic delirium in 11,308 drug-treated psychiatric inpatients was increased by 50% when APs were combined with antiparkinson agents, and by 100% when APs and ADs were co-administered, as compared to the incidence on APs alone. The need to underscore the increased risk of SEs from multiple drugs is made clear by several studies. Grohmann et al. (1984) monitored approximately 5,000 patients treated over 3 years in several German cities and found that patients received an average of 3.8 psychotropic medications, although it is unclear how often these were administered simultaneously. These patients were not on research protocols and were treated purely on clinical grounds. It is instructive to note that Grohmann et al. found 60.4% of their patients had SEs, with discontinuation of the drug being required in 9%–15% of all patients, a rate that is higher than that for individual drugs. Apsler and Rothman's (1984) survey of 459 outpatients on psychotropics found that 66% of patients took 1 prescription drug, 22% took 2, 11% took 3, and 2% took 4 or more drugs.

We next look at the impact of drug SEs on the physician, the patient, and the treatment process. In the clinical context, how do physicians see the development of SEs? Because there are no studies that shed light on this, it may be useful to look at SEs in the larger medical context, keeping in mind that most psychotropics are prescribed by nonpsychiatric physicians. First, it is usual within the medical context that patients suffer additional, iatrogenic pain during the course of their diagnostic workup and treatment, as witness blood drawings, spinal taps, examination by "scopes" of all kinds, surgical incisions, and so forth. Second, major psychiatric illnesses carry an increased risk of morbidity and mortality from suicides, accidents, and physical illnesses not attributed to treatment with psychotropics (Murphy, Monson, Olivier,

Sobol, & Leighton, 1987; Tsuang & Simpson, 1985). For instance, in those
with depression the mortality rate is one and a half times greater than expected
in a comparable normal population (Murphy et al., 1987). Consequently,
physicians compare the risk of SEs against the inherent risks of the disorder
itself. In this regard, Craig and Lin (1981) note that the advent of psychotropics has not had an adverse effect on the overall mortality of psychiatric
inpatients and that the substantial decline in mortality in the post-drug era
needs further study in order to tell if this is because of the drugs or changes
in health care. Third, physicians see themselves as prescribing a helpful
remedy to a hurting patient, a drug that is both appropriate and often urgently
needed (Baldessarini, 1985b; Benson, 1984). It is also automatically assumed
that any drug on the U.S. market must meet the fundamental Federal Drug
Administration (FDA) criteria of being acceptably safe relative to its benefits.
Fourth, psychiatric drugs are a small portion of a physician's armamentarium.
What else does the little black bag carry? In it, we find numerous drugs, all
with some SEs. We should emphasize that, whereas some drugs can be fairly
benign, physicians routinely prescribe a host of very toxic but unfortunately
common drugs, for example, anti-cancer drugs. Given this background and
the physician's focus on treatment efficacy, the appearance of a SE typically
has minimal impact on clinical practice. A SE is usually "managed" while
drug treatment is maintained.

Physicians also attempt to prevent SEs. In addition to complying with the
adage "the least amount for the shortest time for a relevant indication"
(Ananth, 1987), prevention can be furthered by education of both doctors
and patients. This has already paid dividends as illustrated by the reduction
of seizures from maprotiline as the result of lowering the maximum daily dose
(Gelzer, 1986); decreased hypotension on ADs due to the greater use of
nortriptyline; and decreased mortality from neuroleptic malignant syndrome,
down from 22% before 1984 to 4% in 1984–1986 and 0%–1.4% since (Keck,
Pope, & McElroy, 1987; Pope et al., 1986). The literature also suggests that
SEs could be further prevented if clinicians were to use drug blood levels to
monitor for SE potential, because it is known that SEs but not efficacy are
definitely related to blood levels. For instance, there is a strong relationship
between blood levels of ADs and the occurrence of delirium. Closer monitoring in those most susceptible, for example, medically ill, elderly, depressed
patients, could be very beneficial (Preskorn & Simpson, 1982). In this spirit—
"educate not legislate" (Marks, 1985)—the FDA has recommended that
benzodiazepine AAs not be used for more than 4 months in order to reduce
the potential for addiction. This is more likely to modify physicians' behavior
than the legislated mandatory use of triplicate prescription forms.

Fortunately, the recent or imminent introduction in each psychotropic
class of a new drug with reportedly fewer SEs has focused attention on SEs
and their reduction. Buspirone, the nonbenzodiazepine AA without addictive

potential (Lader, 1987; Newton, Marunycz, Alderdice, & Napoliello, 1986), could help to alleviate the concerns and distress associated with the major problem of benzodiazepine AAs, withdrawal. Numerous studies have found the AD fluoxetine to have markedly fewer SEs (especially orthostatic hypotension, weight gain, sedation, and anticholinergic) than other ADs (Feighner, 1985; Stark & Hardison, 1985; Wernicke, 1985). The AP clozapine is considered particularly efficacious in patients who have failed to respond to other APs. In numerous studies, including one with a 13-year follow-up, no extrapyramidal symptoms or TD have been reported as a consequence of taking clozapine (although there is a single case report of TD). However, clozapine does have an infrequent but potentially lethal SE (agranulocytosis) that precludes it from becoming a drug of choice (Gerlach & Casey, 1988; Lindstrom, 1988). Clearly, these newer drugs are improvements and offer additional options but are not to be considered panaceas.

How do patients see the development of SEs? It appears that the majority of them do not allow SEs to interfere with the treatment they are receiving, although a small group may become noncompliant. In every study that we reviewed, SEs judged by spontaneous patient complaints yielded the lowest incidence, leading us to conclude that the majority of patients with even troublesome SEs such as akathisia, akinesia (Van Putten & Marder, 1987), or TD (Alexopoulos, 1979; Munetz & Roth, 1985) would continue their medication without even raising the complaint of SEs with the physician. It is unclear from the literature whether these patients merely accept a SE as a necessary evil, consider it as acceptable within the risk-benefit context, see it as a sign that "the drug is working," think that the doctor would not want to hear about their complaints, think that these "new symptoms" are part of their disease, become noncompliant (Van Putten & May, 1978), or choose some other option. It has even been suggested that patients do not relate their SEs to their taking medication. In a study of SEs in patients taking the AD amitriptyline, the majority (54.8%) of those on the drug for a short time attributed their new physical symptoms to the medication (i.e., identified these as SEs of the medication) as compared to a minority of the long-term patients (17.6%) making the same attribution (Bryant et al., 1987). It is also known that psychosis may be another factor leading patients to obscure the link between their medication and their physical problems. It has been reported that of the patients with TD who seem to be unaware of their disorder, a majority were actively delusional or hallucinating (Alexopoulos, 1979).

Those who do complain of SEs are generally reassured that the symptom will soon go away due to tolerance developing; or have their medication decreased; or have another drug added. If relief is not obtained within a few days or sooner, the patient is switched to another drug with theoretically less potential to cause that SE. However, in research protocols, this switch in drugs is recorded as patient dropout or medication discontinuation.

It should be emphasized here that the "drop-out" rates from studies variously reported from 1% to 40% do not mean that treatment in such instances is always terminated. Because the subjects were unable to tolerate the protocol, clinical options would allow such patients to be treated with another drug individualized to their needs. Therefore, although the drop-out rate tells us something about the seriousness of the SE, it does not give a clue as to the final therapeutic outcome. This is emphasized by Rabkin et al.'s (1984) findings. In their study of three ADs, patients who had to stop a drug due to serious SEs were started on another one. The results are consistent with the clinical impression that this is usually a successful gambit, because it is "relatively uncommon to have [serious] SEs on more than one drug" (p. 273).

In many studies, drop-out rates for the drug group (due to SEs) did not differ from those of the placebo group (due to ineffectiveness) as in the NIMH Collaborative Study (1964), Liebowitz et al. (1988), Rickels et al. (1987), and Pecknold et al. (1988). Looked at from another vantage point, because approximately 60%–70% of all patients on psychotropics suffer SEs but only 5%–10% discontinue medication, the majority of patients continue pharmacotherapy despite having experienced a SE, including some that may have been quite troublesome. Given that noncompliance from all causes is a major issue in treatment, what is the contribution due to SEs? Blackwell (1982) reviewed the literature on compliance and found that six studies showed SEs to reduce compliance whereas four others showed SEs to have no effect. While recognizing the importance of noncompliance, he argued that SEs are merely one of many factors contributing to it and that important factors include drug efficacy, patients' attitude and belief about their condition and its treatment, and the relative availability of drugs and psychotherapy. However, in a series of studies, Van Putten and associates (Van Putten & May, 1987; Van Putten, May, Marder, & Wittman, 1981) showed that a subjective dysphoric response 4 hours after a single test dose of an AP was associated with less favorable short-term outcome, objective increase in akinesia, increased incidence of akathisia, greater drowsiness, and increased rate of medication refusal. They found a good objective outcome was less likely if the patient continues to experience akathisia, which is of concern because it was treatment resistant in 53% of patients and experienced by them as depression or anxiety. They conclude that "AP drugs have always been more popular with the physician than with the patient. There are numerous reasons for this, but unrecognized akathisia has, we believe, something to do with it" (p. 1039). Further, Apsler and Rothman (1984), in a study of 459 patients, found that fear of dependency and concern about unhealthy SEs were two factors that were reported as causes for noncompliance (primarily a decrease in the use of medication). Patients who were well educated, from a higher socioeconomic stratum, and who perceived themselves as generally healthy took less than prescribed; those at the lower end of the scale on these factors most often endorsed the idea that "medications cause problems" yet took more than prescribed. The authors emphasize that both groups were, however, noncompliant.

Given the potential for frequent and even serious SEs, should patients being started on psychotropics be informed about them? To what extent? Whereas we strongly recommend that all patients be routinely given information about the potential risks and benefits of the drug being recommended, one study (Benson, 1984) found that only one third of psychiatrists surveyed disclosed the risk for major SEs and TD to patients on APs. More disturbing was the finding that about 1 in 10 thought it better not to discuss this with patients. Myers and Calvert (1984) found that patients given information about either SEs or beneficial effects of the drug being prescribed had a higher rate of compliance than those patients who were merely told that the drug was being given to treat their depression. However, it is of particular interest that patients given information only regarding the beneficial effects complained of fewer SEs than patients who received information about SEs or no information at all.

Finally, what is the clinical impact of SEs on the therapeutic process? Is there any? It was reported that roughly 85% of patients on AAs, 40% on ADs, and 25%–40% on APs have no SEs. For the rest, SEs add an unwanted cost to the distress of their illness. This cost, we have seen, can be quite insignificant or extraordinarily high, varying from tolerable to intolerable, from a mere nuisance to infrequent death. Beyond this personal burden is the financial price from prolonged illness, lengthened hospitalization, and disability. One reaction to SEs is that the medication is stopped. Either the physician discontinues it or the patient becomes noncompliant. Blackwell (1982) noted that noncompliance is as much a problem with psychotropics as with other drugs used in chronic medical conditions. However, the majority of patients on psychotropics continue their medication despite a high rate of SEs. Some patients, especially those with mild SEs, simply accept them; others continue treatment with a dose reduction, addition of an antidote, or a change to another drug. Undoubtedly, physicians encourage and support continuation (Van Putten et al., 1981), finding most SEs as "acceptable" within the risk-benefit paradigm (Baldessarini et al., 1988). This is reflected in the relationship among the frequency of use, potential dangers, and primary indication for psychotropics. Among the three psychotropic classes, the APs, which are the least prescribed, are most likely to cause serious SEs and are used for one of the most severe disorders, schizophrenia. The AAs, by far the most prescribed, are the safest and used for the least severe indication, anxiety. The ADs, prescribed for depression, fall in between. Overall, we have found from our review that although SEs have recently gained more research attention focused on their definition, incidence, and treatment, the study of their impact on the therapeutic process has been largely neglected. Perhaps this parallels the surprising conclusion that, based on both the patients' and physicians' behavior, SEs appear to have a less than expected impact on the treatment process considering the high frequency of SEs encountered.

Given the lack of good data in numerous areas relating to the study of SEs, there are still some basic questions to be addressed. The potency and dose equivalence of all psychotropic drugs, but particularly the APs, need to be clarified. Within each class, a more precise understanding of which drug causes the most and least SEs is needed. Objective criteria to diagnose some SEs such as akathisia or akinesia are urgently needed because the possibility has been raised that the majority of patients with these two SEs are undiagnosed, erroneously diagnosed, or wrongly treated (Van Putten & Marder, 1987). We also need further evidence on what the rates of SEs are in inpatients versus outpatients. And finally a great deal more needs to be learned regarding the impact of SEs. For instance, how severe are they? How soon are the SEs typically detected by the clinician? How are they treated? Can they be prevented? How long do SEs take to improve or resolve? How does the patient experience them? How often do they contribute to noncompliance? Only then will we begin to comprehend the true impact of SEs on a patient's life and treatment and increase the possibility of sending home Woody Allen's character while he can still tell the difference between his brother and two soft-boiled eggs.

## REFERENCES

Abbott, R. J., & Loizou, L. A. (1986). Neuroleptic malignant syndrome. *British Journal of Psychiatry, 148,* 47–51.

Addonizio, G., Susman, V. L., & Roth, S. D. (1986). Symptoms of neuroleptic malignant syndrome in 82 consecutive inpatients. *American Journal of Psychiatry, 1431,* 1587–1590.

Akiskal, H. S. (1986). The clinical management of affective disorders. In J. O. Cavenar, Jr. (Ed.), *Psychiatry,* (chap. 61). Philadelphia: Lippincott.

Alexopoulos, G. S. (1979). Lack of complaints in schizophrenics with tardive dyskinesia. *Journal of Nervous and Mental Disease, 167,* 125–127.

Allen, W. (1980). *Side effects.* New York: Ballantine Books.

Ananth, J. (1987). Benzodiazepines: Selective administration. *Journal of Affective Disorders, 13,* 99–108.

Angst, J. (1987). Switch from depression to mania, or from mania to depression: Role of psychotropic drugs. *Psychopharmacology Bulletin, 23,* 66–67.

Apsler, R. & Rothman, E. (1984). Correlates of compliance with psychoactive prescriptions. *Journal of Psychoactive Drugs, 16,* 193–199.

Asatoor, A. M., Levi, A. J., & Milne, M. D. (1963). Tranylcypromine and cheese. *Lancet, 2,* 733–734.

Ayd, F. J. (1961). A survey of drug-induced extrapyramidal reactions. *Journal of the American Medical Association, 175,* 1054–1060.

Baldessarini, R. J. (1984). Antipsychotic drugs. In the American Psychiatric Association Commission on Psychiatric Therapies, T. B. Karasu (Chair), *The psychiatric therapies* (pp. 119–170). Washington, DC: American Psychiatric Association.

Baldessarini, R. J. (1985a). Drugs and the treatment of psychiatric disorders. In A. Gilman, L. Goodman, T. Rall & F. Murad (Eds.), *The pharmacological basis of therapeutics* (pp. 387–445). New York: Macmillan.

Baldessarini, R. J. (1985b). *Chemotherapy in psychiatry: Principles and practice.* Cambridge, MA.: Harvard University Press.

Baldessarini, R. J., & Cohen, B. M. (1986). Regulation of psychiatric practice. *American Journal of Psychiatry, 143,* 750–751.

Baldessarini, R. J., Cohen, B. M., & Teicher, M. H. (1988). Significance of neuroleptic dose and plasma level in the pharmacological treatment of Psychoses. *Archives of General Psychiatry, 45,* 79–91.

Baldessarini, R. J., Katz, B., & Cotton, P. (1984). Dissimilar dosing with high-potency and low-potency neuroleptics. *American Journal of Psychiatry, 141,* 748–752.

Balmer, R., Battegay, R., & Von Marschall, R. (1981). Long term treatment with diazepam. *International Pharmacopsychiatry, 16,* 221–234.

Ban, T. A. (1978). *Pharmacology of thiothixene.* New York: Raven Press.

Baum, C., Kennedy, D. L., Knapp, D. E., Faich, G. A. & Anello, C. (1987). *Drug utilization in the U.S.—1986: Eighth annual review.* Springfield, VA: U.S. Department of Commerce.

Benson, P. R. (1984). Informed consent: Drug information is closed to patients prescribed antipsychotic medication. *Journal of Nervous and Mental Disease, 172,* 642–653.

Berger, P. A. (1977). Antidepressant medications and the treatment of depression. In J. Barchas, P. Berger, R. Ciaranello, & G. Elliot (Eds.), *Psychopharmacology: From theory to practice* (pp. 174–207). New York: Oxford University Press.

Bernstein, J. G. (1987). Induction of obesity by psychotropic drugs. *Annals of New York Academy of Science, 499,* 203–15.

Bernstein, J. G. (1988). *Handbook of drug therapy in psychiatry* (2nd ed.). Littleton, MA: PSG Publishing.

Blackwell, B. (1963). Tranylcypromine. *Lancet, 2,* 414.

Blackwell, B. (1982). Antidepressant drugs: Side effects and compliance. *Journal of Clinical Psychiatry, 43,* 14–18.

Blackwell, B., Marley, E., Price, J., & Taylor, D. (1967). Hypertensive interactions between monoamine oxidase inhibitors and foodstuffs. *British Journal of Psychiatry, 11,* 349–365.

Boston Collaborative Drug Surveillance Program: (1972). Adverse reactions to the tricyclic-antidepressant drugs. *Lancet, 1,* 529–531.

Boston Collaborative Drug Surveillance Program (1973). Clinical depression of the central nervous system due to diazepam and chlordiazepoxide in relation to cigarette smoking and age. *New England Journal of Medicine, 288,* 277–280.

Bourgeois, M., Bouilh, P., Tignol, J., & Yesavage, J. (1980). Spontaneous dyskinesias vs. neuroleptic-induced dyskinesias in 270 elderly subjects, *Journal of Nervous and Mental Disease, 168,* 177–178.

Browne, J. L., & Hauge, K. J. (1986). A review of alprazolam withdrawal. *Drug Intelligence and Clinical Pharmacology, 20,* 837–839.

Bryant, S. G., Fisher, S., & Kluge, R. M. (1987). Long-term versus short-term amitriptyline side effects as measured by a postmarketing surveillance system. *Journal of Clinical Psychopharmacology, 7,* 78–82.

Burckhardt, D., Raeder, E., Muller, V., Imhof, P., & Neubauer, H. (1978). Cardiovascular effects of tricyclic and tetracyclic antidepressants. *Journal of the American Medical Association, 239,* 213–216.

Busfield, B. L., Jr., Schneller, P. & Capra, D. (1962). Depressive symptom or side effect? A comparative study of symptoms during pre-treatment and treatment periods of patients on three antidepressant medications. *Journal of Nervous and Mental Disease, 134,* 339–345.

Bush, P. J., Spector, K. K. & Rabin, D. L. (1984). Use of sedatives and hypnotics prescribed in a family practice. *Southern Medical Journal, 77,* 677–681.

Caroff, S. N. (1980). The neuroleptic syndrome. *Journal of Clinical Psychiatry, 41,* 79–83.

Cole, J. O., & Clyde, D. J. (1961). Extrapyramidal side effects and clinical response to the phenothiazines. *Review of Canadian Biology, 20,* 565–573.

Cole, J. O., & Davis, J. M. (1975). Antidepressant drugs. In A. Freedman, H. Kaplan & B. Sadock (Eds.), *Comprehensive textbook of psychiatry* (2nd ed., pp. 1941–1956). Baltimore: Williams & Wilkins.

Craig, T. J., & Lin, S. P. (1981). Mortality among psychiatric inpatients: Age-adjusted comparison of populations before and after psychotropic drug era. *Archives of General Psychiatry, 38,* 935–938.

Davidson, J., & Turnbull, C. D. (1986). The effect of isocarboxazid on blood pressure and pulse. *Journal of Clinical Psychopharmacology, 6,* 139–143.

Davies, R. K., Tucker G. J., Harrow, M., & Detre, T. P. (1971). Confusional episodes and antidepressant medication. *American Journal of Psychiatry, 128,* 95–99.

Davis, J. M. (1985). Antipsychotic drugs. In H. Kaplan & B. Sadock (Eds.), *Comprehensive textbook of psychiatry* (4th ed., pp. 1481–1512). Baltimore: Williams & Wilkins.

Dean, C. (1987). Tardive dyskinesia: A serious side effect? *American Journal of Psychiatry, 144,* 261–262.

Delay, J., & Deniker, P. (1968). Drug-induced extrapyramidal syndromes. In D. Vinken & G. Bruyn (Eds.), *Handbook of clinical neurology. Diseases of the basal ganglia* (Vol. 6, pp. 248–266). New York: Elsevier.

DeLeo, D., & Magni, G. (1983). Sexual side effects of antidepressant drugs. *Psychosomatics, 24,* 1076–1082.

DeVeaugh-Geiss, J. (1979). Informed consent for neuroleptic therapy. *American Journal of Psychiatry, 136,* 959–962.

DiMascio, A., Shader, R., & Giller, D. R. (1970). Behavioral toxicity. In R. Shader & A. DiMascio (Eds.), *Psychotropic drug side effects* (pp. 132–141). Baltimore: Williams & Wilkins.

Downing, R. W., & Rickels, K. (1967). Self report of hostility and the incidence of side reactions in neurotic outpatients treated with tranquilizing drugs and placebo. *Journal of Consulting Psychology, 1,* 71–76.

Elia, J., Katz, I. R., & Simpson, G. M. (1987). Teratogenicity of psychotherapeutic medications. *Psychopharmacology Bulletin, 23,* 531–586.

Evans, D. L., Davidson, J., & Raft, D. (1982). Early and late side effects of phenelzine. *Journal of Clinical Psychopharmacology, 2,* 208–210.

Feighner, J. P. (1985). A comparative trial of fluoxetine and amitriptyline in patients with major depressive disorder. *Journal of Clinical Psychiatry, 46,* 369–372.

Finkle, B. S., McCloskey, K. L., & Goodman, L. S. (1979). Diazepam and drug associated deaths: A U.S. and Canadian survey. *Journal of the American Medical Association, 242,* 429–434.

Friedel, R. O. (1978). Pharmacokinetics in the gero-psychiatric patient. In M. A. Lipton, A. DiMascio, & K. F. Killan (Eds.), *Psychopharmacology: A generation of progress* (pp. 1499–1505). New York: Raven Press.

Galbrecht, C. R., & Klett, C. J. (1968). Predicting response to phenothiazines: The right drug for the right patient. *Journal of Nervous and Mental Disease, 147,* 173–83.

Gardos, G., & Cole, J. O. (1983). The prognosis of tardive dyskinesia. *Journal of Clinical Psychiatry, 44,* 177–79.

Gardos, G., Cole, J. O., Haskell, D., Marby, D., Paine, S. S., & Moore, P. (1988). The natural history of tardive dyskinesia. *Journal of Clinical Psychopharmacology, 8,* 31S–37S.

Gelzer, J. (1986). Limits to chemotherapy of depression. *Psychopathology, 19* (2), 108–117.

Gerlach, J., & Casey, D. E. (1988). Tardive dyskinesia. *Acta Psychiatrica Scandinavica, 77*, 369–378.

Glassman, A. H., & Bigger, J. T., Jr. (1981). Cardiovascular effects of therapeutic doses of tricyclic antidepressants: A review. *Archives of General Psychiatry, 38*, 815–820.

Glassman, A. H., Giardina, E. V., Perel, J. M., & Davies, M. (1979). Clinical characteristics of imipramine-induced orthostatic hypotension. *Lancet, 1*, 468–472.

Glassman, A. H., Johnson, L. L., Giardina, E. G. V., Walsh, T., Roose, S. P., Cooper, T. B., & Bigger, J. T., Jr. (1983). The use of imipramine in depressed patients with congestive heart failure. *Journal of the American Medical Association, 250*, 1997–2001.

Gopalaswamy, A. K., & Morgan, R. (1985). Too many chronic mentally disabled patients are too fat. *Acta Psychiatrica Scandinavica, 72*, 254–258.

Gordon, H., Law, A., Hohman, K. E., & Groth, C. (1960). The problem of overweight in hospitalized psychiatric patients. *Psychiatric Quarterly, 34*, 69–82.

Greenblatt, D. J. (1976). Antianxiety agents. In R. Miller & D. Greenblatt (Eds.), *Drug effects in hospitalized patients* (pp. 193–204). New York: Wiley.

Grohmann, R., Dirschedl, P., Scherer, J., Schmidt, L. G., & Wunderlich, O. (1985). Reliability of adverse drug reaction assessment in psychiatric inpatients. *European Archives of Psychiatry and Neurological Sciences, 235*, 158–163.

Grohmann, R., Hippius, H., Muller-Oerlinghausen, B., Ruther, E., Scherer, J., Schmidt, L. G., Strauss, A., & Wolf, B. (1984). Assessment of adverse drug reactions in psychiatric hospitals. *European Journal of Clinical Pharmacology, 26*, 727–734.

Gutheil, T. G. (1982). The psychology of pharmacology. *Bulletin of the Menninger Clinic, 46*, 321–330.

Guze, B. H., & Baxter, L. R., Jr. (1985). Neuroleptic malignant syndrome. *New England Journal of Medicine, 313*, 163–166.

Gwirtsman, H. E., Ahles, S., Halaris, A., DeMet, E., & Hill, M. A. (1983). Therapeutic superiority of maprotiline versus doxepin in geriatric depression. *Journal of Clinical Psychiatry, 44*, 449–453.

Hansell, N., & Willis, M. A. (1977). Outpatient treatment of schizophrenia. *American Journal of Psychiatry, 134*, 1082–1085.

Harrison, W. M., Rabkin, J. G., Ehrhardt, A. A., Stewart, J. W., McGrath, P. J., Ross, D., & Quitkin, F. M. (1986). Effects of antidepressant medication on sexual function: A controlled study. *Journal of Clinical Psychopharmacology, 6*, 144–149.

Hayes, J. R., Born, G. F., & Rosenbaum, A. H. (1977). Incidence of orthostatic hypotension in patients with primary affective disorders treated with tricyclic antidepressants. *Mayo Clinic Proceedings, 52*, 509–512.

Hayes, R. L., Gerner, R. H., Fairbanks, L., Moran, M., & Waltuch, L. (1983). ECG findings in geriatric depressives given trazodone, placebo, or imipramine. *Journal of Clinical Psychiatry, 44*, 180–183.

Hermesh, H., Shalev, A. & Munitz, H. (1985). Contribution of adverse drug reaction to admission rates in an acute psychiatic ward. *Acta Psychiatrica Scandinavica, 72*, 104–110.

Herrington, R., & Lader, M. (1981). Antipsychotic drugs. In H. vanPraag (Ed.), *Handbook of biological psychiatry* (Part V, pp. 73–104). New York: Marcel Dekker.

Hesbacher, P. T., Rickels. K., Gordon, P. E., Gray, B., Meckeinburg, R., Weise, C. C., & Vandervort, W. (1970a). Setting, patient, and doctor effects on drug response in neurotic patients. I. Differential attrition, dosage deviation, and side reaction response to treatment. *Psychopharmacologia, 18*, 180–208.

Hesbacher, P. T., Rickels, K., Hutchinson, J., Raab, E., Sablosky, L., Whalen, E., & Phillips, F. (1970b). Setting, patient, and doctor effects on drug response in neurotic patients. II. Differential improvement. *Psychopharmacologia, 18*, 209–215.

Hollister, L. E. (1983). *Clinical pharmacology of psychotherapeutic drugs* (2nd ed.). New York: Churchill Livingstone.

Hollister, L. E. (1988). Antipsychotics & mood stabilisers. In H. Goldman (Ed.), *Review of General Psychiatry* (pp. 580–591). Norwalk: Appleton & Lange.

Jarvik, L. F., Read, S. L., Mintz, J., & Neshkes, R. E. (1983). Pretreatment orthostatic hypotension in geriatric depression: Predictor of response to imipramine and doxepin. *Journal of Clinical Psychopharmacology, 3,* 368–372.

Kane, J. M., & Smith, J. J. (1982). Tardive dyskinesia: Prevalence and risk factors: 1959 to 1979. *Archives of General Psychiatry, 39,* 473–481.

Kane, J. M., Woerner, M., Borenstein, M., Wegner, J. & Lieberman, E. (1986). Integrating incidence and prevalence of tardive dyskinesia. *Psychopharmacology Bulletin, 22,* 254–258.

Kane, J. M., Woerner, M., & Lieberman, J. (1984). Tardive dyskinesia. In D. V. Jeste & R. J. Wyatt (Eds.), *Neuropsychiatric movement disorders* (pp. 97–118). Washington, DC: American Psychiatric Association Press.

Kane, J. M., Woerner, M., & Lieberman, J. (1988). Tardive dyskinesia: Prevalence, incidence, and risk factors. *Journal of Clinical Psychopharmacology, 8,* 52S–56S.

Kaplan, H. I., & Sadock, B. (1988). *Clinical psychiatry.* Baltimore: Williams & Wilkins.

Keck, P., Pope, H., & McElroy, S. (1987). Frequency and presentation of neuroleptic malignant syndrome: A prospective study. *American Journal of Psychiatry, 144,* 1344–1346.

Klein, D. F., Gittelman, R., Quitkin, F., & Rifkin, A. (1980). *Diagnosis and drug treatment of psychiatric disorders: Adults and children* (2nd ed.). Baltimore: Williams & Wilkins.

Klein, D. F., & Rosen, B. (1973). Premorbid asocial adjustment and response to phenothiazine treatment among schizophrenic inpatients. *Archives of General Psychiatry, 29,* 480–485.

Kronig, M. H., Roose, S. P., Walsh, B. T., Woodring, S., & Glassman, A. H. (1983). Blood pressure effects of phenelzine. *Journal of Clinical Psychopharmacology, 3,* 307–10.

Lader, M. (1987). Assessing the potential for buspirone dependence or abuse and effects of its withdrawal. *American Journal of Medicine, 82,* 20–26.

Lader, M. H. (1984). Antianxiety drugs. In The American Psychiatric Association Commission on Psychiatric Therapies, B. T. Karasu (Chair). *The psychiatric therapies* (pp. 53–84) Washington, DC: American Psychiatric Press.

Langou, R. A., Van Dyke, C., Tahan, S. R., & Cohen, L. S. (1980). Cardiovascular manifestations of tricyclic antidepressant overdose. *American Heart Journal, 100,* 458–464.

Learoyd, B. M. (1972). Psychotropic drugs and the elderly patient. *Medical Journal of Australia, 1,* 1131–1133.

Letemendia, F. J. J., & Harris A. D. (1959). The influence of side-effects on the reporting of symptoms. *Psychopharmacologia, 1,* 39–47.

Levine, J., & Schooler, N. R. (1986). SAFTEE: A technique for the systematic assessment of side effects in clinical trials. *Psychopharmacology Bulletin, 22,* 343–381.

Levinson, P., Malen, R., Hogben, G., & Smith, H. (1978). Psychological factors in susceptibility to drug-induced extrapyramidal symptoms. *American Journal of Psychiatry, 135,* 1375–76.

Levitt, A. J., Joffe, R. T., Esche, I., & Sherret, D. (1987). The effect of desipramine on body weight in depression. *Journal of Clinical Psychiatry, 48,* 27–28.

Lewis, J. L., & Winokur, G. (1987). The induction of mania: A natural history study with controls. *Psychopharmacology Bulletin, 23,* 74–78.

Liebowitz, M. R., Quitkin, F. M., Stewart, J. W., McGrath, P., Harrison, W., Markowitz, J., Rabkin, J., Tricamo, E., Goetz, D., & Klein, D. (1988). Antidepressant specificity in atypical depression. *Archives of General Psychiatry, 45,* 129–137.

Lin, K. M., & Finder, E. J. (1983). Neuroleptic dosage in Asians. *American Journal of Psychiatry, 140,* 490–491.

Lin, K. M., Poland R. E., & Lesser, I. M. (1986). Ethnicity and psychopharmacology. *Culture, Medicine, and Psychiatry, 10,* 151–165.

Lindstrom, L. H. (1988). The effect of long-term treatment with clozapine in schizophrenia: A retrospective study in 96 patients treated with clozapine for up to 13 years. *Acta Psychiatrica Scandinavica, 77,* 524–529.

Lingjaerde, O., Ahlfors, G., Bech, P., Dencker, J., & Elgen, K. (1987). The UKU side effect rating scale: Results. *Acta Psychiatrica Scandinavica, 76,* 37–63.

Livingston, R. L., Zucker, D. K., Isenberg, K. & Wetzel, R. D. (1983). Tricyclic antidepressants and delirium. *Journal of Clinical Psychiatry, 44,* 173–176.

Luchins, D. J. (1983). Review of clinical and animal studies comparing the cardiovascular effects of doxepin and other tricyclic antidepressants. *American Journal of Psychiatry, 140,* 1006–1009.

Marcos, L. R., & Cancro, R. (1982). Pharmacotherapy of Hispanic depressed patients. *American Journal of Psychotherapy, 36,* 505–512.

Marks, J. (1985). *The benzodiazepines: Use, overuse, abuse.* (2nd Edition.) Lancaster, England: University of Cambridge.

Marshall, J. B., & Forker, A. D. (1982). Cardiovascular effects of tricyclic antidepressant drugs: Therapeutic usage, overdose, and management of complications. *American Heart Journal, 103,* 401–414.

Mason, A. S., & Granacher, R. P. (1980). *Clinical handbook of antipsychotic drug therapy.* New York: Brunner Mazel.

Mathew, R. J., Weinman, M., & Claghorn, J. L. (1980). Tricyclic side effects without tricyclics in depression. *Psychopharmacology Bulletin, 16,* 58–60.

McGrath, P. J., Blood, D. K., Stewart, J. W., Harrison, W., Quitkin, F. M., Tricamo, E., & Markowitz, J. (1987). A comparative study of the electrocardiographic effects of phenelzine, tricyclic antidepressants, mianserin, and placebo. *Journal of Clinical Psychopharmacology, 7,* 5335–5339.

Meador-Woodruff, J. H., Akil, M., Wisner-Carlson, R., & Grunhaus, L. (1988). Behavioral and cognitive toxicity related to elevated plasma tricyclic antidepressant levels. *Journal of Clinical Psychopharmacology, 8,* 28–32.

Mellinger, G. D. & Balter, M. B. (1981). Prevalence and patterns of use of psychotherapeutic drugs: Results from a 1979 national survey of American adults. In G. Tognoni, C. Bellantuono & M. Lader (Eds.), *Epidemiological impact of psychotropic drugs* (pp. 117–135). Amsterdam: Elsevier/North Holland.

Meyers, B. S., & Mei-Tal, V. (1983). Psychiatric reactions during tricyclic treatment of the elderly reconsidered. *Journal of Clinical Psychopharmacology, 3,* 2–6.

Miller, R. R. (1974). Hospital admissions due to adverse drug reactions. *Archives of Internal Medicine, 134,* 219–223.

Mitchell, J. E., & Popkin, M. K. (1983). Antidepressant drug therapy and sexual dysfunction in men: A review. *Journal of Clinical Psychopharmacology, 3,* 76–79.

Mogul, K. M. (1985). Psychological considerations in the use of psychotropic drugs with women patients. *Hospital and Community Psychiatry, 36,* 1080–1085.

Munetz, M. R., & Roth, L. H. (1985). Informing patients about tardive dyskinesia. *Archives of General Psychiatry, 42,* 866–871.

Murphy, J. M., Monson, R. R., & Olivier, D. C., Sobol, A. M., & Leighton, A. H. (1987). Affective disorders and mortality: A general population study. *Archives of General Psychiatry, 44,* 473–480.

Myers, E. D., & Calvert, E. J. (1984). Information, compliance and side-effects: A study of patients on antidepressant medication. *British Journal of Clinical Pharmacology, 17,* 21–25.

National Institute of Mental Health Psychopharmacology Service Center Collaborative Study Group. (1964). Phenothiazine treatment in acute schizophrenia. *Archives of General Psychiatry, 10,* 246–261.

Nelson, J. C., Jatlow, P. J., Boch, J., Quinlam, D. M., & Bowers, M. B., Jr. (1982). Major adverse reactions during desipramine treatment: Relationship to plasma drug concentrations, concomitant antipsychotic treatment, and patient characteristics. *Archives of General Psychiatry, 39,* 1055–1061.

Newton, R. E., Marunycz, J. D., Alderdice, M. T., & Napoliello, M. J. (1986). A review of the SE profile of buspirone. *American Journal of Medicine, 80,* 17–21.

Nies, A., & Robinson, D. S. (1982). Monoamine oxidase inhibitors. In E. S. Paykel (Ed.), *Handbook of affective disorders* (pp. 246–261). New York: Guilford Press.

Noble, P., & Lader, M. (1971). Salivary secretion and depressive illness: A physiological and psychometric study. *Psychological Medicine, 1,* 372–376.

Parry, H. J., Balter, M. B., Mellinger, G. D., Cisin, I. H. & Manheimer, D. I. (1973). National patterns of psychotherapeutic drug use. *Archives of General Psychiatry, 28,* 769–783.

Pearlman, C. A. (1986). Neuroleptic malignant syndromes: A review of the literature. *Journal of Clinical Psychopharmacology, 6,* 257–273.

Pecknold, J. C., Swinson, R. P., Kuch, K. & Lewis, C. P. (1988). Alprazolam in panic disorder and agoraphobia: Results from a multicenter trial. III. Discontinuation effects. *Archives of General Psychiatry, 45,* 429–436.

Petursson, H., & Lader, M. (1984). *Dependence on tranquilizers.* Oxford: Oxford University Press.

Pitts, W. M., Fann, W. E., Sajadi, C. & Snyder, S. (1983). Alprazolam in older depressed patients. *Journal of Clinical Psychiatry, 44,* 213–215.

Pope, H. G., Jr., Keck, P. E., & McElroy, S. L. (1986). Frequency and presentation of neuroleptic malignant syndrome in a large psychiatric hospital. *American Journal of Psychiatry, 143,* 1227–1233.

Popkin, M. K., Callies, A. L. & Mackenzie, T. B. (1985). The outcome of antidepressant use in the medically ill. *Archives of General Psychiatry, 42,* 1160–1163.

Potkin, S. G., Shen, Y., & Pardes, H. (1984). Haloperidol concentrations elevated in Chinese patients. *Psychiatry Research, 12,* 167–172.

Prescott, L. P. (1983). Safety of the benzodiazepines. In E. Costa (Ed.), *The Benzodiazepines: from molecular biology to clinical practice* (pp. 253–266). New York: Raven Press.

Preskorn, S. H., & Simpson, S. (1982). Tricyclic-antidepressant-induced delirium and plasma drug concentration. *American Journal of Psychiatry, 139,* 822–823.

Preskorn, S. H., Weller, E., Jerkovich, G., Hughes, C. W., & Weller, R. (1988). Depression in children: Concentration-dependent CNS toxicity of tricyclic antidepressant. *Psychopharmacology Bulletin, 24,* 140–142.

Prien, R. F., & Cole, J. O. (1968). High dosage chlorpromazine therapy in schizophrenia. *Archives of General Psychiatry, 18,* 482–495.

Quitkin, F., Rifkin, A., Gochfeld, L, & Klein, D. F. (1977). Tardive dyskinesia: Are the first signs reversible? *American Journal of Psychiatry, 134,* 84–87.

Rabkin, J., Quitkin, F., Harrison, W., Tricamo, E. & McGrath, P. (1984). Adverse reactions to monoamine oxidase inhibitors. Part I. A comparative study. *Journal of Clinical Psychopharmacology, 4,* 270–278.

Rabkin, J., Quitkin, F. M., McGrath, P., Harrison, W. & Tricamo, E. (1985). Adverse reactions to monoamine oxidase inhibitors. Part II. Treatment correlates and clinical management. *Journal of Clinical Psychopharmacology, 5,* 2–9.

Reed, K., Smith, R. C., Schoolar, J. C., Hu, R., Leelavath, D. E., Mann, E., & Lippman, L. (1980). Cardiovascular effects of nortriptyline in geriatric patients. *American Journal of Psychiatry, 137,* 986–989.

Rhoades, H. M., & Overall, J. E. (1984). Side effect of different antipsychotic and antidepressant drugs. *Psychopharmacology Bulletin, 20,* 83–88.

Rickels, K., Chung, H. R., Csanalosi, I. B., Hurowitz, A. M., London, J., Wiseman, K., Kaplan, M., & Amsterdam, J. D. (1987). Alprazolam, diazepam, imipramine, and placebo in outpatients with major depression. *Archives of General Psychiatry, 44,* 862–866.

Risch, S. C., Groom, G. P., & Janowsky, D. S. (1981). Interfaces of psychopharmacology and cardiology—Part one. *Journal of Clinical Psychiatry, 42*, 23–34.

Roose, S. P., Glassman, A. H., Giardina, E. G. V., Walsh, B. T., Woodring, S., & Bigger, J. T., Jr. (1987). Tricyclic antidepressants in depressed patients with cardiac conduction disease. *Archives of General Psychiatry, 44*, 273–275.

Rosenbaum, J. F. (1984). Treatment of outpatients with desipramine. *Journal of Clinical Psychiatry, 45*, 17–21.

Rudorfer, M. V., Ross, R. J., Linnoila, M., Sherer, M. A., & Potter, W. Z. (1985). Exaggerated orthostatic responsivity of plasma norepinephrine in depression. *Archives of General Psychiatry, 42*, 1865–1192.

Rush, A. J., Erman, M. K., Schlesser, M. A., Roffwarg, H. P., Vasavada, N., Khatami, M., Fairchild, C., & Giles, D. E. (1985). Alprazolam vs. amitriptyline in depressions with reduced REM latencies. *Archives of General Psychiatry, 42*, 1154–1159.

Sarwer-Foner, G. J. (1960). Recognition and management of drug-induced extrapyramidal reactions and "paradoxical" behavioral reactions in psychiatry. *Canadian Medical Association Journal, 83*, 312–318.

Schmidt, L. G., Grohmann, R., Helmchen, H., Langscheid-Schmidt, K., Muller-Oerling-hausen, B., Poser, W., Ruther, E., Scherer, J., Strauss, A., & Wolf, B. (1984). Adverse drug reactions: an epidemiological study at psychiatric hospitals. *Acta Psychiatrica Scandinavica, 70*, 77–89.

Schmidt, L. G., Grohmann, R., Strauss, A., Spiess-Kiefer, C., Lindmeier, D. & Muller-Oerlinghausen, B. (1987). Epidemiology of toxic delirium due to psychotropic drugs in psychiatric hospitals. *Comprehensive Psychiatry, 28*, 242–249.

Schneider, L. S., Sloane, R. B., Staples, F. R., & Bender, M. (1986). Pretreatment orthostatic hypotension as a predictor of response to nortriptyline in geriatric depression. *Journal of Clinical Psychopharmacology, 6*, 172–176.

Sederer, L. (1986). Schizophrenic disorders. In L. Sederer (Ed.), *Inpatient psychiatry* (2nd ed., pp. 53–80). Baltimore: Williams & Wilkins.

Seeman, M. V. (1983). Interaction of sex, age, and neuroleptic dose. *Comprehensive Psychiatry, 24*, 125–128.

Shapiro, A. K. (1971). Placebo effects in medicine, psychotherapy, and psychoanalysis. In A. E. Bergin & S. L. Garfield (Eds.), *Handbook of psychotherapy and change* (pp. 439–473). New York: Wiley.

Smith, R. C., Chojnacki, M., Hu, R., & Mann, E. (1980). Cardiovascular effects of therapeutic doses of tricyclic antidepressants: Importance of blood level monitoring. *Journal of Clinical Psychiatry, 41*, 57–63.

Snyder, S. H., & Yamamura, H. I. (1977). Antidepressants and the muscarinic acetylcholine receptor. *Archives of General Psychiatry, 34*, 236–239.

Stark, P. & Hardison, C. D. (1985). A review of multicenter controlled studies of fluoxetine vs. imipramine and placebo in outpatients with major depressive disorder. *Journal of Clinical Psychiatry, 46*, 53–58.

Sternberg, D. E. (1986). Neuroleptic malignant syndrome: The pendulum swings. *American Journal of Psychiatry, 143*, 1273–1275.

Svenson, S. E. & Hamilton, R. G. (1966). A critique of over emphasis on side effects with the psychotropic drugs: An analysis of 18,000 chlordiazepoxide treated cases. *Current Therapy & Research, 8*, 455–464.

Szabadi, E., Grazner, P. & Bradshaw, C. M. (1980). The peripheral anticholinergic activity of tricyclic antidepressants: comparison of amitriptyline and desipramine in human volunteers. *British Journal of Psychiatry, 137*, 433–439.

Tesar, G. E., Rosenbaum, J. F., Biederman, J., Weilburg, J. B., Pollack, M. H., Gross, C. C., Falk, W. E., Gastfriend, D. R., Zusky, P. M., & Bouckoms, A. (1987). Orthostatic hypotension and antidepressant pharmacotherapy. *Psychopharmacology Bulletin, 23*, 182–186.

Tessler, J. F., Stokes, S. R., & Pietras, M. (1978). Consumer response to Valium. *Drug Therapy, 8*, 179–186.

Tomb, D. A. (1988). *Psychiatry for the house officer* (3rd ed.). Baltimore: Williams & Wilkins.

Tsuang, M. T. & Simpson, J. C. (1985). Mortality studies in psychiatry: Should they stop or proceed? *Archives of General Psychiatry, 42*, 98–103.

Tyrer, P., Owen, R., & Dowling, S. (1983). Gradual withdrawal of diazepam after long term therapy. *Lancet, 1*, 1402–1406.

Uhlenhuth, E. H., Balter, M. B. & Lipman, R. S. (1978). Minor tranquilizers. Clinical correlates of use in an urban population. *Archives of General Psychiatry, 35*, 650–655.

Uhlenhuth, E. H., Balter, M. B., Mellinger, G. D., Cisin, I. H., & Clinthorne, J. (1983). Symptom checklist syndromes in the general population. *Archives of General Psychiatry, 40*, 1167–1173.

U.S. Bureau of the Census (1986). *Statistical abstract of the United States: 1987 (107th ed.)*. Washington, DC: U.S. Government Printing Office.

van der Kolk, B. A., Shader, R. I., & Greenblatt, D. J. (1978). Autonomic effects of psychotropic drugs. In M. A. Lipton, A. DiMascio, & K. F. Killam (eds.). *Psychopharmacology: A generation of progress* (pp. 1009–1021). New York: Raven Press.

Van Putten, T., & Marder, S. R. (1987). Behavioral toxicity of antipsychotic drugs. *Journal of Clinical Psychiatry, 48*, 13–19.

Van Putten, T., Marder, S. R., Mintz, J., & Poland, R. E. (1988). Haloperidol plasma levels and clinical response: A therapeutic window relationship. *Psychopharmacology Bulletin, 24*, 172–175.

Van Putten, T., & May, P. R. A. (1978). Subjective response as a predictor of outcome in pharmacotherapy: The consumer has a point. *Archives of General Psychiatry, 35*, 477–480.

Van Putten, T., May, P. R. A., & Marder, S. R. (1984). Akathisia with haloperidol and thiothixene. *Archives of General Psychiatry, 41*, 1036–1039.

Van Putten, T., May, P. R. A., Marder, S. R., & Wittman, L. A. (1981). Subjective response to antipsychotic drugs. *Archives of General Psychiatry, 38*, 187–190.

Veith, R. C., Raskind, M. A., Caldwell, J. H., Barnes, R. F., Gumbrecht, G., & Ritchie, J. L. (1982). Cardiovascular effects of tricyclic antidepressants in depressed patients with chronic heart disease. *New England Journal of Medicine, 306*, 954–959.

Vestergaard, P. (1983). Clinically important side effects of long-term lithium treatment: A review. *Acta Psychiatrica Scandinavica, 67*, 1–33.

Wehr, T. A., & Goodwin, F. K. (1987). Can antidepressants cause mania and worsen the course of affective illness? *American Journal of Psychiatry, 144*, 1403–1411.

Wernicke, J. F. (1985). The side effect profile and safety of fluoxetine. *Journal of Clinical Psychiatry, 46*, 59–67.

Williams, P., Murray, J., & Clare, A. (1982). A longitudinal study of psychotropic drug prescription. *Psychological Medicine, 12*, 201–206.

Winstead, D. K., Anderson, A., Eilers, M. K., Backwell, B. & Zaremba, A. L. (1974). Diazepam on demand. Drug seeking behavior in psychiatric inpatients. *Archives of General Psychiatry, 30*, 349–351.

Yesavage, J. A., Tanke, E. D., & Sheikh, J. I. (1987). Tardive dyskinesia and steady-state serum levels of thiothixene. *Archives of General Psychiatry, 44*, 913–15.

Ziegler, V. E., & Biggs, J. T. (1977). Tricyclic plasma levels: Effect of age, race, sex, and smoking. *Journal of the American Medical Association, 238*, 2167–2169.

# 7 | PERSONALITY FACTORS IN THE MEDIATION OF DRUG RESPONSE

Sidney E. Cleveland
*Baylor College of Medicine*

Paradoxical or idiosyncratic response to drugs and medication has been noted clinically for years. The lay person is familiar with the differential response to alcohol by some people ingesting approximately equivalent alcohol dosage. Thus, there have always been belligerent drunks, weeping drunks, loquacious drunks, and mute drunks. It has usually been assumed that the range of response to alcohol relates in some way to the personal makeup of the individual. With the advent of the tranquilizer drugs in the mid-1950s such anecdotal observations drew the attention of clinicians who noted differential response, given equivalent dosage, to drugs intended to calm the patient but which only created more agitation and unrest rather than tranquility for some patients. Accordingly, studies were directed at identification of factors either within the individual or in the environment related to or possibly responsible for the aberrant drug response. Experiments were undertaken to explore the mediation of drug response by situational factors, motivation, attitude toward medication, self-image, suggestibility, and personality. It is with the latter factor that this chapter is concerned. All of these influences are often referred to collectively as nonspecific in contrast to the specific or pharmacological action of a drug (Fisher, 1970a).[1]

---

[1] For the sake of clarification it should be noted that the Seymour Fishers cited in these reviews are two separate individuals. Seymour Fisher (a) was located at Boston University School of Medicine and now is at the University of Texas School of Medicine, Galveston, Texas, while Seymour Fisher (b) was and is located at the State University of New York Health Science Center, Syracuse, New York.

Stimulated initially by the variant response of psychiatric patients to the phenothiazenes and later by the variant response to other of the psychoactive medications, a steady stream of research was launched, intended to explore the role of personality in drug response.

This research, which produced a continuous literature stretching from the 1950s and for the next 30 or so years, is reviewed in this chapter. These studies appear to have had one, two, or even three purposes, not all studies being concerned with all three goals. First there is the intent in most of the research to demonstrate that persons differing on some personality dimension show significantly different psychological, behavioral, or physiological response to a given drug or medication. Second, some of these studies also were aimed at demonstrating the relationship of the personality trait to efficacy of the prescribed drug. Finally, some studies, having found drug response to be mediated by personality, concerned themselves with an explanation as to how this could be, what theoretical position was possible in explaining how a psychological orientation (personality trait) could influence a physiological response (drug reaction)? This latter question invoked the age-old dilemma, for some investigators, of the body-mind relationship.

This chapter observes certain limits on the survey of the drug response literature. There is no review of research studies on the physiological or behavioral effects of drugs per se. That is, the literature reporting the effect of drugs on personality is not reviewed. Neither is the literature on the response to placebos reviewed unless the study involves placebo response as mediated by personality. Finally, the chapter does not concern itself with response to illicit drugs unless the research was carried out before the drug was ruled illicit (as in the case of LSD).

The relevant literature is reviewed and critiqued, especially as to the methodological and statistical shortcomings that characterized many of the studies in this area, particularly the early ones.

Presumably the original intent stimulating research interest in the role of personality in drug response was to discover personality patterns so persuasive of positive response ("The right drug for the right patient," Klett & Moseley, 1965) that a clinician, before reaching for a prescription blank, would order a personality analysis for the patient. That this happy occurrence did not ensue from the research studies, despite some promising findings, is of interest, and this chapter will examine why this fortunate payoff from the research did not follow. Also, although there was a fairly steady flow of publications in this area, extending over a 30-year or longer period, the research literature in the past few years has nearly disappeared, suggesting a loss of interest in the topic. In this chapter speculation is offered as to possible reasons why interest in the role of personality in drug response has languished.

## COMPLEXITIES OF PERSONALITY–DRUG RESPONSE
## RESEARCH

Experimentation intended to relate personality factors to drug response is an enormously complicated affair. It is probably too harsh a criticism to characterize such attempts as efforts designed to correlate one unknown with a second unknown. But often the results of such research seem to approach that extreme. Eysenck (1983) has provided a service to all experimenters in this area by contributing a listing of possible variables influencing drug response, of which personality represents only one factor out of many. Eysenck pointed out that in addition to such obvious factors as the nature of the drug under consideration, including dosage and its frequency, mode of introduction, and so forth, other personal and situational factors must be considered. These may include situational stresses, motivation of the subject for participating in the experiment, prior drug experience, subject's sex, age, physical and mental health, doctor–patient relationship, and the social environment of the experiment. Presumably the experimenter must be sensitive to the possible presence of all these variables in the research study, any one or combination of which might imbalance the experiment and confound the results. Because it is virtually impossible to control all variables precisely, the need for employing large numbers of subjects in these experiments, in the hopes that any bias introduced will be balanced out, is especially important. As we see, many of the published studies used very small subject samples.

Eysenck (1983) goes on to cite other factors that may confound personality–drug research outcome. These include drug tolerance and an opposite effect "kindling," time of day effect, and biphasic drug effects, that is, differential drug effect at different dosages and an interaction with different personality types.

Another hazard inherent in psychopharmacological research and one not directly addressed by Eysenck involves the use of volunteers as research subjects. Lasagna (1963) reminds us that the motivation of research volunteers may influence research outcome. For example, money, hope for self-therapy, desire for professional advice, escape from personal problems, even self-destructive impulses may motivate subjects to participate. Not mentioned, but possibly important because mental set toward the experiment of those forced to participate in the research is unknown, is that of "volunteers" who by their status (e.g., students or prisoners) must serve as subjects.

Eysenck (1983) also provided another helpful guideline to research psychopharmacologists in emphasizing the point that personality–drug response research should proceed from a theory-oriented position rather than a pragmatic or empirical point of view. Unfortunately, his advice comes much too late for the majority of studies in this field. As we see, there has been little uniformity in the approaches selected by researchers, each experimenter or team of experimenters pursuing their own favorite personality trait and comparing it to their drug of choice, resulting in an often confusing array of findings.

Of course, in recommending a theory-oriented point of departure for research, Eysenck (1983) selected his own theory of personality as the proper launching pad. In the Eysenckian scheme of things there are only three dimensions or areas of personality; and despite the bewildering array of personality measures available, these can all be encompassed within three axes. These are (a) Psychoticism versus Impulse control (P), (b) Extraversion versus Introversion (E), and (c) Neuroticism versus Emotional stability (N). These factors can be obtained from the Maudsley Personality Inventory (Eysenck, 1947). Eysenck (1983) also reasoned that drugs can be classified in such a way that behavior will be influenced in a specific direction. Thus, P behavior will be increased by a hallucinogenic drug such as LSD. Major tranquilizers, like the phenothiazines, should decrease P behavior. Stimulant drugs will result in more introversion and depressants, more extraversion, whereas adrenergetic drugs will be associated with N activation. Eysenck (1983) turned these equations around and in a sampling of published studies demonstrates by selecting subjects according to their standing on his personality axes that they respond to certain drugs differentially. For example, he described an experiment by Heinze (1983) where low N scorers improved under placebo or tranquilizer and high N scorers declined under a tranquilizer. However, many of Eysenck's citations involve laboratory studies that have at best only peripheral clinical application. It is unclear just how accurate Eysenck's theory is in predicting drug response from his theoretical position. Eysenck claimed (Zubin & Katz, 1964) that a review of "100 random articles" reveals the number of his successful predictions to be "well above the 80 percent level" (p. 375). However, Zubin and Katz (1964) demur. Although they agree with Eysenck that research on personality and drug effect may best proceed from a theoretical base, their review of Eysenck's work reveals his predictions to have failed as often as they succeeded, or 50%. But one should note that these are only estimates of the success–failure rate drawn from the published literature. Because negative or inconclusive research findings seldom are published, the real failure–success rate is unknown. The often-mentioned *Journal of Negative and Inconclusive Results* has never been published.

Also, work by von Felsinger, Lasagna, and Beecher (1955) indicates that drug response does not always proceed according to any straight line formula with atypical drug response (e.g., dysphoria in a response to a stimulant) being nearly as common as the typical or expected response (euphoria).

Fisher (1970a) suggested that not all of the so-called nonspecific factors influencing drug outcome, such as personality, are necessarily psychological in nature although as social scientists we tend to infer such an influence. Actually, he points out, there are very few drugs whose effects are entirely "specific" patient to patient and within each patient. He mentioned, as did

Eysenck (1983), other possible "nonspecific" factors, a list approximating the latter's. Fisher also discussed in greater detail some of these factors: for example, the pathologic state of the subjects, including the reliability of diagnosis and milieu of the drug administration, especially the doctor–patient or subject–experimenter relationship and expectation of outcome on the part of both. Fisher believed it is important to distinguish between drug response (behavioral change under drugs) from drug effect (direct drug pharmacodynamic action) and between placebo response (behavioral change) and placebo effect (that portion of behavioral change due to receiving medication). One assumes that we are being reminded here that all drugs, in addition to their pharmacological effect, also carry a placebo effect. Finally, Fisher posed four general principles psychopharmacologists should observe:

1. The more the response system being measured involves cortical processes such as awareness, consciousness and subjective feelings, the greater will be the role of nonspecific factors influencing drug response. (p. 35)

2. Many apparent nonspecific influences may be reducible to (i.e., explained by) simple physiologic and pharmacologic factors. (p. 36)

3. The more "potent" a drug is, the less sensitive it will be to nonspecific factors. (p. 36) (Carried to the extreme, if a drug is potent enough, all response will be the same regardless of personality or any other nonspecific factor; the patient will be toxic, probably unconscious or dead.)

4. Most available data suggest that the maximum drug response can be obtained by administering the drug in the presence of the most favorable "placebogenic" (all nonspecific) factors. (p. 37)

Yehuda (1976) covered some of the same complexities of drug research as do Eysenck (1983) and Fisher (1970a). In addition, he pointed to an experiment by Schachter (1964) who demonstrated that varying instructions to subjects regarding expected drug response modifies reaction of the subject to a drug.

Brehm and Back (1968) and Back and Sullivan (1978) were interested in the expectations of individuals about drug effects and the relationship of these expectations to certain aspects of personality. Following factor analysis of response to a questionnaire regarding attitude toward drug taking, willingness to change oneself using drugs and self-body attitudes, Brehm and Back (1968) identified five factors related to willingness to change oneself using chemicals. These were:

1. Insecurity, that is, a desire to change distressing symptoms by chemical means;

2. Fear of loss of control, that is, fear of one's actions under drugs or of becoming dependent on drugs;

3. Sick role, that is, seeking external help under stress;
4. Denial of drug effects;
5. Curiosity.

Brehm and Back found in a youthful population an association between attitudes toward self and expressed willingness to take drugs but a different pattern for males versus females. Working with a middle-aged to elderly group Back and Sullivan (1978) also found personal attitudes to be related to use of drugs and medicine but in different ways than was true for youth. These two studies underline the need for psychopharmacologists to pay heed to sex and age in their search for personality–drug response relationships, a precautionary note not always followed by the researchers.

Aaronson (1970) worried that personality–drug response research findings raise the problem of mind–body dualism and challenge the "monastic orientation" of science. But he resolves this dilemma by noting that both drug response and personality traits are handled (measured) in identical fashion, that is, by observing behavior. He stated: "Concepts of methods of study developed in the area of personality are equally applicable to studying drugs and pharmacological methods may be profitably used to clarify problems of personality theory" (p. 816).

Downing and Rickels (1978) also reviewed published research on the role of nonspecific factors over the prior decade and pointed to the often confusing and sometimes inconsistent results encountered in attempting to relate personality and many other variables to response to mild tranquilizers, the anxiolytic drugs. They express concern about the generalizability of findings using small homogeneous patient groups in studies on personality–drug response.

Two other caveats should be noted in reviewing the literature in this area. These limiting factors were not cited in the studies reviewed but may be relevant in evaluating the findings. First, many of the studies in order to maximize the chances for positive results used as research subjects only the upper and lower 10%–20% of persons scoring on a particular psychological test. This procedure, while understandable, raises questions about the majority of the population rejected from the research because they were not "pure" individuals. Would the hypotheses still have been confirmed in a general group as measured on a particular personality trait? How broadly can the findings be generalized? For example, Heniger, DiMascio, and Klerman (1964–1965) were interested in the differential response to phenothiazines by Type A versus Type B students as determined by MMPI scores. Eight Type A and 8 Type B subjects were selected from a pool of 120 volunteers. One wonders what the effect on the experimental results were following such a highly selective subject procedure.

Finally, attention should be directed to a possible distinction between statistical significance in an experiment and clinical significance. One is reminded of studies on biofeedback training, for example, Friedman, Cleveland, and Baer (1980), where post-myocardial infarction patients were trained to change voluntarily their heart rate to a statistically significant average degree of one or two heart beats per minute. But does such a finding have any clinical significance? Probably not many cardiologists would be impressed. The same question can be raised about statistically significant drug response differences among subjects selected for their variance along a particular personality dimension.

The published literature on personality–drug response, as will be seen, has not been able to demonstrate with any consistency a convincing relationship between the personality trait under study and treatment effect. In fact, some studies present a confusing clinical picture of outcome, with some patients improving and some getting worse (e.g., Frostad, Forrest, & Bakker, 1965–1966; Sarwer-Foner, 1957). Many studies used nonclinical subjects with no clinical relevance. Thus, the research in this area sent no compelling message to clinicians that attention to the personality of their patients would materially influence treatment outcome.

## REVIEW OF THE LITERATURE ON MEDIATION OF DRUG RESPONSE BY PERSONALITY FACTORS

Over a 30-year period, numerous investigators have invoked the use of a variety of personality traits and behavioral characteristics as possible predictors of drug response. In a few instances the choice of personality trait has been guided by a theory involving the interaction of personality and drugs. However, most studies appear to have been either exploratory in choice of a particular trait or a matter of convenience with an easily administered personality test available. At the same time some studies chose as the independent variable either a personality test that was cumbersome and time consuming (MMPI) or one requiring specialized expertise to administer, score, and interpret (Rorschach) or required special laboratory equipment (Rod and Frame Test or Tilting Room and Tilting Chair Test—Witkin et al., 1954). Such highly specialized procedures would not be readily available to the practicing clinician to be used prior to drug treatment.

This is not an exhaustive survey of the literature but a representative sampling of studies exploring a variety of personality traits pursued in the hopes of clarifying the phenomenon of paradoxical drug response. For earlier literature reviews in this area see Eysenck (1983), Zubin and Katz (1966), and Yehuda (1976).

## Psychoanalytic

Because traditionally psychoanalysis shuns biochemical or physical explanations of behavior and adheres to a psychological approach, it is a bit surprising to find that psychoanalytic theory guided some of the earlier studies on personality and drug response. Sarwer-Foner (1957) and Sarwer-Foner and Ogle (1956) treated patients with "affect disorders" using reserpine or chlorpromazine and observed that men who feared passivity usually employed energetic activity as a defense against their passivity. According to Sarwer-Foner, these drugs, with their sedative properties, interfered with the rigorous, masculine activity employed by such men, and their major ego defense was thus impaired, resulting in their becoming more anxious and upset. Of the 55 patients studied, 16 were judged to fall within this category and the poor results obtained with these 16 were considered to follow from threat to their ego posed by the passivity forced on them by a tranquilizing drug. Other patients (number not cited) interpreted drug side effects as representing an altered body image and feared losing body control. Depressed patients, restricted in their interpersonal relations by the sedative effects of the drugs, become more depressed, anxious, and agitated (number not provided). Unfortunately, confirmation of an interesting hypothesis, namely that the psychological meaning of a drug to a patient may weaken ego defense, receives questionable support in these studies because of the faulty methodology employed. For example, in addition to drug therapy many of these patients were receiving psychotherapy, and the confounding effects of this variable are unknown. Also, there was no double-blind procedure employed, and therapists were also evaluators of drug response. No details are provided as to the method or reliability of patient evaluations. Drug dosage varied greatly among patients. Some patients received only 1 mg or less of reserpine a day and the highest dose was 40 mg a day. Average duration of dosage is given as 26 days but varied from less than 24 hours to 66 days. Some patients received the drug orally and some by injection. How these considerable variations in dosage, method of dosage, and duration of dosage influenced drug response is unknown. Finally, although the theory may contribute to an understanding of why some patients worsen in drug therapy, it says nothing as to why patients improve with drugs.

## Reactors and Nonreactors

The concept of Reactors versus Nonreactors originated in the empirical studies on placebo response to pain. Jellinek (1946) and Beecher, Keats, Mosteller, and Lasagna (1953), for example, observed that in working with oral analgesics for relief of pain some persons obtained as much relief from an inert placebo as from a drug (aspirin, codeine, or morphine). These persons were termed Reactors and were also usually found to obtain more relief from analgesics than did Nonreactors. Reactors had difficulty discriminating between a drug and a placebo, a finding that is of interest as is seen in examining other research studies. In subsequent studies (Lasagna, Mosteller, von Felsinger, & Beecher, 1954; von Felsinger et al., 1955) the personality of Reactors and Nonreactors (determined by response to a placebo) was described using interviews, Rorschach testing, and the Vocabulary subtest of the Wechler–Bellevue Intelligence Scale. Reactors–Nonreactors did not differ as to intelligence (measured by the Vocabulary subtest) but did differ on the Rorschach and on demographic data obtained from interviews. On the basis of certain Rorschach "signs" the researchers described Reactors as more anxious, more self-centered, more emotionally labile, and more "talkative" than the Nonreactors. The latter, however, were not seen as normal, as they were described as more rigid and emotionally controlled than the "average," but still not as deviant as the Reactors. In the von Felsinger et al. (1955) study personality deviance (measured by the Rorschach) correlated with atypical drug response. That is, subjects who reacted to a drug such as amphetamine with dysphoria or to morphine with euphoria displayed deviant personalities as revealed by interview and Rorschach performance. But these personality–drug interactions were post hoc, not predicted from Rorschach signs or interview data and involved only small numbers of subjects, like 2 or 4 out of the total group of 20 subjects. Seven subjects with normal, mature personalities, based on Rorschach records, reacted typically to the drugs.

There are a number of problems associated with the Reactor–Nonreactor studies. For example, interview data differentiating the two groups are not well defined (e.g., Reactors were rated as greater "talkers" than Nonreactors but no definition of a talker was provided.) Reactors gave a greater number of responses to the Rorschach Test than did Nonreactors. Since most of the Rorschach "signs" differentiating the personality characteristics of the two groups are directly dependent on the total number of responses produced, one can only conclude that the Reactors were the more verbally expressive to the test. One of the difficulties with the Reactor–Nonreactor concept is the matter of constancy. Are Reactors always Reactors and to all drugs and placebos or only to certain ones at certain times? Are Nonreactors always Nonreactors? The answers to these questions are not reassuring. In the Lasagna et al. study (1954), for example, among 93 postoperative patients only 21% were consistently Nonreactors, never being relieved of pain by a placebo, whereas only 14% were consistent Reactors, always relieved of pain. Two thirds of the subjects thus could not be consistently placed into the Reactor–Nonreactor categories.

In an ambitious study Joyce (1959) set out to replicate the Lasagna et al. (1954) findings using medical students and their response to either cyclizine hydrochloride, mecolzine hydrochloride, perphenazine, prochlorperazine, or a placebo (lactose). A large number of psychological tests and procedures were given including the Bernreuter Personality Inventory (Flanagan, 1935); an intelligence test (Group Test for High Grade Intelligence; Heim, 1956); the Moreno Sociogram (Moreno, 1935), and the Assessment of Autonomic Activity Awareness (Mandler, Mandler, & Uviller, 1958).

The study contained two phases. In the first, 48 men and 11 women reported symptoms following drug administration, using a questionnaire. In Phase 2 a new sample of medical students comprising 50 men and 9 women also took the same psychological tests and their status as Reactors or Nonreactors was predicted from their test results. Two of the tests discriminated between Reactors and Nonreactors, the Bernreuter and the Autonomic Awareness Questionnaire. In Phase 1 Reactors were initially identified by their response to a "dummy" (placebo). Results of the Bernreuter test revealed Reactors to be less self-confident and less dominant than Nonreactors, while being more sociable and extraverted.

The Autonomic Awareness (AA) questionnaire was used only in Phase 2 of the experiment. Subjects with high AA scores, that is, those who reported more bodily symptoms such as bowel movements or sweating, were significantly more likely to be Reactors to a placebo than Nonreactors. The author concluded that the results of his studies should be considered in prescribing medication for Reactors or Nonreactors. For example, according to Joyce, a placebo may be sufficient for a favorable response with a Reactor, whereas a Nonreactor may need an active drug to cope with the same symptom. Also, Joyce warned that in the evaluation of new drugs the proportion of Reactors and Nonreactors in the experimental group must be obtained in order to measure the true effectiveness of the drug.

There are some unexplained puzzles in the results of this study. In Phase 1 only 50% of the men could be identified as "consistent Reactors or Nonreactors" and 36% of the women. In Phase 2, 62% of the men and 100% of the women were reported as "consistent Reactors." One wonders what the "real" distribution of Reactors and Nonreactors in any population may be, given these variable numbers. In view of other studies (e.g., Brehm & Back, 1968; Fast & Fisher, 1971b) that found men and women to differ in drug response and attitudes toward drugs, why did Joyce bother to include women in these experiments, given the small numbers used, 11 in Phase 1 and 9 in Phase 2? Or, having included women, why was a separate analysis of their results not done?

The study is commendable in that a replication of the experiment was contained in the second phase. Also, personality hypotheses were not limited to psychological test results, but attempts were made to verify the personality style of Reactors or Nonreactors from actual behavior such as sociometric ratings and classroom behavior. The investigator considers the findings to validate the Lasagna et al. (1954) results. But if this was the intent of the experiment, why were the same measures and procedures (Rorschach Test and interviews) not used? Also, the investigator applies the rather liberal probability level of .10 as indicating statistical significance and treats "tendencies" as if they were statistically significant differences. Psychological test score distributions and $p$ values for their differences between groups are not displayed or reported, making it impossible to discern their patterns. The investigator makes the curious point that a factor analysis of the test measures was not attempted because the measures were "notional" or empirical, not based on theory. One would think this would be all the more reason to do a factor analysis in order to specify which factors were contributing to the variance in the subject groups. Finally, the use of medical students required to participate in the studies raises questions about their knowledge of drugs and drug effects and whether such knowledge played any role in the results.

## MMPI

Several investigators have seized upon MMPI scores as the independent variable in studying drug response.

Kornetsky and Humphries (1957) undertook an ambitious study comparing the reactions of normal volunteers, ages 18–23 but not otherwise identified, to a variety of drugs and dosages: sodium barbital, meperdine, chlorpromazine, and LSD. Only 10 subjects were used, 6 men and 4 women. A variety of psychomotor tasks were employed as dependent measures; and MMPI scores on the hysteria, hypochrondrias, depression, and psychathenia scales were correlated with "subjective drug response" (number of symptoms reported) and "objective drug effects" (performance on mental and psychomotor tasks). Rank order correlations are reported between MMPI scores and objective and subjective drug effects. No indication is given as to the statistical significance of these correlations. The investigators considered the effect of the drugs to be dependent on the "reaction pattern" of the subject and related to MMPI score. It was found that those subjects most affected by one drug were also most affected by the other drugs. The more deviant was a subject's MMPI score, the greater was the drug effect. However, because of the extremely small number of subjects (10), the mix of men and women, and the failure to measure pre-drug mental and psychomotor performance, such conclusions must be regarded with caution. Although the investigators believed that the more deviant a subject's MMPI score, the greater would be the drug effect, no indication was made as to what constituted MMPI deviance.

Klerman, DiMascio, Greenblatt, and Rinkel (1959) reported on the response to three agents, 400 mg of phenyltoloxamine, 5 mg of reserpine, or an inert placebo, by 15 male college students. The investigators were interested in the differential response to these drugs by Type A versus Type B subjects as determined by MMPI scores. Type A subjects scored high on the Manic and

Ego Strength MMPI scales and low on the Introversion, Depression, and Manifest Anxiety scales. Type A subjects behaviorally were assertive and athletic and lacked interest in intellectual and artistic endeavors. In some of these characteristics they were similar to Sarwer-Foner's action-oriented patients. Type B subjects scored low on the MMPI Manic and Ego Strength scales and high on the Introversion, Depression, and Anxiety scales. They tended to be passive and invested in intellectual pursuits. Of the original subjects only 5 were judged to be Type A and 5, Type B. Thus, the analyses rested on the differential response to drugs of only 5 persons in each group. Type A subjects disliked sedative drugs (e.g., phenyltoloxamine) and responded negatively to them. Klerman et al. (1959) reasoned that sedation was threatening to this group because of their reliance on muscular activity and the threat to their self-image that inactivity posed. This interpretation follows the Sarwer-Foner (1957) activity–passivity theory regarding the effect of sedatives on action-oriented persons. The contrasting group (Type B), reacted negatively to reserpine, finding the visceral effects of reserpine unpleasant because of their hypochondriacal concerns and sensitivity about their health. This latter finding also follows the lead provided by Sarwer-Foner (1957).

Klerman et al. (1959) state that the differences observed in reaction by Type A and Type B subjects to the drug employed were "statistically significant." However, no information was provided as to what statistical procedures were applied, only that they were "nonparametric." The level of significance also was not indicated.

In a paper delivered by Klerman (1961) reporting on the Klerman et al. (1959) study, he also notes that both Type A and Type B subjects reacted to a placebo and so the question was raised as to whether both groups were placebo Reactors. Klerman rejected the Reactor concept as being "highly relative and dependent upon the exact definition of the anticipated [drug] response in a specified situation" (p. 5.). One assumes that Klerman is here calling into question the reliability of the Reactor concept.

Like Sarwer-Foner, Klerman et al. (1959) reason that on ingesting a drug a person perceives, with or without awareness, changes in central nervous system and peripheral physiological functions due to the drug's effect and assigns meaning to these changes according to his or her personality type.

Extending the prior study, Heninger et al., (1964–65) assigned male student volunteers to either the Type A or the Type B group on the basis of the previously described MMPI scores.

Drugs with sedative properties (e.g., chlorpromazine) were more disrupting to the psychomotor activity of Type A subjects and produced lessening of self-confidence and greater sleepiness than in Type B subjects. Sedation improved rapport with the examiner in the Type B group according to these group members. The investigators contended on the basis of their results that the psychological meaning of a drug and its effects were responsible for an individual's response to the drug, again following the hypotheses of the Sarwer-Foner (1957) studies. That is, assertive, extroverted subjects were threatened by sedatives that disturbed their ego defenses organized around pushing against their environment, whereas introverted, passive subjects welcomed and were not threatened by sedation.

A study by Klapper, McColloch, and Merkey (1973) used MMPI and Army General Classification Test scores to test tolerance to an irritant. Nine army enlisted personnel more tolerant of exposure to a chemical irritant had lower MMPI scores and higher IQ scores than less tolerant personnel. The 9 subjects with the longest time exposure to the irritant had significantly lower L, K, Hy, R, and Lb scores on the MMPI than did the 9 subjects with less tolerance. The investigators concluded that the high MMPI scores of the less tolerant subjects represented concern about health issues and intolerance to pain, a conclusion reminiscent of the Type B subjects in the previously described MMPI studies where Type Bs were concerned about health issues and expressed hypochondriacal complaints. The tolerance displayed by the subjects with higher IQs was unexpected, and the investigators speculated that they were more motivated to perform in test situations.

## Suggestibility

Heller, Walton, and Black (1957) were interested in the personality variable, suggestibility, and its role in the response to the tranquilizer meprobomate. Thirty-two patients, hospitalized for symptoms of "tension," were divided into two groups of 16 each, unevenly represented by men and women, one group receiving meprobomate and one group, a placebo for 4 weeks. The Taylor Manifest Anxiety Scale (TMAS; Taylor, 1953) and MMPI were administered and patients were matched for anxiety, headache, and tension scores before assignment to control or experimental groups. In addition, using Eysenck's (1947) diagnostic grouping, patients were labeled hysteric or dysthymic. Finally, suggestibility was assessed by attempting "light" hypnosis. Not surprisingly, in view of the small number of subjects, the need to divide these into still smaller subgroups for statistical analyses, and the relatively short drug trial period, the results were inconclusive. To answer the questions posed, a much larger subject population should have been employed and a more sophisticated statistical analysis used in order to assign the proper contribution made by each of the many variables under study.

## Acquiescence

Another trait receiving the attention of several researchers attempting to identify personality determinants to drug response is that of Acquiescence. Based on a questionnaire developed by Bass (1956), the Bass Social Acquiescence Scale, the respondent is required to indicate agreement or disagreement with a series of proverbs or clichés. Degree of agreement with or rejection of these statements measures behavioral conformity or a need to be nice and please others, according to Bass (1956) and Fisher and Fisher (1963b). The latter investigators found high Acquiescers to report more of the experimentally suggested body effects of a placebo than did Nonacquiescers. Employed in the study were 33 men and 39 women, all college undergraduates. No sex differences were found either for Acquiescence score or for reported body changes in response to the placebo. Fast and Fisher (1971b) reported on the response by 15 men and 15 women, paid volunteers, to placebo and epinephrine administered intramuscularly to high and low Acquiescers. They found high Acquiescers to be more disturbed by an active drug (more anxiety) than by a placebo. However, the study used simple univariate statistical analyses rather than multiple variate analyses where multiple variables were at play (men vs. women, definite vs. indefinite body image, and high vs. low Acquiescers), so that the results may have been confounded by factors other than Acquiescence standing.

A study by McNair, Fisher, Kahn, and Droppleman (1970a) and an earlier study by these same investigators (McNair et al., 1966a) also found high Acquiescers to respond more positively (less tension-anxiety) to a placebo than to an active drug (diazepam). Low Acquiescers, on the other hand, responded more favorably to the drug. Thus, the two sets of experimenters agreed in their findings that Acquiescence is a mediating factor in response to placebo or an active drug. But the experimenters did not agree in their interpretation of what Acquiescence is. Fisher and Fisher (1963b) and Fast and Fisher (1971b) view Acquiescence as measuring conformity of behavior. However, McNair et al (1966a) do not accept this view of Acquiescence as measured by the Bass Scale. To the contrary, they found their Acquiescers to be anything but conforming behaviorally, displaying greater noncompliance to the research protocol than Nonacquiescers. McNair et al. (1966a) preferred to see Acquiescence as a measure of uncritical thinking in thoughtless and nondiscriminating individuals. They also pointed to studies by Rickels and Downing (1965) and McGee (1962) linking verbal ability (measured by vocabulary performance) to Acquiescence, where low verbals reacted to drugs and placebos as did high Acquiescers. In other words, McNair et al. (1966a) are suggesting that Acquiescence may be more a cognitive factor than a personality trait and may be correlated with verbal ability.

In any event, these various studies using the Acquiescence scale seem to agree that something associated with a differential response to a placebo or to certain drugs is being measured. The effect of the Acquiescence variable persists with different subject populations, college students or psychiatric patients, men or women, and with different medications. If we accept the assertion of Bass (1956) and Fisher and Fisher (1963b) that the Acquiescence scale is a measure of social conformity or a desire to please, then perhaps the underlying personality dynamic at play in these studies is suggestibility.

Finally, it is important to note that not only did McNair et al. (1966b) find differential response to a placebo or diazepam associated with Acquiescence score but they also found this score related to improvement of their psychiatric outpatients depending on whether they received a placebo or diazepam. Low Acquiescers responded more favorably to the active drug diazepam than to a placebo. In a later study (McNair et al., 1970a), similar findings were obtained with 8 female patients using a placebo and a mild tranquilizer (chlordiazepoxide). The investigators accounted for these findings by characterizing high Acquiescers as "poor witnesses," that is, as "thoughtless and nondiscriminating individuals" who misinterpreted and misreported the somatic changes induced by the active drug. The McNair et al. (1966a, 1970a) studies are commendable for their use of sophisticated statistical analyses. Also, along with the Sarwer-Foner (1957) work these are among the few reported research efforts to find a link between a personality variable and clinical outcome following drug treatment.

## Action–Nonaction Orientation and High-Low Anxiety

These two conceptual aspects of personality are discussed within the same section because three different studies included one or both in their experiments. First, Frostad et al. (1965–1966) hypothesized that assertive, "action-oriented" persons would respond differently to certain drugs compared with more passive, non-action-oriented individuals. However, action orientation was not determined as were Klerman's (1961) Type A group by MMPI scores or by Sarwer-Foner's (1957) Rorschach signs and psychiatric interviews but instead on the basis of the Cattell and Stice (1963) 16 Personal Factors Questionnaire (IPAT). From a volunteer group of 225 men, 60 were selected, 30 with action-oriented personalities as measured by the IPAT and 30 as non-action-oriented. Also, the Taylor Manifest Anxiety Scale (TMAS) (1953) was used to further divide the 60 subjects into high- and low-anxiety groups. Frostad et al. (1965–1966) considered a TMAS of 10 and above as representing high anxiety and 9 and below, low anxiety. But in a different study to be described presently, DiMascio and Barrett (1965) used a TMAS score of 7 and below for low anxiety and 20 and above, high anxiety, cutoff scores in line with TMAS published norms. Subjects in the Frostad et al. study were administered either diazepam or a placebo for 3 days and were also subjected to a stress situation that included electric shock and a mathematics test. Non-action-oriented, low-anxiety subjects were most adversely affected by diazepam, especially as to intellectual performance. This group also had the highest number of reported drug side effects. However, the experimental results were confusing and often contradictory. As is seen presently, many methodological questions have been raised about this study, rendering the results questionable.

DiMascio and Barrett (1965) compared drug response in 60 volunteer students rated high or low on the TMAS scale. Either meprobamate, oxazepam, or a placebo was given double blind for a week to groups of 10 each scoring high or low anxiety before drug trials. The Scheier–Cattell Anxiety Battery (1960) was also given pre- and post-drug administration, and scores on these performance tests were used as determinants of drug-induced change in anxiety. High-anxious subjects reduced anxiety with oxazepam while low-anxious subjects increased in anxiety. The authors attempted to explain the latter unexpected result by reasoning that the low-anxious subjects may have been neurotics who did not show their anxiety but who produced "undesirable drug effects." It is important to note that in the DiMascio and Barrett study two separate anxiety measures were used, the TMAS to determine the high-low anxiety groupings and the Scheier and Cattell Anxiety Battery Institute for Personality and Ability Testing (1960) to measure change in anxiety from pre- to post-drug administration. We are not informed whether the TMAS high and low subjects were still high and low anxiety following drug administration.

In an unusual publication, McDonald (1967), himself an investigator of personality–drug interaction, took the Frostad et al. (1965–1966) study to task for its methodological shortcomings. He enumerates at least 10 major defects in the research, ranging from failure to replicate with a larger subject population, failure to provide IPAT cutoff scores, failure to adhere to normative TMAS scores for high anxiety so that the study probably contained no high-anxiety subjects, introduction of experimental stress conditions that seemed to serve no purpose, use of simple *t* tests rather than analysis of variance in the statistical handling of the data, and failure to obtain baseline (pre-drug) measures such a GSR and mental performance. Although McDonald did not single out any other specific publication for such criticism, he indicates that many published studies to date on the personality–drug response question are flawed to a degree, rendering results and conclusions suspect.

## Field Dependence–Independence

Witkin, Dyke, Faterson, Goodenough, and Karp (1962) in a long series of research studies developed a behavioral continuum of field independency–dependency (FI & FD). Based originally on performance tests measuring ability to orient oneself in space and later extended to other behavioral dimensions, FI individuals proved to be the more integrated and differentiated as to self, to need less support and guidance from others as compared to FD persons, and to be inner directed as opposed to FDs who are outwardly directed.

Special equipment is usually used to measure FI or FD status including tasks that measure a person's ability to orient to the vertical. In a situation providing few visual clues such as adjusting a tilted luminous rod in a darkened room to the vertical or adjusting oneself in a tilted chair in a tilted room, people vary in their ability to achieve the vertical.

Silverman, McGough, and Bogdonoff (1967) applied the FI–FD concept to physiological response to insulin. In this experiment, 10 FI men and 10 FD men, college students, responded differently to hypoglycemic insulin injection with differential change in measures such as blood pressure, pulse rate, and free fatty acid level. FIs displayed pulse rate rise, systolic blood pressure rise, and diastolic fall unlike FDs who showed hyporesponsivity. The investigators interpreted these findings as suggesting that FD subjects are chronically more alerted than FIs and have poorer ability to assess both internal and external stimuli.

In a later study Silverman and McGough (1969) extended the FI–FD concept to response to epinephrine. Sixty male volunteers were distributed among FIs, FDs, and "middles." In this experiment FI and FD subjects did not differ significantly on cardiovascular response following epinephrine administration, but FI subjects did show greater GSR activity. The authors note that again FD subjects are less responsive to adrenergic stimuli than FIs. The investigators concluded that FD subjects are less responsive to adrenergic stimuli than FI subjects and, being chronically alerted, are less able to interpret stimuli such as body changes resulting from drug effect.

## Femininity

Greenberg, Fisher, and Shapiro (1973b) explored the relationship between what they termed sex-role development and response to taking medication. Psychiatric inpatients, 20 men and 15 women, were given the California Psychological Inventory Femininity scale (Gough, 1964). Nurses rated patients' resistance to taking tranquilizer medication, enumerated the reported adverse side effects to medication, and rated patients on whether medication was effective. For women, high femininity was related to low resistance to taking medication, fewer reported side effects, and fewer reported body distortions. For men, such relationships did not reach a level of statistical significance. The authors concluded that prior research demonstrated women as being more secure about their bodies than men, which rendered them more immune to adverse effects of medication. However, no information was available on dosage or frequency of medication, which could have influenced results. Other studies have demonstrated that so-called Reactors report more symptoms in response to medication than do Nonreactors (Joyce, 1959). In the Greenberg et al. (1973b) study, a low femininity score in women was associated with more reported side effects to medication than a high femininity score. For men the direction was the same though only at the .10 probability level. Is there thus a relationship between Reactors and low femininity, both groups responding with greater side effects to medication?

Acquiescence is still another personality variable demonstrated in other studies (e.g., Fast & Fisher, 1971b; McNair et al., 1970a) to be associated with drug side effect complaints. One wonders that in research linking personality variables such as femininity, Acquiescence, or "Reactor" status to drug response, how much variance is being introduced by each trait in each study? It should be kept in mind that although research subjects may be selected on the basis of one personality variable, for example Acquiescence, those same subjects also carry an unmeasured and unknown degree of other personality traits, for example, Type A or anxiety. Only a very large study with large number of subjects and employing sophisticated statistical analyses could identify all the possible contributions to outcome findings made by the various traits. Only a large-scale study using a factor analytic approach could tease out the interrelations among the various personality traits.

## Body Image

The perception of one's body as a psychological object is referred to as one's body image. How this image is perceived may take many different forms including size (big–small), adequacy (weak–strong), and well differentiated versus vague and diffuse. A number of devices have been employed to gauge these different aspects of body image. For example, extensive research by Fisher and Cleveland (1968b) indicated that persons differ in the degree to which they perceive their bodies as possessing a boundary well articulated versus diffuse and indeterminate. A measure of boundary definiteness (Barrier Score) based on inkblot percepts (Rorschach Test responses) was developed by these investigators, and position on this boundary dimension (high vs. low barrier) was found to be associated with a wide range of behavioral responses including differential awareness of body areas (e.g., exterior vs. interior), reported effect on body symptoms produced by a placebo or a drug (epinephrine), and channeling of neurophysiological response to various body areas. In general, persons with high barrier scores when asked to focus on their body tended to emphasize their awareness of body areas representing psychologically the body exterior (skin and muscles), whereas low barrier scorers were more attuned to the body areas representing the interior (gut and heart).

It has already been mentioned that some of the earlier work by Sarwer-Foner (1957) found that men who entertained a poor body image (worried about their body as determined in psychiatric interview) interpreted physiological changes produced by a drug (reserpine or chlorpromozine) as impairment of their bodies. Klerman (1961), it will be recalled, found that his Type B subjects, who on the MMPI displayed marked concern about bodily health, reacted negatively to drugs that produced perceptible effects on autonomic and visceral functions. In other words, excessive somatic concern indicative of a poor body image was associated with a characteristic response to certain drugs.

The study by Fast and Fisher (1971b) has also been referred to earlier in connection with the response of high and low Acquiescers to epinephrine and a placebo. These investigators in the same experiment looked at their data in respect to the role of body image in response to epinephrine and a placebo. They utilize the boundary or barrier score developed by Fisher and Cleveland (1968b) and found that some drug and placebo effects could be predicted from the barrier score. In the Fast and Fisher (1971b) study, high male (but not female) barrier scorers tended to report more body exterior symptoms following injection of both placebo and epinephrine. An inverse relationship was found between barrier score and acceptance of suggestions of interior body symptoms following placebo injection. The investigators concluded that a number of hypotheses linking body attitude and specific response to a drug or placebo had been verified. A problem with the study, however, is that the research subjects totaled 15 men and 15 women, while a large number of variables were being evaluated concomitantly (Acquiescence, barrier score, men vs. women, drug–placebo). Simple correlations were used to analyze the findings. A much larger subject population and the application of multivariate analysis might have been more helpful in specifying the contribution made by the different personality elements.

Clausen and Fisher (1973b) studied 75 normal paid female volunteers, separated into five groups, each of which received orally either 200 or 100 mg of pentobarbital, placebo, or 20 or 10 mg d-amphetamine. The barrier score was again employed as a measure of body boundary definition. Other body image measures were also applied, a Body Distortion Questionnaire developed by Fisher (1970b) that inquires about a subject's perception of 82 of his or her body areas. A Body Focus Questionnaire also developed by Fisher (1970b) was used that required the subject to compare relative prominence of 108 paired body areas. Results from ingestion of drug or placebo included heightened body awareness and increase in boundary definiteness. Also, a heightened sense of depersonalization was reported. In other words, following drug or placebo ingestion, subjects apparently experiencing unpleasant somatic effects of the ingestion deal with such experiences by denying them to be a part of themselves (depersonalization). The project examined a number of body image-drug response relationships not germane to this review. Of interest, however, is the finding of a differential relationship between body image and the two drugs and dosages under study. For example, barrier score correlated positively, although only moderately so, with increase in depersonaliza-

tion (reported disturbing body sensations) following d-amphetamine ingestion, but not so for pentobarbital. The authors speculate that the former
drug increases alertness, which, in turn, enhances boundary differentiation,
whereas the latter drug, a sedative, diminishes alertness and diffuses body
boundary definiteness. The authors employed analysis of variance for their
basic statistical data treatment and report only their significant findings. It
would also have been helpful to have known how many total analyses were
performed so as to be able to determine whether the significant results reported
exceeded those expected by chance. The investigators regard the study as "a
rough exploratory effort."

Cassell and Hemingway (1970) also explored body attitudes as mediators
of response to phenobarbital and caffeine citrate. In an initial study, 9 men
and 9 women ingested 30 mg of phenobarbital and responded to Fisher's
(1970b) Body Focus Questionnaire. Sedation of this nature produced an
increased awareness of the head as opposed to other body areas, especially
peripheral ones. Mild stimulation (five 65 mg tablets of caffeine citrate) with
37 additional subjects established a relationship between degree of arousal
and prominence in awareness of outer and right-side body areas. In a third
study, the Fisher–Cleveland (1968b) barrier score was related to ingestion of
the same drugs. (Findings in the earlier reported studies were upheld as to
sedation–arousal and body image changes.) Also, high barrier score was
correlated with increased sedation following phenobarbital ingestion. The
investigators concluded that these novel body image measures provided a
different perspective on the relationship of body attitudes and drug reactions.
But whether body image was mediating drug reaction or drug effects were
influencing body image is not always clear.

## Intelligence

Intelligence is not ordinarily considered to be a component of personality.
Rather it is held to be a measure of cognitive or problem-solving ability.
Nonetheless, several investigators have included a measure of intelligence as
part of their psychological screening of subjects responding to a drug. This
was done not to ascertain the drug's effect on IQ but to see whether high- or
low-IQ persons responded differently to the drug. Usually the IQ measure
employed was a vocabulary test such as the vocabulary subtest in the Wechsler–Bellevue Intelligence Scale. Results of these attempts to relate IQ to
differential drug response were as inconsistent as similar attempts with personality traits. For example, Klapper et al. (1973) found, contrary to their
expectation, that U.S. Army volunteers with high IQs were more tolerant of
pain induced by a potent irritant (orthochloro-benzylidene-malonitrile) than
low-IQ subjects. The investigators speculated that the unexpected finding
could be explained as due to higher motivation to perform by high IQs,

although no measure of motivation was at hand. They also speculated that the low IQs had more psychiatric abnormalities, although no measure of psychiatric symptoms or deviance was available. Mean MMPI clinical scores for both groups were well below 70.

Joyce (1959) found placebo Reactors and Nonreactors in one experiment not to differ on a test of intelligence, but in a second, to differ at the .05 level of significance. Lasagna et al. (1954) found no difference between Reactors and Nonreactors on IQ. Rickels and Downing (1965) found that clinic patients with low verbal ability (low IQ), in contrast to patients with higher verbal ability, responded as favorably to ineffective medication and placebo as they did to more effective medication. Actually, the variance in this study was being contributed by the low-verbal subjects who responded more favorably to placebo or an ineffective drug, whereas high-verbal subjects were split as to improvement on all treatment methods (effective drug, placebo, and ineffective drug). Treatment evaluation of patients was not blind, as psychiatrists treating patients also did the evaluations, which could have biased the data.

On an a priori basis there is no reason to assume that, at least within the normal range of intelligence, IQ should have any relationship to drug response. Results of the few studies employing IQ as a predictor of drug response must be classified as inconclusive.

## Significance of the Research

What is to be made of all these studies? Do they advance our knowledge and understanding of the interaction between "mind" and "body," and have the results provided direction in the clinical field that would assist in selection of the right drug for the right patient? As far as the latter part of this question is concerned, there is no evidence that outcome of the personality–drug response studies has had any impact on the prescription of medication in clinical settings. As to the first part of the question regarding contribution to the theory of "mind–body" relationships, this reviewer would tend to agree with Zubin and Katz (1964), who, in reviewing the status of the field nearly three decades ago, concluded:

Our survey of the relation between psychopharmacology and personality change has forced us to realize that neither of these two fields is sufficiently defined to enable us to make definitive conclusions regarding their interaction at the present time. Both fields are themselves at a low level of articulation and any attempt at studying their interaction is very hazardous. (p. 394)

A difficulty with many of the studies cited involves the faulty methodology employed, the application of simplistic statistical analyses where more sophisticated multivariate analyses would have been indicated, the use of very small and often highly selected subject populations, and the failure to replicate studies, especially where small numbers of research subjects were used. Eysenck (1983), Fisher (1970a), Lasagna (1963), and others have listed the many nonspecific factors in addition to personality that may influence drug response. With many variables at play, not all of which can be controlled, a sizable number of research subjects should be included in the personality–drug response studies in the hopes that nonspecific factors other than personality will be balanced out.

There is another curiosity in all these published studies. It seems not to matter as to positive results that all manner of dependent variable measures (personality tests) were used and different independent variables (drugs) as well. Projective tests, psychiatric interviews, paper-and-pencil tests, and perceptual tasks used to ascertain highs and lows on personality typologies all resulted in differential drug response. If we are to accept all the research findings at face value, some powerful and generalized (but unidentified) personality factor must be at play to account for the positive results across such a broad range.

In a few instances there were consistent and replicated findings linking a personality score with a specific placebo or drug response. These included Acquiescence score and Action Orientation versus Passive Orientation. What theory can explain the findings in these cases? If we accept, for the sake of argument, that high Acquiescence is a form of Passive Orientation and low Acquiescence the opposite, perhaps we are dealing here with a single personality dimension. Then the theory encompassing these studies can be explained in simple terms fitting both Eysenck's (1983) or Sawer-Foner's (1957) position—namely, that a drug will act in an opposing direction to the patient's major personality trait. That is, an action-oriented person will be disturbed by a drug that lessens activity, whereas a passively oriented person will adjust easily to a sedative or tranquilizer. But this formula applies only to a narrow band of personality traits and a narrow band of drugs.

If the criterion for success of the research in this area rests on its influence in guiding clinical practice, one must conclude that little was accomplished. Certainly practitioners, faced with the responsibility of prescribing this drug or that one for this mental condition or that one, received no mandate from the results of this array of studies to dictate their clinical practice. No imperative findings emerge to compel clinicians to order a personality analysis for their patients before prescribing a treatment drug. And the dwindling numbers of published research on personality–drug response in recent years suggest that the researchers themselves have become discouraged either by their tangle of findings or by the failure of practitioners to adopt any of their conclusions for their practice.

That hoped-for influence on clinical practice is not too strict a criterion by which to judge the importance and success of these studies is attested to by the closing remarks of some of these researchers in their articles. For example, McNair et al. (1970), having found the Acquiescence score to be predictive of drug response, concluded: "The results support an earlier recommendation that level of Acquiescence be considered in the methodology of out-patient drug trials" (p. 135). Or consider the closing remarks of Shaw-cross and Tyer (1985):

> Personality characteristics therefore constitute an important factor in predicting response to antidepressant drugs. If, in an individual case, there seems to be little to choose between treatment with a TCA (Tricyclic antidepressant) or a MAOI (monoamine oxidase inhibitor) a personality assessment may help provide a decision. Behavioral and psychological responses to drugs are influenced in large part by the character structure and defenses of the individual, features which may be found in patients in different psychiatric diagnostic categories. Awareness of these personality mechanisms is necessary for proper understanding of the effects of drugs in clinical situations. (p. 561)

Finally, Klerman et al. (1959) considered the role of personality in drug response thusly:

> Behavioral and psychological responses to drugs are influenced in large part by the character structure and defenses of the individual, features which may be found in patients in different psychiatric diagnostic categories. Awareness of these personality mechanisms is necessary for proper understanding of the effects of drugs in clinical situations. (p. 237)

That these warnings or hopes expressed by the researchers went largely un-heeded by the practitioners is interesting and the reasons worthy of specu-lation.

First, perhaps the implications of the research findings on personality–drug response were not followed by clinicians simply because the published studies were not read by them. Researchers do research and clinicians practice their art and in many instances there is little communication between the two groups. But, assuming the publications were read, at least in part, perhaps the clinicians were dismayed by the simplicity of many of the studies or were discouraged by the bewildering list of personality factors reported as influenc-ing drug response. It seems that nearly every personality factor studied "worked," that is, was found to be associated with drug response. So, which factor should the practitioner use to refine his or her drug prescriptions?

The practitioner is aware that each of his or her patients possesses more than a single personality variable. The patient who scores high on Acquies-cence also scores somewhere on Type A, Type B, "Action Oriented," and so forth. As Zubin and Katz (1964) observed: "When one is attempting to link up a single trait with drug response, he has, however, to contend with the fact that his subjects, though having one personality trait in common, are likely to differ in other traits and thus make it impossible to relate the trait in question to the drug" (p. 372). In addition, the practitioner will see that many of the studies linking personality and drug response selected only the extremes on a certain trait in order to maximize positive results. What about the majority of the clinician's patients? How do they fare in this personality–drug business?

Clinicians reading the personality–drug literature must have reacted with dismay to the measuring instruments used to measure this or that personality trait. The psychological tests or instruments used were either time consuming (MMPI), highly specialized (Rorschach) or required unusual equipment (Rod and Frame Test). Could the busy practitioner afford the time or expertise necessary to carry out the personal analyses? Also the clinician may have wondered about the age of the personality tests involved. (The Rorschach has been around since 1921, the MMPI since 1951, the Bernreuter since 1935, and the Taylor Manifest Anxiety Scale since 1953.) Perhaps the practitioner asked, "Are there no modern, easily administered, scored and interpreted tests that would fit my busy practice?" It may have been a combination of these problems that for the most part turned clinicians off from incorporating personality trait analysis on a regular basis into their practice of dispensing drugs.

Finally, clinicians reading this literature closely may have been puzzled by what seemed a commonality among some of the personality traits under study as well as the characteristics of the drug response to these traits even though the traits may have carried different labels and were measured differently. To note just a few confusing similarities: Type A subjects used by Klerman et al. (1959) were defined as having interest in athletics and "active mastery of the environment," and Type B subjects were "passive and intellectually inclined." McDonald's (1967) Type A subjects measured by the 16 PF were described as "extroverted and self-assertive." High barrier scorers were characterized as being invested in "pushing against their surroundings and being self-steering." Silverman et al. (1967) refer to field independent persons as "taking an intellectual and impersonal approach to problems and with little need for guidance from others." Reactors, described by Joyce (1959), were identified on the Bernreuter as "extroverted," "sociable," and "uncritical." Acquiescers were identified by McNair et al. (1966) as being "thoughtless, uncritical and nondiscriminating." The subjects with similar sounding personality traits but with differing labels also tended to react similarly to drugs or placebo. One is reminded of the proverbial blind men examining an elephant. There is some commonality in there but each investigator pictures it differently. One suspects that there is a degree of correlation among all the traits used by the different investigators. A factor analytic study would have been helpful in identifying the basic variables at play, but one never seems to have been carried out.

## Prescription for the Future

As weather forecasters have found out many times over, prediction of future events is an extremely hazardous business. Research into personality–drug response appears to have come pretty much to a dead end. The payoff for both research investigators and practitioners has not been rewarding enough. What of the future? Will there be a revival of this type of study? In this reviewer's opinion, the answer is probably no.

Opportunity to conduct a definitive study on the relationship of personality to drug response, at least with the antipsychotic drugs, was lost in the 1950s–1960s when the Veterans Administration (VA) conducted its large-scale, nationwide studies on the efficacy of the new antipsychotic drugs, the phenothiazines. Prior to 1956 only a few scattered clinical studies by single investigators reporting on results with a single drug and a few cases were available in the literature. In 1956 a series of cooperative studies in chemotherapy were launched by the VA, using its vast network of hospitals and psychiatric patients, to provide a large subject population and one well distributed geographically (Lasky, 1960). The priorities of these studies were (a) to demonstrate the superior efficacy of the antipsychotics compared to a placebo and (b) to compare the relative efficacy of the antipsychotics. Unfortunately, the role of personality in determining drug response or drug efficacy was understandably not a priority for the VA. Studies similar to the VA cooperative project were also conducted by the Spring Grove State hospital group, Baltimore, MD (Hanlon, Michaux, Ota, Shaffer, & Kurland, 1965; Kurland, Michaux, Hanlon, Ota, & Simopoulos, 1962). These studies, like the VA series, enjoyed the use of large subject populations and the application of sophisticated statistical analyses, but again, the focus of the experiments was the establishment of the superiority of antipsychotic drugs over placebo and the evaluation of the relative effectiveness of the various drugs. The State Hospital studies did include personality measures (e.g., MMPI) but not as drug response predictors. Rather, personality score changes were measured pre-post treatment as indicators of drug effect.

If there should be a revolution in the theory and practice of personality measurement, the study of personality–drug response might be resumed. Pharmacology has had its revolution and forged ahead with an ever evolving, not to mention bewildering, array of drugs for each and every symptom, syndrome, and diagnosis. It would seem an insurmountable task to evaluate personality using the cumbersome measures now available, as it interacts with the enormous list of drugs available, and an impossible task for the clinician to take into consideration personality analyses as he administers to patients from the nearly endless formulary available.

## REFERENCES

Aaronson, B. S. (1970). Drugs: Personality: Personality: Drugs. *Psychological Reports, 26,* 811–818.

Back, K. W., & Sullivan, D. A. (1978). Self-image, medicine and drug use. *Addictive Diseases: An International Journal, 3*(3), 373–382.

Bass, B. (1956). Development and evaluation of a scale for measuring social acquiescence. *Journal of Abnormal and Social Psychology, 53,* 296–299.

Beecher, H. K., Keats, A. S., Mosteller, F., & Lasagna, L. (1953). The effectiveness of oral analgesics (morphine, codeine, acetylsalicylic acid) and the problem of placebo "reactors" and "nonreactors." *Journal of Pharmacology and Experimental Therapeutics, 109,* 393–400.

Brehm, M. L., & Back, K. W. (1968). Self-image and attitudes toward drugs. *Journal of Personality, 36,* 299–314.

Cassell, W. A., & Hemingway, P. (1970). Body consciousness in states of pharmacological depression and arousal. *Neuropharmacology, 9,* 169–173.

Cattell, P. B., & Stice, G. F. (1963). *The 16 Personality Factor Questionnaire* (2nd ed.) Champaign, IL: Institute for Personality and Ability Testing.

Clausen, J., & Fisher, S. (1973b). Effects of amphetamine and barbituate on body experience. *Psychosomatic Medicine, 35,* 390–405.

DiMascio, A., & Barrett, J. (1965). Comparative effects of oxazepam in "high" and "low" anxious student volunteers. *Psychosomatics, 6,* 298–302.

Downing, R. W., & Rickels, K. (1978). Nonspecific factors and their interaction with psychological treatment in pharmacotherapy. In M. A. Kipton, A. DiMascio, & K. R. Killan (Eds.), *Psychopharmacology: A generation of progress* (pp. 1419–1428). New York: Raven Press.

Eysenck, H. J. (1947). *Dimensions of personality.* London: Keegan, Trench, Trubner.

Eysenck, H. J. (1983). Drugs as research tools in psychology: Experiments with drugs in personality research. *Neuropsychobiology. 10,* 29–43.

Fast, G. J., & Fisher, S. (1971b). The role of body attitudes and acquiescence in epinephrine and placebo effects. *Psychosomatic Medicine, 33,* 63–84.

Fisher, S. (1970a) Nonspecific factors as determinants of behavioral response to drugs. In A. DiMascio & R. I. Shader (Eds.), *Clinical handbook of psychopharmacology* (pp. 17–39). New York: Science House.

Fisher, S. (1970b) *Body experience in fantasy and behavior.* New York: Appleton-Century-Crofts.

Fisher, S., & Cleveland, S. E. (1968b). *Body image and personality.* New York: Dover Press.

Fisher, S., & Fisher, R. L. (1963b). Placebo response and acquiescence. *Psychopharmacologia, 4,* 298–301.

Flanagan, J. C. (1935). *Factor analysis in the study of personality.* Palo Alto: University Press.

Friedman, E. P., Cleveland, S. E., & Baer, P. (1980). Heart rate control following myocardial infarction. *American Journal of Clinical Feedback, 3,* 35–41.

Frostad, A. L., Forrest, G. L., & Bakker, C. B. (1965–1966). Influence of personality type on drug response. *American Journal of Psychiatry, 122,* 1153–1158.

Gough, H. G. (1964). *California Psychological Inventory.* Palo Alto: Consulting Psychologists Press.

Greenberg, R. P., Fisher, S., & Shapiro, J. (1973b). Sex-role development and response to medication by psychiatric in-patients. *Psychological Reports, 33,* 675–677.

Hanlon, T. E., Michaux, M. H., Ota, K. Y., Shaffer, J. W., & Kurland, A. A. (1965). The comparative effectiveness of eight phenothiazines. *Psychopharmacologia, 7,* 89–106.

Heim, A. W. (1956). *Manual for the Group Test of High Grade Intelligence A.H. 5.* London: National Foundation for Educational Research.

Heinze, U., Kastner, I., & Kulka, H. (1983). Differential effects of a tranquilizing drug and personality traits. In W. Janke (Ed.), *Response variability to psychotropic drugs* (pp. 203–208). Oxford: Pergamon Press.

Heller, G. C., Walton, D., & Black, D. A. (1957). Meprobamate in the treatment of tension states. *Journal of Mental Sciences, 103,* 581–588.

Heninger, G., DiMascio, A., & Klerman, G. L. (1964–1965). Personality factors in variability of response to phenothiazines. *American Journal of Psychiatry, 121,* 1091–1094.

Jellinek, E. M. M. (1946). Clinical tests on comparative effectiveness of analgesic drugs. *Biometrics Bulletin, 2,* 87–89.

Joyce, C. R. B. (1959). Consistent differences in individual reactions to drugs and dummies. *British Journal of Pharmacology, 14,* 512–521.

Klapper, J. A., McColloch, M. A., & Merkey, R. P. (1973). The relationship of personality to tolerance of an irritant compound. *Journal of Personality and Social Psychology, 26,* 110–112.

Klett, C. J., & Moseley, E. (1965). The right drug for the right patient. *Journal of Consulting Psychology, 29,* 546–551.

Klerman, G. L. (1961). *The influence of personality factors on phrenotropic agent effects.* Paper presented at the sixth annual Veterans Administration research conference, Cincinnati, OH.

Klerman, G. L., DiMascio, A., Greenblatt, M., & Rinkel, M. (1959). The influence of specific personality patterns on the reactions of phenotopic agents. In J. M. Masserman (Ed.), *Biological Psychiatry* (pp. 224–238). New York, London: Grune & Stratton.

Kornetsky, C., & Humphries, O. (1957). Relationship between effects of a number of centrally acting drugs and personality. *AMA Archives of Neurology and Psychiatry, 77,* 325–327.

Kurland, A. S., Michaux, M. H., Hanlon, T. E., Ota, K. Y. & Simopoulos, A. M. (1962). The comparative effectiveness of six phenothiazine compounds, phenobarbital and inert placebo in the treatment of acutely ill patients: Personality dimensions. *Journal of Nervous and Mental Diseases, 134,* 48–61.

Lasagna, L. (1963). The relation of drug induced changes to personality. In M. Rinkel (Ed.), *Specific and non-specific factors in psychopharmacology* (pp. 114–129). New York: Philosophical Library.

Lasagna, L., Mosteller, F., von Felsinger, J. M., & Beecher, H. K. (1954). A study of the placebo response. *American Journal of Medicine, 16,* 770–779.

Lasky, J. J. (1960). Veterans Administration cooperative chemotherapy projects and related studies. In L. Uhr & J. G. Miller (Eds.), *Drugs and behavior* (pp. 540–554). New York: Wiley.

McDonald, R. L. (1976). The effects of personality type on drug response. *Archives of General Psychiatry, 17,* 680–686.

McDonald, R. L. (1967). Influence of personality type on drug response: A critical reply. *Journal of Psychology, 65,* 123–129.

McGee, R. K. (1962). Response style as a personality variable: By what criterion? *Psychological Bulletin, 4,* 284–295.

McNair, D. M., Fisher, S., Kahn, R. J., & Droppleman, L. F. (1970a). Drug-personality and interaction in intensive outpatient treatment. *Archives of General Psychiatry, 22,* 128–135.

McNair, K. M., Kahn, R. J., Droppleman, L. F., & Fisher, S. (1966a). *Patient acquiescence and drug effects.* Paper read at IV World Congress of Psychiatry, Madrid.

Mandler, G., Mandler, J. M., & Uviller, E. T. (1958). The perception of autonomic activity. *Journal of Abnormal and Social Psychology, 56,* 367–373.

Moreno, J. L. (1935). *Who shall survive?* New York: Beacon House.

Rickels, K., & Downing, K. (1965). Verbal ability (intelligence) and improvement in drug therapy of neurotic patients. *Journal of New Drugs, 5,* 303–307.

Sarwer-Foner, G. J. (1957). Psychoanalytic theories of activity-passivity conflicts and of the continuum of ego defenses. *Archives of Neurology and Psychiatry, 78,* 413–418.

Sarwer-Foner, G. J., & Ogle, W. (1956). Psychodynamic aspects of reserpine: Its uses and effects in open psychiatric settings. *Developments in Social Therapy, 1,* 11–17.

Sarwer-Foner, G. J., & Ogle, W. (1955). The use of reserpine in an open psychiatric setting. *Canadian Medical Association Journal, 73,* 187–191.

Schachter, S. (1964). The interaction of cognitive and physiological determinants of emotional state. In P. H. Leiderman & D. Shapiro (Eds.), *Psychobiological approaches to social behavior* (pp. 138–173). London: Tavistock.

Scheier, I. H., & Cattell, R. B. (1960). *IPAT 8-Parallel form anxiety battery.* Champaign, IL: Institute of personality and ability testing.

Silverman, A. J., & McGough, W. E. (1969). Epinephrine response differences in field-dependent and field-independent subjects. *Biological Psychiatry, 1,* 185–188.

Silverman, A. J., McGough, E., & Bogdonoff, M. D. (1967). Perceptual correlates of the physiological response to insulin. *Psychosomatic Medicine, 29,* 252–264.

Shawcross, C. R., & Tyrer, P. (1985). Influence of personality on response to monoamine oxidase inhibitors and tricyclic anti-depressants. *Journal of Psychiatric Research, 19,* 557–562.

Taylor, J. A. (1953). A personality scale of manifest anxiety. *Journal of Abnormal and Social Psychology, 48,* 285–290.

von Felsinger, J. M., Lasagna, L., & Beecher, H. K. (1955). Drug-induced mood changes in man. 2. Personality and reactions to drugs. *Journal of the American Medical Association, 157,* 1113–1119.

Witkin, H. A., Dyke, R. B., Faterson, H. F., Goodenough, R., & Karp, S. A. (1962). *Psychological differentiation,* New York: Wiley.

Witkin, H. A., Lewis, H. B., Hertzman, M., Machover, K., Meissner, P. B., & Wapner, S. (1954). *Personality through perception.* New York: Harper.

Yehuda, S. (1976). The influence of behavioral and environmental factors on drug effect. In D. I. Mostofsky (Ed.), *Behavior control and modification of physiological activity* (pp. 297–313). Englewood Cliffs, NJ: Prentice-Hall.

Zubin, J., & Katz, M. M. (1964). Psychopharmacology & Personality. In P. Worchel & D. Byrne (1964) (Eds.), *Personality and change* (367–395). New York: Wiley.

# 8 | ANALYSIS OF STATISTICAL PROCEDURES AND DESIGNS COMMONLY USED IN DRUG RESEARCH STUDIES

Silas Halperin
*Syracuse University*

In this chapter, the state of the anxiety and depression drug research literature is examined from a statistician's perspective. The critique is based on 49 articles dealing with the somatic treatment of either anxiety or depression. The articles were selected randomly from a computer list of recent publications in these areas.

The research papers were reviewed with two purposes in mind. First, commonly encountered positive features of the design and analysis were collected and are discussed. Second, problem areas were identified and studied, and specific recommendations are made to correct such deficiencies.

## COMMONLY ENCOUNTERED POSITIVE FEATURES

There were some critically important issues that were present in virtually every paper. Each experiment contained a control group of some type. In most control groups, a placebo was administered, although it was rare for the exact composition of the placebo to be reported. Most of the articles provide some statement of the randomization process by which subjects were assigned to either the control group or one of the treatment groups. The importance of a randomized control group cannot be overemphasized in drug treatment experiments of the type considered here. It is well documented (Prien & Levine, 1984) that, based on self-report instruments, a placebo is sufficient to elicit improvement of a variety of conditions. Without some form of comparison group, it is usually impossible to interpret observed treatment

263

effects. The randomization does much to ensure that observed differences are not attributable to differential subject characteristics, rather than to the treatment.

As randomization reduces the risk of rival explanations of results, so too does the inclusion of double blindness. Fortunately, a special attempt was made in almost every experiment to ensure that both the assessors and the subjects were blind to the treatment. Of course, subjects can often guess that they are receiving a placebo if that placebo is inert. The issue of whether a placebo should be devoid of therapeutic value is both an ethical and a design issue, and many trade-offs need to be considered, as are discussed in Prien and Levine (1984).

One distinctive feature of the clinical trial is its susceptibility to damage from attrition. Subject mortality occurred in every experiment reviewed, and the topic was usually pursued by the authors at some length. It is important that authors provide a thorough explanation for why subjects leave a trial, and some assessment of the bias created by this attrition. It is also desirable to describe the implications of missing data to the process of statistical analysis. It is clear that attrition increases the complexity of statistical procedures, and the literature varies in the quality with which this issue is considered.

A number of ad hoc methods have been devised to analyze incomplete data from a drug trial. Some authors cope with attrition by limiting their analysis only to those cases that are complete. This policy suffers from the disadvantage that much information may be lost, and because of this, the risk of bias may be increased (Little & Rubin, 1987, p. 6). Another strategy that is employed is the use of "endpoint" analysis. Here, each subject's final observation is used as the dependent variable in the analysis. The disadvantage of this approach is that comparisons are made among dissimilar observations. Differential attrition in drug and placebo samples could easily confound effects based on such endpoints. For example, if steady improvement is expected across the trial for each sample, the sample that incurs greater attrition will be placed at a disadvantage. That sample is usually the one that receives the inert placebo, and such analysis will then overstate the relative advantage of the drug.

A third ad hoc strategy used in the analysis of incomplete data is to compare each week's results to the baseline. This has the disadvantage that it leads to a proliferation of tests, referred to later as the problem of multiplicity. Also, each successive comparison is based upon a shrinking number of more persistent subjects.

Some authors try more than one of these ad hoc approaches and report whether each provided essentially the same conclusions. This combination strategy is better than any one of the three strategies by itself, but it is not the best that can be done.

Conspicuously absent from any article were model-based statistical techniques that were designed for incomplete longitudinal data (e.g., Ware, 1985). Models of growth (Goldstein, 1979; Grizzle & Allen, 1969) are appropriate to drug trials, yet are not being used. Polynomial growth cure models are especially attractive when used in conjunction with the iterative EM Algorithm (Dempster, Laird, & Rubin, 1977; Little & Rubin, 1987; Laird & Ware, 1982) for appropriate analysis of incomplete data. In the case of polynomials, the suggestion of Cook and Ware (1983) is especially relevant:

> In growth curve analysis, an unbalanced design can result either from missing data or from variation in measurement times among subjects. The random effects model extends to this setting, and the family of random effects models described by Laird and Ware includes polynomial growth models with arbitrary patterns of observation times. In many situations, however, this iterative analysis is closely approximated by a very simple analysis in which we fit a polynomial growth curve for each individual, then analyze the effect of individual characteristics and time-invariant exposure variables on these coefficients by ordinary linear regression, using the coefficients as summary statistics. Especially when the patterns of observations are similar among individuals, we recommend this two-step analysis both for efficiency and ease of interpretation. (p. 16)

An alternative model-based approach to growth curve analysis of incomplete data is provided by successive differences (Schwertman & Heilbrun, 1986). This represents a departure from past practice, and further development of the successive differences may be required.

If the data are incomplete in a nested (or monotone) pattern, other model-based procedures are available. A nested pattern occurs when, once a subject has left a trial, the subject does not return. Such data can be organized into a triangular pattern and analysis can proceed using a likelihood ratio test derived by Bhargava (1975).

Another approach to the analysis of incomplete data from a drug trial is appropriate if the restrictive assumptions of repeated measures analysis of variance (Kirk, 1982) can be defended. The approach, originally developed by Yates (1933) for use in agricultural experiments, was extended by Bartlett (1937) and is discussed and illustrated in the work of Coons (1957).

These model-based procedures were developed especially for the analysis of incomplete data, and thus, unlike the ad hoc procedures now used in drug trials, make use of all the available data in a consistent and integrated fashion. Model-based methods do not create the disadvantages cited above for the ad hoc methods. However, these methods assume that values are *missing at random* (Little & Rubin, 1987); if data are not randomly missing, bias may be introduced by the attrition. In that case, the validity of the experiment may be compromised in a manner that no statistical procedure can cure.

Our ability to draw conclusions from an experiment depends heavily on the characteristics of the subjects, the details of the treatments, and the form of assessing treatment effects. These issues were considered in most of the articles examined. There is good evidence that members of the research community appreciate the importance of these issues and are working to design good experiments. Unfortunately, the articles report results that suggest that double-blindness is something seldom achieved in trials using an inert placebo.

## PROBLEM AREAS OF DESIGN AND ANALYSIS

### Multiplicity

The most pervasive statistical problem encountered in reviewing the articles was an almost total lack of concern for the overall risk of committing a Type I error. Kirk (1982) defined the experimentwise error rate as "the probability that one or more erroneous statements will be made in an experiment" (p. 103). If those statements are conclusions from tests of hypotheses, and if those tests are statistically independent, the experimentwise error rate can be determined. For example, if 10 independent tests are to be performed, each at a .05 level of significance, the experimentwise error rate would be $(1—.95^{10})$, or .401.

Unfortunately, if the tests are not independent, as happens in most experiments, the experimentwise error cannot in general be determined. However, an upper limit on the experimentwise error rate can be set using the Bonferroni inequality (Dunn, 1961). In the illustration of 10 related tests, each performed at a .05 level of significance, the upper limit to the experimentwise error would be $(10 \times .05)$, or .50. If 20 related tests were performed at the .05 level, the best we can say is that the experimentwise error rate is no more than 100%. This comment, that the error rate is no more than 100%, applies to many of the articles that deal with drug research. It should be viewed as unacceptable, and remedies are offered later for this serious problem.

Control over the experimentwise error rate is lost when an excessive number of statistical tests are performed. In the statistics literature, performing too many tests is known as multiplicity. Diaconis (1985) attributed much of the finding of the ESP literature to multiplicity.

Multiplicity in the drug treatment literature occurs when experiments include an abundance of variables. For example, consider the description of variables contained in Rickels et al. (1982):

> During the pretreatment period, demographic and illness history data were collected. At pre- and post-treatment, a battery of laboratory tests, including SMA-12, CBC, urinalysis, and electrocardiogram, and a physical examination were performed. At posttreatment, the physician completed a disposition form in which

he assessed global improvement, recorded reasons for dropouts, and rated several indirect measures of patient satisfaction with study medication. Each week, the physician completed the Hamilton Rating Scale for Anxiety (HAM-A), which provides a psychic and somatic cluster as well as a total score, the Hamilton Rating Scale for Depression (HAM-D), and a global estimate of anxious psychopathology. The physician also recorded information about dosage schedule, concurrent illness, concomitant medication, and vital signs. A side effect checklist was not used; side effects were recorded only when volunteered by the patient. The patients completed the Hopkins Symptom Checklist (HSCL) and the Profile of Mood Scale (POMS) weekly. (p. 82)

The thoroughness of their assessment is laudable, but performing statistical tests on this multitude of variables must create an experimentwise error rate approaching 100%.

What choices are available to us when we have so many variables? Several possibilities are suggested by Diaconis (1985). As one remedy, Diaconis suggested we might *publish some results without "p-values."* Salsburg (1985), in his American Statistician article entitled "The Religion of Statistics as Practiced in Medical Journals," wrote of the heretical nature of this suggestion.

After 17 years of interacting with physicians, I have come to realize that many of them are adherents of a religion they call *Statistics.* It bears some resemblance to the mathematical theories and practices of statistics as described in journals like this one, using many of the same words, but it reflects activity in only a small portion of the statistical world—the use of hypothesis tests. To the physician who practices this religion, Statistics refers to the seeking out and interpretation of p values. Like any good religion, it involves vague mysteries capable of contradictory and irrational interpretation. It has a priesthood and a class of mendicant friars. And it provides Salvation: Proper invocation of the religious dogmas of Statistics will result in publication in prestigious journals. This form of Salvation yields fruit in this world (increases in salary, prestige, invitations to speak at meetings) and beyond this life (continual references in the citation indexes). (p. 220)

If we find it difficult to give up the comforts of significance testing, we may find solace in a distinction that is being endorsed by a growing segment of the statistical community. Many recommend that a distinction be drawn between confirmatory and exploratory analysis. It is probably wise to remind ourselves that not all of our variables are of equal interest or stature. Some, probably only a few, are "Key" variables, upon which strong theoretical interest can be centered in the form of research hypotheses. A larger set of variables are "Promising" on a priori grounds, and what remain, a vast "Haystack" of variables, possess few intrinsic properties upon which defensible research hypotheses may be formulated. This trichotomy was suggested by Mosteller and Tukey (1977, p. 393) in a different, but related, context.

If such a classification scheme can be imposed upon the variables, testing can be limited to those variables categorized as either Key or Promising. Reducing the number of variables submitted to confirmatory analysis will, of course, reduce the multiplicity inherent in the study. The Haystack should be submitted to exploratory analysis (Tukey, 1977) without the inclusion of $p$-values, and findings from these analyses should be viewed as the foundation of hypotheses to be tested in future research.

Even after eliminating the Haystack from inferential consideration, a sizable number of confirmatory analyses may remain. The multiplicity may now be controlled by a number of possible methods. Some would suggest using multivariate analysis of variance, the significance of which would be prerequisite to further univariate analysis (Morrison, 1976). A viable alternative suggested by many, including Diaconis (1985, p. 16), is the use of the Bonferroni inequality. This inequality is the basis of a method by Dunn (1961), which specifies an experimentwise error rate and then divides it among the several significance tests to be performed. For example, if 10 related tests are to be performed, and it is desired to place a limit of .10 on the experimentwise error rate, each test could be performed at the .01 level of significance. This subdivision places an upper limit on the true experimentwise error rate, thus controlling the multiplicity. It should be recognized that the Dunn procedure does not require an equal subdivision and readily allows a larger allocation of error rate to the Key variables than to the Promising variables. For instance, 3 tests could be performed, each at the .025 level, and the remaining 7 less interesting tests could use the .025/7 = .0036 level.

Still another source of multiplicity lurks in the clinical trial. Many authors, when confronted with weekly assessments, do pairwise significance tests. Such an analytic strategy may be found, for example, in Wheatley (1982), who tested differences in consecutive weeks, and in Saul, Jones, Edwards, and Tweed (1985), who compared each weekly value to the baseline. Others (e.g., Jacobson, Goldstein, Dominguez, & Steinbook, 1983) investigate the significance of treatment differences at each week separately. The proliferation of tests from these analytic strategies could be avoided by treating them as simple main effects (Kirk, 1982) and post hoc contrasts, following the finding of an interaction from a factorial analysis.

## The Appearance of Model Misspecification

Certain statistical procedures are especially susceptible to misuse, as is documented in work such as Lewis and Burke (1949). When such a procedure is encountered, it is natural to question whether it has been applied correctly. It is for this reason that any vagueness in the description of the statistics employed in an article should be avoided. Statements such as that found in

Goldberg and Finnerty (1982) are simply not sufficient: "All of the data were analyzed using appropriate statistical techniques" p. 87.

Most statistical procedures were developed by assuming independence of observations. For example, we might have two different samples resulting from random assignment to a condition (drug or placebo). Any comparison between these two conditions involves a comparison between different subjects as well. When the difference between conditions is confounded by differences in subjects, the conditions variable is often called a "between-subjects" variable. Such "completely randomized" designs might be analyzed using the two-sample $t$ test, one-way analysis of variance, or the Mann–Whitney test.

Not all statistical tests require observations to be independent, however. Correlated observations are the basis of some tests (e.g., correlated $t$ test, repeated measures analysis of variance, Wilcoxon matched pairs signed-ranks test). Many phrases are used in place of "correlated observations": paired observations, matched data, blocked data, repeated measures. Paired observations come about when subjects arrive in pairs, as with married couples, siblings, or littermates. Matched (blocked) data occur when subjects are paired on the basis of some variable and then, within each pair, are assigned at random to conditions. For example, matched pairs could be formed from a baseline assessment. One member of the pair would then be randomly assigned to the drug treatment and the other member would be assigned to the placebo. Repeated measures occur when each subject is observed under each condition. All of these designs lead to observations that can be correlated across the conditions, and comparisons between conditions do not involve comparisons of independent subjects. Such a conditions variable is often called a "within-subjects" variable.

Sometimes, authors treat "within-subjects variables" as if they were "between-subjects variables." Often, not enough care is exercised to convince the reader that within-subjects factors were treated properly. For example, Dorman (1983) appeared to have created a within-subjects treatment variable by a process described as blocking. This is an excellent research strategy. Unfortunately, the author provides no clear description of the statistical analysis, and the reader is left wondering if techniques suited to between-subjects variables were incorrectly applied to a within-subjects treatment variable. A clear statement of the form of statistical analysis could remove that doubt and strengthen the impact of the article.

Another statistical technique that is occasionally misused is the factorial analysis of variance. The factorial model should reflect the design of the experiment as precisely as possible. If the design calls for data to be collected from different sources (e.g., multicenter cooperative studies; Prien & Levine, 1984), those sources should be incorporated into the model. For example, if drug trials were held at three centers and the two conditions (drug vs. placebo) were compared over 6 weeks, the proper model for analysis of the data would be a 3 × 2 × 6 repeated measures analysis of variance. Alternatively, if sample sizes are quite large, we can afford to use the various sources as a type of replication, or for purposes of cross-validation. It is less appropriate to simply pool data from various sources, following preliminary significance tests, as was done by Rickels, Feighner, and Smith (1985). In this article, sample sizes were sufficient to treat the design as three replicates of an experiment, providing the opportunity to demonstrate a consistency of results that could dispel conjectures that findings are the result of multiplicity.

## Crossover Designs

Occasionally, a clinical trial is planned as a crossover design. Examples of crossover designs may be found in Munjack et al. (1985) and Noyes et al. (1984). In the crossover design, each subject is randomly assigned to either a treatment or a control group and observed for some time. Then, after a sufficient washout period, each subject's assignment is reversed, and the subject is followed for more time. Use of this design provides within-subjects information concerning the treatment effects. Because within-subjects effects are usually estimated more precisely than between-subjects effects, this design provides some natural advantages.

Some trade-offs are encountered in crossover designs, however. One disadvantage of this design is the potential for a carry-over effect, especially for those who receive the placebo last. Another disadvantage is the relatively long length of a trial in crossover designs. There are other means of creating a within-subjects treatment variable that do not suffer from these disadvantages. One possibility involves blocking or matching on some relevant variable (e.g., a baseline measure of anxiety or depression) and forming many blocks, each containing as many subjects as conditions to be compared. Blocking does provide improvement over use of uncorrelated observations and does not have the disadvantages of carry-over effects and very long trials. There are some disadvantages to creating "condition" as a within-subjects variable by blocking rather than using repeated measures. For one, blocking probably does not reduce the error variance as effectively as repeated measures. Secondly, more subjects are required for blocking, because, with repeated measures, subjects are re-used. More of these correlated designs should be used in drug trial experimentation.

## Violation of Assumptions

Stevens (1946) defined a hierarchy of scales of measurement, based on permissible mathematical operations. Only those having ratio scale properties should be used to form ratios. Consider, for example, the measurement of temperature inside the core of an overheating nuclear reactor. If the reactor was located in the United States, we might measure its temperature in degrees Fahrenheit to be 636, or 3.000 times the temperature of boiling water. If the reactor was located in Canada, its temperature would be measured in degrees Celsius to be 335.55, or 3.356 times the temperature of boiling water. Which is correct? Neither, since neither degrees Fahrenheit nor degrees Celsius form a ratio scale of measurement. A ratio scale requires an origin, where zero represents the absence of what is being measured. The Kelvin (absolute) scale of temperature is a ratio scale. On the Kelvin scale, the temperature of the reactor is 1.632 times the temperature of boiling water. Many authors assume that the Hamilton Rating Scales for measuring level of depression possess ratio scale properties and take ratios to express those scales in terms of percentages. This practice is weak at best and should be discontinued.

Many articles rely on statistical techniques whose validity and/or interpretability depend upon distributional assumptions. It is rare to find an author who questions those assumptions, but, in one article (Dunner, Ishiki, Avery, Wilson, & Hyde, 1986), a search for an outlying observation was performed and one was discovered. It would be helpful if more experimenters would make it a regular practice to search for distributional anomalies such as outliers and skewness. Even descriptive statistics can reflect the disruptive influence of distributional abnormalities (Halperin, 1986).

## CONCLUSIONS

From a statistical perspective, the literature concerned with drug treatment of anxiety and depression is vulnerable to bias. Three factors point to the strong possibility that reported drug effects are spuriously large.

1. The good intentions to include double blindness in experiments may not be effective. Systematic evidence suggests we might doubt whether subjects really did not know they were receiving an inert substance.

2. If strong improvement is expected in the control group, the use of ad hoc statistical methods such as discarding incomplete cases or "endpoint" analysis exacerbates the effect of greater attrition in the placebo sample.

3. The multiplicity rampant in this literature yields experimentwise error rates that are unacceptable. The fact that Type I errors must occur regularly, and probably favor the drug over the placebo, adds to the bias.

Specific recommendations were made to improve the literature with regard to the second and third points. Regarding the first point, it seems clear that a different choice for the placebo is one possible solution to the problem; this prospect will require the attention of those people who contribute to this research literature.

Other things can be done to improve the statistical aspects of the literature. For one, more designs should be used where the treatment/control condition is a within-subjects variable. An increased use of crossover designs and designs that incorporate blocking on a baseline measure would be desirable.

I also strongly encourage experimenters, when publishing their results, to devote more time to describing their statistical analyses. I had the impression that statisticians assisted in performing the statistical analyses, but were excluded from writing the final report. I think researchers in this area would be wise to involve statisticians not only in the analysis, but also in the design of the experiment and in the final reporting of results.

## REFERENCES

Bartlett, M. S. (1937). Some examples of statistical methods of research in agriculture and applied biology. *Journal of the Royal Statistical Society Supplement, 4,* 137–170.

Bhargava, R. P. (1975). Some one-sample testing problems when there is a monotone sample from a multivariate normal population. *Annals of the Institute of Statistical Mathematics, 27,* 327–339.

Cook, N. R., & Ware, J. H. (1983). Design and analysis methods for longitudinal research. *Annual Review of Public Health, 4,* 1–23.

Coons, I. (1957). The analysis of covariance as a missing plot technique. *Biometrics, 13,* 387–405.

Dempster, A. P., Laird, N. M., & Rubin, D. B. (1977). Maximum likelihood from incomplete data via the EM algorithm. *Journal of the Royal Statistical Society, Series B, 39,* 1–22.

Diaconis, P. (1985). Theories of data analysis: From magical thinking through classical statistics. In D. C. Hoaglin, F. Mosteller, & J. W. Tukey (Eds.), *Exploring data tables, trends, and shapes* (pp. 1–36). New York: Wiley.

Dorman, T. (1983). A multi-centre comparison of prazepam and diazepam in the treatment of anxiety. *Pharmatherapeutica, 3,* 433–440.

Dunn, O. J. (1961). Multiple comparisons among means. *Journal of the American Statistical Association, 56,* 52–64.

Dunner, D. L., Ishiki, D., Avery, D. H., Wilson, L. G., & Hyde, T. S. (1986). Effect of alprazolam and diazepam on anxiety and panic attacks in panic disorder: A controlled study. *Journal of Clinical Psychiatry, 47,* 458–460.

Goldberg, H. A., & Finnerty, R. (1982). Comparison of buspirone in two separate studies. *Journal of Clinical Psychiatry, 43*(12), 87–91.

Goldstein, H. (1979). *The design and analysis of longitudinal studies.* New York: Academic Press.

Grizzle, J. E., & Allen, D. M. (1969). Analysis of growth and dose response curves. *Biometrics, 25,* 357–382.

Halperin, S. (1986). Spurious correlations—causes and cures. *Psychoneuroendocrinology, 11,* 3–13.

Jacobson, A. F., Goldstein, B. J., Dominguez, R. A., & Steinbook, R. M. (1983). A placebo-controlled, double-blind comparison of clobazam and diazepam in the treatment of anxiety. *Journal of Clinical Psychiatry, 44,* 296–300.

Kirk, R. E. (1982). *Experimental design: Procedures for the behavioral sciences* (2nd ed.). Belmont, CA: Brooks/Cole.

Laird, N. M., & Ware, J. H. (1982). Random-effects models for longitudinal data. *Biometrics, 38*, 963–974.

Lewis, D., & Burke, C. J. (1949). The use and misuse of the chi-square test. *Psychological Bulletin, 46*(6), 433–489.

Little, R. J. A., & Rubin, D. B. (1987). *Statistical analysis with missing data.* New York: Wiley.

Morrison, D. F. (1976). *Multivariate statistical methods* (2nd ed.). New York: McGraw-Hill.

Mosteller, F., & Tukey, J. W. (1977). *Data analysis and regression.* Reading, MA: Addison-Wesley.

Munjack, D. J., Rebal, R., Shaner, R., Staples, F., Braun, R., & Leonard, M. (1985). Imipramine versus propranolol for the treatment of panic attacks: A pilot study. *Comprehensive Psychiatry, 26*, 80–89.

Noyes, R., Jr., Anderson, D. J., Clancy, J., Crowe, R. R., Slymen, D. J., Ghoneim, M. M., & Hinrichs, J. V. (1984). Diazepam and propranolol in panic disorder and agoraphobia. *Archives of General Psychiatry, 41*, 287–292.

Prien, R. F., & Levine, J. (1984). Research and methodological issues for evaluating the therapeutic effectiveness of antidepressant drugs. *Psychopharmacology Bulletin, 20*, 250–257.

Rickels, K., Case, W. G., Downing, R. W., & Fridman, R. (1986). One-year follow-up of anxious patients treated with diazepam. *Journal of Clinical Psychopharmacology, 6*, 32–36.

Rickels, K., Case, W. G., Downing, R. W., & Winokur, A. (1983). Long-term diazepam therapy and clinical outcome. *Journal of the American Medical Association, 250*, 767–771.

Rickels, K., Feighner, J. P., & Smith, W. T. (1985). Alprazolam, amitriptyline, doxepin, and placebo in the treatment of depression. *Archives of General Psychiatry, 42*, 134–141.

Rickels, K., Weisman, K., Norstad, N., Singer, M., Stoltz, D., Brown, A., & Danton, J. (1982). Buspirone and diazepam in anxiety: A controlled study. *Journal of Clinical Psychiatry, 43*(12), 81–86.

Salsburg, D. S. (1985). The religion of Statistics as practiced in medical journals. *The American Statistician, 39*, 220–223.

Saul, P., Jones, B. P., Edwards, K. G., & Tweed, J. A. (1985). Randomized comparison of atenolol and placebo in the treatment of anxiety: A double-blind study. *European Journal of Clinical Pharmacology, 28*, 109–110.

Schwertman, N. C., & Heilbrun, L. K. (1986). A successive difference method for growth curves with missing data and random observation times. *Journal of the American Statistical Association, 81*, 912–916.

Stevens, S. S. (1946). On the theory of scales of measurement. *Science, 103*, 677–680.

Tukey, J. W. (1977). *Exploratory data analysis.* Reading, MA: Addison-Wesley.

Ware, J. H. (1985). Linear models for the analysis of longitudinal studies. *The American Statistician, 39*, 95–101.

Wheatley, D. (1982). Buspirone: Multicenter efficacy study. *Journal of Clinical Psychiatry, 43*(12), 92–94.

Yates, F. (1933). The analysis of replicated experiments when the field results are incomplete. *Empirical Journal of Experimental Agriculture, 1*, 129–142.

# 9 | THE EFFICACY OF ELECTROCONVULSIVE THERAPY IN THE TREATMENT OF MAJOR DEPRESSIVE DISORDER

Harold A. Sackeim
*Columbia University*

Electroconvulsive therapy (ECT) was first used in 1938 in the treatment of psychiatric patients. Prior to the introduction of electricity as a means of eliciting seizures, pharmacological methods were used. In 1934, Laszlo Meduna first administered camphor in solution intramuscularly with the aim of provoking cerebral seizures. Meduna held the view, now since discarded, that there was an antagonism between epilepsy and schizophrenia, such that schizophrenia was underrepresented in patients with epilepsy and that epilepsy was rare in schizophrenic patients. He reasoned that there may be therapeutic benefit to artificially inducing epileptic-like seizures in schizophrenic patients. On the basis of clinical observations in a fairly substantial number of patients, Meduna (1935) reported that indeed the procedure was of benefit in relieving psychotic symptomatology.

Despite the introduction of malarial or fever therapy by Wagner-Jauregg in 1917 for treatment of general paresis, the era in which convulsive therapy was introduced was characterized by therapeutic nihilism. Within biological perspectives of psychopathology, the dominant belief was that the major psychiatric disturbances were untreatable and reflected primary genetic and/ or neuropathological disturbance. Meduna's findings were treated in some camps with considerable skepticism. Indeed, his direct contradiction of the view that psychotic conditions were untreatable led to his losing his clinical and academic appointments. However, within a matter of a few years other somatic treatments were developed. Insulin coma therapy was first used in 1933 by Sakel, followed in 1935 by Moniz's introduction of psychosurgery. The reported success of these procedures in ameliorating psychopathological states (Sakel, 1938) ushered in an era of new therapeutic optimism, setting the stage for the development of the psychopharmacological approaches in the 1950s.

The introduction of psychopharmacological agents was strongly related to the virtual abandonment of insulin coma treatment and the marked reduction in use of psychosurgery. However, convulsive therapy has remained, and is now considered the form of somatic treatment with the longest continuous history of use in psychiatry. Soon after Meduna's report, it was recognized that other pharmacological agents could more reliably and safely induce seizures than camphor. In the 1930s and 1940s, pentylenetetrazol (Cardiozol, Metrazol) was frequently used. Cerletti and Bini were responsible for the substitution of an electrical stimulus for a chemical convulsant agent, and comparative trials evaluating efficacy and side effects of the two approaches continued until the 1960s (Small, 1974). In the 1950s, administration of a muscle relaxant and general anesthesia became commonplace, so that patients are unconscious during the procedure and protected from violent convulsive movements of the body. In the 1960s, a series of studies began evaluating the relevant benefits and risks of administering the electrical stimulus either to one side of the head (unilateral ECT) or bilaterally, on both sides of the head. To date, there have been in excess of 40 such comparative trials, with research in this area continuing. In the 1970s and 1980s considerable attention was given to the nature of the electrical stimulus, with new devices introduced to minimize the electrical intensity required to elicit seizures, with the hope of thereby lessening side effects. With respect to mechanisms of action, there have been concerted attempts since the 1940s to identify the critical neurophysiological and neurochemical consequences of ECT.

Despite its long history of use and the continuing attention ECT has received from the research community, this form of treatment remains the most controversial in psychiatry. There are a variety of factors that have fueled this controversy (Sackeim, 1985), a number of which only indirectly bear on the issue of efficacy. However, in this chapter, the focus is on evaluating what is known about the therapeutic properties of ECT. Specific topics are reviewed, specifically in relation to the use of ECT in treatment of major depressive disorder. Attention is given to comparisons of ECT with experimental conditions involving only administration of anesthetic agents or with subconvulsive electrical stimulations. Comparisons of the differential therapeutic effects of different forms of ECT and comparisons of the therapeutic effects of ECT and antidepressant medications are examined. This discussion concludes with a review of the problem of relapse following clinical response to ECT.

## REAL VERSUS SHAM ECT

It has long been argued that the elicitation of a generalized tonic-clonic seizure in the brain provides the necessary and sufficient conditions for the efficacy of ECT (d'Elia, Ottosson, & Strömgren, 1983; Ottosson, 1960). This view stipulates that the neurophysiological changes that ensue with seizures are fundamental to mechanisms of antidepressant response. This position rules out a number of psychological theories regarding efficacy.

Some psychological theories point out that ECT can be highly ritualized. Prior to starting a course of treatments, patients typically undergo a series of medical examinations to uncover conditions that may increase risk (e.g., space-occupying lesions). They fast from the evening before a treatment until its completion. With modern technique, at the treatment session they are attended to by staff that usually includes a psychiatrist, an anesthesiologist, nurses, and aides. Prior to induction of anesthesia and until the completion of the treatment they are monitored with EKG and often EEG. The treatment involves administration of a number of medications, principally a short-acting barbiturate anesthetic (e.g., methohexital), so that patients are unconscious for the few minutes that the procedure requires, and a muscle relaxant (e.g., succinylcholine), so that motor manifestations of the seizure are blunted. This intricate set of activities is repeated at either a two or a three treatments per week schedule.

Some psychological theories of efficacy have focused on the notion that this repetitive, intricate set of operations instills a magical quality to ECT, not only making the procedure the most "medical" or "surgical" of current psychiatric treatments, but also satisfying patient needs for attention and dependence. Related views emphasize that the expectations regarding positive clinical outcome are so high with ECT, with patients typically informed that the response rate in depressed patients is approximately 80% to 90%, that this combined with the intricate set of operations makes for a maximal placebo effect. Other theories have focused on the presumed need of depressed patients to experience real or symbolic punishment. Such views emphasize that patients may be fearful of the treatment and unconsciously identify the passage of current through the brain, the elicitation of a seizure, and other aspects of the procedure as punitive acts, thereby satisfying needs for self-directed or introjected anger. Still other theories emphasize the repeated experience of loss of consciousness, either as a result of seizure elicitation or anesthesia. The reconstitution that is established upon awakening with the gradual dissipation of confusion and disorientation is viewed as in some way restorative. Regardless of the focus, such theories reject the belief that the physiological changes that accompany seizure elicitation are intrinsic to the antidepressant properties of ECT (see Fink, 1979, and Miller, 1967, for reviews of psychological theories).

A method that has been used extensively to test the plausibility of such notions is the "real versus sham ECT" comparison. Such studies involve random assignment of patients to conditions in which they receive either a typical course of ECT ("real") or a course in which the same procedures are followed, including the repeated induction of anesthesia and application of electrodes, but no current is passed and consequently no seizure is elicited. When conducted properly such studies are double-blind, given that neither patients nor those engaged in clinical evaluation are aware of assignment to real or sham conditions. Superiority of real ECT, relative to sham conditions, would strongly suggest that either the passage of electricity or the elicitation of a seizure is critical to efficacy. Equivalence in therapeutic response would suggest that such factors are irrelevant to antidepressant effects, providing indirect support for some of the psychological theories just described.

A number of such comparative trials were conducted in the 1950s and early 1960s (Brill, Crumpton, Eiduson, Grayson, & Hellman, 1959; Fahy, Imiah, & Harrington, 1963; Harris & Robin, 1960; Sainz, 1959; Ulett, Smith, & Gleser, 1956). The findings from such studies have been reviewed elsewhere (Barton, 1977; Fink, 1979, 1980; Janicak et al., 1985; Scovern & Kilmann, 1980). In general, the results of these investigations indicated superior short-term clinical outcome with real versus sham ECT. However, these findings were inconsistent across studies and a number of methodological problems characterized much of the work. In particular, in some studies patient samples that were heterogeneous with respect to diagnosis included patients with chronic schizophrenic conditions, and did not involve random assignment or blind evaluation with objective instruments; in much of this work sample sizes were exceedingly small. In the 1970s and 1980s a spate of new studies emerged, all conducted in the United Kingdom.

The impetus for much of this new work was a report by Lambourn and Gill (1978) that found equivalent efficacy for real ECT compared to repeated anesthesia alone (see Table 9.1) and concern about the methodological inadequacies in the studies from the prior era. Given the clinical implications, several independent groups conducted new trials. The characteristics and findings of the studies in depressed patients are summarized in Table 9.1. Across these trials, it is evident that short-term clinical outcome was superior with real compared to sham ECT. Given the cumulative experience over the last 30 years, the issue as to whether ECT is more efficacious in major depressive disorder than repeated anesthesia alone is now clearly determined. The medical risks of ECT with respect to morbidity and mortality largely center on the administration of anesthetic agents. It has been argued that new real versus sham ECT trials directed at addressing these same issues would be difficult to justify on either ethical or scientific grounds (Sackeim, 1986).

TABLE 9.1
Recent Comparative Studies of Real Versus Sham ECT

| Study | Methods | # Of Pts. | | Outcome | Comments |
|---|---|---|---|---|---|
| | | Started | Completed | | |
| Freeman et al. (1978) | Random Double-blind 2 Sham vs. 2 Real ECT followed by Real ECT | 20 20 | 14 18 | > Hamilton scores after 2 sham vs. 2 real ECT; more subsequent real ECT given the initial sham group | TCAs and BZD given during trial; Handling of dropout may have enhanced real ECT efficacy |
| Lambourn & Gill (1978) | Random Double-blind 6 sham ECT vs. 6 real ECT | 16 16 | 16 16 | Nonsignificant outcome differences favoring real ECT | BZD given during trial; Use of low dose, unilateral ECT may have weak efficacy; restriction to 6 treatments unlike clinical practice and too severe |
| West (1981) | Randomness and Blindness Uncertain 6 sham ECT vs. 6 real ECT | 12 13 | 11 11 | Marked advantage for real ECT; after 6 treatments 10 of 11 sham and no real patients switched to new treatment | TCA and BDZ; Limited methodology details available, with unresolved issues about sample selection and blindness; small sample size |

*(continued)*

TABLE 9.1
(continued)

| Study | Methods | # Of Pts. | | Outcome | Comments |
|---|---|---|---|---|---|
| | | Started | Completed | | |
| Johnstone et al. (1980) | Random Double-blind 8 sham ECT 8 real ECT | 35 35 | 31 31 | Small advantage for real ECT; Substantial clinical response to sham ECT; delusional patients responded better to real ECT; neurotic depressives had no difference | BDZ; High percentage of ward admissions entered in the trial |
| Brandon et al. (1984) | Random Double-blind Up to 8 sham ECT Up to 8 real ECT | 42 53 | 29 43 | Marked advantage for real ECT, particularly in delusional/retarded patients | BDZ; Relatively high dropout rate |
| Gregory et al. (1985) | Random Double-blind sham ECT vs. real bilateral ECT vs. real unilateral ECT No. treatments determined by clinical need | 23 23 23 | 20 21 19 | Marked advantage for both bilateral and unilateral ECT in improvement and number of treatments; bilateral required fewer treatments than unilateral ECT | BDZ; Unclear how dropout was handled |

TCA = Tricyclic antidepressant; BZD = Benzodiazepine.

Several important factors should be considered in evaluating this work. First, the negative findings of Lambourn and Gill (1978) were puzzling. Even given the small sample size (16 real patients, 16 sham patients), it was unclear at the time why equal rates of clinical response were obtained in the two conditions. Lambourn and Gill used a form of ECT that has subsequently been identified as weak in therapeutic properties. They administered unilateral right (nondominant) ECT with an electrical stimulus characterized by low intensity and ultra-brief pulse width. Sackeim, Decina, Kanzler, Kerr, and Malitz (1987; Malitz, Sackeim, Decina, Kanzler, & Kerr, 1986) contrasted unilateral right and bilateral ECT, with extremely low stimulus intensity determined by adjusting stimulus dose for each patient to be just above seizure threshold. In this double-blind, random assignment trial, using conservative outcome criteria, 70% of patients were classified as responding to low dosage bilateral ECT. However, only 28% of patients responded to low dosage unilateral right ECT. This led to the suggestion discussed further later, that at low stimulus intensity, unilateral ECT may lose a good deal of its efficacy. Concerned with this possibility, Gill and colleagues (Gregory, Shawcross, & Gill, 1985) completed another real versus sham ECT trial, this time comparing both bilateral and unilateral ECT to sham conditions, and using higher levels of stimulus intensity. The findings of this study indicated that both real ECT modalities were clearly superior in efficacy to the sham condition, although patients needed fewer treatments to achieve comparable therapeutic gains with bilateral than unilateral ECT.

The findings of Sackeim, Decina, Kanzler et al., (1987) are relevant in this context for another reason. The magnitude of the efficacy difference obtained between bilateral and unilateral ECT was dramatic. Yet patients in the unilateral right ECT condition not only experienced repeated anesthesia, but had generalized seizures of the same duration as the bilateral group. The acute cardiovascular changes that accompany seizure elicitation were equivalent in the two treatment conditions (Prudic et al., 1987). Nonetheless, the response rate obtained with low dose unilateral right ECT was the same or less than that reported in the comparative studies for sham ECT conditions. Such findings indicate that it is highly unlikely that the psychological theories described above provide sufficient conditions for the efficacy of ECT. As discussed later, this particular set of findings also suggested that factors over and above seizure elicitation per se are critical in accounting for the efficacy of the treatment.

Across the recent series of real versus sham ECT trials, relative uniformity was observed in rates of response to real ECT conditions. The magnitude of differences between the conditions in rates of therapeutic response seemed more tied to variability in the "effectiveness" of the sham treatment. Why might this be and what might it suggest regarding the nature of response to ECT?

Sham ECT is usually intended to serve as a placebo condition. The intricate procedures involved in performing ECT would necessarily unblind patients to whether they were receiving active treatment, if the "placebo" condition was like that in pharmacological trials and involved administering a pill. Consequently, all aspects of traditional ECT were followed in these studies, except for passage of current and seizure induction. The variability observed in rate of response to "sham" ECT suggests three alternatives: rater effects, sampling differences, and intrinsic antidepressant properties to anesthesia induction.

One might account for the intertrial differences in rates of response to repeated anesthesia by presuming that different clinical research centers differed in criteria for determining good outcome and/or in expectations for overall positive results. The relative lack of variability with respect to real ECT outcome rates makes this alternative less attractive. A more likely possibility pertains to differences among the trials in patient characteristics. Although undocumented, it is commonly believed that there are national differences in the extent to which ECT is used as a treatment of first choice or as a treatment of last resort. Even more likely are physician and clinical center differences along this dimension. The typical rate of placebo response in psychopharmacological trials in major depression is approximately 30% (e.g., Klein, Gittelman, Quitkin, & Rifkin, 1980). One might anticipate that those centers that administer ECT principally to medication-resistant patients would have a considerably lower rate of "placebo" response. The reason for this is that the medication-resistant patient has already experienced one, and often many, extended trials of biological treatment and should have already manifested a placebo response were it to occur. Unfortunately, information on the rates of medication-resistance in the recent series of real versus sham ECT trials is for the most part lacking, and has never been examined in relation to different rates of response to ECT versus anesthesia alone. It has been commented, however, that one of the trials (Johnstone et al., 1980) that overall showed a smaller advantage than typical for real ECT included a remarkably high rate of consecutive admissions with major depression in the study (Kendell, 1981).

The third alterative is that sham ECT or repeated administration of anesthesia should not be considered as an "active placebo," but as a weak antidepressant treatment. In psychopharmacological trials, an inactive placebo is inert and essentially has no effects on the individual. Active placebos share many of the side effects of the psychotropic medication with which they are compared, but lack efficacy with regard to the psychopathological condition being treated. For example, in studies of the effects of scopolamine, a central anticholinergic agent, it is often useful to administer methscopolamine as placebo. The latter is also an anticholinergic agent in the periphery, but does not cross the blood brain barrier. The avowed intention in using repeated anesthesia as a contrast condition is to provide an active placebo. Not only are patients thereby blind to whether or not they experienced seizure induction, but many of the acute effects of traditional ECT are mimicked, including a period of disorientation following awakening and some somatic side effects. However, there are some reasons to believe that repeated anesthesia may have therapeutic properties. Although never subject to rigorous evaluation of efficacy, the administration of barbiturates and the use of chemically induced sleep therapy was an accepted mode of treatment for various forms of psychopathology prior to the introduction of ECT and other somatic treatments (Kalinowsky & Hippius, 1972). On theoretical grounds, the view has been raised that antidepressant effects may be obtained by acting on the same neurochemical systems that subserve the principal mode of action of the barbiturate anesthetics (Lloyd, Morselli, & Bartholini, 1987; Sackeim, 1986; Sackeim, Decina, Prohovnik, Malitz, & Resor, 1983). It is also noteworthy that the dosage of anesthetic agent used in the real versus sham ECT trials seemed roughly correlated with the obtained rate of therapeutic response. For example, Brandon, et al., (1984), reporting one of the lowest response rates to sham ECT (20%), used 1.0 mg/kg of methohexital, whereas Johnstone et al. (1980) had a response rate of 40% and used 1.5 mg/kg of the same agent. Finally, in an earlier literature on treatment of depression, comparisons of ECT efficacy are available with medication placebo or no-treatment conditions (e.g., Greenblatt, Grooser, & Wechsler, 1964; Kiloh, Child, & Latner, 1960). It is noteworthy that for the most part these biologically inactive conditions yielded smaller response rates than those obtained with sham ECT and typically even larger differences with ECT.

In summary, at this point it is incontrovertible that ECT is an effective antidepressant agent and considerably more so than administration of repeated anesthesia. This focuses the issues of accounting for efficacy on other questions. These include the aspects of ECT that are critical to antidepressant response, that is, the passage of an electrical current, the areas of the brain stimulated (e.g., bilateral vs. unilateral ECT), the induction of seizures; the longevity of therapeutic response, that is, relapse rates; and the issue of the relative efficacy of ECT compared to other treatments of depression.

## STIMULUS INTENSITY AND ECT EFFICACY

The traditional view of the mechanisms of action of ECT stipulates that characteristics of the electrical stimulus are incidental to therapeutic outcome. The critical agent is the induction of a generalized, tonic-clonic seizure. Regardless of how such seizures are produced, electrically or chemically, as long as they are generalized and of adequate duration they will have strong antidepressant properties. This view is usually expressed with the corollary that the intensity of the ECT electrical stimulus plays a role in determining the magnitude of cognitive side effects. As might be intuitively expected, more intense electrical stimuli are believed to result in more extensive and severe acute and subacute cognitive effects. Consequently this pair of propositions is not only relevant for considerations of antidepressant mechanisms, but of relevance for determining the nature of practice. As evidenced, for example, in the report of the National Institute of Health Consensus Development Conference on ECT (Rose, 1985), adoption of this view leads to the recommendation that practitioners should use stimulus intensities that require the least amount of electrical charge to produce adequate seizures.

The notion that the quantity of electricity used was independent of the therapeutic effects of ECT derived from three sources of evidence. The first concerned the comparative trials of electrical and chemical seizure induction (e.g., Small, 1974). Generally speaking, chemical induction of seizures was found to be as effective as electrical induction in treatment of depression. Indeed, although never documented, some clinicians believe that a subgroup of patients who fail trials of ECT may nonetheless respond to chemical-induction techniques. Although this evidence indirectly supports the view that, independent of the method, the elicitation of a generalized seizure is necessary for antidepressant response, it does not address the question of whether the quantity of electricity used in ECT is related to speed or quality of clinical outcome. Indeed, given that electrical and chemical induction involve inherently different classes of agents, there is no obvious way of determining the "doses" of electrical and chemical induction to be compared.

The second area of evidence concerns studies that contrasted ECT with techniques that followed all the same procedures, including the passage of current, but used stimulus intensities sufficiently weak so that seizures were not produced. This is referred to as subconvulsive treatment. Such comparative studies take a step beyond real versus sham ECT trials not only in having some form of electrical stimulation in all groups, but also in being likely to produce more comparable cognitive side effects in the comparative conditions. Although never documented, it is known that some patients following subconvulsive stimulation will experience confusional states that are more intense and prolonged than what they experience following convulsive treatments. The probability of such events is likely to be a function in part of the electrical intensity of the subconvulsive stimulus.

There have been relatively few trials comparing subconvulsive and convulsive electrical stimulation (Fink, Kahn, & Green, 1958; Ulett, Smith, & Gleser, 1956). Further, methodological limitations regarding the nature of random assignment, diagnostic heterogeneity, and the evaluation of outcome weaken somewhat the force of this work. Nonetheless, the findings in this area supported the view that induction of seizures leads to better clinical response than administration of subconvulsive electrical stimuli. It should be noted, however, that such findings do not address the issue as to whether the intensity of electrical stimulus used with convulsive treatments contributes to efficacy. Indeed, were there such a contribution one would also expect that subconvulsive treatments would be less efficacious.

The third source of evidence came from the classic studies of Ottosson (1960). The critical research he conducted involved a three-group comparison. Patients received either a form of ECT that was considered moderately suprathreshold or a form of ECT that was grossly suprathreshold, and a third group was given the moderately suprathreshold electrical intensity with simultaneous administration of lidocaine. Lidocaine is an anticonvulsant agent, and it resulted in marked reduction in the length and altered the characteristics of the cerebral seizure discharge, as evaluated with EEG techniques. Evaluation of short-term outcome at the end of the trial revealed that the moderately and grossly suprathreshold groups achieved comparable rates of remission. The lidocaine group had inferior clinical response. In contrast, studies of cognitive side effects indicated that the grossly suprathreshold condition was most deleterious, with lower and comparable levels in the moderately suprathreshold and lidocaine-modified groups. The standard interpretation that emerged from this work is that the occurrence of a full, generalized seizure is critical to antidepressant response. Indeed on the basis of these findings, many in the field of ECT focused on the duration of seizures as a predictive measure of the likely efficacy of the treatment (e.g., Maletzky, 1968). Characteristics of the electrical stimulus, particularly with respect to intensity, were viewed as irrelevant in accounting for efficacy. On the other hand, electrical parameters, in addition to the neurobiological effects of seizure elicitation, were believed to be related to side effect profiles.

Although still the dominant perspective, new developments in ECT research have suggested reinterpretations of the Ottosson findings. The minimal electrical intensity needed to elicit seizures in the human varies dramatically. Using a psychophysical threshold titration technique with an electrically efficient waveform, Sackeim, Decina, Portnoy, Neeley, and Malitz (1987) reported that the range in seizure threshold in a homogeneous population of elderly, drug-free patients with major depression was 12-fold. Working with a wider range of diagnoses, age, medical, and medication conditions, they reported that the range in clinical practice is likely to be on the order of 40-fold. Practically, this means that patients with the highest seizure threshold require a minimum electrical intensity to produce seizure that is 40 times greater than that required by patients with the lowest thresholds. Ottosson's moderately suprathreshold condition involved use of a relatively inefficient waveform and was sufficiently intense so that virtually all patients had seizures at first application. In other words, for the large majority of patients, this condition was grossly above threshold. The failure to find marked differences between this condition and the "grossly" suprathreshold condition may have been due to the fact that both forms of ECT used electrical intensities beyond the range of an electrical intensity/clinical response therapeutic window. Nonetheless, even though end-point evaluations indicated comparable efficacy, in this trial there was evidence that from evaluations conducted after the fourth treatment speed of clinical response was faster in the grossly suprathreshold group.

A new interpretation has also been recently offered for the findings of the lidocaine-condition (Devanand & Sackeim, 1988). It has been suggested not only that lidocaine may abort the seizure discharge and modify its characteristics, but there are strong animal and human data indicating that it can raise seizure threshold. Indeed, this may have been evidenced in the Ottosson trial to the extent that the instances in which the "moderately" suprathreshold stimulus failed to elicit seizure at first application were in the lidocaine-modified group and that the variance in the electrical dose administered to this group at seizure elicitation was substantially and significantly greater than that in the straightforward moderately suprathreshold condition. This would suggest that the lidocaine group received electrical intensities closer to their seizure threshold, given that it was elevated pharmacologically. Sackeim, Decina, Kanzler et al. (1987a) and Sackeim, Decina, Prohovnik, and Malitz (1987) have suggested that the critical factor in ECT electrical dose/response relations is not the absolute intensity of electrical stimulation, but the degree to which stimulation exceeds seizure threshold. In part, this was suggested because the bulk of the electrical stimulus administered is shunted across the scalp, between the ECT electrodes, and does not enter the brain. A great deal of the variability both in estimates of seizure threshold and in the absolute dosage administered has to do with individual differences in skull anatomy and consequent degree of shunting (Sackeim, Decina, Portnoy et al., 1987; Weaver et al., 1976; Weaver & Williams, 1986). With respect to cognitive side effects, there are animal data that likewise indicate that the degree to which electrical dosage exceeds threshold is more critical than absolute dosage per se (e.g., Gold, Macri, & McGaugh, 1973). By this view, the weaker therapeutic results obtained in the lidocaine condition resulted from treatment of patients closer to threshold. In this respect, it is possible to reinterpret the Ottosson work as actually supporting the notion that stimulus-intensity factors contribute to the efficacy of ECT.

The final area of evidence that has been taken as justification for the view that stimulus-dosing factors are irrelevant to ECT efficacy concerns comparisons of electrical waveforms that differ in their efficiency in eliciting seizures. A variety of types of electrical stimuli have been employed in ECT. For example, for an extended period of time in the United States, the sine wave was the predominant type of electrical stimulus. This waveform is in most essential features identical to that available at wall sockets, that is, a 60 Hz, alternating current. The characteristics of this waveform make it inefficient in eliciting seizures. During a 1-sec stimulus duration, 60 positive and 60 negative going waves would be delivered, with each excursion from baseline lasting 8.33 msec. The nature of the unmodified sine wave is such that it takes considerable time for each wave to reach peak intensity (4.167 msec) and there is considerable time for offset. It is believed that the leading edge of a wave is responsible to neuronal depolarization, and that following the depolarization of a neuron there is a refractory period until subsequent depolarization can occur (e.g., Weiner, 1980). Stimuli that reach peak intensity rapidly, offset quickly, and are characterized by intervals of no electrical current between waves should be considerably more efficient electrically in seizure-eliciting properties. Recognizing this, a variety of modified sine wave and brief pulse devices have been introduced. The typical brief pulse device delivers a square wave stimulus that instantaneously reaches peak values and has durations between 1 and 2 msec. During a 1-sec train of pulses, approximately 800 to 900 msec may involve no stimulation to the brain. Comparative trials of sine wave and brief pulse stimulation have shown that approximately one-third the electrical intensity is needed to elicit seizures with brief pulse unmodified than sine wave stimuli (e.g., Weiner, 1980).

A series of studies have compared less efficient (e.g., sine wave) and more efficient (e.g., brief pulse) stimuli in side effect profiles and efficacy (Carney & Sheffield, 1974; Cronholm & Ottosson, 1963; Kendall, Mills, & Thale, 1956; Robin & deTissera, 1982; Valentine, Keddie, & Dunne, 1968; Weaver, Ives, Williams, & Nies, 1977; Weiner, Rogers, Davidson, & Squire, 1986; Welch et al., 1982). Almost without exception (Warren & Groome, 1984), the findings with regard to acute and subacute side effects have been uniform. More efficient electrical stimulation results in a marked reduction of cognitive side effects. These differences can be substantial during the immediate post-ECT period (Daniel & Crovitz, 1986; Sackeim et al., 1986) and impact on clinical management.

The bulk of investigations that provided efficacy comparisons of electrically efficient and less efficient waveforms did not observe differences in therapeutic properties. However, these negative findings are complicated by two concerns. In many of these trials, the stimulus intensity used was considerably supra-threshold for all patients, regardless of waveform, therefore possibly obscuring intensity-related effects. Second, waveforms differ in a number of electrical properties (e.g., constant current vs. constant voltage, electrical efficiency, phase duration, etc.) that may be of neurobiological consequence and compromise the value of waveform comparisons in addressing issues of efficacy. Nonetheless, there are some important indications in this literature that intensity and/or waveform characteristics may be fundamental to therapeutic response. Cronholm and Ottosson (1963) contrasted a traditional chopped sine wave stimulus with an ultra-brief pulse. The configuration of the latter (ultra-brief pulse width, high pulse intensity, low pulse frequency over long pulse train duration) was such that extremely low levels of stimulus intensity were needed to elicit seizure. This condition was found to be therapeutically inferior to traditional methods. Robin and deTissera (1982) contrasted three different waveforms: high-intensity, sine wave stimulation, high-intensity, brief pulse, and low-intensity, ultra-brief pulse. The two high-intensity conditions were equivalent in efficacy measures, whereas, the low-intensity condition required more treatments to achieve an equivalent level of outcome. Both of these trials used only the bilateral electrode placement. As indicated earlier, the results of Sackeim, Decina, Kanzler et al. (1987) suggested that stimulus intensity factors may be particularly critical in determining the rate of response with unilateral right ECT. The findings of Robin and deTissera (1982), in line with the indications in the original Ottosson (1960) work, suggested that stimulus intensity may impact on speed of response (therapeutic efficiency) even with bilateral ECT.

Clearly, what is needed in this area are trials in which low-intensity and high-intensity stimulation are contrasted, keeping the electrical waveform constant. Two such trials are underway. The Columbia University study involves random assignment of depressed patients to two crossed factors, unilateral versus bilateral ECT, and low- and high-stimulus intensity. The low-dose groups are treated at intensity levels just above seizure threshold, whereas the high-intensity groups are treated at levels 150% above (2.5 times) the seizure threshold established at the beginning of the ECT course. Preliminary findings from this trial replicate the remarkably poor rate of efficacy of low-dose, unilateral ECT and indicate that at higher intensity rate of therapeutic response to unilateral ECT is substantially enhanced. The preliminary findings also suggest that, independent of electrode placement, higher stimulus intensity speeds clinical response, that is, patients require fewer treatments to achieve maximal clinical benefit (Sackeim, in press). Robin and colleagues are likewise engaged in a trial in which the same waveform is used at differing intensity levels in patients receiving bilateral ECT. The preliminary findings in this work also suggest that speed of clinical response is superior at higher intensity (Robin, in press).

At present there appear to be strong indications that the original view is incorrect that stimulus intensity is independent of clinical outcome. Such a determination has fundamental theoretical and applied implications. The classic view that stimulus intensity was independent of efficacy focused attention on neurobiological changes intrinsic to seizure elicitation in accounting for the mechanisms of therapeutic action of ECT (Ottosson, 1985). The findings that low-intensity, unilateral right ECT elicits full generalized seizures, comparable in duration to those elicited with other conditions, and yet is notably weak in efficacy, indicate that seizure elicitation per se may be less critical to antidepressant response than previously believed. These findings also offer new methods for investigating the neuropsychobiology of ECT response. Seizure elicitation in the human produces so large a variety of physiological changes that an inherent difficulty in the study of ECT mechanisms has been identification of those events critical to outcome relative to those events that are independent of response (Sackeim, 1988). The fact that full seizures can be elicited that reliably have very weak therapeutic properties provides an opportunity to dissect the physiological changes that accrue generally with seizure elicitation from those that occur with seizures associated with strong therapeutic properties.

At the applied level, the indications that stimulus intensity impacts on efficacy has serious implications for practice. It had been common for practitioners to use routinely the same stimulus intensity for virtually all patients. Given that the range in seizure threshold in unselected patients is probably about 40-fold (Sackeim, Decina, Portnoy et al., 1987; Sackeim, Decina, Prohovnik et al., 1987), and the use of inefficient electrical waveforms, such practice can result in patients with low seizure thresholds receiving at each treatment stimulus intensities that exceed the minimum necessary to produce seizure by several thousand percent. In pharmacological practice, with most psychotropic agents one would expect toxicity were patients to receive doses 40 times that necessary for therapeutic action, and the evidence has been fairly consistent that ECT stimulus intensity is related to cognitive side effects. It would appear that a good deal of the cognitive side effects of ECT can be moderated by adopting more rational electrical dosing strategies (e.g., Sackeim, Portnoy, Neeley, Steif, Decina, & Malitz, 1986). However, the available evidence indicates that electrical intensity contributes to rate and/ or speed of clinical response. Minimal stimulus intensities may not be as therapeutic. Adoption of a standard high-intensity setting for all patients will not deal with this problem. Patients with high seizure thresholds would nonetheless be treated with an electrical dose quite close to threshold, with a reduction in efficacy, and patients with low thresholds would likely receive intensities well in excess of that needed to be within an electrical dose/ response therapeutic window. In this circumstance, it would appear that what is needed is titration of stimulus intensity relative to the seizure threshold of each patient. In this way, the practitioner can be assured that the stimulus is suprathreshold, while at the same time moderating the electrical dose to the minimum needed to ensure good therapeutic response. Such titration strategies have recently been suggested (MECTA, 1987). They offer the possibility of using stimulus intensities considerably lower than that that has characterized standard practice, thereby lowering side effects, but at the same time being conservatively suprathreshold in order to ensure clinical response.

## BILATERAL VERSUS UNILATERAL ECT

No other set of issues in the field of ECT has received more research attention than the comparative efficacy and side effects of bilateral and unilateral ECT. Although unilateral ECT techniques had previously been employed, the first comparative trial of unilateral and bilateral techniques was reported by Lancaster, Steinert, and Frost (1958). This report ushered in a wave of clinical trials with its suggestion that unilateral ECT may have a considerable advantage with respect to a lower side effect profile, while being equal in efficacy to bilateral ECT.

Bilateral ECT involves placement of stimulus electrodes symmetrically, on both sides of the head. In virtually all studies in the modern era, the same electrode placement has been used for bilateral ECT, that is, frontotemporal. This placement results in a current density path in the brain, which shows a marked anterior-posterior (caudality) gradient in the cortex. The anterior prefrontal pole is likely to receive the greatest current density, with a sharp drop-off in more posterior tissue (Rush & Driscoll, 1968; Sackeim & Mukherjee, 1986; Weaver et al., 1977). Relative to unilateral ECT, bilateral placement is likely to result in greater current density in deep, subcortical structures. A variety of electrode placements have been used for unilateral ECT (d'Elia & Raotma, 1975). The most common have been the Lancaster and d'Elia placements. All unilateral ECT placements involve positioning one of the electrodes in the same frontotemporal position as in bilateral ECT. The second electrode has varied in its placement over the ipsilateral hemisphere. The d'Elia placement involves positioning slightly down from the vertex, over parietal cortex. The Lancaster placement positions the electrode a few centimeters below the d'Elia placement, over temporoparietal areas. Regardless of exact placement, current density with unilateral ECT will be substantially greater in the hemisphere ipsilateral than contralateral to the electrodes. Although in gross motor and EEG manifestations, seizures induced with unilateral ECT will appear to be generalized, fine-grained quantitative analyses of EEG can demonstrate asymmetries in the onset of seizures, the amplitude of the seizure discharge, and in postictal EEG slowing (e.g., d'Elia, 1970; Staton, Hass, & Brumback, 1981). Asymmetric transient neurological signs have also been observed following unilateral ECT (Kriss, Halliday, & Pratt, 1980). Within each hemisphere, unilateral ECT is likely to have a relatively even current density distribution over the anterior two thirds of the cortex. This difference in current density paths between the electrode placements is most likely due to the patterns of current shunting across the scalp. Therefore, bilateral and unilateral placements differ not only in lateralization but also in regionality of current density distributions. Although not fully appreciated in the literature, this patterning suggests that differences between the modalities in behavioral consequences should not be assumed to be only a function of functional brain asymmetry.

Differences in the side effect profiles between bilateral and unilateral right ECT are well established. The extent and duration of disorientation are greater with bilateral ECT (Daniel & Crovitz, 1986; Sackeim et al., 1986). Although not documented, it is most likely that the probability of developing an organic brain syndrome (prolonged period of clouded consciousness) is significantly greater with bilateral ECT. Verbal anterograde and retrograde amnestic deficits are also greater with bilateral ECT immediately following a treatment and several days following the end of the treatment course. It is controversial whether bilateral ECT also results in greater disruption of nonverbal memory functions, and in particular those subserved to a greater extent by the right hemisphere. Evidence that this might be the case was reported by Squire and Slater (1978), although the "nonverbal" task used in this study, memory for geometric designs, could have been readily subject to verbal coding. Sackeim et al. (1986) suggested that the issue of whether bilateral and unilateral ECT differ in nonverbal amnestic deficits may be an oversimplification. They found that bilateral ECT produced greater retrograde amnesia for nonsense shape recognition, but was equivalent to unilateral right ECT in producing anterograde and retrograde deficits for face recognition. Given the differences between the modalities in current density paths and, as a likely result, in patterns of seizure discharge within the right hemisphere, it may be that findings of equivalent or differential right hemisphere deficits are task dependent.

Once patients recover from the acute postictal disorientation, the cognitive effects of ECT are highly selective with respect to memory functions. Other aspects of cognitive performance typically are unchanged or improved (e.g., Malloy, Small, Miller, & Milstein, 1982). In particular, tasks highly dependent on attention and concentration reveal deficient performance in depressed patients prior to ECT and often enhanced performance following the ECT course, with the extent of change related to measures of therapeutic response. On the other hand, retrieval of information learned shortly before or during the ECT course or retrieval of information newly learned but tested after a delay will be areas of clear impairment (Cronholn & Ottosson, 1961; Sackeim & Steif, 1988; Steif, Sackeim, Portnoy, Decina, & Malitz, 1986). Traditionally, beyond a week following the ECT course, differences between the modalities in cognitive effects have been difficult to document. This may be because the cognitive effects of ECT are most intense immediately following seizure induction and there is sharp recovery of functioning as time from ECT increases. Consequently, regardless of modality, there is remarkably little objective evidence of persistent cognitive deficits a few weeks beyond the end of the ECT course (e.g., Squire, 1986; Weiner, 1984). An exception is likely to be a spottiness in memory for personal and impersonal events that occurred within the months preceding and the weeks following the ECT course. In this domain, there well may be permanent loss, with the interpretation that ECT interferes with the consolidation of recent memories (Squire, 1986). Indeed, recently a greater long-term memory loss was documented for bilateral relative to unilateral ECT. Weiner et al. (1986) observed that compared both to non-ECT-depressed patient controls and to patients who had received unilateral ECT, bilateral ECT patients had a persistent deficit in memory for personal events, particularly those that occurred within the year preceding ECT. Therefore, given the established difference in short-term side effects and a possible difference in long-term cognitive profiles, the decision to use unilateral or bilateral ECT has important implications for risk/benefit considerations.

This summary concerned contrasts between bilateral and unilateral right ECT. Unilateral left ECT is a technique rarely used in treatment of major depression. With respect to orientation and verbal memory functions, early studies indicated that unilateral left ECT had a side effect profile similar to bilateral ECT (Daniel & Crovitz, 1982; d'Elia, 1970; Halliday, Davison, Browne, & Kreeger, 1968; Lancaster et al., 1958). Particularly because these deficits are most bothersome to patients, unilateral left ECT was essentially abandoned. It should be noted also that of six comparative studies that examined efficacy of unilateral left and right ECT, three investigations had findings that suggested superior antidepressant response with electrode placement over the right hemisphere (see Malitz, Sackeim, & Decina, 1982, for a discussion). Such findings are supportive of the view that functional brain asymmetry contributes to manifestation of affective disorder (e.g., Sackeim et al., 1982), in addition to being critical in understanding the nature of ECT modality side effects profiles.

Despite a history of more than 35 comparative trials of the relative efficacy of unilateral and bilateral ECT, this area continues to be a source of controversy. Indeed, most academic reviews (with important exceptions, see Abrams, 1986a; Overall & Rhoades, 1986) have concluded that if differences in efficacy exist they are slight, statistical in nature, and of doubtful clinical consequence. The report of the Task Force of the American Psychiatric Association (Frankel et al., 1978) strongly recommended the use of unilateral right ECT, and some have questioned whether bilateral ECT is ever indicated (Strömgren, 1984). In contrast, surveys of clinical practice suggest that clinicians predominantly rely on bilateral ECT (e.g., Frankel et al., 1978; Pippard & Ellam, 1981).

The literature on the comparative efficacy of bilateral and unilateral ECT has been subject to a number of reviews and has been subject to meta-analysis (Abrams, 1986b; d'Elia & Raotma, 1975; Fink, 1979; Janicak et al., 1985; Overall & Rhoades, 1986; Pettinati, Mathisen, Rosenberg, & Lynch, 1986). Rather than recover this well-worn ground, a number of considerations are offered here to aid in interpreting this literature.

The large bulk of studies in this area failed to find significant efficacy differences between the modalities, although the majority reported trends favoring bilateral ECT. This has been interpreted variously as indicating a nonmeaningful efficacy difference (d'Elia & Raotma, 1975) or as signaling a difference of clinical consequence. Likewise, meta-analyses of the same studies have yielded rather different conclusions (Janiack et al., 1985; Overall & Rhoades, 1986), partly because of reliance on different statistical techniques for assessing interstudy findings. It should be noted here that the median sample size of studies comparing bilateral and unilateral ECT has been only 20 patients per treatment condition. Particularly in the major meta-analytic approaches, efficacy was determined by examining the categorical rate of response in each group. This means, of course, that the power in most comparative trials was remarkably low, lessening the confidence in null results. Further, dichotomous classification as responders or nonresponders is inherently insensitive to the issue as to whether the modalities differ in quality of response (i.e., the nature and extent of residual symptomatology in patients who have sustained clinical benefit).

A few studies have shown clear-cut efficacy differences, and with notable exception (e.g., Welch et al., 1982), these effects have favored bilateral ECT. Of more concern, some studies have obtained large differences favoring bilateral ECT (Abrams et al., 1983; Gregory et al., 1985; Sackeim, Decina, Kanzler et al., 1987), and these studies are among those that used the strictest methodological conditions and are among the most recent. Indeed, given the recent history of findings, it is probably no longer viable to frame the question as to whether bilateral and unilateral ECT are equal in efficacy. Instead, the issue should be identification of the conditions under which unilateral ECT can be as effective as bilateral ECT.

There are a number of possibilities that may explain why more recent work has demonstrated more robust therapeutic advantages for bilateral ECT. Two factors that are raised here concern patient selection and technical factors in the administration of the treatment. Although there was at one time a host of studies that examined patient factors that predict response to ECT generally (e.g., Carney, Roth, & Garside, 1965; Mendels, 1967), there has been very limited work discerning whether unilateral and bilateral ECT differ in patient factors related to outcome. One exception is a study by Heshe, Roeder, and Theilgaard (1978), which found that bilateral ECT held a particular advantage for elderly patients. Although not well documented, it is likely that the nature of patient populations receiving ECT in academic and clinical settings has changed over the last two or more decades. Not only has there been diagnostic refinement regarding what constitutes major depressive disorder, but it is likely that ECT practice has increasingly centered on medication-resistant or medication-intolerant patients. Particularly in the United States, a major indication for ECT has become failure to respond to adequate trials with antidepressant medication or inability to sustain such trials due to side effect considerations (e.g., Frankel et al., 1978). As discussed later, there are no data documenting relative rates of response to ECT in medication-resistant patients and in those who have not failed adequate medication trials. Intuitively, one might expect that those who failed prior courses of antidepressant treatment would be less likely to respond to ECT than those who had not. Speculatively, it may also be the case that a larger representation of medication-resistant patients in research conducted at often tertiary academic centers magnifies efficacy differences between unilateral and bilateral ECT. A related possibility concerns patients with delusional or psychotic depression. There is a fair documentation that at high rates such patients fail to respond to monotherapy with antidepressants or antipsychotics (e.g., Spiker et al., 1985), and that they respond at high rates to bilateral ECT (Avery & Lubrano, 1979; Crow & Johnstone, 1986). Some have contended that psychosis involves perturbation of left hemisphere processes (e.g., Flor-Henry, 1983), which could suggest a preferential response to bilateral ECT. In turn, if both the factors of medication-resistant and psychosis have become more represented in ECT samples, this may result in patient groups that are older, and with greater representation of highly recurrent affective disorder.

It has been suggested that a major methodological confound has characterized virtually all comparative trials of unilateral and bilateral ECT (Sackeim, Decina, Kanzler et al., 1987). The typical paradigm has been to have ECT devices deliver the same electrical intensity to all patients, regardless of modality. Although this equates treatment conditions in terms of the raw amount of electricity being administered, it produces inequality in the amount that reaches the brain. With constant-current, brief pulse devices, seizure threshold is lower with right unilateral ECT (d'Elia placement) than with bilateral ECT (Sackeim, Decina, Portnoy et al., 1987). Consequently, if the same electrical dose is administered to both conditions, it will exceed seizure threshold to a greater extent with unilateral than bilateral ECT. Previously, the hypothesis was described that both the therapeutic and adverse effects of ECT are more related to the degree to which stimulus intensity exceeds seizure threshold than the absolute dose administered (Sackeim, Decina, Prohovnik et al., 1987c). By this view, much of the previous comparative work was biased in favor of the efficacy of unilateral right ECT (underestimated therapeutic differences). This view also suggests that the side effect profile differences were also underestimated. In addition, it has been argued that for unilateral ECT to be efficacious, it, in particular, must be delivered with stimulus intensity that clearly exceeds threshold.

This perspective has been applied in analyses of extant findings regarding efficacy differences between bilateral and unilateral ECT (Abrams, 1986a; Pettinati et al., 1986). There are suggestions that trials that found advantages for bilateral ECT had greater representation of older patients, male patients, used shorter interelectrode distances for unilateral ECT, and/or permitted use of benzodiazepines during the ECT course for anxiolytic or hypnotic purposes. Each of these factors is associated with an increased seizure threshold. Therefore, given the hypothesized sensitivity of unilateral ECT to electrical dosage effects, such practices may have weakened the efficacy of this condition. The most recent studies are more likely to have used ECT devices that delivered more electrically efficient and less intense stimulation. This would have the same result.

If ongoing trials sustain this perspective, it is possible that the conditions under which unilateral and bilateral ECT are equally effective can be specified. Investigation in this area should also be revealing of mechanisms of therapeutic action of ECT. If stimulus intensity needs to be more grossly suprathreshold for unilateral ECT to be equivalent in efficacy, the question arises as to whether the greater efficacy is tied to the increased current density (or seizure discharge) in the ipsilateral or contralateral hemisphere. Do neurophysiological and neuropsychological studies reveal increased or decreased asymmetry when stimulus intensity is enhanced with unilateral ECT? At the practical level, this work will also require reassessment of whether there is a differential advantage with regard to cognitive side effects when each modality is delivered at the minimal intensity level that it requires to produce maximal clinical benefit.

## ECT VERSUS ANTIDEPRESSANT MEDICATIONS

During the 1960s a series of trials were conducted that examined the relative efficacy of ECT compared to tricyclic antidepressants (TCAs) and monoamine oxidase inhibitors (MAOIs) (Bruce et al., 1960; Fahy et al., 1963; Greenblatt et al., 1964; Harris & Robin, 1960; Kiloh et al., 1960; Robin & Harris, 1962; Shepherd, 1965; Wilson, Vernon, Guin, & Sandifer, 1963). These trials were conducted soon after the introduction of the pharmacological agents, and the major American (Greenblatt et al., 1964) and British (Shepherd, 1965) studies in particular were geared to using ECT as a "gold standard" by which to measure the relative efficacy of the medications.

This literature has also been the subject of a number of recent reviews (e.g., Fink, 1980; Janiack et al., 1985; Rifkin, 1988). Broadly speaking there is consensus that across this work ECT was found to be as effective or more effective than any other treatment for depression. On the basis of their meta-analysis, Janiack et al. (1985) summarized the literature as indicating that across studies that compared ECT to any other type of treatment, there was a 78% response rate to ECT, a 28% rate for sham ECT, a 37.6% for medication placebo conditions, a 64.3% rate for TCAs, and a 32% rate of response to

MAOIs. Within the same set of studies, ECT had a 20% advantage in response rate over TCAs.

However, the situation is more complex. In most of this work and in the most critical studies, double-blind conditions did not pertain to the ECT groups. When patients receiving ECT and pharmacotherapy are being compared, it is impossible to disguise treatment conditions unless repeated anesthesia is administered to pharmacotherapy patients (e.g., Wilson et al., 1963). Such a procedure would not conform to clinical practice, it would enhance risks and conceivably it could interfere with medication effects. An alternative is to videotape clinical evaluations. References to or display of side effects that would indicate form of treatment (e.g., memory complaints or complaints of dry mouth, dizziness, etc.) can be edited out, with the tapes rated by clinicians blind to treatment and time period during the study (i.e., time-blind). Such procedures provide some control over rater bias, but not over differential patient expectancy and related placebo effects, and have been implemented recently in comparative studies of ECT and pharmacotherapy in the treatment of acute mania (Mukherjee, Sackeim, & Lee, 1988; Small et al., 1986).

As detailed by Rifkin (1988), the studies contrasting ECT and antidepressant medications also had limitations with respect to the nature of pharmacological treatment and statistical analyses. Since these studies were conducted, the standards for what are considered adequate trials of TCAs and MAOIs have been revised upwards. This has been based on findings that higher dosage and longer duration of treatment are associated with higher clinical response rate (e.g., Quitkin, Rabkin, Ross, & McGrath, 1984). Therefore, by current standards one might question whether the superiority obtained for ECT was due to weak medication conditions. Further, in some trials that reported significant therapeutic advantages for ECT compared to specific comparative conditions, a significant between-group difference across all the conditions tested was not established prior to performing specific comparisons. This criticism loses some force when collapsing data across studies for purposes of meta-analysis.

Rifkin (1988) suggested that there is a pressing clinical need to determine more conclusively whether ECT is more effective than antidepressant medications. He argued that if, indeed, rates of ECT response exceed those with TCAs or MAOIs by approximately 20%, patients and clinicians should be informed of the greater likelihood of response with ECT. One can add to this that it is widely accepted that rates of medical morbidity and mortality are lower with ECT than with antidepressant medications, even though ECT is often used in patients with medical complications who cannot tolerate TCAs or MAOIs. However, this portrayal is also an oversimplification.

As described in the next section, current clinical practice dictates that following response to ECT, patients who have recovered from episodes of major depression receive antidepressant medications for a period of at least several months to prevent relapse of the same episode (e.g., Klein et al., 1980). Given that patients will in any case be exposed to antidepressant medications, it can be argued that unless there are other pressing indications for ECT, failure to respond to medications during the acute phase of illness typically should be established first. This would limit the extent of polytherapy and thereby decrease risks.

Another problem with how this literature has been framed concerns the fact that a large proportion of patients who receive ECT are therapeutically resistant to, or medically intolerant of, antidepressant medications. In evaluating the relative efficacy of these medications and ECT, it would be unfair to randomly assign a typical ECT sample to either ECT or medication conditions. Only a small proportion of medication-resistant patients would be expected to respond to the same class of drug if they already failed adequate trials during the same episode. Accordingly, one would expect a substantially higher response rate for ECT. On the other hand, one might concentrate work on patients untreated during that episode. Such research would be impractical or of limited meaning for three reasons. First, the nature of political climate surrounding ECT, at least in the United States, is such that one should expect high refusal rates in previously untreated patients for participation in a random assignment trial to medication or ECT. The outcome of such work may be compromised by a serious selection bias. Second, the availability of previously untreated patients, with depressions of sufficient severity to require ECT, is likely to be too low at academic centers to sustain this type of research. Third, such samples would not be representative of current ECT practice.

Assessment of the relative value of antidepressant and ECT treatment of depression is complicated by additional factors. Reviews of the comparative trials have centered on determining whether rate of clinical response differed for ECT or medications (e.g., Janiack et al., 1985; Rifkin 1988). For the most part, this involved contrasts of the number of patients in the treatment conditions who were globally rated as improved. Traditionally, it has been claimed that not only is the rate of clinical response superior with ECT, but also the quality of clinical response. It is believed that patients considered improved or substantially improved will show less residual symptomatology, that is, more complete remission, if treated with ECT relative to medications. If true, this is a critical issue because residual symptomatology observed following maximal antidepressant response may be long persisting and possibly predictive of relapse. Unfortunately there are limited data regarding this issue. Hamilton (1982) reported an open, naturalistic study contrasting in his practice the distributions of the proportion of symptom score reductions with ECT and pharmacological treatment. Response to ECT was more bimodal than with antidepressant medications, with ECT characterized by a greater proportion of complete or near-complete remissions. From the point of view of prospective patients, the likely extent of residual symptoms may be as critical as the relative probability of sustaining improvement.

Finally, any evaluation of the relative merits of antidepressant medications and ECT must consider their respective side effect profiles. To some extent this is like comparing apples and oranges. The major concerns with the medications, particularly in the elderly, are systemic medical side effects, and in a small proportion, mortality. ECT has a marked advantage with regard to this domain. However, the frequency of such complications with medications is far lower than the universal acute cognitive side effects of ECT. Although research on the cognitive effects of TCAs and MAOIs is presently assuming more attention, it is unlikely that improvements in ECT technique in the near future will moderate acute cognitive side effects to a level that approaches the sustained effects of antidepressant medications. Further, within the domain of cognition there is likely to be specification by type of treatment, with differences between the medications and ECT in the areas affected. Indeed with ECT, the type and extent of cognitive side effects manifested are strongly related to when patients are assessed relative to their last treatment (e.g., Steif et al., 1986).

In summary, with a number of limitations, the comparative trials of ECT and TCAs or MAOIs are supportive of the view that ECT is the most effective antidepressant available. However, even assuming relative superiority in rates of clinical response, other factors must be considered in determining the priority of somatic treatments in relieving major depressive disorder. The issue as to whether quality of antidepressant response is also superior with ECT requires investigation. The increasing use of ECT in medication-resistant patients also poses issues of efficacy. It is established that medication-resistant patients respond to ECT at high rates (e.g., Avery & Lubrano, 1979). It has never been determined, however, whether their rate or quality of response is equivalent to that of patients who did not fail adequate medication trials in the same episode. It would be useful at the clinical level to determine whether established medication-resistance impinges on ECT response rates. Indeed, it would be highly unusual in therapeutics for patients who have failed adequate trials of accepted treatment for a condition to have equal probability of responding to another class of treatment, as patients not determined to be treatment resistant. If in fact this factor bears no relation to ECT outcome there would also be implications with respect to considerations of mechanisms of antidepressant action of ECT. A prominent approach in the study of such mechanisms has been the identification of the similarities between ECT and TCAs in neurophysiological effects (e.g., Sackeim, 1988). If previous failure to respond to adequate TCA trials is irrelevant with regard to efficacy of ECT, then it would seem less likely that ECT exerts its therapeutic properties via the same mechanisms as TCAs.

## RELAPSE FOLLOWING RESPONSE TO ECT

This chapter has focused on a variety of issues concerning the short-term efficacy of ECT. After 50 years of investigation, with comparisons to sham treatment, subconvulsive stimulation, and placebo and active drug conditions, and within ECT, studies of a variety of technical factors, there is little room for doubt that ECT is a highly effective antidepressant treatment. From my viewpoint, the most pressing clinical question is not whether ECT works, but how best to prevent relapse.

Following response to antidepressant medications, relapse rates on the order of 50% are expected over the ensuing first several months if somatic treatment is discontinued at the point of clinical response (Mindham, Howland, & Shepherd 1973; Prien, Klett, & Caffey, 1973). This accords with notions that somatic treatment suppresses expression of the affective episode, but that the underlying neurobiological abnormality persists until there is spontaneous remission. Relapse rates following a period of 6 months of sustained euthymia are expected to be considerably lower because by that point patients who have remained well are believed to be out of the index episode. Commonly, relapse after a sustained period of remission is considered a recurrence, that is, the expression of a new episode. This formulation results in the distinction among acute phase treatment, continuation phase treatment directed at preventing relapse, and maintenance or prophylactic phase treatment directed at preventing the occurrence of new episodes (e.g., Klein et al., 1980; Prien et al., 1984).

The available evidence indicates that continuing the same antidepressant medication to which patients responded during the acute phase will reduce relapse rate in the ensuing 6 months from approximately 50% to 20% (e.g., Mindham et al., 1973; Prien et al., 1973). The same type of pattern is believed to occur with ECT. If antidepressant treatment is not instituted following response, the evidence strongly indicates that relapse rates will be approximately 50% in the ensuing 4 to 6 months (e.g., Sackeim et al., in preparation; Snaith, 1981). The standard view is that administration of TCAs or MAOIs following ECT reduces this rate to approximately 20%.

This view emanated from three comparative trials conducted in England during the 1960s (Imlah, Ryan, & Harrington, 1965; Kay, Fahy, & Garside, 1970; Seager & Bird, 1962). Table 9.2 presents the essential characteristics of these studies. These trials were conducted with two purposes in mind. The first was to determine whether concomitant treatment with antidepressant medications during the ECT course would result in need for fewer ECT treatments, that is, more rapid clinical response. This work and other studies indicated that proportion and speed of clinical response were not influenced by concomitant antidepressant treatment. The second goal was to determine

TABLE 9.2
Prospective Studies of TCA Continuation Therapy Following
Antidepressant Response to ECT

| Study | Methods | # of Pts. | Followup | Relapse | |
|---|---|---|---|---|---|
| Seager & Bird (1962) | Random Double-blind Imipramine Placebo | entered 40 completed followup 28 | 6 mo | IMI 16% (2/12) | PLACEBO 68% (11/16) |
| Imlah et al. (1965) | Random Not Blind Imipramine Phenelzine No Medication | entered 150 completed followup 111 | 6 mo | IMI & PHZ 21% (15/70) | NO MEDS 51 (21/41) |
| Kay et al. (1970) | Random Double-blind Amitriptyline Diazepam | entered 132 completed followup 115 | 6 mo | AMI 15% (8/52) | DIAZEPAM 38% (24/63) |

whether continuing the antidepressant medications following response to ECT reduced rates of relapse.

The bulk of patients in these trials received TCAs or MAOIs during the ECT course. In the majority of patients the continuation treatment phase did not involve being newly randomly assigned to medication or placebo (or no drug) conditions. Rather, patients continued to receive the same pharmacological agent (or lack thereof) as during the ECT course. This raises the possibility that patients who benefited from the antidepressants as acute phase treatment also sustained benefit during the continuation phase. This problem is compounded by the fact that these trials were conducted soon after the introduction of the antidepressant medications, and at the time, ECT was often used as a treatment of first choice. Accordingly, one would expect that a fairly high proportion of depressed patients responded to the medications as acute phase treatment. As noted earlier, an increasing proportion of ECT practice centers on medication-resistant patients, and in many centers such patients comprise the great majority of those treated with ECT for depression. Nonetheless, the standard of practice in the field is to administer a TCA following clinical response to ECT, regardless of whether patients were found to be TCA-resistant during the acute phase of illness. Indeed, some have recommended that ECT be reserved for TCA-resistant patients and that all patients receive TCA continuation therapy following response to ECT (Klein et al., 1980).

Conceptually it is possible that patients benefit from use of a medication as a continuation treatment that they failed to benefit from as an acute phase treatment. This circumstance rarely arises in psychopharmacological practice, because patients would ordinarily be continued on the same medication they responded to while in the acute phase. The rationale for such practice in the case of ECT centers on either the possibility that what needs to be accomplished from a neurobiological viewpoint differs during the acute and continuation phases or that prior ECT alters the neurobiological substrate such that the requisite pharmacological action can now be obtained (Sackeim, 1986).

To provide an initial examination of this issue, the Columbia group conducted a prospective, naturalistic study (Sackeim et al., in preparation). Patients were monitored until relapse or for one year following clinical response to ECT. Several methods were used to evaluate relative medication resistance during the index depressive episode. Following ECT, somatic and psychotherapeutic treatment was uncontrolled and determined largely at the discretion of patients' referring clinicians. Across the sample, the relapse rate was high and clustered in the first 4 months following clinical response. If patients sustained remission beyond this point, relapse was rare. Regardless of method of evaluation, medication-resistance during the index episode was predictive of a substantially higher rate of relapse. In patients who were found to be medication-resistant prior to receiving ECT, adequacy of post-ECT pharmacotherapy had no relation to relapse rates. In particular, there was no evidence that patients who failed an adequate TCA trial prior to receiving ECT benefited from adequate TCA treatment following clinical response. On the other hand, adequate post-ECT pharmacotherapy was significantly associated with a lower relapse rate in patients who had not received an adequate medication trial prior to ECT. It is likely that a number of these patients would have responded to antidepressant medications had they received adequate trials prior to ECT.

These findings are suggestive that medication-resistance is predictive of a high relapse rate following ECT and that the standard pharmacological strategy of administering the same class of medication as continuation therapy that patients failed to respond to during the acute phase may be ineffective. Considerable caution is necessary in generalizing from these data. As in any naturalistic, uncontrolled study, it is conceivable that levels of treatment and patient characteristics are confounded. Although in this work such factors could not be identified, it is possible that treating clinicians instituted more vigorous continuation therapy in patients who were believed to be at higher risk of relapse. What is sorely needed in this area are prospective, random assignment, placebo-controlled evaluation of the utility of standard pharmacological continuation treatment in medication-resistant ECT-responsive patients. One such trial is ongoing.

It is noteworthy that ECT is the only somatic treatment of major depression that is typically discontinued following clinical response. Little date are available concerning the efficacy of continuing ECT on an intermittent basis following antidepressant response (e.g., Decina, Guthrie, Sackheim, Kahn, & Malitz, 1987; Stevenson & Geoghegan, 1951), although the case reports and clinical experience suggest that this approach can be highly effective in preventing relapse. The severity of cognitive side effects would be expected to be substantially moderated by such a procedure because their magnitude is linked to the temporal spacing of treatments (e.g., three times per week during the acute phase versus once every 2 or 3 weeks during continuation treatment). The difficulties in this area are largely psychosocial. With euthymia, patients are frequently resistant to return periodically to hospitals to undergo anesthesia and seizure induction. An alternative is to evaluate the efficacy of different pharmacological treatment interventions to prevent relapse. This may involve use of standard classes of antidepressants for which medication-resistance was not established during the acute phase. Further, new classes of agents require attention. Particularly in light of developments in the study of the mechanisms of action of ECT, it would seem reasonable to attempt to sustain pharmacologically the same type of neurobiological effects as those produced by ECT in the first place. Ultimately such research offers the promise of replacing ECT with psychopharmacological interventions. This is a formidable task. With the clear exception in the area of cognitive side effects, the safety profile of ECT regarding medical morbidity and mortality and its remarkable short-term therapeutic efficacy present a standard approached by few other interventions in medicine.

## ACKNOWLEDGMENTS

This work was supported in part by grant MH35636 from the National Institute of Mental Health. I thank Richard P. Brown, M.D., Paolo Decina, M.D., D. P. Devanand, M.D., Sidney Malitz, M.D., and Joan Prudic, M.D. for critical discussions of various issues raised here and Victoria P. Maddatu for editorial assistance.

## REFERENCES

Abrams, R. (1986a). A hypothesis to explain divergent findings among studies comparing unilateral and bilateral ECT in depression. *Convulsive Therapy, 2*, 253–258.

Abrams, R. (1986b). Is unilateral electroconvulsive therapy really the treatment of choice in endogenous depression? *Annals of the New York Academy of Sciences, 462*, 50–55.

Abrams, R., Taylor, M., Faber, R., Tso, T., Williams, R., & Almy, G. (1983). Bilateral vs unilateral electroconvulsive therapy: Efficacy in melancholia. *American Journal of Psychiatry, 140*, 463–465.

Avery, D., & Lubrano, A. (1979). Depression treated with imipramine and ECT: The DeCarolis study reconsidered. *American Journal of Psychiatry, 136*, 559–562.

Barton, J. (1977). ECT in depression: The evidence of controlled studies. *Biological Psychiatry, 12*, 687–695.

Brandon, S., Cowley, P., McDonald, C., Neville, P., Palmer, R., & Wellstood-Eason, S. (1984). Electroconvulsive therapy: Results in depressive illness from the Leicestershire trial. *British Medical Journal, 228*, 22–25.

Brill, N. Q., Crumpton, E., Eiduson, S., Grayson, H. M., & Hellman, L. I. (1959). Predictive and concomitant variables related to improvement with actual and simulated ECT. *Archives of General Psychiatry, 1*, 263–272.

Bruce, E. M., Crone, N., Fitzpatrick, G., Frewin, S. J., Gillis, A., Lascelles, C. F., Levene, L. J., & Mersky, H. A. (1960). A comparative trial of ECT and Tofranil. *American Journal of Psychiatry, 117*, 76.

Carney, M. W. P., Roth, J., & Garside, R. F. (1965). The diagnosis of depressive syndromes and the prediction of E.C.T. response. *British Journal of Psychiatry, 111*, 659–674.

Carney, M. W. P., & Sheffield, B. F. (1974). The effects of pulse ECT in neurotic and endogenous depression. *British Journal of Psychiatry, 125*, 91–94.

Cronholm, B., & Ottosson, J. -O. (1961). Memory functions in endogenous depression before and after electroconvulsive therapy. *Archives of General Psychiatry, 5*, 193–199.

Cronholm, B., & Ottosson, J. -O. (1963). Ultrabrief stimulus technique in electroconvulsive therapy. II. Comparative studies of therapeutic effects and memory disturbances in treatment of endogenous depression with the Elther ES electroshock apparatus and Siemens Konvulsator III. *Journal of Nervous and Mental Disease, 137*, 268–276.

Crow, T. J., & Johnstone, E. C. (1986). Controlled trials of electroconvulsive therapy. *Annals of the New York Academy of Sciences, 462*, 12–29.

Daniel, W. F., & Crovitz, H. F. (1982). Recovery of orientation after electroconvulsive therapy. *Acta Psychiatrica Scandinavica, 66*, 421–428.

Daniel, W. F., & Crovitz, H. F. (1986). Disorientation during electroconvulsive therapy: Technical, theoretical, and neuropsychological issues. *Annals of the New York Academy of Sciences, 462*, 293–306.

Decina, P., Guthrie, E. B., Sackeim, H. A., Kahn, D., & Malitz S. (1987). Continuation ECT in the management of relapses of major affective episodes. *Acta Psychiatrica Scandinavica, 75*, 559–562.

d'Elia, G. (1970). Unilateral electroconvulsive therapy. *Acta Psychiatrica Scandinavica (Supplement), 215*, 5–98.

d'Elia, G., Ottosson, J. -O., & Strömgren, L. (1983). Present practice of electroconvulsive therapy in Scandinavica. *Archives of General Psychiatry, 40*, 577–581.

d'Elia, G., & Raotma, H. (1975). Is unilateral ECT less effective than bilateral ECT? *British Journal of Psychiatry, 126*, 83–89.

Devanand, D. P., & Sackeim, H. A. (1988). Seizure elicitation blocked by pretreatment with lidocaine. *Convulsive Therapy, 4*, 225–229.

Fahy, P., Imiah, N., & Harrington, J. A. (1963). A controlled comparison of electroconvulsive therapy, imipramine and thiopentone sleep in depression. *Journal of Neuropsychiatry, 4*, 310–314.

Fink, M. (1979). *Convulsive therapy: Theory and practice.* New York: Raven Press.

Fink, M. (1980). Convulsive therapy and endogenous depression. *Pharmakopsychiatria, 13*, 49–54.

Fink, M., Kahn, R. L., & Green, M. A. (1958). Experimental studies of the electroshock process. *Diseases of the Nervous System, 19*, 113–118.

Flor-Henry, P. (1983). *Cerebral basis of psychopathology.* Boston: John Wright.

Frankel, F. H., Bidder, T. G., Fink, M., Mandel, M. R., Small, I. F., Wayne, G. J., Squire,

L. R., Dutton, E. N., & Gurel, L. (1978). *Electroconvulsive Therapy: Report of the Task Force on Electroconvulsive Therapy of the American Psychiatric Association.* Washington, DC: American Psychiatric Association.

Freeman, C. P., Basson, J. V., & Crighton, A. (1978). Double-blind controlled trial of electroconvulsive therapy (E.C.T.) and simulated E.C.T. in depressive illness. *Lancet, l,* 738–740.

Gold, P. E., Macri, J., & McGaugh, J. L. (1973). Retrograde amnesia gradients: Effects of direct cortical stimulation. *Science, 179,* 1343–1345.

Greenblatt, M., Grooser, G. H., & Wechsler, H. A. (1964). Differential response of hospitalized depressed patients in somatic therapy. *American Journal of Psychiatry, 120,* 935–943.

Gregory, S., Shawcross, C. R., & Gill D. (1985). The Nottingham ECT study: A double-blind comparison of bilateral, unilateral and simulated ECT in depressive illness. *British Journal of Psychiatry, 146,* 520–524.

Halliday, A., Davison, K., Browne, M., & Kreeger, L. (1968). A comparison of the effects on depression and memory of bilateral ECT and unilateral ECT to the dominant and nondominant hemispheres. *British Journal of Psychiatry, 114,* 997–1012.

Hamilton, M. (1982). The effect of treatment on the melancholias (depressions). *British Journal of Psychiatry, 140,* 223–230.

Harris, J. A., & Robin, A. A. (1960). A controlled trial of phenelzine in depressive reactions. *Journal of Mental Science, 106,* 1432–1437.

Heshe, J., Roeder, F., & Theilgaard, A. (1978). Unilateral and bilateral ECT: A psychiatric and psychological study of therapeutic effect and side effects. *Acta Psychiatrica Scandinavica [Supplement], 275,* 1–180.

Imiah, N. W., Ryan, E., & Harrington, J. A. (1965). The influence of antidepressant drugs on the response to electroconvulsive therapy and on subsequent relapse rates. *Neuropsychopharmacology, 4,* 438–442.

Janicak, P. G., Davis, J. M., Gibbons, R. D., Ericksen, S., Chang, S., & Gallagher, P. (1985). Efficacy of ECT: A meta-analysis. *American Journal of Psychiatry, 142,* 297–302.

Johnstone, E. C., Deakin, J. F. W., Lawler, P., Frith, C. D., Stevens, M., McPherson, K., & Crow, T. J. (1980). The Northwick Park electroconvulsive therapy trial. *Lancet, ii,* 1317–1320.

Kalinowsky, L. B., & Hippius, H. (1972). *Pharmacological, convulsive and other treatments in psychiatry.* New York: Grune & Stratton.

Kay, D. W., Fahy, T., & Garside, R. F. (1970). A 7-month double-blind trial of amitriptyline and diazepam in ECT-treated depressed patients. *British Journal of Psychiatry, 117,* 667–671.

Kendall, B. S., Mills, W. B., & Thale, T. (1956). Comparison of two methods of electroshock in their effect on cognitive functions. *Journal of Consulting Psychology, 20,* 423–429.

Kendell, R. E. (1981). The present status of electroconvulsive therapy. *British Journal of Psychiatry, 139,* 265–283.

Kiloh, L. G., Child, J. P., & Latner, G. (1960). A controlled trial of iproniazid in the treatment of endogenous depression. *Journal of Mental Science, 106,* 1139–1144.

Klein, D., Gittelman, R., Quitkin, G., & Rifkin, A. (1980). *Diagnosis and drug treatment of psychiatric disorders: Adults and children.* Baltimore: Williams & Wilkins.

Kriss, A., Halliday, A. M., & Pratt, R. (1980). Neurological asymmetries immediately after unilateral ECT. *Journal of Neurology, Neurosurgery, and Psychiatry, 41,* 1135–1144.

Lambourn, J., & Gill, D. (1978). A controlled comparison of simulated and real ECT. *British Journal of Psychiatry, 133,* 514–519.

Lancaster, N., Steinert, R., & Frost, I. (1958). Unilateral electroconvulsive therapy. *Journal of Mental Science, 104,* 221–227.

Lloyd, K. G., Morselli, P. L., & Bartholini, G. (1987). GABA and affective disorders. *Medical Biology, 65,* 159–165.

Maletzky, B. M. (1978). Seizure duration and clinical effect in electroconvulsive therapy. *Comprehensive Psychiatry, 19*, 541–580.

Malitz, S., Sackeim, H. A., & Decina, P. (1982). ECT in the treatment of major affective disorders: Clinical and basic research issues. *Psychiatric Journal of the University of Ottawa, 7*, 126–134.

Malitz, S., Sackeim, H. A., Decina, P., Kanzler, M., & Kerr, B. (1986). The efficacy of ECT: Dose-response interactions with modality. *Annals of the New york Academy of Sciences, 462*, 58–64.

Malloy, F. W., Small, I. F., Miller, M. J., & Milstein, V. (1982). Changes in neuropsychological test performance after electroconvulsive therapy. *Biological Psychiatry, 17*, 61–67.

MECTA Corporation (1987). *Instruction manual: SR and JR models.* Portland, OR: MECTA Corporation.

Meduna, L. J. (1935). Versuche uber die biologische Beeinflussung des Abaufes der Schizophrenia: Camphor und Cardiozolkrampfe. *Zeitschrift Gesamte Neurologie Psychiatrie, 152* 235–262.

Mendels, J. (1967). The prediction of response to electroconvulsive therapy. *American Journal of Psychiatry, 124*, 153–159.

Miller, E. (1967). Psychological theories of ECT: A review. *British Journal of Psychiatry, 113*, 301–311.

Mindham, R. H. S., Howland, C., & Shepherd, M. (1973). An evaluation of continuation therapy with tricyclic antidepressants in depressive illness. *Psychological Medicine, 3*, 5–17.

Mukherjee, S., Sackeim, H. A., & Lee, C. (1988). Unilateral ECT in the treatment of manic episodes. *Convulsive Therapy, 4*, 74–80.

Ottosson, J. -O. (1960). Experimental studies of the mode of action of electroconvulsive therapy. *Acta Psychiatrica Scandinavica [Supplement], 145*, 1–141.

Ottosson, J. -O. (1985). Use and misuse of electroconvulsive treatment. *Biological Psychiatry, 20*, 933–946.

Overall, J. E., & Rhoades, H. M. (1986). A comment on the efficacy of unilateral versus bilateral ECT. *Convulsive Therapy, 2*, 245–251.

Pettinati, H. M., Mathisen, K. S., Rosenberg, J., & Lynch, J. F. (1986). Meta-analytical approach to reconciling discrepancies in efficacy between bilateral and unilateral electroconvulsive therapy. *Convulsive Therapy, 2*, 7–17.

Pippard, J., & Ellam, L. (1981). *Electroconvulsive treatment in Great Britain.* London: Gaskell.

Prien, R. F., Klett, C. J., & Caffey, E. M. J. (1973). Lithium carbonate and imipramine in prevention of affective episodes: A comparison in recurrent affective illness. *Archives of General Psychiatry, 29*, 420–425.

Prien, R., Kupfer, D., Mansky, P., Small, J., Tuason, V., Voss, C., & Johnson W. (1984). Drug therapy in the prevention of recurrences in unipolar and bipolar affective disorders. *Archives of General Psychiatry, 41*, 1096–1104.

Prudic, J., Sackeim, H. A., Decina, P., Hopkins, N., Ross, F. R., & Malitz, S. (1987). Acute effects of ECT on cardiovascular functioning: Relations to patient and treatment variables. *Acta Psychiatrica Scandinavica, 75*, 344–351.

Quitkin, F. M., Rabkin, J. G., Ross, D., & McGrath, P. J. (1984). Duration of antidepressant drug treatment: What is an adequate trial? *Archives of General Psychiatry, 41*, 238–245.

Rifkin, A. (1988). ECT versus tricyclic antidepressants in depression: A review of the evidence. *Journal of Clinical Psychiatry, 49*, 3–7.

Robin, A. (in press). Current policy and rising trends. In B. Lerer (Ed.), *New Directions in Research in Affective Disorders.* New York: Elsevier.

Robin, A., & Harris, J. A. (1962). A controlled trial of imipramine and electroplexy. *Journal of Mental Science, 106*, 217–219.

Robin, A., & deTissera, S. (1982). A double-blind controlled comparison of the therapeutic effects of low and high energy electroconvulsive therapies. *British Journal of Psychiatry, 141,* 357–366.

Rose, R. (1985). Consensus conference: Electroconvulsive therapy. *JAMA, 254,* 2103–2108.

Rush, S., & Driscoll, D. (1968). Current distribution in the brain from surface electrodes. *Anesthesia and Analgesia, 47,* 717–723.

Sackeim, H. A. (1985). The case for ECT. *Psychology Today, 19,* 36–40.

Sackeim, H. A. (1986). The efficacy of ECT. *Annals of the New York Academy of Sciences, 462,* 70–75.

Sackeim, H. A. (1988). Mechanisms of action of electroconvulsive therapy. In R. E. Hales, & J. Frances (Eds.), *Annual Review of Psychiatry, Vol. 7,* (pp. 436–457). Washington, DC: American Psychiatric Press.

Sackeim, H. A. (in press). Stimulus intensity and ECT outcome. In B. Lerer (Ed.), *New directions in research in affective disorders.* New York: Elsevier.

Sackheim, H. A., Decina, P., Kanzler, M., Kerr, B., & Malitz, S. (1987). Effects of electrode placement on the efficacy of titrated, low-dose ECT. *American Journal of Psychiatry, 144,* 1449–1455.

Sackeim, H. A., Decina, P., Portnoy, S., Neeley, P., & Malitz, S. (1987). Studies of dosage, seizure threshold, and seizure duration in ECT. *Biological Psychiatry, 22,* 249–268.

Sackeim, H. A., Decina, P., Prohovnik, I., & Malitz, S. (1987c). Seizure threshold in ECT: Effects of sex, age, electrode placement and number of treatments. *Archives of General Psychiatry, 44,* 355–360.

Sackeim, H. A., Decina, P., Prohovnik, I., Malitz, S., & Resor, S. (1983). Anticonvulsant and antidepressant properties of ECT: A proposed mechanism of action. *Biological Psychiatry, 18,* 1301–1310.

Sackeim, H. A., Greenberg, M. S., Weiman, A. L., Gur, R. C., Hungerbuhler, J. P., & Geschwind, N. (1982). Hemispheric asymmetry in the expression of positive and negative emotions: Neurologic evidence. *Archives of Neurology, 39,* 210–218.

Sackeim, H. A., & Mukherjee, S. (1986). Neurophysiological variability in the effects of the ECT stimulus. *Convulsive Therapy, 2,* 267–276.

Sackeim, H. A., Portnoy, S., Neeley, P., Steif, B., Decina, P., & Malitz, S. (1986). Cognitive consequences of low dosage ECT. *Annals of the New York Academy of Sciences, 462,* 398–410.

Sackeim, H. A., Prudic, J., Devanand, D. P., Decina, P., Kerr, B., & Malitz, S. (in preparation). *Relapse following response to ECT in major depressive disorder.*

Sackeim, H. A., & Steif, B. L. (1988). The neuropsychology of depression and mania. In A. Georgotas & R. Cancro (Eds.), *Depression and mania* (pp. 265–289). New York: Elsevier.

Sainz, A. (1959). Clarification of the action of successful treatment in the depressions. *Diseases of the Nervous System (Supplement), 20,* 53–57.

Sakel, M. (1938). *Pharmacological treatment of schizophrenia.* New York: Nervous and Mental Disease Publishing.

Scovern, A. W., & Kilmann, P. R. (1980). Status of electroconvulsive therapy: Review of the outcome literature. *Psychological Bulletin, 87,* 260–303.

Seager, C. R., & Bird, R. L. (1962). Imipramine with electrical treatment in depression—a controlled trial. *Journal of Mental Science, 108,* 704–707.

Shepherd, M. (1965). Clinical trial of the treatment of depressive illness. *British Medical Journal, 1,* 881–886.

Small, I. F. (1974). Inhalant convulsive therapy. In M. Fink, S. Kety, J. McGaugh, & T. A. Williams (Eds.), *Psychobiology of convulsive therapy* (pp. 65–77). Washington, DC: Winston & Sons.

Small, J. G., Milstein, V., Klapper, M. H., Kellams, J. J., Miller, M. J., & Small, I. F. (1986). Electroconvulsive therapy in the treatment of manic episodes. *Annals of the New York Academy of Sciences, 462,* 37–49.

Snaith, R. P. (1981). How much ECT does the depressed patient need? In R. L. Palmer (Ed.), *Electroconvulsive therapy: An appraisal* (pp. 61–64). New York: Oxford University Press.

Spiker, D. G., Weiss, J. C., Dealy, R. S., Griffin, S. J., Hanin, I., Neil, J. F., Perel, J. M., Rossi, A. J., & Soloff, P. H. (1985). The pharmacological treatment of delusional depression. *American Journal of Psychiatry, 142,* 430–436.

Squire, L. R. (1986). Memory functions as affected by electroconvulsive therapy. *Annals of the New York Academy of Sciences, 462,* 307–314.

Squire, L. R., & Slater, P. (1978). Bilateral and unilateral ECT: Effects on verbal and nonverbal memory. *American Journal of Psychiatry, 135,* 1316–1320.

Staton, R. D., Hass, P. J., & Brumback, R. A. (1981). Electroencephalographic recording during bitemporal and unilateral non-dominant hemisphere (Lancaster Position) electroconvulsive therapy. *Journal of Clinical Psychiatry, 42,* 264–269.

Steif, B. L., Sackeim, H. A., Portnoy, S., Decina, P., & Malitz, S. (1986). Effects of depression and ECT on anterograde memory. *Biological Psychiatry, 21,* 921–930.

Stevenson, G. H., & Geoghegan, J. J. (1951). Prophylactic electroshock: A five-year study. *American Journal of Psychiatry, 107,* 743–748.

Strömgren, L. (1984). Is bilateral ECT ever indicated? *Acta Psychiatrica Scandinavica, 69,* 484–490.

Ulett, G., Smith, K., & Gleser, G. (1956). Evaluation of convulsive and subconvulsive shock therapies utilizing a control group. *American Journal of Psychiatry, 112.* 795–802.

Valentine, M., Keddie, K., & Dunne, D. (1968). A comparison of techniques in electroconvulsive therapy. *British Journal of Psychiatry, 114,* 989–996.

Warren, E. W., & Groome, D. H. (1984). Memory test performance under three different waveforms of ECT for depression. *British Journal of Psychiatry, 144,* 370–375.

Weaver, L. A. J., Ives, J. O., Williams, R., & Nies, A. (1977). A comparison of standard alternating current and low-energy brief pulse electrotherapy. *Biological Psychiatry, 12,* 525–544.

Weaver, L. A. J., & Williams, R. W. (1986). Stimulus parameters and electroconvulsive therapy. *Annals of the New York Academy of Sciences, 462,* 174–185.

Weaver, L., Williams, R., & Rush, S. (1976). Current density in bilateral and unilateral ECT. *Biological Psychiatry, 11,* 303–312.

Weiner, R. D. (1980). ECT and seizure threshold: Effects of stimulus waveform and electrode placement. *Biological Psychiatry, 15,* 225–241.

Weiner, R. D. (1984). Does electroconvulsive therapy cause brain damage? *Behavioral and Brain Sciences, 7,* 1–54.

Weiner, R. D., Rogers, H. J., Davidson, J. R. T., & Squire, L. R. (1986). Effects of stimulus parameters on cognitive side effects. *Annals of the New York Academy of Sciences, 462,* 315–325.

Welch, C. A., Weiner, R. D., Weir, D., Cahill, J. F., Rogers, H. J., Davidson, J., Miller, R. D., & Mandel, M. R. (1982). Efficacy of ECT in the treatment of depression: Waveform and electrode placement considerations. *Psychopharmacological Bulletin, 18,* 31–34.

West, E. D. (1981). Electric convulsive therapy in depression: A double-blind controlled trial. *British Medical Journal, 282,* 355–357.

Wilson, I. C., Vernon, J. T., Guin, T., & Sandifer, M. G. (1963). A controlled study of treatments of depression. *Journal of Neuropsychiatry, 4,* 331–337.

# 10 | A SECOND OPINION: RETHINKING THE CLAIMS OF BIOLOGICAL PSYCHIATRY

Seymour Fisher
Roger P. Greenberg
*State University of New York*
*Health Science Center*

Multiple probes into the "somatic treatment" literature have been provided by the preceding chapters. Careful scrutiny has been devoted to the somatic therapies invented to cope with the various forms of "mental" distress. We would like to stand off a bit and attempt an integration of the cumulative observations and conclusions that have unfolded. What generalizations seem reasonable? What are the most persistent puzzles? What can one reasonably say about the overall state of the art with respect to the treatments that have been analyzed?

After immersing ourselves in the assorted data, we have emerged with a sense that statements about the results of somatic treatment approaches for "psychiatric disorder" should be viewed with caution and perhaps, even more appropriately, with a fair amount of skepticism. An almost startling complexity faces anyone who seeks to judge the efficacy of the various somatic treatments. The complexity is in part due to the multiple variables influencing any therapeutic outcome and is partially the result of specific troubling inadequacies in current methods for appraising the somatic approaches. We have learned from past literature reviews and discussions with current proponents and opponents of the therapies that the very same set of apparently scientific findings concerning efficacy can be interpreted in quite divergent ways as a function of whichever "theoretical" positions pre-exist. We have personally been startled to read research reports that seemed ostensibly to indicate a quite limited advantage for a particular drug as compared to a placebo, but then to find such reports hailed in another context as proof the drug is highly effective. The impact of bias is bad enough when one is trying to clarify theoretical issues, but takes on a more immediate seriousness when it influences the treatments of large numbers of distressed humans.

The stark fact is that our ability to evaluate therapeutic power remains in a somewhat primitive state. If one cuts through the reams of platitudes, cautions, and principles that have been promulgated concerning the measurement of the efficacy of the somatic treatments, it becomes apparent that the entire structure is more fragile and limited in potency than publicly acknowledged. One already gets premonitions of this fragility from historical accounts of the rise and fall of various treatment modalities. Treatments like insulin shock therapy or lobotomy for schizophrenia have come and gone, after first being hailed and apparently documented as highly successful. Widely accepted and "scientifically founded" successes have mysteriously dissipated with time. Cramond (1987) provided us with a detailed account of this fading process with respect to insulin shock, as has Valenstein (1986) for lobotomy. More currently, we find controversies that assert at one extreme that the Attention Deficit Disorder category (ADD) is not only inadequately treated with stimulant drugs but does not even exit as a syndrome; whereas practitioners at the other extreme confidently treat huge numbers of presumably ADD children with stimulant drugs for extended periods.

It would be well at this point to review the major complexities and deficiencies described in the previous chapters that plague the therapeutic appraisal process. They add up to a formidable array (see Table 10.1).

TABLE 10.1
Summary of Difficulties Complicating Conclusions Concerning the
Effectiveness of Biological Psychiatry Treatments

Unknown degree of transparency of the double-blind design
Failure to use active placebos
Widespread adoption of "washout" procedures that bias measurement of placebo effects
Extreme selectivity of sampling procedures
Vagueness of quantitative definitions of what is a meaningful "therapeutic effect"
Overuse of multiple outcome measures and statistical tests
Not infrequent contradictions in results from different sites in multicenter studies
Fair amount of indifference about high recurrence rates
Focus on short-term rather than long-term outcome
The not inconsiderable prevalence of serious side effects
Failure to establish substantial correlations between blood levels of drugs and their
    therapeutic power
Applying treatments to parts of the patient spectrum to which they are not really applicable
Existence of alternative psychological treatments that may be equally as effective and less
    somatically damaging

## DOUBLE-BLIND

As earlier noted, the sine qua non of a research design for assaying a therapy is a strategy for preventing the bias of the therapist or the patient from coloring the apparent treatment outcome. The double blind and related techniques have been employed toward this end. It is presumed that "double-blind" designs prevent the therapist or the patient from knowing when an active agent as contrasted to a placebo is being administered. The need for such concealment is not only obvious on a commonsense basis but also because previous research has shown that the more poorly a study controls sources of potential bias the more it produces results favoring the therapeutic agent being evaluated (e.g., Smith, Traganza, & Harrison, 1969; Wechsler, Grosser, & Greenblatt, 1965). No matter how great their scientific integrity, researchers who are invested in the success of a particular treatment will manage to exaggerate its power if their biases are not curbed.

In fact, double-blind paradigms have proven to be riddled with doubt.[1] A number of studies (e.g., Hughes & Krahn, 1985; Rabkin et al., 1986; Stallone, Mendlewicz, & Fieve, 1975) have shown that there is considerable potential for the patients and personnel involved in testing a drug treatment to distinguish it from placebo by either its therapeutic or side effects or still other cues. It is worthwhile in this respect to consider in a bit of detail the report by Rabkin et al. (1986). This project was carried out by a group in the Department of Psychiatry at Columbia University and includes participants like Frederick Quitkin and Donald Klein who have taken strong positive positions concerning the validity of data emerging from double-blind studies. The design of the study involved asking physicians and patients (treated for depression in a university research clinic) to guess at the end of 6 weeks of treatment (involving either imipramine, phenalzine, or placebo) whether an active or inactive substance had been administered. Both patients and physicians were able to make correct identifications at well beyond chance levels (79% and 87% respectively). Patients were more accurate in their identifications of active drug versus placebo when they were on the active drug rather than placebo (over 80% vs. 59%). The physicians did equally well in their identifications no matter whether the patient was on an active drug or placebo. When the patients were dichotomized into those who had or had not clearly improved during treatment, it was found that the overall rate of correct identification by patients was significantly higher in the case of those who were in the "responder" as compared to the "nonresponder" category. The physicians did not differ in their accuracy of identification in the context of the responder–nonresponder differentiation.

---

[1]Hill, Nunn, and Fox (1976) have even documented the fact that many studies are so careless that the drug and placebo preparations offered to patients can be distinguished by fairly casual inspection.

Although an effort was made to examine the relationship of correct identification to the character of the side effects experienced by the patients, the methodology was so flawed that the findings in this area are really worthless. Thus, side effects were not quantitatively evaluated until after 6 weeks of treatment had occurred. Also, only about half of the total sample was included in the side effects analysis. In the context of these flaws, the authors shift back and forth between asserting that side effects play little role in the accuracy of identification and cautioning that the results are inadequate to form any rational opinion about this issue. In the end, they conclude that side effects probably do play a role in correct identification, but to some unknown degree. The basic thrust of their paper is to suggest that the major variable mediating identification is degree of improvement. They imply that if this is so, then the breaking of the double blind is not serious since it merely reflects a realistic awareness of the actual degree of improvement occurring. However, an examination of their data indicates that viewing correct identification as simply a reflection of awareness of the improvement process is untenable. Consider that it was found that physicians were highly successful (84% correct) in identifying those patients who were nonresponders but who were taking an active drug! How could the physicians possibly have used signs of improvement to identify the patients who were on an active drug when there were no signs of improvement? The only cues available indicated (nonresponse) nonimprovement! Clearly, significant sources of information were available beyond signs of improvement that guided the physicians in their penetration of the double blind.

In the face of such data, the authors somehow manage to conclude "We do not believe that the internal validity of a clinical trial is compromised when this occurs" (p. 86). But in the very next sentence they add, "Nevertheless, the assumption that the double blind effectively conceals treatment conditions by the end of the trial, from either doctor or patient, appears unfounded" (p. 86). Indeed, they go on to say: "Finally, *active placebo medication* (our italics)—may help to conceal treatment assignments and should be considered as design options" (p. 86). Despite their ambivalence this group of investigators, which includes stalwarts of the drug therapy establishment, ultimately admit that the usual attempts to maintain the double blind have failed and that the use of an active placebo is advisable. So far as we can tell, subsequent research projects still have not taken such advice about using active rather than passive placebos.

The simple truth is that as drug trials are presently conducted there is no reasonable way to estimate the degree to which they are biased. The extent to which the double blind will be breached is probably mediated by a whole host of factors, such as the intensity of motivation to influence the results, the zeal of treatment personnel in sniffing out suggestive cues, and the degree to which patients are motivated or induced to reveal how the effects of the presumed "drug" are being experienced by them. The considerable prevalence of such breaches is suggested by the wide variations in drug versus placebo effectiveness reported in the literature, the incredible differences in apparent efficacy that not infrequently appear among multiple centers when they participate in a drug evaluation, and the hefty shifts in published descriptions of effectiveness of a drug over time as sentiments toward it alter in response to new theoretical or political paradigms. With respect to this last point, it is interesting how quickly the officially defined effectiveness of the shock treatments for schizophrenia nose-dived as soon as the antipsychotic drugs were introduced.

Hughes and Krahn (1985) have been so impressed with the vulnerability of double-blind designs, not only in the case of "psychoactive" but also "nonpsychoactive" drugs, that they have proposed a formal series of procedures and analyses as counter-measures. They suggest that upon completion of the drug trails the subjects be asked whether they believe they received an active drug or a placebo or are uncertain. Subjects are then assigned to one of six cells in a 2 x 3 table contrasting actual drug group (placebo versus active drug) and accuracy of drug identification (correct versus incorrect versus uncertain). This table is used for three sets of analyses. First, the blindness of the study is ascertained by comparing the numbers of subject who correctly and incorrectly identify their drug assignment. Second, a determination is made as to whether any failure to maintain blindness affected the validity of the results. This is done by comparing the sizes of the drug effects (i.e., the difference in active drug and placebo among subjects who correctly or incorrectly identify the drug they received and also those who are uncertain in this respect). Presumably, if drug identification impacted the validity of the results, then the drug effect should vary significantly among the three groups. Third, the size of the drug effect, with identification held constant, is determined by ascertaining drug effects within particular groups (e.g., those definitely blind because they are truly "uncertain"). We would urge that all presumably double-blind enterprises make use of such procedures to "check up" on how significantly the data have been compromised by the breaking of the code.

## ACTIVE VERSUS INACTIVE PLACEBO

The vulnerability of the double-blind design is heightened by the fact that, with few exceptions, the placebo control "drugs" used in such designs are inactive. That is, when patients involved in drug trials ingest the placebo they experience considerably fewer "physiological" effects than do those who ingest the active therapeutic agent. The subject impact of the placebo is obviously different from that of the active substance (e.g., Brune et al., 1962; Lipman, Park, & Rickels, 1966). This means that cues are provided as to whether one is receiving a placebo or something more active. Actually, little research attention has been given to this potentially highly important matter. We (Greenberg and Fisher) have already cited earlier studies (e.g., Thomson, 1982) suggesting that the use of an active placebo (e.g., atropine) in designs evaluating the effectiveness of tricyclics for treating depression reduces the apparent therapeutic advantage of active drug over placebo. We pointed out too that there is a growing literature indicating that amount of self-awareness mediates important response systems and it is logical to expect that agents intensifying body sensations will also increase self-body awareness. An active drug may not only be more easily recognized as a "real" treatment but also stimulate special "self-feelings" that can influence various levels of behavior. As earlier mentioned, increased self-awareness can have effects like magnifying self-disapproval or making individuals more realistically aware of their feelings and motivations or simply enhancing the vividness of one's emotional experiences. The mere fact that blindly ingesting a placebo is a perceptibly different experience than taking an active agent means that there is only an illusory experimental parity between the two conditions. The level of control assumed to prevail in the experiment is not there.

It is already documented that response to a drug can be tied to some extent to its body experiential context. A modest example is provided in a study by Clausen and Fisher (1973). They found that shifts in mood initiated by drugs like Pentobarbital or d-Amphetamine are correlated with changes in the degree to which subjects experience an increase or decrease in their sensory awareness of the boundary versus interior regions of the body. Although the data were correlational and therefore not interpretable in causal terms, they do indicate a promising link between how a drug influences one to redistribute attention toward various parts of one's body and certain mood states (e.g., anxiety, depression) that would be of importance when treating psychiatric patients. However, the way in which the issue of active versus inactive placebo has been handled dramatizes the determination of drug researchers to ignore the experiential aspects of drug therapies.[2] They have been utterly intrigued with a concept of treatment as an objective enterprise that directly manipulates biochemical systems. There has been little room in their schemas for the mediating impact of the multiple ways humans can interpret things done to their bodies. No one has taken the time to get at the elementary issue of what it means to be given an active versus inactive placebo. This is astounding. Vast amounts of energy are devoted by drug researchers to controlling an array of variables, but they have ignored the quite obvious fact that an inactive

---

[2]It should be indicated that researchers concerned with the efficacy of Electric Convulsive Therapy (ECT) have taken the active placebo issue seriously and have done their best to construct experiments in which ECT is compared with a procedure that mimics it closely, albeit, in structure, but not in lasting side effects. Sackeim provided details concerning this matter in his chapter. Interestingly, he noted considerable variability in the therapeutic power of sham shock as a function of such factors as clinical setting and modes of selection of patients.

placebo cannot possibly be experienced in a fashion equivalent to a physiologically active drug! To ignore the active placebo problem is even more inexplica-
ble when one considers that there have already been papers published strongly
hinting that therapeutic outcome can be influenced by the degree to which
a placebo arouses bodily sensations that mimic the "real thing." Persons who
participate in a drug study and who receive only an inactive placebo might
have a wide range of interpretations of the fact that the body sensations they
experience are not commensurate with their expectations of a "real medicine."
The most obvious is that they have not received a potent treatment but rather
an inconsequential placebo. This would, of course, initiate such thoughts as
"I am not getting treatment" or "Nothing is being done for me." But other
interpretations concerning the absence of "active" body sensations might
range from "This is wonderful. I am taking a medicine that doesn't hurt" to
"My body is so strong it barely feels the medicine" to "The doctor is trying to
fool or deceive me in some way." The point is that the interpretations could
be highly individualistic and unpredictable. No one has systematically tried
to map out the actual patterns of modal reactions and to relate them to
therapeutic consequences.

The entire matter of whether and how the body experiences associated
with a specific drug (or placebo) affect its therapeutic impact remains to be
clarified. There are some interesting notions with which one can play. On
the one hand, as already noted, if such body experiences are too limited or
sparse (as is the case with an inactive placebo), this might create an expectation of "no effect." At the other extreme, if the sensations induced are
too vivid or powerful or unpleasant, they might foster negative, avoidant,
antitherapeutic attitudes. The potential power of such attitudes to cancel out
the direct biochemically derived therapeutic effects of agents may be greater
than we know. We also earlier suggested that the locale of the body sensations
stimulated by an agent may play some role in that agent's impact. There is
evidence that accentuating awareness of specific body sectors (landmarks)
may selectively tune individuals to certain feelings or fantasies. For example,
when males are made more aware of the back of the body they become more
sensitive to stimuli with anal or dirt connotations. Or when they are rendered
more aware of their eyes they have accentuated responses to oral stimuli
(Fisher, 1986). If, then, a drug like imipramine induces a strong "dry mouth"
feeling, this would presumably magnify awareness of the mouth region, which
in turn could, as earlier described, produce a selective intensified response to
certain themes that, in psychodynamic terms, conceivably play a role in the
etiology of depression. Certainly we do quite routinely interpret sensations
from specific body areas (e.g., stomach, genitals) as signals of particular needs;
and it is not farfetched to consider that drug-induced accentuation of defined
body locales may be analogously interpreted.

It is also possible that agents that inhibit the functions of specific body areas would have selective antitherapeutic effects. For example, if a drug affects the legs and interferes with motility it might prove to be particularly threatening to an individual whose self-concept is constructed around notions of being independent and free. Or if a drug creates strange, confusing sensations in the head region (which is the perceived site of intellectuality), this could be antitherapeutically threatening to those who attach heightened import to possessing superior cognitive prowess. The possibility of drugs taking on especially negative connotations if they threaten to undermine salient goals or personality styles is certainly suggested by Cleveland's chapter in which he reviews the psychological mediators of drug response. Although Cleveland presents us with a somewhat discouraging picture concerning the dependability of the accumulated research in this area, he does point out that several studies indicate a trend for drugs that act in a direction opposite to an individual's "major personality trait" to be unusually disturbing.

Overall, the present orientation of those espousing "somatic" treatments implicitly hardens the meaningless separation between "mind" and "body." The so-called physiological effects of a drug are treated as if they were of an entirely different class from the "psychological" ones. "Placebo effects" are regarded as a nuisance to be screened out. Obviously, "psychological effects"[3] are fully as physiological as those attributed to a drug's biochemical action.

---

[3] Are psychological factors truly important in mediating the effects of the biologically oriented treatments? Obviously, the mere fact that placebo controls are necessary in order to appraise the effectiveness of an agent means the question must be answered in the affirmative. It is true that Cleveland, in his chapter reviewing the research dealing with the role of psychological factors in drug response, came up with a small yield of reliable findings. Although numerous individual significant findings have been described, Cleveland cautioned that they often derive from experimental methods that are possibly defective. Some of the difficulty in this area of research seems to derive from the fact that much of the work was carried out decades ago when less exacting standards of design and analysis prevailed. However, there remain a number of studies, deserving of follow-up, that suggest such variables as acquiescence (Fisher & Fisher, 1963; McNair, Fisher, Kahn, & Droppleman, 1970), extraversion–introversion (Eysenck, 1983), and body boundary definiteness (Clausen & Fisher, 1973; Fast & Fisher, 1971) may contribute significantly to how drugs are experienced and perhaps even to their therapeutic prowess. In addition, many personality and attitudinal variables have not been explored that one might intuitively expect to influence drug responses. Illustratively, there is good evidence that males and females differ in their attitudes toward body events and medical procedures (Fisher, 1986), and so one might anticipate that the dimension of masculinity–femininity would enter meaningfully into each individual's response to drug therapy experiences. Or consider that the decision to undergo drug therapy involves, at some levels, a willingness to put one's fate in the hands of an authority figure who "promises" that ingestion of a chemical will lead to a "cure." The decision to go this route rather than a psychotherapeutic one would seem to be mediated by attitudes concerning how much one can individually control one's own fate. Indeed, there has been some interesting empirical work showing that the choice of a medical or psychological help-seeking path is significantly influenced by the degree to which an individual adopts a masculine or feminine (independent or dependent) sex-role orientation (Greenberg & Fisher, 1977; Zeldow & Greenberg, 1979, 1980).

Placebo responses occur in tissue and are physiologically "real." However, the current set among biologically oriented researchers is to act as if one category of drug action is real and the so-called psychological aspect is imaginary, verging on the fictional. One can understand the attitude of biological researchers whose goal is to create an agent that selectively eliminates a "psychiatric symptom" by initiating changes in some biochemical system. Their focus is on the events in that system and other potential influences are extraneous. However, human response patterns cannot be separated into such neat categories, and in fact, we know little about the potential amount of spread of the physiological events, representing the psychological experience of taking a particular drug, to the specific biochemical system that drug is supposed to influence "directly." Indeed, if one considers that the typical aim of the somatic treatments is to alter targeted "psychological" experiences (e.g., depression, anxiety), any insistence on sharply segregating "psychological" and "somatic" factors becomes misleading.

## SAMPLING PROBLEMS

In reviewing numerous studies in the "somatic therapy" literature, we were struck with the fluctuating vicissitudes characterizing sample selection. Aside from the usual sampling problems pertaining to the selectivity of which persons are originally willing to come forward to seek treatment for their discomfort, and, in addition, to volunteer as subjects for a study, there are others of serious consequence. Most prominent is the relatively high proportion of patients who "drop out" before the completion of their treatment programs. Numerous of the dropouts are in response to unpleasant side effects. There are many published studies in which as many as 35% or more of the patients fail to complete the research protocol (Baekeland & Lundwall, 1975). Various procedures have been developed to deal fairly with the question of how to classify the therapeutic outcomes of dropouts, but none can vitiate the simple fact that the final sample of fully treated patients has often been drastically reduced. Further, as already described, the design of many more current studies includes a preliminary "washout" phase during which patients who are uncooperative or placebo responsive or spontaneously in remission are eliminated. The numbers of "washouts" range widely and may be modally in the vicinity of 20%. There are, of course, still other filters that increase sample selectivity. For example, Karon points out in his chapter dealing with schizophrenia that studies often lose sizable segments of their samples by not including patients who are too disorganized to participate in certain phases of the research protocol (e.g., respond to formal psychological tests). One can also find decisions not to permit particular racial groups to be represented in samples or to avoid using subjects below a given educational level. So we end up wondering about the final survivors in the average drug trial. To what degree do they typify the average individual in "real life" who seeks treatment? How much can one generalize from a treatment sample that is made up of the "leftovers" from multiple depleting processes? Are we left with a relatively narrow band of those most willing to conform to the rather rigid demands of the research establishment? Are the survivors those most accepting of a dependent role? The truth is that there are probably multiple kinds of survivors, depending upon the specific local conditions prevailing where the study was carried out. We would guess that some of the striking differences in results that appear in multicenter drug studies could be traced back to specific forms of sampling bias. We do not know, in any satisfactorily systematic way, how psychologically unique the persons are who get recruited into, and stick with, drug research enterprises. We are not the first to raise this question, but we probably take more seriously the potential implications. Although drug researchers try to get representative samples, their problems of recruitment and their own filtering customs (e.g., "washout" screening) do get them into trouble. We wonder how damaging the problem truly is. In the laboratory minimal concern seems to prevail. Serious study of the matter may lead to a rude awakening. It is even possible that the instability in improvement rates shown over time by various therapeutic agents is due to changes in the types of patients who get caught in the research net at different temporal points.

## THE PROBLEM OF A MEANINGFUL MAGNITUDE OF THERAPEUTIC EFFECT

The decision as to whether a particular treatment mode is "sufficiently" better than a placebo is fraught with subjectivity. Obviously, the fact that a treatment is better than placebo at a statistically significant level can turn out to be meaningless at the clinical level. Conceivably, a difference as small as a few percent might be statistically significant, but it would be insignificant when viewed against the vagaries of real life. As earlier noted, one has to decide what level of difference between active agent and placebo it is reasonable to expect. Is a 10% difference reasonable? Should it be 20% or 30% or 40% or 50% or even greater? There is no scientific way to settle such an issue. "Better" in this context is in the eyes of beholders who come to the scene with a variety of agendas and expectations. The cutting point at which the active agent is declared to be effective will vary as a function of such parameters as the long-term consequences of not instituting any "treatment" at all, the seriousness of the side effects produced by the active agent, the cost of the treatment, the durability of the improvement achieved, and so forth. There are infinite combinations and permutations of these parameters with reference to how they might mediate the choice of a therapy. Let us be more specific and consider just one contextual aspect of a decision to use a tricyclic for treating a depressive state. What if the true difference in efficacy between placebo and tricyclic is somewhere between 20% and 30%? Does such an advantage outweigh the potential threat of a side effect like drug-induced psychosis? If there is a potential 5%–6% probability of being rendered psychotic (albeit temporarily) by an antidepressant drug, should one seriously hesitate about accepting it as a reasonable treatment? Incidentally, we do not know what long-term effects a tricyclic-induced delirium has upon individuals. Do such individuals, as a result, suffer persistent elevations in anxiety about their future stability (e.g., "I am crazy" or "I am a person who can become crazy")? How much of a risk of psychosis is it worth taking to gain relief from moderate or even severe depression, which typically has a fairly self-limiting course? Related questions arise for each therapeutic drug in relation to its own peculiar side effects. What is the impact upon a schizophrenic man who becomes impotent as the result of taking an antipsychotic drug? How devastating is such an episode of impotence upon long-term sexual self-regard? Does it introduce permanent doubts about one's sexual functioning? Does this, in turn, feed back and increase the likelihood of future psychotic disruptions? Analogous questions come to mind for an agent like cloipramine that gives improvement rates (30%–40%) significantly greater than placebo for obsessive-compulsive behavior, but which apparently in most instances also leads to partial or total anorgasmia.

The matter of defining an agent's therapeutic efficacy is often viewed unidimensionally in terms of how much better than placebo it appears to be. However, considerably more complexity is actually involved. To begin with, as earlier described, many studies have used multiple measures of improvement and it is not unusual to find that some of the measures give better results than the others. Indeed, Murray noted in an earlier chapter than even supposedly equivalent formal measures of depression may give disparate results when used to evaluate the effectiveness of an antidepressant agent. So, we are faced with the fact of a relativity of outcome results varying as a function of the outcome measures employed. It needs to be underscored that there are countless studies in which one set of measures shows an agent to be effective, but another set ends up with nonsignificant results. This species of relativity is rarely captured in broad statements about how effective an agent is. Relatedly, the stability of observed differences between active agent and placebo as a function of place and time is rarely, if ever, spelled out. In multicenter studies an agent may do very well in certain locales but be of indifferent effectiveness in others. The differences among centers can be truly impressive. It will be recalled that one study (Feighner, Aden, Fabre, Rickels, & Smith, 1983) concerned with comparing imipramine, alprazolam, and placebo in the treatment of depression in five different settings found amazing variability in outcomes.

Although the pooled data indicated the drugs were more effective than placebos, more detailed inspection revealed that after 6 weeks of treatment every one of the six outcome measures showed imipramine to be equivalent to placebo in two or more of the five centers! Two of the centers detected a difference favoring imipramine on only 1 of 12 comparisons! We ought to keep an accurate box score of this kind of variability because it might provide a rough index of the degree to which the agent's effectiveness is modified by local variations in procedure, attitudes toward patient, and so forth. Incidentally, when large differences in therapeutic effects appear that are linked to locale, one should look for hints as to whether the "best" or "worst" sites are closer to the clinical reality in which that agent is most likely to be administered. Any shifts in effectiveness over broad time periods should also be monitored. A trend for declining results over a 10-year span might mean that hidden placebo effects are becoming less powerful. Or they might mean that more contemporary cohorts of patients have characteristics (e.g., ethnic, educational) different from earlier ones that render them less able to benefit from the agent. We suggest that it be formally required that each agent's effectiveness be tracked from decade to decade so as to minimize inertia in eliminating treatment procedures that have somehow lost their potency (and there have been many).

There are still other aspects of an agent's effectiveness that should be formally defined as part of an overall statement concerning its therapeutic power. We need to know with some precision the actual part of the diagnostic spectrum to which it is truly applicable. For example, in the case of the antidepressants there is now reasonably good data indicating that they are not particularly useful for treating persons with mild to moderate depression and similarly ineffective for depressed individuals who are delusional. This leaves a relatively narrow band of the total depressive population within which the antidepressants are meaningfully applicable. In actual clinical practice this limitation is frequently ignored; and we obviously need a more vigorous affirmation and enforcement of it. As one scans the literature dealing with the presumed effectiveness of drugs for various diagnostic categories, one sees again and again that there is over generalization and a resistance to clearly differentiated statements of limitation. This is flagrantly obvious for certain of the antianxiety drugs (see Lipman's review chapter) that are prescribed for a wide range of conditions in which anxiety is prominent, but which in actuality have proven to be the treatment of choice in only a few limited instances.

Further, a definition of therapeutic power should provide a statement of the modal length of time required for an agent to initiate improvement and, perhaps more importantly, the modal amount of time improvement persists while the treatment is continued and also after it is discontinued. An agent could theoretically produce a spectacular amount of improvement for a week or two and then fade to a zero level. Karon points out in his chapter that antipsychotic drugs may result in fairly dramatic improvement in schizophrenic symptoms within the protected confines of a psychiatric ward (where passive-compliant behavior is the ideal), but be significantly less effective in maintaining reasonable integration once the patient emerges into the hurly-burly world. He noted too that the antipsychotics may give a short-term therapeutic advantage, but a long-term disadvantage as compared to other therapeutic maneuvers (e.g., psychotherapy). Recall too that Lipman in his chapter describes certain of the antianxiety drugs as providing significant alleviation of distress for only a quite brief period.[4] Indeed, relapse rates over a period of 1 to 2 years are high for the antidepressants and also for ECT.

This is a logical point to raise the issue of how the therapeutic power of a "somatic therapy" should be described for potential consumers. When psychiatrists recommend to patients that they undergo a specific "course of treatment," what parameters of the treatment agent should they spell out? One could urge that each of the dimensions relating to effectiveness described above should be delineated in ways that can be understood. This would mean that patients would be told such things as how much better than placebo the agent is likely

---

[4]Somewhat tangentially, we would at least like to raise the question of whether the public statements (i.e., published reports) concerning the therapeutic advantage of most of the treatment agents have been systematically overblown because negative findings are less likely to get published than positive ones. For example, one could speculate that the average "drug researcher" who has a stake in proving "his drug" works would be reluctant to publicize instances in which it has failed to show therapeutic power. Of course, this is the kind of accusation that is easy to make but difficult to document. However, there is a report by Overall and Rhoades (1982) that provides some borderline documentation for such potential bias. They present data derived from the Biometrics Laboratory at George Washington University that was supported for more than a decade by the Psychopharmacology Research Branch of the National Institute of Mental Health in order to provide data management assistance for researchers in the clinical psychopharmacology area. These data are unique because they represent studies that were carried out irrespective of whether the results were ever formally published. Although most of the data registered in this computer center were obtained in certain standardized ways, there were some exceptions; and so for the purpose of this report Overall and Rhoades included only studies in which there was a pretreatment baseline rating on the Brief Psychiatric Rating Scale (BPRS) and a rating on the BPRS at 6–12 weeks after the onset of the clinical trial. Also, only data from studies involving sample sizes of six or more per treatment group were included. Improvement was defined as 50% reduction in BPRS total score. In that part of their analysis concerned with four categories of depressed patients (anxious, retarded, agitated, hostile) Overall and Rhoades looked at the impact of "recognized antidepressant drugs" on 515 patients and of placebo on 54 patients. The average improvement in the drug treated samples was 47.8% and the average in the placebo samples was 50%. Overall and Rhoades caution that the placebo patients and the active drug patients did not participate in the same studies and so there are problems concerning the comparability of the data pertaining to each group. They also caution that some of the studies involved "new drugs" that "were not actually found to be effective." But even so, it is startling to find in this aggregation of data not yet put through the selective sieve of publication that the placebo rate of improvement is at least as great as that for the active antidepressant agents!

to be, how long it usually takes for improvement to be initiated, and under what conditions improvement can be maintained. They would be told if the agent has shown unusual instability in its effects (e.g., with reference to place or time). Perhaps, too, information would be offered as to alternative psychosocial treatments that are generally equally effective. If those who administer a therapeutic agent are called upon to provide such detailed input, this might increase the likelihood that they would keep themselves knowledge-able about the pertinent research literature. But having made these points, the fact remains that the decision as to what information "should" be provided to patients is not a scientific one. If one could demonstrate experimentally that giving or not giving certain classes of information influences the therapeutic outcome, one might have an empirical base for action in this area. However, little or no pertinent solid data exist. The decision as to how much and what kinds of data to supply patients becomes a political one linked to one's values about such things as "democracy," "telling the truth," and "knowing what is best for the patient."

## SUMMARY STATEMENT

As just reviewed, there have been formidable obstacles to arriving at a fair, rational evaluation of the therapies current in biological psychiatry. These obstacles variously involve the inadequacies of the double-blind design, the failure to employ active placebos, the extreme selectivity of the samples studied, and the miasmic vagueness of the definitions of what represents a "therapeutic" level of effect. In the face of such complexities it requires a certain amount of foolhardiness to assert with confidence that an agent is unquestionably therapeutic for a given syndrome. It would seem the better part of wisdom to speak cautiously, tentatively, and modestly. It will be recalled that Halperin, in his chapter dealing with the statistical problems in drug therapy research, urged that many of the findings of multivariable drug studies be viewed as suggestions and hypotheses rather than as statistically proven facts. We do not have any reason to be comfortably secure about any of the major therapeutic findings that guide biological psychiatry today. What will the picture look like when we have available test designs less biased than the so-called double blind or when we employ more equitable versions of placebos? That such skepticism is justified is affirmed not only by the "successful" treatments that have monotonously come and gone in the past but also the considerable variability and vagueness one finds in probing the current research literature. It would be more honest and fairer if it were publicly acknowledged that there are serious deficiencies in the state of our knowledge about what is therapeutic for psychological distress. The basic truth at this point in time is that biological psychiatry is swimming in uncertainty. It is deceptive to give "patients" the impression that we know with any certainty what will help them to "get better." Of course, it is difficult for any discipline that has been charged by the culture with assuming the responsibility for correcting or curing certain undesirable states to admit its limitations. The pressure to pretend to mythic powers and capabilities is intense and unfortunately often irresistible. As one counts the "cures" that have appeared and disappeared, one gets the impression of a persistent, pressing need to conjure up illusory, comforting medicalized images about what can be done to alleviate "pathology."

We have been impressed with how often studies reporting negative findings concerning treatment effects are indignantly attacked as inadequate for their presumed deficiencies with respect to such variables as sample size, low dose levels, and restricted duration of treatment (e.g., Klein, Gittelman, Quitkin, & Rifkin, 1980). In actuality, there is little evidence that most negative findings can be explained away in this fashion. For example, as we showed in our chapter dealing with the treatment of depression, the apparent therapeutic efficacy of the antidepressants has not increased in recent studies (more closely observing supposedly optimum design and treatment conditions) as compared to earlier projects. If anything, the apparent more recent efficacy seems to be less than in the earlier supposedly flawed efforts. It is our view that once a treatment mode gets a foothold any contrary data that are uncovered are smothered with an unending series of stereotyped objections relating to their less than optimum quality. Since no study, particularly those involving treatment modes, can be carried out to perfection, there are always objections that can be conjured up and provide rationalizations for ignoring negative evidence. This point may be seen as applying so broadly to all research as to be meaningless to raise in the present context. However, we think it deserves to be reiterated with a dash of passion. Our personal experience has been that when we have asked members of the biological psychiatry establishment to consider some of the negative trends in the treatment research literature they have typically retreated behind a barrage of multiple generalized criticisms based on presumed departures from ideal treatment conditions. There seems always to be one more reason why negative results can be explained away or treated as being of little import.

## THE STATE OF THE ART

The doubt and uncertainty that surface when one appraises the existing publications concerned with biological psychiatry therapies have been visible in many of the chapters in this book. Let us scan the gist of what has surfaced. McGuinness' analysis of the overall data pertinent to the success of stimulant medications for the ADD (formerly "hyperactive") syndrome leaves us with grave doubts. She took a strong position that the so-called ADD category is a fiction and that the presumed power of stimulant drugs to help "ADD children" has yet to be demonstrated convincingly. Even if it eventually turns out that McGuinness is too severe in her criticisms, there can be no dispute that she does raise substantially important questions. We should note that other reviewers have sounded similar alarms about the lack of evidence to support a unique diagnostic syndrome labeled ADD (Prior & Sanson, 1986; Rutter, 1983).

When we turn to Lipman's appraisal of the therapies employed to deal with the spectrum of "anxiety disorders," we find a mixed state of affairs. We are told, first of all, that the conventional anxiolytic drugs have been largely discredited and yet are still being used despite their failure from a scientific perspective. We are also provided with information indicating that no really satisfactory drug treatment has been empirically validated for "social phobias" or the post-traumatic syndrome or obsessive-compulsive symptoms. Certain antidepressants are described as significantly therapeutic for long-term General Anxiety Disorder symptoms and Panic/Agoraphobia. In the instance of Panic/Agoraphobia, it is noted that the addition of "behavioral treatment" is an important component of any therapeutic regimen aiming for a high level of success. Actually, as one follows Lipman's exposition of his conclusions about certain drugs' effectiveness, it is hedged about with "ifs" and "buts" relating to the possible negative impact of side effects and the need for a supportive contribution from non-drug agents.

Karon's chapter dealing with the treatment of schizophrenia does not systematically probe the therapeutic potency of the antipsychotic drugs as compared to placebos, but does extensively examine their potency in relation to a psychotherapeutic approach. Karon leads us through a number of lines of evidence indicating that there may be disadvantages (without even considering side effects) to the use of the antipsychotics linked to their long-term decline in effectiveness for individual patients and also the resultant eventual greater financial cost of treatment. He also points out defects in some of the designs of major past explorations of the therapeutic effectiveness of the antipsychotics. Among such defects, he enumerates failure to secure representative samples, use of improper measures, and also inappropriate modes of statistical analysis.

The search that we conducted in our chapter of the antidepressant research findings was not reassuring. We discovered that the actual difference in therapeutic power between a drug like imipramine and a passive placebo is more on the order of 25% (as evidenced by more recent studies) than the 35% to 45% usually touted. We noted too the high rates of recurrence of depressive symptoms following cessation of drug therapy and the quite limited relationships between effectiveness and such variables as dosage and the actual blood level of the drug. Of course, we also raised numerous questions about the dependability of the research design used to evaluate the antidepressants and criticized the neglect of the meanings patients may attach to the body sensations and experiences induced by an intended therapeutic agent.

The most salutary appraisal appears in Sackeim's discussion of the value of Electric Convulsive Therapy (ECT) for depression. He concludes that ECT is more effective than sham shock and also significantly more effective than the antidepressant drugs. The research described is exemplary in its use of an active placebo (sham shock) against which to compare the active treatment, although we should note that sham shock does not create the same level of side effects that ECT does. Sackeim does point out that because many of the patients referred for ECT have previously done poorly on antidepressant medication, they may as a group have lower potentiality for placebo response ("the medication-resistant patient has already experienced one and often many extended trials of biological treatment and should have already manifested a placebo response were it to occur"). If so, the placebo response to sham shock would be artificially reduced and the net difference in improvement between sham and real ECT unrealistically inflated. Sackeim notes too that symptom recurrence is high if no additional treatment[5] is supplied following the completion of an ECT series; and he refers to an as yet not clearly defined degree of memory loss resulting from the impact of the electrical current upon brain tissue. Interestingly, the relative potency of ECT for depression dramatizes the unstable political factors that may mediate whether a treatment will be applied. That is, although ECT seems to clear up depressive symptoms more efficiently than the antidepressant drugs, it is still employed far less often in most therapy settings.

The dominant image of these core reviews is that of a patchwork of findings, with inconsistency and inconclusiveness prevailing. As mentioned, the one exception to such uncertainty is the Sackeim analysis of ECT. The overall state of our knowledge concerning the drug therapies obviously leaves much to be desired. We are impressed with the narrowness of the perspective typifying the drug research literature.[6] By "narrow" we mean that there is

---

[5]Sackeim criticized the practice of many clinicians of putting post ECT patients on an antidepressant regimen even though such patients were previously unresponsive to an antidepressant series. He cited data suggesting this practice is probably ineffective in preventing relapse.

[6]The narrowness of the treatment literature leaves us uninformed about certain fundamentals. We may have rough estimates of how much better than placebo various treatments are, but we have lost a vision of the "natural history" of most of the "mental symptom" syndromes. We do not know with any confidence how much more improvement the current treatments produce than would occur spontaneously if the affected individuals simply make it on their own (with the support of their own social networks).

relatively little interest in the findings of neighboring disciplines (particularly psychology) that might be helpful in understanding the wide range of responses to drug medications persons display. We have earlier mentioned the neglect by researchers of the many studies dealing with the effects of enhanced self-awareness. In addition, there has been neglect of the potential contribution of attribution theory (e.g., Harvey & Weary, 1984); of past findings concerning accuracy in perceiving physiological events within one's own body (e.g., Fisher, 1986); of literature bearing on the interaction of suggestibility and body experience (e.g., Fast & Fisher, 1971); and of the existing data (e.g., Pennebaker, 1982) clarifying how the social-interpersonal context influences reports of personal discomfort. The neglected areas just cited all provide ideas and techniques of investigation that should be valuable to anyone who is trying to understand the reactions of individuals to highly charged social situations in which they are being asked by an authority figure to ingest substances with mysterious properties that will presumably "improve" how they "feel."

It is surprising that we are still so confused about major issues despite the tremendous quantities of energy and money that have been invested in drug research projects. Issues arise again and again; are rarely resolved, and spasmodically reappear. Knowledge in this realm is fugacious. Just at random, note that researchers are perennially and futilely looking for evidence that the antidepressants are differentially therapeutic for "endogenous" versus "exogenous" depression (even presuming that there is a way of getting agreement as to what these terms mean). Note that the long-engrained distinction between agents that are useful for depressive as compared to anxiety syndromes is fading—almost gone. Note that long-established dicta to the effect that antidepressant drug effects cannot be detected until the completion of several weeks of treatment have now been challenged (Katz et al., 1987). Note that Karon knowledgeably raised doubts about the widely propagated stance that drug therapy is superior to psychotherapy in treating schizophrenics. Note that Lipman concluded, as did Solomon and Hart (1978), that one cannot find substantial reason to use most of the conventional, popularly accepted anxiolytic agents. Note that we are hearing (e.g., Baldessarini & Davis, 1980; Marder, 1983) that well-established dose levels for antipsychotic agents can probably be revised drastically downward. Note that it has relatively suddenly become acceptable to view the tardive dyskinesia side effects of the antipsychotics as truly serious (perhaps even bad enough to suggest discontinuance of the antipsychotics). Note that after all these years of widespread use of stimulant drugs to treat the "hyperactive" child (or now more euphemistically referred to as ADD) the possibility is presenting itself that the presumed therapeutic effects are quite small or even zero. It is amazing that clinicians manage to operate with even moderate rationality in the midst of such unresolved and also shifting discrepancies.

## COMPARING PSYCHOSOCIAL AND DRUG TREATMENTS

It is ironic that the efforts put forth in this book to assess the effectiveness of psychotropic medications have uncovered so much empirical support for the success of psychosocial approaches in dealing with such problems as depression, anxiety, and schizophrenia. Comparatively, psychotherapeutic treatments have in most instances proven to either equal or surpass the outcomes attained with medication. Recall that our (Greenberg & Fisher) overview of treatments for depression showed that, when placed side by side in the same studies, depression specific psychotherapies more often than not eclipsed the results obtained with drugs (five out of eight trials). Psychotherapy proved to be the equal of medication in those instances where it was not superior. Furthermore, research revealed that most of the time adding drugs to a psychotherapy approach did not enhance the outcome. This assessment is consistent with a statistical meta-analysis which demonstrated that, on average, comparisons of control groups with psychotherapy groups or medication groups favored the potency of psychotherapy approaches (Steinbrueck, Maxwell, & Howard, 1983). Of course, this does not mean that drugs are not of value or would never enhance the treatment of depression. But it does suggest that medications may be resorted to more frequently, more quickly, and more ubiquitously than the evidence can justify.

Similarly, Lipman's review of remedies for anxiety-related conditions indicated that drugs were often not the treatment of choice. A psychosocial approach appeared to be sufficient to deal with most cases of simple phobia, social phobia, agoraphobia and, obsessive compulsive symptomology. Nonpharmacologic treatment for generalized anxiety disorders were seen as "promising," and a behavioral treatment approach (combined with antidepressant medication) was viewed as the "most effective" means of reducing panic attacks. In general, although one can point to certain consistent trends, a reading of Lipman's chapter leaves the impression that there is room for future well-controlled studies that will lead to firmer conclusions about the relative merits of psychotherapy versus drugs for treating anxiety. In terms of current practice, attempts to compare psychotherapy outcome to medication results are complicated by the fact that drug treatments for anxiety disorders most often involve anxiolytic agents whose efficacy is not well supported by the research literature.

Perhaps most surprising, since it flies in the face of commonly held beliefs, is Karon's carefully researched conclusion that psychosocial treatment, rendered by therapists with relevant training and experience, is the "optimal" method for dealing with schizophrenia. Medication was found to have value mainly as a means to achieve short-term compliance and manageability, whereas psychotherapy produced more long-term adaptability and stability. Karon persuasively argued that much of the past research on psychotherapy for schizophrenia has been diluted by its reliance on therapists who were not sufficiently invested in or trained for the task and its use of methodology that on occasion operated against the attainment of significant treatment effects.

Overall, the chapters on treatment for depression, anxiety, and schizophrenia reveal that well thought out, active, focused psychosocial treatments can be effective. Yet some might question whether these approaches are as cost-effective as the seemingly simple administration of medications. Aside from the greater physical, emotional, and economic costs engendered by drug side effects, the work reviewed suggests that there are other reasons to believe that psychotherapies may be at least as cost-efficient as medications and possibly more so in the long run. For example, duration of treatment is not consistently longer for psychotherapy approaches than for biological treatments, and there are even signs in the literature that psychotherapy can sometimes achieve stronger effects than drugs in a briefer time period. Recall that in the meta-analysis of treatments for depression (Steinbrueck et al., 1983) the psychosocial treatment achieved about twice the effect size that drug treatment did in almost half the time. Similarly, Karon showed that within 6 months, experienced therapists working with schizophrenics achieved results superior to those characterizing patients receiving medication alone.

Also promoting psychosocial treatments as a cheaper solution to emotional problems is the fact that they can be delivered by a wider array of well-trained professionals. Because drug administration presently requires medical training and because psychiatrists are both the fewest in number and the most costly of all workers in the mental health field, any approach that depends solely on their medical expertise is likely to be both less available and more expensive.

Perhaps the most overriding reasons to consider the cost benefit advantages of approaches that do not rely primarily on medication are the growing findings concerning relapse and long-term improvements. The evidence reviewed within this book indicates that there is a problem of recurring symptoms and inability to maintain adjustment in substantial numbers of patients biologically treated for depression, anxiety, or schizophrenia. Although this is also a problem for psychosocial treatments, some studies are now beginning to show that psychosocial therapies may be of particular value in maintaining improved patients and helping them learn how to cope with stressful conflicts and ward off the reappearance of symptoms. Both the work on depression relapse that we (Greenberg & Fisher) have cited and Karon's review of the extended outlook for treated schizophrenic patients intimate that long-term stability is more enhanced for those patients who have had a course of psychotherapeutic treatment.

A few words of caution need to be injected about attempts to compare outcomes for psychotherapeutic and biological approaches. For pharmacological treatments a double-blind, placebo-controlled paradigm has been considered essential for separating out the specific effects of "active ingredients" from the effects of placebos or inert substances. As we have noted in our antidepressant chapter, the closer research designs have come to fulfilling these conditions, the smaller the specific drug effects seem to become. On the other hand, despite the psychotherapy researchers' awareness of the placebo issue (e.g., Klein & Rabkin, 1984; Shapiro & Morris, 1978; Prioleau, Murdock, & Brody, 1983) and despite creative attempts to construct realistic psychotherapy placebo groups (e.g., Critelli & Newman, 1984; Klein & Rabkin, 1984), psychotherapy researchers have not, for the most part, been able to match the level of blindness and the apparent comparability of treatments that occur in pharmaceutical research. Butler and Strupp (1986), in discussing attempts to separate the illusive specific from nonspecific effects, have argued that doing psychotherapy is not analogous to the administration of drugs and that psychotherapy unlike medication cannot be delivered as a "contextless" agent. For them the active ingredients of psychotherapy cannot be separated from the interpersonal relationship in which the treatment takes place. They conclude that new research strategies need to be developed to study psychotherapy.

In any event, since psychotherapy research typically has not attained the degree of blindness characteristic of drug investigations and because the distinction between specific and nonspecific therapeutic factors is blurred in psychotherapy treatments, comparisons between control groups and treatment groups may be open to different degrees of bias in psychotherapy research and in drug research. Thus, checking the outcome rates in separate controlled studies of psychotherapy and of drugs to see how they measure up against each other (as was done in the Steinbrueck et al. meta-analysis we cited) may be unfair because the drug treatments, having been conducted under blinder conditions, are likely to appear less potent. Alternatively, because the active and inactive ingredients of psychotherapy have not proven to be easily separable, the argument that drug trials are more stringent can be countered by the notion that the control groups in psychotherapy studies may frequently also contain active treatment ingredients. This lessens the chances of finding psychotherapy superior in outcome to its control condition. At present we have no way of knowing whether it is easier to find treatment superiority in the typical controlled drug study or the usual psychotherapy outcome investigation. Fortunately, the comparison of drug and psychotherapy outcomes is not as obscured when both treatments appear in the *same* study. Here the cross-checking of outcome magnitudes against each other is direct and not hampered by the question of comparability to their respective placebo controls.

Incidentally, it is possible to argue that nonmedication approaches may have value in treating psychiatric disorders even if the disorders are considered to have a substantial biological component. Significant research is emerging which documents that individuals who enter into psychotherapy subsequently require fewer visits to practitioners for medical problems, fewer days of hospitalization for any reason, and lower subsequent medical expenses (e.g., Jones & Vischi, 1980; Mumford, Schlesinger, & Glass, 1981). The fact that relationships, self-exploration, and disclosure can create somatic changes in people is amply exhibited by the many studies showing that environmentally induced emotions can alter physiology (e.g., Goldstein, Edelberg, Meier, & Davis, 1988; Sommers-Flanagan & Greenberg, 1989), the investigations concluding that social support can enhance physical health (e.g., Cohen & Syme, 1985), and the intriguing work demonstrating that the revelation of traumatic experiences can positively affect the immune system (Pennebaker, Kiecolt-Glaser, & Glaser, 1988).

## SIDE EFFECTS

All the somatic treatments produce what are referred to as *side effects.* That is, they cause a variety of forms of physiological disturbance and discomfort. This is well documented in the chapter by Dewan and Koss. The term *side effect* is a euphemism in that it implies a minor, inconsequential ("side") impact on the individual involved. However, the truth is that side effects can variously lead to death, brain damage, serious dysfunction in specific organ systems, and psychosis (to mention only a few of the serious possibilities). Many side effects are reversible, but some (e.g., death) obviously are not. Most side effects occur in only a small percentage of the cases treated, but if one computes the total number of individuals treated with a specific agent in the world, even a small percentage can add up to a quite impressive number of persons. One must also not lose sight of the fact that some serious side effects (e.g., tardive dyskinesia) do occur in relatively large percentages of treated individuals and so world-wide there is a massive prevalence. As Dewan and Koss pointed out, physicians are accustomed to witnessing side effects because of the frequency with which they employ drug treatments. One finds in discussions with physicians that they are inclined to gloss over the fact that a side effect occurs. For them it is typically an expected epiphenomenon. We have talked with psychiatrists about the 5% to 6% likelihood[7] of setting off a psychotic delirium when administering certain tricyclics and been impressed with their professionalized belle indifference. They assured us that such psychotic episodes are "brief" and "reversible." A similar belle indifference has impressed us when discussing other side effects that would presumably be intensely personally threatening, like impotence or impaired ability to main-

---

[7]In their chapter, Dewan and Koss cited data that raise the possibility that as many as 20% of a Black population might respond to tricyclic mediation by developing a psychotic level of disturbance.

tain equilibrium. As earlier noted, side effects are rarely viewed from the perspective of the individuals experiencing them. Such individuals are probably perceiving the side effects as "in" their bodies and as potentially of large proportions. They probably do not know if the side effects are *really* reversible. They may only know that they feel "strange" and are experiencing sensations stereotypically associated with "something is wrong" or "I am sick." As indicated, we lack information as to the immediate or long-term psychological consequences of "having" one of the more serious side effects over a period of time. We have not been able to find consistent data defining whether severity of side effects has implications for the probability of future "recovery" or significant changes in attitude toward self ("My body is fragile" or "I am sexually inadequate").[8] In the case of depressed individuals we certainly have ample evidence that they amplify the negativity of events, and it would not be surprising if they dramatized the negative body implications of certain of the side effects associated with antidepressant medications. It goes almost without saying that systematic studies of what side effects mean to patients are badly needed.

As we have learned more about the ubiquitous side effects, we have begun to speculate about their possible role in the recovery process. Obviously, they can be very threatening and disturbing. However, we have also wondered whether the sudden creation of a body "symptom" by a medication might not in certain instances serve paradoxically as a distractor that can draw attention away from the immediate psychological distress and therefore induce a sense of "Yes, I have an acute physical discomfort, but my depression or my bad psychological state now seems less pressing." Under these circumstances the medicated individual might conclude, "Yes, my body hurts but I feel less disturbed and mixed up psychologically." Is there any precedent for such a possibility? In fact, we have come upon analogous prototypes while exploring the pertinent literature.

Let us begin the exploration of this matter by considering a study by Cowden and Brown (1956). These investigators intensively observed the impact upon one hospitalized schizophrenic man of dramatizing a somatic symptom. They theorized that they could decrease psychological distress in this man if they could somehow get him to channel his anxiety into a "physical symptom" rather than into an unrealistic delusion formation. They capitalized upon an early back injury incurred by this individual; and asked all hospital personnel in contact with him to focus upon the highlighting of possible pain or discomfort he might be experiencing in his back (and also to suggest

---

[8]Mathew, Weinman, Thapar, Beck, and Claghorn (1983) do report significant positive correlations in depressed patients between number and severity of side effects produced by antidepressants and degree of state anxiety. One cannot deduce causality but it may be that intensifying side effects can, indeed, increase anxiety.

remedies like physical therapy). As a result, he became very preoccupied with his back and simultaneously his psychotic behavior decreased significantly— to the point that he was discharged from the hospital and was adjusting well at home. Apparently, the highlighting of his somatic discomfort diminished his psychological distress. In a parallel fashion, it is conceivable that when psychologically distressed patients are given a medication that produces a salient side effect, some of them may displace their anxiety to a somatic site and thereby begin to feel "mentally" relieved ("improved").

It is interesting in this context to think about a considerable literature that describes a condition labeled as "masked depression." This condition presumably involves the concealment of "clinically significant depression" (e.g., Fish, 1987; Paykel & Norton, 1982) behind "masks" like drug abuse and sociopathic behavior, but most commonly behind "somatic complaints." Masking of depression by somatization is portrayed (Fisch, 1987) as "Selective focusing on the body manifestations of stress rather than dealing with the psychosocial stress itself." It "may be a way to escape, consciously or unconsciously, from conflict and active coping" (pp. 371–372). The inwardly depressed persons are said to "use" somatic complaints to defend themselves against both the experience of depressive affect and the conflicts considered to underlie that affect. Is it possible that the instant somatic symptoms provided by the side effects of medications can acquire an analogous "masking" function? One could metaphorically even view the side effect as providing an instant "conversion symptom," with all of the defensive (repressive) power presumably associated with a conversion strategy (Ford, 1983).

The material just cited is largely anecdotal and clinical. However, more empirical data exist that suggest not only the value of distraction for decreasing psychological distress, but even more specifically the value of physical symptomatology for minimizing such distress. Several reports (e.g., Fennell & Teasdale, 1984; Fennell, Teasdale, Jones, & Damle, 1987) have shown that if depressed patients are exposed to a source of distraction their affect becomes less depressed. In such studies depressed patients are given distracting tasks (e.g., describing a series of pictures) and measures are secured of the frequency with which "depressing thoughts" are entertained and also the intensities of "depressed mood." Changes in such experimental patients during the distraction procedure are compared with those occurring in a control group of depressed patients who are subjected to a neutral intervention. The experimental groups demonstrate significantly less distress as a function of having been exposed to distraction.

Spence, Pilowsky, and Minniti (1985–86) carried out a project in which they appraised persons with chronic pain whose "somatic origin" was questionable. A questionnaire was used to classify these persons with reference to the degree to which they seemed to be "conversion" oriented. Those with the highest conversion scores were found to "acknowledge little dysphoric affect and denied life problems apart from physical illness" (p. 1). Focusing on one's physical difficulties was accompanied by diminished awareness of psychological feelings and issues.

However, in an experiment even more telling for the topic on hand, Demjen and Bakal (1986) asked patients with chronic headaches to monitor (write descriptions of) their own thoughts over a series of five headache episodes (just at the outset of and during the worse pain). The thoughts described were categorized as to whether they were headache related (e.g., "I feel helpless with the pain") or referred to nonheadache forms of tension (e.g., "I am critical of another person" or "I am pressed for time"). Analyses indicated that "chronic headache disorders of increased severity are accompanied by a cognitive shift whereby the patient's primary concern moves from situational and interpersonal stress to distress associated with the disorder itself" (p. 187). The patients with the more severe headache symptoms showed a predominance of headache-related thoughts. The higher the intensity of the symptom the fewer were the thoughts about psychological themes. Consider too that those who reported increases in headache-related thoughts tended to be "deniers" (as measured by a questionnaire tapping "denial of present life problems"). Here again one can see how side effects initiated by a medication might recruit a predominance of thought about the somatic discomfort that would, in turn, crowd out thinking about less somatically phrased themes. Incidentally, the fact that Demjen and Bakal detected a link between a denying orientation and focusing on the somatic themes suggests the possibility that the degree to which patients might utilize side effects as a distraction would be mediated by attitudes tied to the repression-sensitization continuum. In any case, we are raising for general consideration the possibility that side effects may in some contexts serve as positive "distractors," whereas in others they may intensify anxiety and interfere with the therapeutic process.

Although we have been critical of the biological psychiatry treatment modes, we are aware that the work of those invested in this area has been marked by good intentions, vigor, and an overall desire to become more scientifically rigorous. We are aware too that the widespread existence of psychological disturbance creates a pressure to create treatments that can be given en masse. People want quick solutions to their nagging anxieties, sadnesses, and feelings of alienation from reality. The medicalization of psychological distress has promised analogous "medical solutions." One particularly tempting aspect of such medicalization is that it conveys to the sufferers that they can be cured without any special efforts on their own part. They need only ingest a powerful agent and the biochemical impact will restore them. It is striking how pervasive the attitude has become that taking a chemical into one's body can relieve any and all discomforts, ranging from the slightest headache to the most severe anguish. One cannot help but be impressed by the metaphorical bridging between this orientation and the widespread hunger for forbidden drug substances (e.g., heroin, cocaine) that are touted for making people feel "good." The medicalized concepts of "drug care" and the addict's fantasies about "drug cure" obviously overlap. There is probably a persistent leakage form the "medical models" to "street models" with respect to ways to generate "cures." However, our position, based on the total material herein presented, is that biological treatments for psychological anguish involve a good deal more uncertainty than popularly envisioned.

## REFERENCES

Baekeland, F., & Lundwall, L. (1975). Dropping out of treatment: A critical review. *Psychological Bulletin, 82*, 738–783.

Baldessarini, R. J., & Davis, J. M. (1980). What is the best maintenance dose of neuroleptics in schizophrenia? *Psychiatry Research, 3*, 115–122.

Brune, G., Morpurgo, C., Bielkus, A., Kobayashi, T., Tourlentes, T., & Himwich, H. (1962). Relevance of drug induced extrapyramidal reactions to behavioral changes during neuroleptic treatment. Treatment with trifluoperazine singly and in combination with trihexyphenidyl. *Comprehensive Psychiatry, 3*, 227–234.

Bulter, S. F., & Strupp, H. H. (1986). Specific and nonspecific factors in psychotherapy: A problematic paradigm for psychotherapy research. *Psychotherapy, 23*, 30–40.

Clausen, J., & Fisher, S. (1973). Effects of amphetamine and barbiturate on body experience. *Psychosomatic Medicine, 35*, 390–405.

Cohen, S., & Syme, S. (Eds.). (1985). *Social support and health.* Orlando, FL: Academic Press.

Cowden, R. C., & Brown, J. E. (1956). The use of a physical symptom as a defense against psychosis. *Journal of Abnormal and Social Psychology, 53*, 133–135.

Cramond, W. A. (1987). Lessons from the insulin story in psychiatry. *Australian and New Zealand Journal of Psychiatry, 21*, 320–326.

Critelli, J. W., & Neuman, K. F. (1984). The placebo: Conceptual analysis of a construct in transition. *American Psychologist, 39*, 32–39.

Demjen, S., & Bakal, D. (1986). Subjective distress accompanying headache attacks: Evidence for a cognitive shift. *Pain, 25*, 187–194.

Eysenck, H. J. (1983). Drugs as research tools in psychology: Experiments with drugs in personality research. *Neuropsychobiology, 10*, 29–43.

Fast, G. J., & Fisher, S. (1971). The role of body attitudes and acquiescence in epinephrine and placebo effects. *Psychosomatic Medicine, 33*, 63–64.

Feighner, J. P., Aden, G. C., Fabre, L. F., Rickels, K., & Smith, W. T. (1983). Comparison of alprazolam, imipramine, and placebo in the treatment of depression. *Journal of the American Medical Association, 249*, 3057–3064.

Fennell, M. J. V., & Teasdale, J. D. (1984). Effects of distraction on thinking and affect in depressed patients. *British Journal of Clinical Psychology, 23*, 65–66.

Fennell, M. J. V., Teasdale, J. D., Jones, S., & Damle, A. (1987). Distraction in neurotic and endogenous depression: An investigation of negative thinking in major depressive disorder. *Psychological Medicine, 17*, 441–452.

Fisch, R. Z. (1987). Masked depression: Its interrelations with somatization, hypochondriasis and conversion. *International Journal of Psychiatry in Medicine, 17*, 367–379.

Fisher, S. (1986). *Development and structure of the body image* (Vols. 1 and 2). Hillsdale, NJ: Lawrence Erlbaum Associates.

Fisher, S., & Fisher, R. L. (1963). Placebo response and acquiescence. *Psychopharmacologia, 4*, 298–301.

Ford, C. V. (1983). *The somatizing disorders.* New York: Elsevier Biomedical.

Goldstein, H. S., Edelberg, R., Meier, C. F., & Davis, L. (1988). Relationship of resting blood pressure and heart rate to experienced anger and expressed anger. *Psychosomatic Medicine, 50*, 321–329.

Greenberg, R. P., & Fisher, S. (1977). The relationship between willingness to adopt the sick role and attitudes toward women. *Journal of Chronic Disease, 30*, 29–37.

Harvey, J. H., & Weary, G. (1984). Current issues in attributions theory and research. In M. R. Rosenzweig & L. W. Porter (Eds.), *Annual review of psychology* (Vol. 35, pp. 427–459). Palo Alto, CA: Annual Reviews, Inc.

Hill, L. E., Nunn, A. J., & Fox, W. (1976, February 14). Matching quality of agents employed in "double blind" controlled clinical trials. *The Lancet*, 352–356.

Hughes, J. R., & Krahn, D. (1985). Blindness and the validity of the double blind procedure. *Journal of Clinical Psychopharmacology, 5*, 138–142.

Jones, K. R., & Vischi, T. R. (1980). Impact of alcohol, drug abuse and mental health treatment on medical care utilization: A review of the literature. *Medical Care, 17*, (Suppl. 2), 1–82.

Katz, M. M., Koslow, S. H., Maas, J. W., Frazer, A., Bowden, C. L., Casper, R., Croughan, J., Kocsis, J., & Redmond, E., Jr. (1987). The timing, specificity and clinical prediction of tricyclic drug effects in depression. *Psychological Medicine, 17*, 297–309.

Klein, D. F., Gittelman, R., Quitkin, F., & Rifkin, A. (1980). *Diagnosis and drug treatment of psychiatric disorders: Adults and children* (2nd ed.). Baltimore: Williams & Wilkins.

Klein, D. F., & Rabkin, J. G. (1984). Specificity and strategy in psychotherapy research and practice. In J. B. W. Williams & R. L. Spitzer (Eds.), *Psychotherapy research: Where are we and where should we go?* (pp. 306–331). New York: Guilford Press.

Lipman, R. S., Park, L. C., & Rickels, K. (1966). Paradoxical influence of a therapeutic side-effect interpretation. *Archives of General Psychiatry, 15*, 462–474.

Marder, S. R. (1983). Maintenance therapy in schizophrenia. *Current Psychiatric Therapies, 22*, 141–150.

Mathew, R. J., Weinman, M. L., Thapar, R., Beck, J. J., & Claghorn, J. I. (1983). Somatic symptoms in depression and anti-depressants. *Journal of Clinical Psychiatry, 44*, 10–12.

McNair, D. M., Fisher, S., Kahn, R. J. & Droppleman, L. F. (1970). Drug-personality and interaction in intensive outpatient treatment. *Archives of General Psychiatry, 22*, 128–135.

Mumford, E., Schlesinger, H. J., & Glass, G. V. (1981). Reducing medical costs through mental health treatment: Research problems and recommendations. In A. Broskowski, E. Marks, & S. H. Budman (Eds.), *Linking health and mental health* (pp. 257–273). Beverly Hills, CA: Sage.

Overall, J. E., & Rhoades, H. M. (1982). Refinement of phenomenological classification in clinical psychopharmacology research. *Psychopharmacology, 77*, 24–30.

Paykel, E. S., & Norton, R. W. (1982). Masked depression. *British Journal of Hospital Medicine, 27*, 151–157.

Pennebaker, J. W. (1982). *The psychology of physical symptoms.* New York: Springer-Verlag.

Pennebaker, J. W., Kiecolt-Glaser, J. K., & Glaser, R. (1988). Disclosure of traumas and immune function: Health implications for psychotherapy. *Journal of Consulting and Clinical Psychology, 56*, 239–245.

Prioleau, L., Murdock, M., & Brody, N. (1983). An analysis of psychotherapy versus placebo studies. *The Behavioral and Brain Sciences, 6*, 275–310.

Prior, M., & Sanson, A. (1986). Attention deficit disorder with hyperactivity: A critique. *Journal of Child Psychiatry and Psychology, 27*, 307–319.

Rabkin, J. G., Markowitz, J. S., Stewart, J., McGrath, P., Harrison, W., Quitkin, F. M., & Klein, D. F. (1986). How blind is blind? Assessment of patient and doctor medication guesses in a placebo-controlled trial of imipramine and phenelzine. *Psychiatry Research, 19*, 75–86.

Rabkin, J. G., Stewart, J. W., McGrath, P. J., Markowitz, J. S., Harrison, W., & Quitkin, F. M. (1987). Baseline characteristics of 10-day placebo washout responders in antidepressant trials. *Psychiatry Research, 21,* 9–22.

Rutter, M. (1983). Behavioral studies: Questions and findings on the concept of a distinctive syndrome: In M. Rutter (Ed.), *Developmental neuropsychiatry* (pp. 259–279). New York: Guilford Press.

Shapiro, A. K., & Morris, L. A. (1978). The placebo effect in medical and psychological therapies. In S. L. Garfield & A. E. Bergin (Eds.), *Handbook of psychotherapy and behavior change* (2nd ed., pp., 369–410). New York: Wiley.

Smith, A., Traganza, E., & Harrison, G. (1969). Studies on the effectiveness of antidepressant drugs. *Psychopharamacology Bulletin, 5,* 1–53.

Solomon, K., & Hart, R. (1978). Pitfalls and prospects in clinical research on antianxiety drugs: Benzodiazepines and placebo—A research review. *Journal of Clinical Psychiatry, 39,* 823–831.

Sommers-Flanagan, J., & Greenberg, R. P. (1989). Psychosocial variables and hypertension. A new look at an old controversy. *Journal of Nervous and Mental Disease, 177,* 15–24.

Spence, N. D., Pilowsky, I., & Minniti, R. (1985–86). The attribution of affect in pain clinic patients: A psychophysiological study of the conversion process. *International Journal of Psychiatry in Medicine, 15,* 1–11.

Stallone, F., Mendlewicz, J., & Fieve, R. (1975). Double blind procedure: An assessment in a study of lithium prophylaxis. *Psychological Medicine, 5,* 78–82.

Steinbrueck, S. M., Maxwell, S. E., & Howard, G. S. (1983). A meta-analysis of psychotherapy and drug therapy in the treatment of unipolar depression with adults. *Journal of Consulting and Clinical Psychology, 51,* 856–863.

Thomson, R. (1982). Side effects and placebo amplification. *British Journal of Psychiatry, 140,* 64–68.

Valenstein, E. S. (1986). *Great and desperate cures.* New York: Basic Books.

Wechsler, H., Grosser, G. H., & Greenblatt, M. (1965). Research evaluating antidepressant medications on hospitalized mental patients: A survey of published reports during a 5-year period. *Journal of Nervous and Mental Disease, 141,* 231–329.

Zeldow, P. B., & Greenberg, R. P. (1979). Attitudes toward women and orientation to seeking psychological help. *Journal of Clinical Psychology, 35,* 473–476.

Zeldow, P. B., & Greenberg, R. P. (1980). Who goes where: Sex role bias in psychological and medical help seeking. *Journal of Personality Assessment, 44,* 433–435.

# Author Index

340

Burrows, G. D., *149*
Busfield, B. L., 48, 67, 217, *227*
Bush, P. J., 214, *228*
Butler, G., 78, 97
Butler, S. F., 329, *334*
Byrne, D., *262*

**C**

Cadow, B., 67
Caffey, E. M. J., 299, *305*
Cahill, J. F., *307*
Caldwell, J. H., *234*
Callies, A. L., 205, *232*
Calvert, E. J., 225, *231*
Campbell, D. T., 141, *147*
Campbell, S. B., 169, *184*
Campeas, R., 77, 98, 99
Cancro, R., 127, *147*, 197, *231*, *306*
Candy, J., 87, *103*
Capponi, R., 57, *64*
Capra, D., 217, *227*
Carney, M. W. P., 287, 293, *303*
Caroff, S., 28, *32*, 203, *228*
Carpenter, W. T., 144, *147*
Carr, V., 43, *64*
Carroll, B. J., 54, *64*
Carroll, E. E., *100*
Carrougher, J., 158, *186*
Carver, C. S., 27, *36*
Case, G., 90, 91, 94, *101, 102*
Case, W. G., 20, *36, 273*
Casey, D. E., 200, 218, 223, *229*
Casper, R., *335*
Cassell, W. A., 254, *260*
Cattell, P. B., 249, *260*
Cattell, R. B., 250, *262*
Cavenar, J. O., Jr., *100*, *226*
Chalmers, T. C., *34*
Chang, S., *304*
Charles, L., 173, 180, *185*
Charney, D. S., 81, 85, 88, 97

Chassan, J. B., 74, 97
Chaudhry, D. R., 85, *101*
Chen, J. J., 83, *102*
Child, J. P., 283, *304*
Chojnacki, M., 209, *233*
Chouinard, G., 87, 96, 97, 108, *147*
Christensen, E. R., 40, 42, 65, 66
Christensen, H., 80, 81, 97
Christiansen, J., *36*
Christie, J. E., 7, *32*
Chung, H. R., *232*
Ciaranello, R., *227*
Cicchetti, D. V., 43, 47, 48, 64
Ciompi, L., 106, *147*
Cisin, I. H., 69, 71, *100, 101, 103*, 201, 213, *232, 234*
Claghorn, J. L., 217, *231*, 331, *335*
Clancy, J., 84, *101, 273*
Clare, A., 213, *234*
Clausen, J., 253, *260*, 314, 316, *334*
Clay, P. M., 4, *36*
Clayton, P. J., 47, *65*
Clements, S. D., 157, *185*
Cleveland, S., 28, *33*, 241, 252, 253, 254, *260*
Clinthorne, J., 69, *103*, 201, *234*
Clyde, D. J., 30, *36*, 197, 198, *228*
Cobb, J., 81, 82, *100*
Cohen, A. S., 97
Cohen, B. M., 190, 192, *227*
Cohen, D., *100*
Cohen, H. W., 4, *33*
Cohen, L. S., 209, *230*
Cohen, N. J., 169, 171, 180, *185*
Cohen, R. M., 99
Cohen, S., 330, *334*
Colb, L. C., 97
Cole, J. O., 2, 3, 10, *32*, 35, 74, 93, 98, *102*, 105, *147*, 192, 197, 198, 200, 201, 205, *228, 232*
Coleman, J. H., *102*

# Subject Index